Guild Court
A London Story

by

George Macdonald

Guild Court
A London Story
by George Macdonald

ISBN: 978-93-62205-63-6

Published by

DOUBLE 9 BOOKS

2/13-B, Ansari Road
Daryaganj, New Delhi – 110002
info@double9books.com
www.double9books.com
Tel. 011-40042856

ABOUT THE AUTHOR

George MacDonald was a Scottish writer, poet, and Christian Congregational clergyman. He established himself as a pioneering figure in modern fantasy writing and mentored fellow writer Lewis Carroll. In addition to his fairy stories, MacDonald wrote various works on Christian theology, including sermon collections. George MacDonald was born on December 10, 1824, in Huntly, Aberdeenshire, Scotland, to manufacturers George MacDonald and Helen McCay or MacKay. His father, a farmer, descended from the Clan MacDonald of Glen Coe and was a direct descendant of one of the families killed in the 1692 massacre. MacDonald was raised in an exceptionally literary household: one of his maternal uncles, Mackintosh MacKay, was a renowned Celtic scholar, editor of the Gaelic Highland Dictionary, and collector of fairy stories and Celtic oral poetry. His paternal grandfather had helped to publish an edition of James Macpherson's Ossian, a contentious epic poem based on the Fenian Cycle of Celtic Mythology that contributed to the birth of European Romanticism. MacDonald's step-uncle was a Shakespeare scholar, while his paternal cousin was also a Celtic intellectual. Both of his parents were avid readers, with his father admiring Isaac Newton, Robert Burns, William Cowper, Chalmers, Samuel Taylor Coleridge, and Charles Darwin, to name a few, and his mother receiving a classical education that encompassed several languages.

CONTENTS

CHAPTER I
THE WALK TO THE COUNTING-HOUSE

In the month of November, not many years ago, a young man was walking from Highbury to the City. It was one of those grand mornings that dawn only twice or thrice in the course of the year, and are so independent of times and seasons that November even comes in for its share. And it seemed as if young Thomas Worboise had at his toilet felt the influences of the weather, for he was dressed a trifle more gayly than was altogether suitable for the old age of the year. Neither, however, did he appear in harmony with the tone of the morning, which was something as much beyond the significance of his costume as the great arches of a cathedral upheaving a weight of prayer from its shadowed heart toward the shadowless heavens are beyond the petty gorgeousness of the needlework that adorns the vain garments of its priesthood. It was a lofty blue sky, with multitudes of great clouds half way between it and the earth, among which, as well as along the streets, a glad west wind was reveling. There was nothing much for it to do in the woods now, and it took to making merry in the clouds and the streets. And so the whole heaven was full of church windows. Every now and then a great bore in the cloudy mass would shoot a sloped cylinder of sun-rays earthward, like an eye that saw in virtue of the light it shed itself upon the object of its regard. Gray billows of vapor with sunny heads tossed about in the air, an ocean for angelic sport, only that the angels could not like sport in which there was positively no danger. Where the sky shone through it looked awfully sweet and profoundly high. But although Thomas enjoyed the wind on his right cheek as he passed the streets that opened into High Street, and although certain half sensations, half sentiments awoke in him at its touch, his look was oftenest down at his light trowsers or his enameled boots, and never rose higher than the shop windows.

As he turned into the church-yard to go eastward, he was joined by an acquaintance a few years older than himself, whose path lay in the same direction.

"Jolly morning, ain't it, Tom?" said he.

"Ye-es," answered Thomas, with something of a fashionable drawl, and in the doubtful tone of one who will be careful how he either praises or condemns anything. "Ye-es. It almost makes one feel young again."

"Ha, ha, ha! How long is it since you enjoyed the pleasing sensation last?"

"None of your chaff, now, Charles."

"Well, upon my word, if you don't like chaff, you put yourself at the wrong end of the winnower."

"I never read the Georgics."

"Yes, I know I was born in the country—a clod-hopper, no doubt; but I can afford to stand your chaff, for I feel as young as the day I was born. If you were a fast fellow, now, I shouldn't wonder; but for one like you, that teaches in the Sunday-school and all that, I am ashamed of you, talking like that. Confess now, you don't believe a word of what you cram the goslings with."

"Charles, you may make game of me as you like, but I won't let you say a word against religion in my presence. You may despise me if you like, and think it very spoony of me to teach in the Sunday-school, but—well, you know well enough what I mean."

"I can guess at it, old fellow. Come, come, don't think to humbug me. You know as well as I do that you don't believe a word of it. I don't mean you want to cheat me or any one else. I believe you're above that. But you do cheat yourself. What's the good of it all when you don't feel half as merry as I do on a bright morning like this? I never trouble my head about that rubbish. Here am I as happy as I care to be—for to-day, at least, and 'sufficient unto the day,' you know."

Thomas might have replied, had he been capable of so replying, that although the evil is sufficient for the day, the good may not be. But he said something very different, although with a solemnity fit for an archbishop.

"There's a day coming, Charles, when the evil will be more than sufficient. I want to save my soul. You have a soul to save, too."

"Possibly," answered Charles, with more carelessness than he felt; for he could not help being struck with the sententiousness of Thomas's reply, if not with the meaning contained in it. As he was not devoid of reverence, however, and had been spurred on to say what he had said more from the sense of an undefined incongruity between Thomas's habits, talk included, and the impression his general individuality made upon him, than from any wish to cry down the creed in which he took no practical interest, he went no farther in the direction in which the conversation was leading. He doubled.

"If your soul be safe, Tom, why should you be so gloomy?"

"Are there no souls to save but mine? There's yours now."

"Is that why you put on your shiny trot-boxes and your lavender trousers, old fellow? Come, don't be stuck up. I can't stand it."

"As you please, Charles: I love you too much to mind your making game of me."

"Come, now," said Charles Wither, "speak right out as I am doing to you. You seem to know something I don't. If you would only speak right out, who knows if you mightn't convert me, and save my soul, too, that you make such a fuss about. For my part, I haven't found out that I have a soul yet. What am I to do with it before I know I've got it? But that's not the point. It's the trousers. When I feel miserable about myself—"

"Nonsense, Charles! you never do."

"But I do, though. I want something I haven't got often enough; and, for the life of me, I don't know what it is. Sometimes I think it's a wife. Sometimes I think it's freedom to do whatever I please. Sometimes I think it's a bottle of claret and a jolly good laugh. But to return to the trousers."

"Now leave my trousers alone. It's quite disgusting to treat serious things after such a fashion."

"I didn't know trousers were serious things—except to old grandfather Adam. But it's not about your trousers I was talking. It was about my own."

"I see nothing particular about yours."

"That's because I'm neither glad nor sorry."

"What *do* you mean?"

"Now you come to the point. That's just what I wanted to come to myself, only you wouldn't let me. You kept shying like a half-broke filly."

"Come now, Charles, you know nothing about horses, I am very sure."

Charles Wither smiled, and took no other notice of the asseveration.

"What I mean is this," he said, "that when I am in a serious, dull-gray, foggy mood, you know—not like this sky—"

But when he looked up, the sky was indeed one mass of leaden gray. The glory of the unconditioned had yielded to the bonds of November, and—*Ichabod*.

"Well," Charles resumed, looking down again, "I mean just like this same sky over St. Luke's Work-house here. Lord! I wonder if St. Luke ever knew what kind of thing he'd give his medical name to! When I feel like that, I never dream of putting on lavender trousers, you know, Tom, my boy. So I can't understand you, you know. I only put on such like—I never had such a stunning pair as those—when I go to Richmond, or—"

"Of a Sunday, I believe," said Worboise, settled.

"Of a Sunday. Just so. The better day, the better deed, you know, as people say; though, I dare say, you don't think it."

"When the deed is good, the day makes it better. When the deed is bad, the day makes it worse," said Tom, with a mixture of reproof and "high sentence," which was just pure nonsense.

How much of Thomas's depression was real, and how much was put on—I do not mean outwardly put on without being inwardly assumed—in order that he might flatter himself with being in close sympathy and harmony with Lord Byron, a volume of whose poems was at the time affecting the symmetry of his handsome blue frock-coat, by pulling down one tail more than the other, and bumping against his leg every step he took—I cannot exactly tell. At all events, the young man was—like most men, young and old—under conflicting influences; and these influences he had not yet begun to harmonize in any definite result.

By the time they reached Bunhill Fields, they were in a gray fog; and before they got to the counting-house, it had grown very thick. Through its reddish mass the gaslights shone with the cold brilliance of pale gold.

The scene of their daily labor was not one of those grand rooms with plate-glass windows which now seem to be considered, if not absolutely necessary to commercial respectability, yet a not altogether despicable means of arriving at such. It was a rather long, rather narrow, rather low, but this morning not so dark room as usual—for the whole force of gas-burners was in active operation. In general it was dark, for it was situated in a narrow street, opening off one of the principal city thoroughfares.

As the young men entered, they were greeted with a low growl from the principal clerk, a black-browed, long-nosed man. This was the sole recognition he gave them. Two other clerks looked up with a *good-morning* and a queer expression in their eyes. Some remarks had been made about them before they entered. And now a voice came from the *penetralia*:

"Tom, I want you."

Tom was disposing of his hat and gloves with some care.

"You hear the governor, Mr. Worboise, I suppose?" said Mr. Stopper, the head clerk, in the same growling voice, only articulated now.

"Yes, I hear him," answered Thomas, with some real and some assumed nonchalance. "I do hear him, Mr. Stopper."

Through a glass partition, which crossed the whole of the room, Mr. Boxall, "the governor," might be seen at a writing-table, with his face toward the exoteric department. All that a spectator from without could see, as he went on writing, was a high forehead, occupying more than its due share of a countenance which, foreshortened, of course, from his position at the table, appeared otherwise commonplace and rather insignificant, and a head which had been as finely *tonsured* by the scythe of Time as if the highest ecclesiastical dignity had depended upon the breadth and perfection of the vacancy. The corona which resulted was iron-gray.

When Thomas was quite ready he walked into the inner room.

"Tom, my boy, you are late," said Mr. Boxall, lifting a face whose full view considerably modified the impression I have just given. There was great brilliance in the deep-set eyes, and a certain something, almost merriment, about the mouth, hovering lightly over a strong upper lip, which overhung and almost hid a disproportionately small under one. His chin was large, and between it and the forehead there was little space left for any farther development of countenance.

"Not very late, I believe, sir," answered Thomas. "My watch must have misled me."

"Pull out your watch, my boy, and let us see."

Thomas obeyed.

"By your own watch, it is a quarter past," said Mr. Boxall.

"I have been here five minutes."

"I will not do you the discredit of granting you have spent that time in taking off your hat and gloves. Your watch is five minutes slower than mine," continued Mr. Boxall, pulling out a saucepan of silver, "and mine is five minutes slower than the Exchange. You are nearly half an hour late. You will never get on if you are not punctual. It's an old-fashioned virtue, I know. But first at the office is first at the winning-post, I can tell you. You'll never make money if you're late."

"I have no particular wish—I don't want to make money," said Thomas.

"But I do," rejoined Mr. Boxall, good-naturedly; "and you are my servant, and must do your part."

Thereat Thomas bridled visibly.

"Ah! I see," resumed the merchant; "you don't like the word. I will change it. There's no masters or servants nowadays; they are all governors and *employees*. What they gain by the alteration, I am sure I don't know."

I spell the italicized word thus, because Mr. Boxall pronounced *employés* exactly as if it were an English word ending in *ees*.

Mr. Worboise's lip curled. He could afford to be contemptuous. He had been to Boulogne, and believed he could make a Frenchman understand him. He certainly did know two of the conjugations out of—I really don't know how many. His master did not see what the curl indicated, but possibly his look made Thomas feel that he had been rude. He sought to cover it by saying—

"Mr. Wither was as late as I was, sir. I think it's very hard I should be always pulled up, and nobody else."

"Mr. Wither is very seldom late, and you are often late, my boy. Besides, your father is a friend of mine, and I want to do my duty by him. I want you to get on."

"My father is very much obliged to you, sir."

"So he tells me," returned Mr. Boxall, with remarkable good humor. "We expect you to dine with us to-morrow, mind."

"Thank you, I have another engagement," answered Thomas, with dignity, as he thought.

Now at length Mr. Boxall's brow fell. But he looked more disappointed than angry.

"I am sorry for that, Tom. I wished you could have dined with us. I won't detain you longer. Mind you don't ink your trousers."

Was Thomas never to hear the last of those trousers? He began to wish he had not put them on. He made his bow, and withdrew in chagrin, considering himself disgraced before his fellows, to whom he would gladly have been a model, if he could have occupied that position without too much trouble. But his heart smote him—gently, it must be confessed—for having refused the kindness of Mr. Boxall, and shown so much resentment in a matter wherein the governor was quite right.

Mr. Boxall was a man who had made his money without losing his money's worth. Nobody could accuse him of having ever done a mean, not to say a dishonest thing. This would not have been remarkable, had he not been so well recognized as a sharp man of business. The more knowing any jobber about the Exchange, the better he knew that it was useless to dream of getting an advantage over Mr. Boxall. But it was indeed remarkable that he should be able to steer so exactly in the middle course that, while he was keen as an eagle on his own side, he should yet be thoroughly just on the other. And, seeing both sides of a question with such marvelous clearness, in order to keep his own hands clean he was not driven from uncertainty to give the other man anything more than his right. Yet Mr Boxall knew how to be generous upon occasion, both in time and money: the ordinary sharp man of business is stingy of both. The chief fault he had was a too great respect for success. He had risen himself by honest diligence, and he thought when a man could not rise it must be either from a want of diligence or of honesty. Hence he was *a priori* ready to trust the successful man, and in some instances to trust him too much. That he had a family of three daughters only—one of them quite a child—who had never as yet come into collision with any project or favorite opinion of his, might probably be one negative cause of the continuance of his openheartedness and justice of regard.

Thomas Worboise's father had been a friend of his for many years—at least so far as that relation could be called friendship which consisted in playing as much into each other's hands in the way of business as they could, dining together two or three times in the course of the year, and keeping an open door to each other's family. Thomas was an only son, with one sister. His father would gladly have brought him up to his own profession, that of the law, but Thomas showing considerable disinclination to the necessary studies, he had placed him in his friend's counting-house with the hope that that might suit him better. Without a word having been said on the subject, both the fathers would have gladly seen the son of the one engaged to any daughter of the other. They were both men of considerable property, and thought that this would be a pleasant way of determining the future of part of their possessions. At the same time Mr. Boxall was not quite satisfied with what he had as yet seen of Tom's business character. However, there had been no signs of approximation between him and either of the girls, and therefore there was no cause to be particularly anxious about the matter.

CHAPTER II
THE INVALID MOTHER

To account in some measure for the condition in which we find Tom at the commencement of my story, it will be better to say a word here about his mother. She was a woman of weak health and intellect, but strong character; was very religious, and had a great influence over her son, who was far more attached to her than he was to his father. The daughter, on the other hand, leaned to her father, an arrangement not uncommon in families.

On the evening of the day on which my story commences, office hours were long over before Tom appeared at home. He went into his mother's room, and found her, as usual, reclining on a couch, supported by pillows. She was a woman who never complained of her sufferings, and her face, perhaps in consequence of her never desiring sympathy, was hard and unnaturally still. Nor were her features merely still—they looked immobile, and her constant pain was indicated only by the absence of all curve in her upper lip. When her son entered, a gentle shimmer of love shone out of her eyes of troubled blue, but the words in which she addressed him did not correspond to this shine. She was one of those who think the Deity jealous of the amount of love bestowed upon other human beings, even by their own parents, and therefore struggle to keep down their deepest and holiest emotions, regarding them not merely as weakness but as positive sin, and likely to be most hurtful to the object on which they are permitted to expend themselves.

"Well, Thomas," said his mother, "what has kept you so late?"

"Oh! I don't know, mother," answered Tom, in whose attempted carelessness there yet appeared a touch of anxiety, which caught her eye.

"You do know, Tom; and I want to know."

"I waited and walked home with Charles Wither."

He did not say, "I waited to walk home."

"How was he so late? You must have left the office hours ago."

"He had some extra business to finish."

It was business of his own, not office business; and Tom finding out that he would be walking home a couple of hours later, had arranged to join him that he might have this account to give of himself.

"You know I do not like you to be too much with that young man. He is not religious. In fact, I believe him to be quite worldly. Does he ever go to church?"

"I don't know, mother. He's not a bad sort of fellow."

"He is a bad sort of fellow, and the less you are with him the better."

"I can't help being with him in the office, you know, mother."

"You need not be with him after office hours."

"Well, no; perhaps not. But it would look strange to avoid him."

"I thought you had more strength of character, Thomas."

"I—I—I spoke very seriously to him this morning, mother."

"Ah! That alters the case, if you have courage to speak the truth to him."

At that moment the door opened, and the curate of St. Solomon's was announced. Mrs. Worboise was always at home to him, and he called frequently, both because she was too great an invalid to go to church, and because they supposed, on the ground of their employing the same religious phrases in their conversation, that they understood each other. He was a gentle, abstracted youth, with a face that looked as if its informing idea had been for a considerable period sat upon by something ungenial. With him the profession had become everything, and humanity never had been anything, if not something bad. He walked through the crowded streets in the neighborhood with hurried step and eyes fixed on the ground, his pale face rarely brightening with recognition, for he seldom saw any passing acquaintance. When he did, he greeted him with a voice that seemed to come from far-off shores, but came really from a bloodless, nerveless chest, that had nothing to do with life, save to yield up the ghost in eternal security, and send it safe out of it. He seemed to recognize none of those human relations which make the blood mount to the face at meeting, and give strength to the grasp of the hand. He would not have hurt a fly; he would have died to save a malefactor from the gallows, that he might give him another chance of repentance. But mere human aid he had none to bestow; no warmth, no heartening, no hope.

Mr. Simon bowed solemnly, and shook hands with Mrs. Worboise.

"How are you to-night, Mrs. Worboise?" he said, glancing round the room, however. For the only sign of humanity about him was a certain weak admiration of Amy Worboise, who, if tried by his own tests, was dreadfully unworthy even of that. For she was a merry girl, who made great sport of the little church-mouse, as she called him.

Mrs. Worboise did not reply to this question, which she always treated as irrelevant. Mr. Simon then shook hands with Thomas, who looked on him with a respect inherited from his mother.

"Any signs of good in your class, Mr. Thomas?" he asked.

The question half irritated Tom. Why, he could not have explained even to himself. The fact was that he had begun to enter upon another phase of experience since he saw the curate last, and the Sunday-school was just a little distasteful to him at the moment.

"No," he answered, with a certain slightest motion of the head that might have been interpreted either as of weariness or of indifference.

The clergyman interpreted it as of the latter, and proceeded to justify his question, addressing his words to the mother.

"Your son thinks me too anxious about the fruits of his labor, Mrs. Worboise. But when we think of the briefness of life, and how soon the night comes when no man can work, I do not think we can be too earnest to win souls for our crown of rejoicing when He comes with the holy angels. First our own souls, Mr. Thomas, and then the souls of others."

Thomas, believing every word that the curate said, made notwithstanding no reply, and the curate went on.

"There are so many souls that might be saved, if one were only in earnest, and so few years to do it in. We do not strive with God in prayer, Mrs. Worboise. We faint and cease from our prayers and our endeavors together."

"That is too true," responded the lady.

"I try to do my best," said Thomas, in a tone of apology, and with a lingering doubt in his mind whether he was really speaking the absolute truth. But he comforted himself with saying to himself, "I only said 'I try to do my best;' I did not say, 'I try my best to do my best.'"

"I have no reason to doubt it, my young friend," returned the curate, who was not ten years older than his young friend. "I only fancied—no doubt it was but the foolish fancy of my own anxiety—that you did not respond quite so heartily as usual to my remark."

The mother's eyes were anxiously fixed on her son during the conversation, for her instincts told her that he was not quite at his ease.

She had never given him any scope, never trusted him, or trained him to freedom; but, herself a prisoner to her drawing-room and bed-room, sought with all her energy and contrivance, for which she had plenty of leisure, to keep, strengthen, and repair the invisible cable by which she seemed to herself to hold, and in fact did hold, him, even when he was out of her sight, and himself least aware of the fact.

As yet again Thomas made no reply, Mr. Simon changed the subject.

"Have you much pain to-night, Mrs. Worboise?" he asked.

"I can bear it," she answered. "It will not last forever."

"You find comfort in looking to the rest that remaineth," responded Mr. Simon. "It is the truest comfort. Still, your friends would gladly see you enjoy a little more of the present—" *world*, Mr. Simon was going to say, but the word was unsuitable; so he changed it—"of the present—ah! dispensation," he said.

"The love of this world bringeth a snare," suggested Mrs. Worboise, believing that she quoted Scripture.

Thomas rose and left the room. He did not return till the curate had taken his leave. It was then almost time for his mother to retire. As soon as he entered he felt her anxious pale-blue eyes fixed upon him.

"Why did you go, Thomas?" she asked, moving on her couch, and revealing by her face a twinge of sharper pain than ordinary. "You used to listen with interest to the conversation of Mr. Simon. He is a man whose conversation is in Heaven."

"I thought you would like to have a little private talk with him, mamma. You generally do have a talk with him alone."

"Don't call it talk, Thomas. That is not the proper word to use."

"Communion then, mother," answered Thomas, with the feeling of aversion a little stronger and more recognizable than before, but at the same time annoyed with himself that he thus felt. And, afraid that he had shown the feeling which he did recognize, he hastened to change the subject and speak of one which he had at heart.

"But, mother, dear, I wanted to speak to you about something. You mustn't mind my being late once or twice a week now, for I am going in for German. There is a very good master lives a few doors from the counting-house; and if you take lessons in the evening at his own lodgings, he charges so much less for it. And, you know, it is such an advantage nowadays for any one who wants to get on in business to know German!"

"Does Mr. Wither join you, Thomas?" asked his mother, in a tone of knowing reproof.

"No, indeed, mother," answered Thomas; and a gleam of satisfaction shot through his brain as his mother seemed satisfied. Either, however, he managed to keep it off his face, or his mother did not perceive or understand it, for the satisfaction remained on her countenance.

"I will speak to your father about it," she answered.

This was quite as much as Thomas could have hoped for: he had no fear of his father making any objection. He kissed his mother on the cheek—it was a part of her system of mortifying the flesh with its affections and lusts that she never kissed him with any fervor, and rarely allowed those straight lips to meet his—and they parted for the night.

CHAPTER III
EXPOSTULATION

Thomas descended to breakfast, feeling fresh and hopeful. The weather had changed during the night, and it was a clear, frosty morning, cold blue cloudless sky and cold gray leafless earth reflecting each other's winter attributes. The sun was there, watching from afar how they could get on without him; but, as if they knew he had not forsaken them, they were both merry. Thomas stood up with his back to the blazing fire, and through the window saw his father walking bareheaded in the garden. He had not returned home till late the night before, and Thomas had gone to bed without seeing him. Still he had been up the first in the house, and had been at work for a couple of hours upon the papers he had brought home in his blue bag. Thomas walked to the window to show himself, as a hint to his father that breakfast was ready. Mr. Worboise saw him, and came in. Father and son did not shake hands or wish each other good-morning, but they nodded and smiled, and took their seats at the table. As Mr. Worboise sat down, he smoothed, first with one hand, then with the other, two long side-tresses of thin hair, trained like creepers over the top of his head, which was perfectly bald. Their arrangement added to the resemblance his forehead naturally possessed to the bottom of a flat-iron, set up on the base of its triangle. His eyebrows were very dark, straight, and bushy, his eyes a keen hazel; his nose straight on the ridge, but forming an obtuse angle at the point; his mouth curved upward, and drawn upward by the corners when he smiled, which gave him the appearance of laughing down at everything; his chin now is remarkable. And there, reader, I hope you have him. I ought to have mentioned that no one ever saw his teeth, though to judge from his performances at the table, they were in serviceable condition. He was considerably above the middle hight, shapeless rather than stout, and wore black clothes.

"You're going to dine at the Boxall's to-night, I believe, Tom? Mr. Boxall asked me, but I can't go. I am so busy with that case of Spender & Spoon."

"No, father. I don't mean to go," said Tom.

"Why not?" asked Mr. Worboise, with some surprise, and more than a hint of dissatisfaction. "Your mother hasn't been objecting, has she?"

"I am not aware that my mother knows of the invitation," answered Tom, trying to hide his discomfort in formality of speech.

"Well, I said nothing about it, I believe. But I accepted for you at the same time that I declined for myself. You saw the letter—I left it for you."

"Yes, sir, I did."

"Well, in the name of Heaven, what do you mean? You answer as if you were in the witness-box. I am not going to take any advantage of you. Speak out, man. Why won't you go to Boxall's?"

"Well, sir, to tell the truth, I didn't think he behaved quite well to me yesterday. I happened to be a few minutes late, and—"

"And Boxall blew you up; and that's the way you take to show your dignified resentment! Bah!"

"He ought to behave to me like a gentleman."

"But how is he, if he isn't a gentleman? He hasn't had the bringing up you've had. But he's a good, honest fellow, and says what he means."

"That is just what I did, sir. And you have always told me that honesty is the best policy."

"Yes, I confess. But that is not exactly the kind of honesty I mean," returned Mr. Worboise with a fishy smile, for his mouth was exactly of the fish type. "The law scarcely refers to the conduct of a gentleman as a gentleman."

This was obscure to his son, as it may be to the reader.

"Then you don't want me to behave like a gentleman?" said Tom.

"Keep your diploma in your pocket till it's asked for," answered his father. "If you are constantly obtruding it on other people, they will say you bought it and paid for it. A gentleman can afford to put an affront in beside it, when he knows it's there. But the idea of good old Boxall insulting a son of mine is too absurd, Tom. You must remember you are his servant."

"So he told me," said Tom, with reviving indignation.

"And that, I suppose, is what you call an insult, eh?"

"Well, to say the least, it is not a pleasant word to use."

"Especially as it expresses a disagreeable fact. Come, come, my boy. Better men then you will ever be have had to sweep their master's office before now. But no reference is made to the fact after they call the office their own. You go and tell Mr. Boxall that you will be happy to dine with him to-night if he will allow you to change your mind."

"But I told him I was engaged."

"Tell him the engagement is put off, and you are at his service."

"But—" began Tom, and stopped. He was going to say the engagement was not put off.

"But what?" said his father.

"I don't like to do it," answered Tom. "He will take it for giving in and wanting to make up."

"Leave it to me, then, my boy," returned his father, kindly. "I will manage it. My business is not so very pressing but that I can go if I choose. I will write and say that a change in my plans has put it in my power to be his guest, after all, and that I have persuaded you to put off your engagement and come with me."

"But that would be—would not be true," hesitated Tom.

"Pooh! pooh! I'll take the responsibility of that. Besides, it *is* true. Your mother will make a perfect spoon of you—with the help of good little Master Simon. Can't I change my plans if I like? We must *not* offend Boxall. He is a man of mark—and warm. I say nothing about figures—I never tell secrets. I don't even say how many figures. But I know all about it, and venture to say, between father and son, that he is warm, decidedly warm—possibly hot," concluded Mr. Worboise, laughing.

"I don't exactly understand you, sir," said Tom, meditatively.

"You would understand me well enough if you had a mind to business," answered his father.

But what he really meant in his heart was that Mr. Boxall had two daughters, to one of whom it was possible that his son might take a fancy, or rather—to express it in the result, which was all that he looked to—a marriage might be brought about between Tom and Jane or Mary Boxall; in desiring which he thought he knew what he was about, for he was Mr. Boxall's man of business.

"I won't have you offend Mr. Boxall, anyhow," he concluded. "He is your governor."

The father had tact enough to substitute the clerk's pseudonym for the obnoxious term.

"Very well, sir; I suppose I must leave it to you," answered Tom; and they finished their breakfast without returning to the subject.

When he reached the counting-house, Tom went at once to Mr. Boxall's room, and made his apologies for being late again, on the ground that his father had detained him while he wrote the letter he now handed to him. Mr. Boxall glanced at the note.

"I am very glad, Tom, that both your father and you have thought better of it. Be punctual at seven."

"Wife must put another leaf yet in the table," he said to himself, as Thomas retired to his desk. "Thirteen's not lucky, though; but one is sure to be absent."

No one was absent, however, and number thirteen was the standing subject of the jokes of the evening, especially as the thirteenth was late, in the person of Mr. Wither, whom Mr. Boxall had invited out of mere good nature; for he did not care much about introducing him to his family, although his conduct in the counting-house was irreproachable. Miss Worboise had been invited with her father and brother, but whether she stayed at home to nurse her mother or to tease the curate, is of no great importance to my history.

The dinner was a good, well-contrived, rather antiquated dinner, within the compass of the house itself; for Mrs. Boxall only pleased her husband as often as she said that they were and would remain old-fashioned people, and would have their own maids to prepare and serve a dinner—"none of those men-cooks and undertakers to turn up their noses at everything in the house!" But Tom abused the whole affair within himself as nothing but a shop-dinner; for there was Mr. Stopper, the head-clerk, looking as sour as a summons; and there was Mr. Wither, a good enough fellow and gentleman-like, but still of the shop; besides young Weston, of whom nobody could predicate any thing in particular, save that he stood in such awe of Mr. Stopper, that he missed the way to his mouth in taking stolen stares at him across the table. Mr. Worboise sat at the hostess's left hand, and Mr. Stopper at her right; Tom a little way from his father, with Mary Boxall, whom he had taken down, beside him; and many were the underbrowed glances which the head-clerk shot across the dishes at the couple.

Mary was a very pretty, brown-haired, white-skinned, blue-eyed damsel, whose charms lay in harmony of color, general roundness, the smallness of her extremities, and her simple kind-heartedness. She was dressed in white muslin, with ribbons precisely the color of her eyes. Tom could not help being pleased at having her beside him. She was not difficult to entertain, for she was willing to be interested in anything; and while Tom was telling her a story about a young lad in his class at the Sunday-school, whom he had gone to see at his wretched home, those sweet eyes filled with tears, and Mr. Stopper saw it, and choked in his glass of sherry. Tom saw it too, and would have been more overcome thereby, had it not been for reasons.

Charles Wither, on the opposite side of the table, was neglecting his own lady for the one at his other elbow, who was Jane Boxall—a fine, regular-featured, dark-skinned young woman. They were watched with stolen glances of some anxiety from both ends of the table, for neither father nor mother cared much about Charles Wither, although the former was too kind to omit inviting him to his house occasionally.

After the ladies retired, the talk was about politics, the money-market, and other subjects quite uninteresting to Tom, who, as I have already said, was at this period of his history a reader of Byron, and had therefore little sympathy with human pursuits except they took some abnormal form— such as piracy, atheism, or the like—in the person of one endowed with splendid faculties and gifts in general. So he stole away from the table, and joined the ladies some time before the others rose from their wine; not, however, before he had himself drunk more than his gravity of demeanor was quite sufficient to ballast. He found Mary turning over some music, and as he drew near he saw her laying aside, in its turn, Byron's song, "She walks in beauty."

"Oh! do you sing that song, Miss Mary?" he asked with *empressement*.

"I have sung it several times," she answered; "but I am afraid I cannot sing it well enough to please you. Are you fond of the song?"

"I only know the words of it, and should so much like to hear you sing it. I never heard it sung. *Do*, Miss Mary."

"You will be indulgent, then?"

"I shall have no chance of exercising that virtue, I know. There."

He put the music on the piano as he spoke, and Mary, adjusting her white skirts and her white shoulders, began to sing the song with taste, and, what was more, with simplicity. Her voice was very pleasant to the ears of Thomas, warbling one of the songs of the man whom, against his conscience, he could not help regarding as the greatest he knew. So much moved was he, that the signs of his emotion would have been plainly seen had not the rest of the company, while listening more or less to the song, been employing their eyes at the same time with Jane's portfolio of drawings. All the time he had his eyes upon her white shoulder: stooping to turn the last leaf from behind her, he kissed it lightly. At the same moment the door opened, and Mr. Stopper entered. Mary stopped singing, and rose with a face of crimson and the timidest, slightest glance at Tom, whose face flushed up in response.

It was a foolish action, possibly repented almost as soon as done. Certainly, for the rest of the evening, Thomas sought no opportunity of again approaching Mary. I do not doubt it was with some feeling of relief that he heard his father say it was time for them to be going home.

None of the parents would have been displeased had they seen the little passage between the young people. Neither was Mary offended at what had occurred. While she sat singing, she knew that the face bending over her was one of the handsomest—a face rather long and pale, of almost pure Greek outline, with a high forehead, and dark eyes with a yet darker fringe. Nor, although the reader must see that Tom had nothing yet that could be called character, was his face therefore devoid of expression; for he had plenty of feeling, and that will sometimes shine out the more from the very absence of a *characteristic* meaning in the countenance. Hence, when Mary felt the kiss, and glanced at the face whence it had fallen, she read more in the face than there was in it to read, and the touch of his lips went deeper than her white shoulder. They were both young, and as yet mere electric jars charged with emotions. Had they both continued such as they were now, there could have been no story to tell about them; none such, at least, as I should care to tell. They belonged to the common class of mortals who, although they are weaving a history, are not aware of it, and in whom the process goes on so slowly that the eye of the artist can find in them no substance sufficient to be woven into a human creation in tale or poem. How dull that life looks to him, with its ambitions, its love-making, its dinners, its sermons, its tailors' bills, its weariness over all—without end or goal save that toward which it is driven purposeless! Not till a hope is born such that its fullfilment depends upon the will of him who cherishes it, does a man begin to develop the stuff out of which a tale can be wrought. For then he begins to have a story of his own—it may be for good, it may be for evil—but a story. Thomas's religion was no sign of this yet; for a man can no more be saved by the mere reflex of parental influences than he will be condemned by his inheritance of parental sins. I do not say that there is no interest in the emotions of such young people; but I say there is not reality enough in them to do anything with. They are neither consistent nor persistent enough to be wrought into form. Such are in the condition over which, in the miracle-play, Adam laments to Eve after their expulsion from Paradise—

"Oure hap was hard, *oure wytt was nesche* (soft, tender) To paradys whan we were brought."

Mr. Boxall lived in an old-fashioned house in Hackney, with great rooms and a large garden. Through the latter he went with Mr. Worboise and Tom to let them out at a door in the wall, which would save them a few hundred yards in going to the North London Railway. There were some old trees in the garden, and much shrubbery. As he returned he heard a rustle among the lilacs that crowded about a side-walk, and thought he saw the shimmer of a white dress. When he entered the drawing-room, his daughter Jane entered from the opposite door. He glanced round the room: Mr. Wither was gone. This made Mr. Boxall suspicious and restless; for, as I have said, he had not confidence in Mr. Wither. Though punctual and attentive to business, he was convinced that he was inclined to be a fast man; and he strongly suspected him of being concerned in betting transactions of different sorts, which are an abomination to the man of true business associations and habits.

Mr. Worboise left the house in comfortable spirits, for Providence had been propitious to him for some months past, and it mattered nothing to him whether or how the wind blew. But it blew from the damp west cold and grateful upon Thomas's brow. The immediate influence of the wine he had drunk had gone off, and its effects remained in discomfort and doubt. Had he got himself into a scrape with Mary Boxall? He had said nothing to her. He had not committed himself to anything. And the wind blew cooler and more refreshing upon his forehead. And then came a glow of pleasure as he recalled her blush and the glance she had so timidly lifted toward his lordly face. That was something to be proud of! Certainly he was one whom women—I suppose he said *girls* to himself—were ready to—yes—to fall in love with. Proud position! Enviable destiny! Before he reached home the wind had blown away every atom of remorse with the sickly fumes of the wine; and although he resolved to be careful how he behaved to Mary Boxall in future, he hugged his own handsome idea in the thought that she felt his presence, and was—just a little—not dangerously—but really a little in love with him.

CHAPTER IV
GUILD COURT

The office was closed, the shutters were up in the old-fashioned way on the outside, the lights extinguished, and Mr. Stopper, who was always the last to leave, was gone. The narrow street looked very dreary, for most of its windows were similarly covered. The shutters, the pavements, the kennels, everything shone and darkened by fits. For it was a blowing night, with intermittent showers, and everything was wet, and reflected the gaslights in turn, which the wind teased into all angles of relation with neighboring objects, tossing them about like flowers ready at any moment to be blown from their stems. Great masses of gray went sweeping over the narrow section of the sky that could be seen from the pavement.

Now and then the moon gleamed out for one moment and no more, swallowed the next by a mile of floating rain, dusky and shapeless. Fighting now with a fierce gust, and now limping along in comparative quiet, with a cotton umbrella for a staff, an old woman passed the office, glanced up at the shuttered windows, and, after walking a short distance, turned into a paved archway, and then going along a narrow passage, reached a small paved square, called Guild Court. Here she took from her pocket a latch-key, and opening a door much in want of paint, but otherwise in good condition, entered, and ascended a broad, dusky stair-case, with great landings, whence each ascent rose at right angles to the preceding. The dim light of the tallow candle, which she had left in a corner of the stair-case as she descended, and now took up with her again, was sufficient to show that the balusters were turned and carved, and the hand-rail on the top of them broad and channeled. When she reached the first floor, she went along a passage, and at the end of it opened a door. A cheerful fire burned at the other end of a large room, and by the side of the fire sat a girl, gazing so intently into the glowing coals, that she seemed unaware of the old woman's entrance. When she spoke to her, she started and rose.

"So you're come home, Lucy, and searching the fire for a wishing-cap, as usual!" said the old lady, cheerily.

The girl did not reply, and she resumed, with a little change of tone—

"I do declare, child, I'll never let him cross the door again, if it drives you into the dumps that way. Take heart of grace, my girl; you're good enough for him any day, though he be a fine gentleman. He's no better gentleman than my son, anyhow, though he's more of a buck."

Lucy moved about a little uneasily; turned to the high mantel-piece, took up some trifle and played with it nervously, set it down with a light sigh, the lightness of which was probably affected; went across the room to a chest of drawers, in doing which she turned her back on the old woman; and then only replied, in a low pleasant voice, which wavered a little, as if a good cry were not far off—

"I'm sure, grannie, you're always kind to him when he comes."

"I'm civil to him, child. Who could help it? Such a fine, handsome fellow! And has got very winning ways with him, too! That's the mischief of it! I always had a soft heart to a frank face. A body would think I wasn't a bit wiser than the day I was born."

And she laughed a toothless old laugh which must once have been very pleasant to her husband to hear, and indeed was pleasant to hear now. By this time she had got her black bonnet off, revealing a widow's cap, with gray hair neatly arranged down the sides of a very wrinkled old face. Indeed the wrinkles were innumerable, so that her cheeks and forehead looked as if they had been crimped with a penknife, like a piece of fine cambric frill. But there was not one deep rut in her forehead or cheek. Care seemed to have had nothing at all to do with this condition of them.

"Well, grannie, why should you be so cross with me for liking him, when you like him just as much yourself?" said Lucy, archly.

"Cross with you, child! I'm not cross with you, and you know that quite well. You know I never could be cross with you even if I ought to be. And I didn't ought now, I'm sure. But I am cross with him; for he can't be behaving right to you when your sweet face looks like that."

"Now don't, grannie, else I shall have to be cross with you. Don't say a word against him. Don't now, dear grannie, or you and I shall quarrel, and that would break my heart."

"Bless the child! I'm not saying a word for or against him. I'm afraid you're a great deal too fond of him, Lucy. What hold have you on him now?"

"What hold, granny!" exclaimed Lucy, indignantly. "Do you think if I were going to be married to him to-morrow, and he never came to the church—do you think I would lift that bonnet to hold him to it? Indeed, then, I wouldn't."

And Lucy did not cry, but she turned her back on her grandmother as if she would rather her face should not be seen.

"What makes you out of sorts, to-night, then, lovey?"

Lucy made no reply, but moved hastily to the window, made the smallest possible chink between the blind and the window-frame, and peeped out into the court. She had heard a footstep which she knew; and now she glided, quiet and swift as a ghost, out of the room, closing the door behind her.

"I wonder when it will come to an end. Always the same thing over again, I suppose, to the last of the world. It's no use telling them what *we* know. It won't make one of them young things the wiser. The first man that looks at them turns the head of them. And I must confess, if I was young again myself, and hearkening for my John's foot in the court, I might hobble—no, not hobble then, but run down the stairs like Lucy there, to open the door for him. But then John was a good one; and there's few o' them like him now, I doubt."

Something like this, I venture to imagine, was passing through the old woman's mind when the room door opened again, and Lucy entered with Thomas Worboise. Her face was shining like a summer now, and a conscious pride sat on the forehead of the young man which made him look far nobler than he has yet shown himself to my reader. The last of a sentence came into the room with him.

"So you see, Lucy, I could not help it. My father—How do you do you do, Mrs. Boxall? What a blowing night it is! But you have a kind of swallow's nest here, for hardly a breath gets into the court when our windows down below in the counting-house are shaking themselves to bits."

It was hardly a room to compare to a swallow's nest. It was a very large room indeed. The floor, which was dark with age, was uncarpeted, save just before the fire, which blazed brilliantly in a small kitchen-range, curiously contrasting with the tall, carved chimney-piece above it. The ceiling corresponded in style, for it was covered with ornaments—

All made out of the carver's brain.

And the room was strangely furnished. The high oak settle of a farm-house stood back against the wall not far from the fire, and a few feet from it a tall, old-fashioned piano, which bore the name of Broadwood under the cover. At the side of the room farthest from the fire stood one of those chests of drawers, on which the sloping lid at the top left just room for a glass-doored book-case to stand, rivaling the piano in hight. Then there was a sofa, covered with chintz plentifully besprinkled with rose-buds; and in the middle of the room a square mahogany table, called by upholsterers a *pembroke*, I think, the color of which was all but black with age and manipulation, only it could not be seen now because it was covered with a check of red and blue. A few mahogany chairs, seated with horse hair, a fire-screen in faded red silk, a wooden footstool and a tall backed easy-chair, covered with striped stuff, almost completed the furniture of the nondescript apartment.

Thomas Worboise carried a chair to the fire, and put his feet on the broad-barred bright kitchen fender in front of it.

"Are your feet wet, Thomas?" asked Lucy with some gentle anxiety, and a tremor upon his name, as if she had not yet got quite used to saying it without a *Mr.* before it.

"Oh no, thank you. I don't mind a little wet. Hark how the wind blows in the old chimney up there! It'll be an awkward night on the west coast, this. I wonder what it feels like to be driving right on the rocks at the Land's End, or some such place."

"Don't talk of such things in that cool way, Mr. Thomas. You make my blood run cold," said Mrs. Boxall.

"He doesn't mean it, you know, grannie," said Lucy meditating.

"But I do mean it. I should like to know how it feels," persisted Thomas—"with the very shrouds, as taut as steel bars, blowing out in the hiss of the nor'wester."

"Yes, I dare say!" returned the old lady, with some indignation. "You would like to know how it felt so long as your muddy boots was on my clean fender!"

Thomas did not know that the old lady had lost one son at sea, and had another the captain of a sailing-vessel, or he would not have spoken as he did. But he was always wanting to know how things felt. Had not his education rendered it impossible for him to see into the state of his own mind, he might, questioned as to what he considered the ideal of life, have replied, "A continuous succession of delicate and poetic sensations." Hence he had made many a frantic effort after religious sensations. But the necessity of these was now somewhat superseded by his growing attachment to Lucy, and the sensations consequent upon that.

Up to this moment, in his carriage and speech, he had been remarkably different from himself, as already shown in my history. For he was, or thought himself, somebody here; and there was a freedom and ease about his manner, amounting, in fact, to a slight though not disagreeable swagger, which presented him to far more advantage than he had in the presence of his father and mother, or even of Mr. Boxall and Mr. Stopper. But he never could bear any one to be displeased with him except he were angry himself. So when Mrs. Boxall spoke as she did, his countenance fell. He instantly removed his feet from the fender, glanced up at her face, saw that she was really indignant, and, missing the real reason of course, supposed that it was because he had been indiscreet in being disrespectful to a cherished article of housewifely. It was quite characteristic of Tom that he instantly pulled his handkerchief from his pocket, and began therewith to restore the brightness of the desecrated iron. This went at once to the old lady's heart. She snatched the handkerchief out of his hand.

"Come, come, Mr. Thomas. Don't ye mind an old woman like that. To think of using your handkerchief that way! And cambric too!"

Thomas looked up in surprise, and straightway recovered his behavior.

"I didn't think of your fender," he said.

"Oh, drat the fender!" exclaimed Mrs. Boxall, with more energy than refinement.

And so the matter dropped, and all sat silent for a few moments, Mrs. Boxall with her knitting, and Tom and Lucy beside each other with their thoughts. Lucy presently returned to their talk on the stair-case.

"So you were out at dinner on Wednesday, Thomas?"

"Yes. It was a great bore, but I had to go.—Boxall's, you know. I beg your pardon, Mrs. Boxall; but that's how fellows like me talk, you know. I should have said Mr. Boxall. And I didn't mean that he was a bore. That he is not, though he is a little particular—of course. I only meant it was a bore to go there when I wanted to come here."

"Is my cousin Mary *very* pretty?" asked Lucy, with a meaning in her tone which Thomas easily enough understood.

He could not help blushing, for he remembered, as well he might. And she could not help seeing, for she had eyes, very large ones, and at least as loving as they were large.

"Yes, she is very pretty," answered Thomas; "but not nearly so pretty as you, Lucy."

Thomas, then, was not stupid, although my reader will see that he was weak enough. And Lucy was more than half satisfied, though she did not half like that blush. But Thomas himself did not like either the blush or its cause. And poor Lucy knew nothing of either, only meditated upon another blush, quite like this as far as appearance went, but with a different heart to it.

Thomas did not stop more than half an hour. When he left, instead of walking straight out of Guild Court by the narrow paved passage, he crossed to the opposite side of the court, opened the door of a more ancient-looking house, and entered. Reappearing—that is, to the watchful eyes of Lucy man[oe]uvring with the window-blind—after about two minutes, he walked home to Highbury, and told his mother that he had come straight from his German master, who gave him hopes of being able, before many months should have passed, to write a business letter in intelligible German.

CHAPTER V
MORE ABOUT GUILD COURT

Mrs. Boxall was the mother of Richard Boxall, the "governor" of Thomas Worboise. Her John had been the possessor of a small landed property, which he farmed himself, and upon which they brought up a family of three sons and one daughter, of whom Richard was the eldest, and the daughter Lucy the youngest. None of the sons showed the least inclination to follow the plow or take any relation more or less dignified toward the cultivation of the ancestral acres. This aversion, when manifested by Richard, occasioned his father considerable annoyance, but he did not oppose his desire to go into business instead of farming; for he had found out by this time that he had perpetuated in his sons a certain family doggedness which he had inherited from one ancestor at least—an obstinacy which had never yet been overcome by any argument, however good. He yielded to the inevitable, and placed him in a merchant's office in London, where Richard soon made himself of importance. When his second son showed the same dislike to draw his livelihood directly from the bosom of the earth, and revealed a distinct preference for the rival element, with which he had made some acquaintance when at school at a sea-port at no great distance from his home, old John Boxall was still more troubled, but gave his consent—a consent which was, however, merely a gloomy negation of resistance. The cheerfulness of his wife was a great support to him under what he felt as a slight to himself and the whole race of Boxalls; but he began, notwithstanding, to look upon his beloved fields with a jaundiced eye, and the older he grew the more they reminded him of the degenerate tastes and heartlessness of his boys. When he discovered, a few years after, that his daughter had pledged herself, still in his eyes a mere child, to a music-master who visited her professionally from the next town, he flew at last into a terrible rage, which was not appeased by the girl's elopement and marriage. He never saw her again. Her mother, however, was not long in opening a communication with her, and it was to her that Edward, the youngest son, fled upon occasion of a quarrel with his father, whose temper had now become violent as well as morose. He followed his second brother's example, and went to sea. Still the mother's cheerfulness was little abated; for, as she said to herself, she had no reason to be ashamed of her children. None of them had done any thing they had to be ashamed of, and why should she be vexed? She had no idea Lucy had so much spirit in her. And if it were not for the old man, who was surely over-fond of those fields of his, she could hold up her head with the best of them; for there was Dick—such a gentleman to be sure! and John, third mate already! and Cecil Burton sought after in London, to give his lessons, as if he were one of the old masters! The only thing was that the wind blew harder at night since Ned went to sea; and a boy was in more danger than a grown man and a third mate like John.

And so it proved; for one night when the wind blew a new hay-rick of his father's across three parishes, it blew Edward's body ashore on the west coast.

Soon after this a neighboring earl, who had the year before paid off a mortgage on his lands, proceeded in natural process to enlarge his borders; and while there was plenty that had formerly belonged to the family to repurchase, somehow or another took it into his head to begin with what might seem more difficult of attainment. But John Boxall was willing enough to part with his small patrimony—for he was sick of it—provided he had a good sum of ready money, and the house with its garden and a paddock, by way of luck-penny, secured to him for his own life and that of his wife. This was easily arranged. But the late yeoman moped more than ever, and died within a twelvemonth, leaving his money to his wife. As soon as he was laid in his natural inheritance of land cubical, his wife went up to London to her son Richard, who was by this time the chief manager of the business of Messrs. Blunt & Baker. To him she handed over her money to use for the advantage of both. Paying her a handsome percentage, he invested it in a partnership in the firm, and with this fresh excitement to his energies, soon became, influentially, the principal man in the company. The two other partners were both old men, and neither had a son or near relative whom he might have trained to fill his place. So in the course of a few years, they, speaking commercially, fell asleep, and in the course of a few more, departed this life, commercially and otherwise. It was somewhat strange, however, that all this time Richard Boxall had given his mother no written acknowledgment of the money she had lent him, and which had been the foundation of his fortune. A man's faults are sometimes the simple reverses of his virtues, and not the results of his vices.

When his mother came first to London, he had of course taken her home to his house and introduced her to his wife, who was a kind and even warm-hearted woman. But partly from prudence, partly from habit, Mrs. Boxall, senior, would not consent to become the permanent guest of Mrs. Boxall, junior, and insisted on taking a lodging in the neighborhood.

It was not long, however, before she left the first, and betook herself to a second; nor long again before she left the second, and betook herself to a third. For her nature was like a fresh, bracing wind, which, when admitted within the precincts of a hot-house, where everything save the fire is neglected, proves a most unwelcome presence, yea, a dire dismay. Indeed, admirably as she had managed and borne with her own family, Mrs. Boxall was quite unfit to come into such habitual contact with another household as followed from her occupying a part of the same dwelling. Her faith in what she had tried with success herself, and her repugnance to whatever she had not been accustomed to, were such that her troublesomeness when she became familiar, was equal to the good nature which at first so strongly recommended her. Hence her changes of residence were frequent.

Up to the time when he became a sleeping partner, Mr. Blunt had resided in Guild Court—that is, the house door was in the court, while the lower part of the house, forming the offices of the firm, was entered from what was properly a lane, though it was called Bagot Street. As soon as mother and son heard that Mr. Blunt had at length bought a house in the country, the same thought arose in the mind of each—might not Mrs. Boxall go and live there? The house belonged to the firm, and they could not well let it, for there was more than one available connection between the two portions of the building, although only one had lately been in use, a door, namely, by which Mr. Blunt used to pass immediately from the glass-partitioned part of the counting-house to the foot of the oak stair-case already described; while they used two of the rooms in the house as places of deposit for old books and papers, for which there was no possible accommodation in the part devoted to active business. Hence nothing better could be devised than that Mrs. Boxall, senior, should take up her abode in the habitable region. This she made haste to do, accompanied by a young servant. With her she soon quarreled, however, and thereafter relied upon the ministrations of a charwoman. The door between the house and the counting-house was now locked, and the key of it so seldom taken from the drawer of Mr. Boxall, that it came to be regarded almost as a portion of the wall. So much for the inner connection of Guild Court and Bagot Street.

Some years after Mrs. Boxall removed to London, Mr. Burton, the music-master, died. They had lived from hand to mouth, as so many families of uncertain income are compelled to do, and his unexpected death left his wife and child without the means of procuring immediate necessities. Inheriting the narrowness and prejudices of his descent and of his social position to a considerable degree, Mr. Boxall had never come to regard his sister's match with a music-master as other than a degradation to the family, and had, in his best humors, never got further in the humanities of the kingdom of heaven, than to patronize his brother-in-law; though if size and quality go for anything in existence itself, as they do in all its accidents, Richard Boxall was scarcely comparable, honest and just man as he was, to Cecil Burton; who, however, except that he was the father of Lucy, and so in some measure accounts for her, is below the western horizon of our story, and therefore need scarcely be alluded to again. This behavior of her brother was more galling to Mrs. Burton than to her husband, who smiled down any allusion to it; and when she was compelled to accept Richard's kindness in the shape of money, upon the death of Mr. Burton, it was with a bitterness of feeling which showed itself plainly enough to wound the self-love of the consciously benevolent man of business. But from the first there had been the friendliest relations between the mother and daughter, and as it was only from her determination to avoid all ground of misunderstanding, that Mrs. Boxall had not consented to take up her abode with the Burtons. Consequently, after the death of Mr. Burton, the mother drew yet closer to the daughter, while the breach between brother and sister was widened.

Two years after the death of her husband, Mrs. Burton followed him. Then Mrs. Boxall took her grandchild Lucy home to Guild Court, and between the two there never arose the question of which should be the greater. It often happens that even a severe mother becomes an indulgent grandmother, partly from the softening and mellowing influences of time, partly from increase of confidence in child-nature generally, and perhaps also, in part, from a diminished sense or responsibility in regard to a child not immediately her own. Hence grandparents who have brought up their own children well are in danger of spoiling severely those of their sons and daughters. And such might have been the case with Mrs. Boxall and Lucy, had Lucy been of a more spoilable nature. But she had no idea of how much she had her own way, nor would it have made any difference to her if she had known it. There was a certain wonderful delicacy of moral touch about her in the discrimination of what was becoming, as well as of what was right, which resulted in a freedom the legalist of society would have called boldness, and a restraint which the same judge would have designated particularity; for Lucy's ways were not, and could not be, her ways, the one fearing and obeying, as she best could, existing laws hard to interpret, the other being a law unto herself. The harmonies of the music by which, from her earliest childhood, her growing brain had been interpenetrated, had, by her sweet will, been transformed into harmonies of thought, feeling, and action. She was not clever, but then she did not think she was clever, and therefore it was of no consequence; for she was not dependent upon her intellect for those judgments which alone are of importance in the reality of things, and in which clever people are just as likely to go wrong as any other body. She had a great gift in music—a gift which Thomas Worboise *had never yet discovered*, and which, at this period of his history, he was incapable of discovering, for he had not got beyond the toffee of the drawing-room sentiment—the song which must be sent forth to the universe from the pedestal of ivory shoulders. But two lines of a ballad from Lucy Barton were worth all the music, "She walks in beauty," included, that Mary Boxall could sing or play.

Lucy had not seen her cousins for years. Her uncle Richard, though incapable of being other than satisfied that the orphan should be an inmate of the house in Guild Court, could not, or at least did not, forget the mildly defiant look with which she retreated from his outstretched hand, and took her place beside her mother, on the sole occasion on which he called upon his sister after her husband's death. She had heard remarks—and being her mother's, she could not question the justice of them. Hence she had not once, since she had taken up her abode with her grandmother, been invited to visit her cousins; and there was no affectation, but in truth a little anxiety, in the question she asked Thomas Worboise about Mary Boxall's beauty. But, indeed, had she given her uncle no such offense, I have every reason to believe that her society would not have been much courted by his family. When the good among rich relations can be loving without condescension, and the good among poor relations can make sufficient allowance for the rich, then the kingdom of heaven will be nigh at hand. Mr. Boxall shook hands with his niece when he met her, asked her after his mother, and passed on.

But Lucy was not dependent on her uncle, scarcely on her grandmother, even. Before her mother's death, almost child as she still was, she had begun to give lessons in music to a younger child than herself, the daughter of one of her father's favorite pupils, who had married a rich merchant; and these lessons she continued. She was a favorite with the family, who were Jews, living in one of the older quarters of the west end of London; and they paid her handsomely, her age and experience taken into account. Every morning, except Saturday, she went by the underground railway to give an hour's lesson to Miriam Morgenstern, a gorgeous little eastern, whom her parents had no right to dress in such foggy colors as she wore.

Now a long farewell to preliminaries.

Lucy was just leaving her home one morning to go to her pupil, and had turned into the flagged passage which led from the archway into the court, when she met a little girl of her acquaintance, whom, with her help, I shall now present to my readers. She was a child of eight, but very small for her age. Her hair was neatly parted and brushed on each side of a large, smooth forehead, projecting over quiet eyes of blue, made yet quieter by the shadow of those brows. The rest of her face was very diminutive. A soberness as of complete womanhood, tried and chastened, lay upon her. She looked as if she had pondered upon life and its goal, and had made up her little mind to meet its troubles with patience. She was dressed in a cotton frock printed with blue rose-buds, faded by many waters and much soap. When she spoke, she used only one side of her mouth for the purpose, and then the old-fashionedness of her look rose almost to the antique, so that you could have fancied her one of the time-belated *good people* that, leaving the green forest-rings, had wandered into the city and become a Christian at a hundred years of age.

"Well, Mattie," said Lucy, "how are you this morning?"

"I am quite well, I thank you, miss," answered Mattie. "I don't call this morning. The church clock struck eleven five minutes ago."

This was uttered with a smile from the half of her mouth which seemed to say, "I know you want to have a little fun with me by using wrong names for things because I am a little girl, and little girls can be taken in; but it is of no use with me, though I can enjoy the joke of it."

Lucy smiled too, but not much, for she knew the child.

"What do you call the morning, then, Mattie?" she asked.

"Well," — she almost always began her sentences with a *Well* — "I call it morning before the sun is up."

"But how do you know when the sun is up? London is so foggy, you know, Mattie."

"Is it? I didn't know. Are there places without fog, miss?"

"Oh, yes; many."

"Well, about the sun. I always know what *he's* about, miss. I've got a almanac."

"But you don't understand the almanac, do you?"

"Well, I don't mean to say I understand all about it, but I always know what time the sun rises and goes to bed, you know."

Lucy had found she was rather early for the train, and from where she stood she could see the clock of St. Jacob's, which happened to be a reliable one. Therefore she went on to amuse herself with the child.

"But how is it that we don't see him, if he gets up when the almanac says, Mattie?"

"Well, you see, miss, he sleeps in a crib. And the sides of it are houses and churches, and St. Paulses, and the likes of that."

"Yes, yes; but some days we see him, and others we don't. We don't see him to-day, now."

"Well, miss, I dare say he's cross some mornings, and keeps the blankets about him after he's got his head up."

Lucy could not help thinking of Milton's line—for of the few poems she knew, one was the "Ode on the Nativity"—

> So, when the Sun in bed,
> Curtain'd with cloudy red,
> *Pillows his chin upon an orient wave.*

But the child laughed so queerly, that it was impossible to tell whether or how much those were her real ideas about the sunrise.

"How is your father?" Lucy asked.

"Do you mean my father or my mother?"

"I mean your father, of course, when I say so."

"Yes, but I have a mother, too."

Lucy let her have her way, for she did not quite understand her. Only she knew that the child's mother had died two or three years ago.

"Well," resumed the child, "my father is quite well, thank God; and so is my mother. There he is, looking down at us."

"Who do you mean, Mattie?" asked Lucy, now bewildered.

"Well, my mother," answered the child, with a still odder half smile.

Lucy looked up, and saw—but a little description is necessary. They were standing, as I have said already, in the flagged passage which led to, and post-officially considered, formed part of Guild Court. The archway from Bagot Street into this passage was as it were tunneled through a house facing the street, and from this house a wall, stretching inward to the first house in the court proper, formed one side of the passage. About the middle, this wall broke into two workshops, the smallest and strangest ever seen out of the east. There was no roof visible—that lay behind the curtain-wall; but from top to bottom of the wall, a hight of about nine feet, there was glass, divided in the middle so as to form two windows, one above the other. So likewise on the right-hand side of the glass were two doors, or hatches, one above the other. The tenement looked as if the smallest of rooms had been divided into two horizontally by a floor in the middle, thus forming two cells, which could not have been more than five feet by four, and four feet in hight. In the lower, however, a little hight had been gained by sinking the floor, to which a single step led down. In this under cell a cobbler sat, hammering away at his lap-stone—a little man, else he could hardly have sat there, or even got in without discomfort. Every now and then he glanced up at the girl and the child, but never omitted a blow in consequence. Over his head, on the thin floor between, sat a still smaller man, cross-legged like a Turk, busily "plying his needle and thread." His hair, which standing straight up gave a look of terror to his thin, pale countenance, almost touched the roof. It was the only luxuriance about him. As plants run to seed, he seemed to have run to hair. A calm, keen eye underneath its towering forest, revealed observation and peacefulness. He, too, occasionally looked from his work, but only in the act of drawing the horizontal thread, when his eyes had momentary furlough, moving in alternate oscillation with his hand. At the moment when the child said so, he was looking down in a pause in which he seemed for the moment to have forgotten his work in his interest in the pair below. He might be forty, or fifty or sixty—no one could tell which.

Lucy looked up, and said, "That is Mr. Spelt; that is not your mother."

"Well, but I call him my mother. I can't have two fathers, you know. So I call Mr. Spelt my mother; and so he is."

Here she looked up and smiled knowingly to the little tailor, who, leaning forward to the window, through which, reaching from roof to floor of his cage, his whole form was visible, nodded friendlily to the little girl in acknowledgment of her greeting. But it was now time for Lucy to go.

As soon as she had disappeared beyond the archway, Mattie turned toward the workshops. Mr. Spelt saw her coming, and before she had reached them, the upper half of the door was open, and he was stretching down his arms to lift her across the shoemaking region, into his own more celestial realm of tailoring. In a moment she was sitting in the farthest and snuggest corner, not cross-legged, but with her feet invisible in a heap of cuttings, from which she was choosing what she would—always with a reference to Mr. Spelt—for the dressing of a boy-doll which he had given her.

This was a very usual proceeding—so much so that Mattie and the tailor sat for nearly an hour without a word passing between them beyond what sprung from the constructive exigencies of the child. Neither of them was given to much utterance, though each had something of the peculiar gift of the Ancient Mariner, namely, "strange power of speech." They would sit together sometimes for half a day without saying a word; and then again there would be an oasis of the strangest conversation in the desert of their silence—a bad simile, for their silence must have been a thoughtful one to blossom into such speech. But the first words Mattie uttered on this occasion, were of a somewhat mundane character. She heard a footstep pass below. She was too far back in the cell to see who it was, and she did not lift her eyes from her work.

"When the cat's away, the mice will play," she said.

"What are you thinking about, Mattie?" asked the tailor.

"Well, wasn't that Mr. Worboise that passed? Mr. Boxall must be out. But he needn't go there, for somebody's always out this time o' day."

"What do you mean, Mattie?" again asked the tailor.

"Well, perhaps you don't understand such things, Mr. Spelt, not being a married man."

Poor Mr. Spelt had had a wife who had killed herself by drinking all his earnings; but perhaps Mattie knew nothing about that.

"No more I am. You must explain it to me."

"Well, you see, young people will be young people."

"Who told you that?"

"Old Mrs. Boxall says so. And that's why Mr. Worboise goes to see Miss Burton, *I* know. I told you so," she added, as she heard his step returning. But Thomas bore a huge ledger under his arm, for which Mr. Stopper had sent him round to the court. Very likely, however, had Lucy been at home, he might have laid a few minutes more to the account of the errand.

"So, so!" said the tailor. "That's it, is it, Mattie?"

"Yes; but we don't *say* anything about such things, you know."

"Oh, of course not," answered Mr. Spelt; and the conversation ceased.

After a long pause, the child spoke again.

"Is God good to you to-day, mother?"

"Yes, Mattie. God is always good to us."

"But he's better some days than others, isn't he?"

To this question the tailor did not know what to reply, and therefore, like a wise man, did not make the attempt. He asked her instead, as he had often occasion to do with Mattie, what she meant.

"Don't you know what I mean, mother? Don't you know God's better to us some days than others? Yes; and he's better to some people than he is to others."

"I am sure he's always good to you and me, Mattie."

"Well, yes; generally."

"Why don't you say *always*?"

"Because I'm not sure about it. Now to-day it's all very well. But yesterday the sun shone in the window a whole hour."

"And I drew down the blind to shut it out," said Mr. Spelt, thoughtfully.

"Well," Mattie went on, without heeding her friend's remark, "he *could* make the sun shine every day, if he liked.—I *suppose* he could," she added, doubtfully.

"I don't think we should like it, if he did," returned Mr. Spelt, "for the drain down below smells bad in the hot weather."

"But the rain might come—at night, I mean, not in the day-time, and wash them all out. Mightn't it, mother?"

"Yes; but the heat makes people ill. And if you had such hot weather as they have in some parts, as I am told, you would be glad enough of a day like this."

"Well, why haven't they a day like this, when they want it?"

"God knows," said Mr. Spelt, whose magazine was nearly exhausted, and the enemy pressing on vigorously.

"Well, that's what I say. God knows, and why doesn't he help it?"

And Mr. Spelt surrendered, if silence was surrender. Mattie did not press her advantage, however, and the besieged plucked up heart a little.

"I fancy perhaps, Mattie, he leaves something for us to do. You know they cut out the slop-work at the shop, and I can't do much more with that but put the pieces together. But when a repairing job comes in, I can contrive a bit then, and I like that better."

Mr. Spelt's meaning was not very clear, either to himself or to Mattie. But it involved the shadow of a great truth—that all the discords we hear in the universe around us, are God's trumpets sounding a *réveillé* to the sleeping human will, which once working harmoniously with his, will soon bring all things into a pure and healthy rectitude of operation. Till a man has learned to be happy without the sunshine, and therein becomes capable of enjoying it perfectly, it is well that the shine and the shadow should be mingled, so as God only knows how to mingle them. To effect the blessedness for which God made him, man must become a fellow-worker with God.

After a little while Mattie resumed operations.

"But you can't say, mother, that God isn't better to some people than to other people. He's surely gooder to you and me than he is to Poppie."

"Who's Poppie?" asked Mr. Spelt, sending out a flag of negotiation.

"Well, there she is—down in the gutter, I suppose, as usual," answered Mattie, without lifting her eyes.

The tailor peeped out of his house-front, and saw a barefooted child in the court below. What she was like I shall take a better opportunity of informing my reader. For at this moment the sound of strong nails tapping sharply reached the ear of Mr. Spelt and his friend. The sound came from a window just over the archway, hence at right angles to Mr. Spelt's workshop. It was very dingy with dust and smoke, allowing only the outline of a man's figure to be seen from the court. This much Poppie saw, and taking the tapping to be intended for her, fled from the court on soundless feet. But Mattie rose at once from her corner, and, laying aside cuttings and doll, stuck her needle and thread carefully in the bosom of her frock, saying:

"That's my father a-wanting of me. I wonder what he wants now. I'm sure I don't know how he would get on without *me*. And that *is* a comfort. Poor man! he misses my mother more than I do, I believe. He's always after me. Well, I'll see you again in the afternoon if I can. And, if not, you may expect me about the same hour to-morrow."

While she thus spoke she was let down from the not very airy hight of the workshop on to the firm pavement below; the tailor stretching his arms with her from above, like a bird of prey with a lamb in his talons. The last words she spoke from the ground, her head thrown back between her shoulders that she might look the tailor in the face, who was stooping over her like an angel from a cloud in the family Bible.

"Very well, Mattie," returned Mr. Spelt; "you know your own corner well enough by this time, I should think."

So saying, he drew himself carefully into his shell, for the place was hardly more, except that he could just work without having to get outside of it first. A soft half smile glimmered on his face; for although he was so used to Mattie's old-fashioned ways, that they scarcely appeared strange to him now, the questions that she raised were food for the little tailor's meditation—all day long, upon occasion. For some tailors are given to thinking, and when they are they have good opportunity of indulging their inclinations. And it is wonderful what a tailor's thinking may come to, especially if he reads his New Testament. Now, strange perhaps to tell, though Mr. Spelt never went to church, he did read his New Testament. And the little tailor was a living soul. He was one of those few who seem to be born with a certain law of order in themselves, a certain tidiness of mind, as it were, which would gladly see all the rooms or regions of thought swept and arranged; and not only makes them orderly, but prompts them to search after the order of the universe. They would gladly believe in the harmony of things; and although the questions they feel the necessity of answering take the crudest forms and the most limited and individual application, they yet are sure to have something to do with the laws that govern the world. Hence it was that the partial misfit of a pair of moleskin or fustian trowsers—for seldom did his originality find nobler material to exercise itself upon—would make him quite miserable, even though the navvy or dock-laborer might be perfectly satisfied with the result, and ready to pay the money for them willingly. But it was seldom, too, that he had even such a chance of indulging in the creative element of the tailor's calling, though he might have done something of the sort, if he would, in the way of altering. Of that branch of the trade, however, he was shy, knowing that it was most frequently in request with garment unrighteously come by; and Mr. Spelt's thin hands were clean.

He had not sat long after Mattie left him, before she reappeared from under the archway.

"No, no, mother," she said, "I ain't going to perch this time. But father sends his compliments, and will you come and take a dish of tea with him and me this afternoon?"

"Yes, Mattie; if you will come and fetch me when the tea's ready."

"Well, you had better not depend on me; for I shall have a herring to cook, and a muffin to toast, besides the tea to make and set on the hob, and the best china to get out of the black cupboard, and no end o' things to see to."

"But you needn't get out the best china for me, you know."

"Well, I like to do what's proper. And you just keep your eye on St. Jacob's, Mr. Spelt, and at five o'clock, when it has struck two of them, you get down and come in, and you'll find your tea a-waiting of you. There!"

With which conclusive form of speech, Mattie turned and walked back through the archway. She never ran, still less skipped as most children do, but held feet and head alike steadily progressive, save for the slightest occasional toss of the latter, which, as well as her mode of speech, revealed the element of conceit which had its share in the oddity of the little damsel.

When two strokes of the five had sounded in the ears of Mr. Spelt, he laid his work aside, took his tall hat from one of the comers where it hung on a peg, leaped lightly from his perch into the court, shut his half of the door, told the shoemaker below that he was going to Mr. Kitely's to tea, and would be obliged if he would fetch him should anyone want him, and went through the archway. There was a door to Mr. Kitely's house under the archway, but the tailor preferred going round the corner to the shop door in Bagot Street. By this he entered Jacob Kitely's domain, an old bookshop, of which it required some previous knowledge to find the way to the back premises. For the whole cubical space of the shop was divided and subdivided into a labyrinth of book-shelves, those in front filled with decently if not elegantly bound books, and those behind with a multitude innumerable of books in all conditions of dinginess, mustiness, and general shabbiness. Among these Jacob Kitely spent his time patching and mending them, and drawing up catalogues. He was not one of those booksellers who are so fond of their books that they cannot bear to part with them, and therefore when they are fortunate enough to lay their hands upon a rare volume, the highest pleasure they know in life, justify themselves in keeping it by laying a manuscript price upon it, and considering it so much actual property. Such men, perhaps, know something about the contents of their wares; but while few surpassed Jacob in a knowledge of the outside of books, from the proper treatment of covers in the varying stages of dilapidation, and of leaves when water-stained or mildewed or dry-rotted to the different values of better and best editions, cut and uncut leaves, tall copies, and folios shortened by the plow into doubtful quartos, he never advanced beyond the title-page, except when one edition differed from another, and some examination was necessary to determine to which the copy belonged. And not only did he lay no *fancy prices* upon his books, but he was proud of selling them under the market value—which he understood well enough, though he used the knowledge only to regulate his buying. The rate at which he sold was determined entirely by the rate at which he bought. Do not think, my reader, that I have the thinnest ghost of a political economy theory under this: I am simply and only describing character. Hence he sold his books cheaper than any other bookseller in London, contenting himself with a profit proportioned to his expenditure, and taking his pleasure in the rapidity with which the stream of books flowed through his shop. I have known him take threepence off the price he had first affixed to a book, because he found that he had not advertised it, and therefore it had not to bear its share of the expense of the catalogue.

Mr. Spelt made his way through the maze of books into the back shop, no one confronting him, and there found Mr. Kitely busy over his next catalogue, which he was making out in a school-boy's hand.

"How are you, Spelt?" he said, in an alto voice, in which rung a certain healthy vigor, amounting to determination. "Just in time, I believe. My little woman has been busy in the parlor for the last hour, and I can depend upon her to the minute. Step in."

"Don't let me interrupt you," suggested Mr. Spelt, meekly, and reverentially even, for he thought Mr. Kitely must be a very learned man indeed to write so much about books, and had at home a collection of his catalogues complete from the year when he first occupied the nest in the passage. I had forgot to say that Mr. Kitely was Mr. Spelt's landlord, and found him a regular tenant, else he certainly would not have invited him to tea.

"Don't let me interrupt you," said Mr. Spelt.

"Not at all," returned Mr. Kitely. "I'm very happy to see you, Spelt. You're very kind to my Mattie, and it pleases both of us to have you to tea in our humble way."

His humble way was a very grand way indeed to poor Spelt—and Mr. Kitely knew that. Spelt could only rub his nervous, delicate hands in token that he would like to say something in reply if he could but find the right thing to say. What hands those were, instinct with life and expression to the finger nails! No hands like them for fine-drawing. He would make the worst rent look as if there never had been a rough contact with the nappy surface.

The tailor stepped into the parlor, which opened out of the back shop sideways, and found himself in an enchanted region. A fire—we always see the fire first, and the remark will mean more to some people than to others—a most respectable fire burned in the grate, and if the room was full of the odor of red herrings, possibly objectionable *per se*, where was the harm when they were going to partake of the bloaters? A consequential cat lay on the hearth-rug. A great black oak cabinet, carved to repletion of surface, for which a pre-Raphaelite painter would have given half the price of one of his best pictures, stood at the end of the room. This was an accident, for Mr. Kitely could not appreciate it. But neither would he sell it when asked to do so. He was not going to mix trades, for that was against his creed; the fact being that he had tried so many things in his life that he now felt quite respectable from having settled to one for the rest of his days. But the chief peculiarity of the room was the number of birds that hung around it in cages of all sizes and shapes, most of them covered up now that they might go to sleep.

After Mattie had bestowed her approbation upon Mr. Spelt for coming exactly to the hour, she took the brown tea-pot from the hob, the muffin from before the fire, and three herrings from the top of it, and put them all one after another upon the table. Then she would have placed chairs for them all, but was prevented by the gallantry of Mr. Spelt, and only succeeded in carrying to the head of the table her own high chair, on which she climbed up, and sat enthroned to pour out the tea. It was a noteworthy triad. On opposite sides of the table sat the meek tailor and the hawk-expressioned bookseller. The latter had a broad forehead and large, clear, light eyes. His nose—I never think a face described when the nose is forgotten: Chaucer never omits it—rose from between his eyes as if intending to make the true Roman arch, but having reached the keystone, held on upon the same high level, and did not descend, but ceased. He wore no beard, and bore his face in front of him like a banner. A strong pediment of chin and a long, thin-lipped mouth completed an expression of truculent good nature. Plenty of clear-voiced speech, a breezy defiance of nonsense in every tone, bore in it a certain cold but fierce friendliness, which would show no mercy to any weakness you might vaunt, but would drag none to the light you abstained from forcing into notice. Opposite to him sat the thoughtful, thin-visaged, small man, with his hair on end; and between them the staid, old-maidenly child, with her hair in bands on each side of the smooth solemnity of her face, the conceit of her gentle nature expressed only in the turn-up of her diminutive nose. The bookseller behaved to her as if she had been a grown lady.

"Now, Miss Kitely," he said, "we shall have tea of the right sort, shan't we?"

"I hope so," answered Mattie, demurely. "Help Mr. Spelt to a herring, father."

"That I will, my princess. There, Mr. Spelt! There's a herring with a roe worth millions. To think, now, that every one of those eggs would be a fish like that, if it was only let alone!"

"It's a great waste of eggs, ain't it, father?" said Mattie.

"Mr. Spelt won't say so, my princess," returned Mr. Kitely, laughing. "He likes 'em."

"I do like them," said the tailor.

"Well, I dare say they're good for him, and it don't hurt them much," resumed Mattie, reflectively.

"They'll go to his brains, and make him clever," said Kitely. "And you wouldn't call that a waste, would you, Mattie?"

"Well, I don't know. I think Mr. Spelt's clever enough already. He's too much for me sometimes. I confess I can't always follow him."

The father burst into a loud roar of laughter, and laughed till the tears were running down his face. Spelt would have joined him but for the reverence he had for Mattie, who sat unmoved on her throne at the head of the table, looking down with calm benignity on her father's passion, as if laughter were a weakness belonging to grown-up men, in which they were to be condescendingly indulged by princesses, and little girls in general.

"Well, how's the world behaving to you, Spelt?" asked the bookseller, after various ineffectual attempts to stop his laughter by the wiping of his eyes.

"The world has never behaved ill to me, thank God," answered the tailor.

"Now, don't you trouble yourself to say that. You've got nobody to thank but yourself."

"But I like to thank God," said Mr. Spelt, apologetically. "I forgot that you wouldn't like it."

"Pshaw! pshaw! I don't mind it from you, for I believe you're fool enough to mean what you say. But, tell me this, Spelt—did you thank God when your wife died?"

"I tried hard not. I'm afraid I did, though," answered Spelt, and sat staring like one who has confessed, and awaits his penance.

The bookseller burst into another loud laugh, and slapped his hand on his leg.

"You have me there, I grant, Spelt."

But his face grew sober as he added, in a lower but still loud voice—

"I was thinking of my wife, not of yours. Folk say she was a rum un."

"She was a splendid woman," said the tailor. "She weighed twice as much as I do, and her fist—" Here he doubled up his own slender hand, laid it on the table, and stared at it, with his mouth full of muffin. Then, with a sigh, he added, "She was rather too much for me, sometimes. She was a splendid woman, though, when she was sober."

"And what was she when she was drunk?"

This grated a little on the tailor's feelings, and he answered with spirit—-

"A match for you or any other man, Mr. Kitely."

The bookseller said, "Bravo, Spelt!" and said no more.

They went on with their tea for some moments in silence.

"Well, princess!" said Mr. Kitely at last, giving an aimless poke to the conversation.

"Well, father," returned Mattie.

Whereupon her father turned to Spelt and said, as if resuming what had passed before—

"Now tell me honestly, Spelt, do you believe there is a God?"

"I don't doubt it."

"And I do. Will you tell me that, if there was a God, he would have a fool like that in the church over the way there, to do nothing but read the service, and a sermon he bought for eighteenpence, and—"

"From you?" asked Spelt, with an access of interest.

"No, no. I was too near the church for that. But he bought it of Spelman, in Holywell Street. Well, what was I saying?"

"You was telling us what Mr. Potter did for his money."

"Yes, yes. I don't know anything else he does but stroke his Piccadilly weepers, and draw his salary. Only I suppose they have some grand name for salary nowadays, out of the Latin Grammar or the Roman Antiquities, or some such, to make it respectable. Don't tell me there's a God, when he puts a man like that in the pulpit. To hear him haw-haw!"

The bookseller's logic was, to say the least of it, queer. But Spelt was no logician. He was something better, though in a feeble way. He could jump over the dry-stone fences and the cross-ditches of the logician. He was not one of those who stop to answer arguments against going home, instead of making haste to kiss their wives and children.

"I have read somewhere—in a book I dare say you mayn't have in your collection, Mr. Kitely—they call it the New Testament—"

There was not an atom of conscious humor in the tailor as he said this. He really thought Mr. Kitely might have conscientious scruples as to favoring the sale of the New Testament. Kitely smiled, but said nothing.

"I've read"—the tailor went on—"that God winked at some people's ignorance. I dare say he may wink at Mr. Potter's."

"Anyhow, I wouldn't like to be Mr. Potter," said the bookseller.

"No, nor I," returned Spelt. "But just as I let that poor creature, Dolman, cobble away in my ground-floor—though he has never paid me more than half his rent since ever he took it—"

"Is that the way of it? Whew!" said Mr. Kitely.

"About and about it," answered the tailor. "But that's not the point."

"What a fool you are then, Spelt, to—"

"Mr. Kitely," interposed the tailor with dignity, "do I pay your rent?"

"You've got my receipts, I believe," answered the bookseller, offended in his turn.

"Then I may make a fool of myself, if I please," returned Spelt, with a smile which took all offense out of the remark. "I only wanted to say that perhaps God lets Mr. Potter hold the living of St. Jacob's in something of the same way that I let poor Dolman cobble in my ground-floor. No offense, I hope."

"None whatever. You're a good-natured, honest fellow, Spelt; and don't distress yourself, you know, for a week or so. Have half a herring more? I fear this is a soft roe."

"No more, I thank you, Mr. Kitely. But all the clergy ain't like Mr. Potter. Perhaps he talks such nonsense because there's nobody there to hear it."

"There's plenty not there to do something for his money," said Kitely.

"That's true," returned the tailor. "But seeing I don't go to church myself, I don't see I've any right to complain. Do you go to church, Mr. Kitely?"

"I should think *not*," answered the bookseller. "But there's some one in the shop."

So saying, he started up and disappeared. Presently voices were heard, if not in dispute, yet in difference.

"You won't oblige me so far as that, Mr. Kitely?"

"No, I won't. I never pledge myself. I've been too often taken in. No offense. A man goes away and forgets. Send or bring the money, and the book is yours; or come to-morrow. I dare say it won't be gone. But I won't promise to keep it. There!"

"Very well, I won't trouble you again in a hurry."

"That is as you please, sir," said the bookseller, and no reply followed.

"That's Mr. Worboise," said Mattie, "I wish father wouldn't be so hard upon him."

"I don't like that young man," said Kitely, reëntering. "My opinion is that he's a humbug."

"Miss Burton does not think so," said Mattie, quietly.

"Eh, what, princess?" said her father. "Eh! ah! well! well!"

"You don't give credit, Mr. Kitely?" said the tailor.

"No, not to my own father. I don't know, though, if I had the old boy back again, now he's dead. I didn't behave over well to him, I'm afraid. I wonder if he's in the moon, or where he is, Mr. Spelt, eh? I should like to believe in God now, if it were only for the chance of saying to my father, 'I'm sorry I said so-and-so to you, old man.' Do you think he'll have got over it by this time, Spelt? You know all about those things. But I won't have a book engaged and left and not paid for. I'd rather give credit and lose it, and have done with it. If young Worboise wants the book he may come for it to-morrow."

"He always pays me—and pleasantly," said Spelt.

"Of course," said Mattie.

"I don't doubt it," said her father; "but I like things neat and clean. And I don't like him. He thinks a deal of himself."

"Surely he's neat and clean enough," said Spelt.

"Now, you don't know what I mean. A man ought always to know what another man means before he makes his remarks. I mean, I like a book to go out of my sight, and the price of it to go into my pocket, right slick off. But here's Dolman come to fetch you, Spelt," said the bookseller, as the cobbler made his appearance at the half-open door of the parlor.

"No, I ain't," said Dolman. "I only come to let the guv'nor know as I'm a going home."

"Where's that?" asked Kitely.

"Leastways, I mean going home with a pair o' boots," answered Dolman, evasively, wiping his nose with the back of his hand.

"Ah!" said the bookseller.

CHAPTER VI
THE MORNING OF CHRISTMAS DAY

It is but justice to Thomas Worboise to mention that he made no opportunities of going to his "governor's" house after this. But the relations of the families rendered it impossible for him to avoid seeing Mary Boxall sometimes. Nor did he make any great effort to evade each meetings: and it must be confessed that it was not without a glow of inward satisfaction that he saw her confusion and the rosy tinge that spread over her face and deepened the color of her eyes when they thus happened to meet. For Mary was a soft-hearted and too impressible girl. "I never said anything to her," were the words with which he would now and then apply an unction to his soul, compounded of self-justification and self-flattery. But he could not keep an outward appearance of coolness correspondent to the real coldness of his selfish heart, and the confusion which was only a dim reflection of her own was sufficient to make poor Mary suppose that feelings similar to her own were at work in the mind of the handsome youth. Why he did not *say* anything to her had not yet begun to trouble her, and her love was as yet satisfied with the ethereal luxuries of dreaming and castle-building.

It had been arranged between Amy Worboise and the Boxall girls, that if Christmas Day were fine, they would persuade their fathers to go with them to Hampstead Heath in the morning. How much of this arrangement was owing to sly suggestion on the part of Mary in the hope of seeing Tom, I do not know. I believe Jane contrived that Charles Wither should have a hint of the possibility. It is enough that the plan was accepted by the parents, and that the two families, with the exception of Mrs. Boxall, who could not commit the care of the Christmas dinner to the servants, and the invalid Mrs. Worboise, who, indeed, would always have preferred the chance of a visit from Mr. Simon to the certainty of sunshine and extended prospect, found themselves, after morning service, on the platform of the Highbury railway station, whence they soon reached Hampstead.

The walk from the station, up the hill to the top of the heath, was delightful. It was a clear day, the sun shining overhead, and the ground sparkling with frost under their feet. The keen, healthy air brought color to the cheeks and light to the eyes of all the party, possibly with the sole exception of Mr. Worboise, who, able to walk uncovered in the keenest weather, was equally impervious to all the gentler influences of Nature. He could not be said to be a disbeliever in Nature, for he had not the smallest idea that she had any existence beyond an allegorical one. What he did believe in was the law, meaning by that neither the Mosaic nor the Christian, neither the law of love nor the law of right, but the law of England as practiced in her courts of justice. Therefore he was not a very interesting person to spend a Christmas morning with, and he and Mr. Boxall, who was equally a believer in commerce, were left to entertain each other.

Mary Boxall was especially merry; Amy Worboise roguish as usual; Jane Boxall rather silent, but still bright-eyed, for who could tell whom she might meet upon the heath? And with three such girls Tom could not be other than gay, if not brilliant. True, Lucy was alone with her old grandmother in dingy Guild Court; but if she loved him, was not that enough to make her or any other woman happy? And he could not help it, besides. And why should he not improve the shining hour because Lucy had no flowers to gather honey from? Besides, was he not going to meet her the very next day, after much contrivance for concealment? So he was resolved to be merry and "freuen sich des Lebens."

They reached the flag-staff. The sun was getting low, and clouds were gathering behind him. Harrow-on-the-Hill was invisible, but the reservoir gleamed coldly far across the heath. A wind was blowing from the northwest; all London lay south and east in clearness wonderful, for two or three minutes. Then a vapor slowly melted away the dome of St. Paul's, and, like a spirit of sorrow, gathered and gathered till that which was full of life to those who were in it, was but a gray cloud to those that looked on from the distant hight. Already the young people felt their spirits affected, and as if by a common impulse, set off to walk briskly to the pines above the "Spaniards." They had not gone far, before they met Charles Wither sauntering carelessly along—at least he seemed much surprised to see them. He turned and walked between Jane and Amy, and Mary and Tom were compelled to drop behind, so as not to extend their line unreasonably and occupy the whole path. Quite unintentionally on Tom's part, the distance between the two divisions increased, and when he and Mary reached the pines, the rest of the party had vanished. They had in fact gone down into the Vale of Health, to be out of the wind, and return by the hollow, at the suggestion of Charles Wither, who wished thus to avoid the chance of being seen by Mr. Boxall. When he had taken his leave of them, just as they came in sight of the flag-staff, where Mr. Worboise and Mr. Boxall had appointed to meet them on their return from the pines, Jane begged Amy to say nothing about having met him.

"Oh," said Amy, with sudden and painful illumination, "I am *so* sorry to have been in the way."

"On the contrary, dear Amy, I should not have known what to say to papa, except you had been with me. I am so much obliged to you."

Thus there was clearly trouble in store for Mr. Boxall, who had never yet known what it was not to have his own way—in matters which he would consider of importance at least.

The two gentlemen had gone into Jack Straw's to have a glass of wine together, in honor of Christmas Day; and while they were seated together before a good fire, it seemed to Mr. Boxall a suitable opportunity for entering on a matter of business.

"What will you say to me, Worboise, when I tell you that I have never yet made a will?"

"I needn't tell you what I think, Boxall. You know well enough. Very foolish of you. Very imprudent, indeed. And I confess I should not have expected it of you, although I had a shrewd suspicion that such was the case."

"How came you to suspect it?"

"To tell the truth; I could not help thinking that as our friendship was not of yesterday, you would hardly have asked any one else to draw up your will but your old friend. So you see it was by no mysterious exercise of intelligence that I came to the conclusion that, not being an unkind or suspicious man, you must be a dilatory, and, excuse me, in this sole point, a foolish man."

"I grant the worst you can say, but you shall say it only till to-morrow— that is, if you will draw up the will, and have it ready for me to sign at any hour you may be at leisure for a call from me."

"I can't undertake it by to-morrow; but it shall be ready by the next day at twelve o'clock."

"That will do perfectly. I must remain 'a foolish man' for twenty-four hours longer—that is all."

"You won't be much the worse for that, except you have an attack of apoplexy to fix you there. But, joking apart, give me my instructions. May I ask how much you have to leave?"

"Oh; somewhere, off and on, about thirty thousand. It isn't much, but I hope to double it in the course of a few years, if things go on as they are doing."

Mr. Worboise had not known so much about his friend's affairs as he had pretended to his son. When he heard the amount, he uttered a slight "Whew!" But whether it meant that the sum fell below or exceeded his expectations, he gave Mr. Boxall no time to inquire.

"And how do you want the sum divided?" he asked.

"I don't want it divided at all. There's no occasion whatever to mention the sum. The books will show my property. I want my wife, in the case of her surviving me, to have the whole of it."

"And failing her?"

"My daughters, of course—equally divided. If my wife lives, there is no occasion to mention them. I want them to be dependent upon her as long as she lives, and so hold the family together as long as possible. She knows my wishes about them in everything. I have no secrets from her."

"I have only to carry out instructions. I have no right to offer any suggestions."

"That means that you would suggest something. Speak out, man."

"Suppose your daughters wished to marry?"

"I leave all that to their mother, as I said. They must be their own mistresses some day."

"Well, call on me the day after to-morrow, and I shall have the draught at least ready."

When the two girls reached the flag-staff, their parents were not there. Jane was glad of this, for it precluded questioning as to the point whence they had arrived. As they stood waiting, large snow-flakes began to fall, and the wind was rising. But they had not to wait long before the gentlemen made their appearance, busily conversing, so busily, indeed, that when they had joined the girls, they walked away toward the railway station without concerning themselves to ask what had become of Mary and Thomas.

When they reached the railway station, Mr. Boxall became suddenly aware that two of their party were missing.

"Why, Jane, where's Mary? And where's Tom? Where did you leave them?"

"Somewhere about the pines. I thought they would have been back long ago."

The two fathers looked at each other, and each seeing that the other looked knowing, then first consented, as he thought, to look knowing himself.

"Well," said Mr. Worboise, "they're old enough to take care of themselves, I suppose. I vote we don't wait for them."

"Serve them right," said Mr. Boxall.

"Oh, don't, papa," interposed Jane.

"Well, Jane, will you stop for them?" said her father.

But a sudden light that flashed into Jane's eyes made him change his tone. He did not know why, but the idea of Charles Wither rose in his mind, and he made haste to prevent Jane from taking advantage of the proposal.

"Come along," he said. "Let them take care of themselves. Come along."

The suspicion had crossed him more than once, that Mr. Wither and Jane possibly contrived to meet without his knowledge, and the thought made him writhe with jealousy; for it lay in his nature to be jealous of everyone of whom his wife or his daughters spoke well—that is, until he began to like him himself, when the jealousy, or what was akin to it, vanished. But it was not jealousy alone that distressed him, but the anxiety of real love as well.

By the time they reached Camden Road station, the ground was covered with snow.

When Tom and Mary arrived at the pines, I have said they found that the rest of their party had gone.

"Oh, never mind," said Mary, merrily; "let us run down into the hollow, and wait till they come back. I dare say they are not far off. They will never go without us."

Partly from false gallantry, partly from inclination, Thomas agreed. They descended the bank of sand in a quite opposite direction from that taken by Jane and her companions, and wandered along down the heath. By this time the sky was all gray and white. Long masses of vapor were driving overhead with jagged upper edges. They looked like lines of fierce warriors stooping in their eager rush to the battle. But down in the hollows of the heath all was still, and they wandered on for some time without paying any heed to the signs of the coming storm. Does my reader ask what they talked about? Nothing worthy of record, I answer; although every word that Thomas uttered seemed to Mary worth looking into for some occult application of the sort she would gladly have heard more openly expressed. At length, something cold fell upon her face, and Thomas glancing that moment at her countenance, saw it lying there, and took it for a tear. She looked up: the sky was one mass of heavy vapor, and a multitude of great downy snow-flakes was settling slowly on the earth. In a moment they were clasped hand in hand. The pleasure of the snow, the excitement of being shut out from the visible, or rather the seeing world, wrapped in the skirts of a storm with a pretty girl for his sole companion, so wrought upon Thomas, who loved to be moved and hated to will, that he forgot Lucy, and stood in delight gazing certainly at the falling snow, and not at Mary Boxall, but holding her hand tight in his own. She crept closer to him, for a little gentle fear added to her pleasure, and in a moment more his arm was about her—to protect her, I dare say, he said to himself.

Now, be it understood that Thomas was too much in love with himself to be capable of loving any woman under the sun after a noble and true fashion. He did not love Lucy a great deal better than he loved Mary. Only Mary was an ordinary pretty blonde, and Lucy was dark, with great black eyes, and far more distinguished in appearance than Mary. Besides, she was poor, and that added greatly to the romance of the thing; for it made it quite noble in him to love her, and must make her look up to him with such deserved admiration, that—without reckoning the fact that the one was offered him, and the other only not forbidden because there was as yet no suspicion of his visits in Guild Court—there was positively no room to hesitate in choice between them. Still the preference was not strong enough to keep his heart from beating fast when he found the snow-storm had closed him in with Mary. He had sense enough, however, to turn at once in order to lead her back toward the road. But this was already a matter of difficulty, for there was no path where the storm found them, and with the gathering darkness the snow already hid the high road across the heath; so that the first question was in what direction to go to find it. They kept moving, however, Mary leaning a good deal on Tom's arm, and getting more and more frightened as no path came in view. Even Tom began to be anxious about what was to come of it, and although he did his best to comfort Mary, he soon found that, before the least suspicion of actual danger, the whole romance had vanished. And now the snow not only fell rapidly, but the wind blew it sharply in their faces, and blinded them yet more than merely with its darkness—not that this mattered much as to the finding the way, for that was all hap-hazard long ago.

After wandering, probably in a circuitous fashion, for more than an hour, Mary burst out crying, and said she could not walk a step farther. She would have thrown herself down had not Tom prevented her. With the kindest encouragement—though he was really down-hearted himself—he persuaded her to climb a little hight near them, which with great difficulty she managed to do. From the top they saw a light, and descending the opposite side of the hill, found themselves in a road, where an empty cab stood by the door of a public-house. After trying to persuade Mary to have some refreshment, to which she refused to listen, insisting on being taken to her mother, Thomas succeeded in getting the cabman to drive them to the station. In the railway carriage, Mary lay like one dead, and although he took off both his coats to wrap about her, she seemed quite unconscious of the attention. It was with great difficulty that she reached her home; for there was no cab at the hackney station, and the streets were by this time nearly a foot deep in snow.

Thomas was not sorry to give her up to her mother. She immediately began to scold him. Then Mary spoke for the first time, saying, with great effort:

"Don't, mother. If it had not been for Thomas, I should have been dead long ago. He could not help it. Good-night, Tom."

And she feebly held up her face to kiss him. Tom stooped to meet it, and went away feeling tolerably miserable. He was wet and cold. The momentary fancy for Mary was quite gone out of him, and he could not help seeing that now he had kissed her before her mother he had got himself into a scrape.

Before morning Mary was in a raging fever.

That night Charles Wither spent at a billiard-table in London, playing, not high but long, sipping brandy and water all the time, and thinking what a splendid girl Jane Boxall was. But in the morning he looked all right.

CHAPTER VII
POPPIE

Thomas woke the next morning with a well-deserved sense of something troubling him. This too was a holiday, but he did not feel in a holiday mood. It was not from any fear that Mary might be the worse for her exposure, neither was it from regret for his conduct toward her. What made him uncomfortable was the feeling rather than thought that now Mrs. Boxall, Mary's mother, had a window that overlooked his premises, a window over which he had no legal hold, but which, on the contrary, gave her a hold over him. It was a window, also, of which she was not likely, as he thought, to neglect the advantage. Nor did it console him to imagine what Lucy would think, or—which was of more weight with Thomas—say or do, if she should happen to hear of the affair of yesterday. This, however, was very unlikely to happen; for she had not one friend in common with her cousins, except just her lover. To-day being likewise a holiday, he had arranged to meet her at the Marble Arch, and take her to that frightful source of amusement, Madame Tussaud's. Her morning engagement led her to that neighborhood, and it was a safe place to meet in—far from Highbury, Hackney, and Bagot Street.

The snow was very deep. Mrs. Boxall tried to persuade Lucy not to go. But where birds can pass, lovers can pass, and she was just finishing her lesson to resplendent little Miriam as Thomas got out of an omnibus at Park Street, that he might saunter up on foot to the Marble Arch.

The vision of Hyde Park was such as rarely meets the eye of a Londoner. It was almost grotesquely beautiful. Even while waiting for a lovely girl, Thomas could not help taking notice of the trees. Every bough, branch, twig, and shoot supported a ghost of itself, or rather a white shadow of itself upon the opposite side from where the black shadow fell. The whole tree looked like a huge growth of that kind of coral they call brain-coral, and the whole park a forest of such coralline growths. But against the sky, which was one canopy of unfallen snow, bright with the sun behind it, the brilliant trees looked more like coral still, gray namely, and dull.

Thomas had not sauntered and gazed for more than a few minutes before he saw Lucy coming down Great Cumberland Street toward him. Instead of crossing the street to meet her, he stood and watched her approach. There was even some excuse for his coolness, she looked so picturesque flitting over the spotless white in her violet dress, her red cloak, her grebe muff. I do not know what her bonnet was; for if a bonnet be suitable, it allows the face to show as it ought, and who can think of a bonnet then! But I know that they were a pair of very dainty morocco boots that made little holes in the snow across Oxford Street toward the Marble Arch where Thomas stood, filled, I fear, with more pride in the lovely figure that was coming to *him* than love of her.

"Have I kept you waiting long, Thomas?" said Lucy, with the sweetest of smiles, her teeth white as snow in the summer flush of her face.

"Oh! about ten minutes," said Thomas. It wasn't five. "What a cold morning it is!"

"I don't feel it much," answered Lucy. "I came away the first moment I could. I am sorry I kept you waiting."

"Don't mention it, Lucy. I should be only too happy to wait for you as long every morning," said Thomas, gallantly, not tenderly.

Lucy did not relish the tone. But what could she do? A tone is one of the most difficult things to fix a complaint upon. Besides, she was not in a humor to complain of any thing if she could help it. And, to tell the truth, she was a little afraid of offending Thomas, for she looked up to him ten times more than he deserved.

"How lovely your red cloak looked—quite a splendor—crossing the snow!" he continued.

And Lucy received this as a compliment to herself, and smiled again. She took his arm—for lovers will do that sometimes after it is quite out of fashion. But, will it be believed? Thomas did not altogether like her doing so, just because it was out of fashion.

"What a delightful morning it is," she said. "Oh! do look at the bars of the railing."

"Yes, I see. The snow has stuck to them. But how can you look at such vulgar things as iron stanchions when you have such a fairy forest as that before you?" said the reader of Byron, who was not seldom crossed by a feeling of dismay at finding Lucy, as he thought, decidedly unpoetical. He wanted to train her in poetry, as, with shame let it flow from my pen, in religion.

"But just look here," insisted Lucy, drawing him closer to the fence. "You are short-sighted, surely, Thomas. Just look there."

"Well, I see nothing but snow on both sides of the paling-bars," returned Thomas.

"Now I am sure you are short-sighted. It is snow on the one side, but not on the other. Look at the lovely crystals."

On the eastern quarter of each upright bar the snow had accumulated and stuck fast to the depth of an inch: the wind had been easterly. The fall had ceased some hours before morning, and a strong frost had set in. That the moisture in the air should have settled frozen upon the iron would not have been surprising; what Lucy wondered at was, that there should be a growth, half an inch long, of slender crystals, like the fungous growth commonly called mold, only closer, standing out from the bar horizontally, as if they had grown through it, out of the soil of the snow exactly opposite to it on the other side. On the one side was a beaten mass of snow, on the other a fantastic little forest of ice.

"I do not care about such microscopic beauties," said Thomas, a little annoyed that she whom he thought unpoetical could find out something lovely sooner than he could; for he was of those in whom a phantasm of self-culture is one of the forms taken by their selfishness. They regard this culture in relation to others with an eye to superiority, and do not desire it purely for its own sake. "Those trees are much more to my mind, now."

"Ah, but I do not love the trees less. Come into the park, and then we can see them from all sides."

"The snow is too deep. There is no path there."

"I don't mind it. My boots are very thick."

"No, no; come along. We shall get to Madame Tussaud's before there are many people there. It will be so much nicer."

"I should like much better to stay here awhile," said Lucy, half vexed and a little offended.

But Thomas did not heed her. He led the way up Oxford Street. She had dropped his arm, and now walked by his side.

"A nice lover to have!" I think I hear some of my girl readers say. But he was not so bad as this always, or even gentle-tempered Lucy would have quarreled with him, if it had been only for the sake of getting rid of him. The weight of yesterday was upon him. And while they were walking up the street, as handsome and fresh a couple as you would find in all London, Mary was lying in her bed talking wildly about Thomas.

Alas for the loving thoughts of youth and maidens, that go out like the dove from the ark, and find no room on the face of the desired world to fold their wings and alight! Olive-leaves they will gather in plenty, even when they are destined never to build a nest in the branches of the olive tree. Let such be strong notwithstanding, even when there are no more olive-leaves to gather, for God will have mercy upon his youths and maidens, and they shall grow men and women. Let who can understand me.

Having thus left the beauties of nature behind them for the horrible mockery of art at Madame Tussaud's, Thomas became aware from Lucy's silence that he had not been behaving well to her. He therefore set about being more agreeable, and before they reached Baker Street she had his arm again, and they were talking and laughing gayly enough. Behind them, at some distance, trotted a small apparition which I must now describe.

It was a little girl, perhaps ten years old, looking as wild as any savage in Canadian forest. Her face was pretty, as far as could be judged through the dirt that variegated its surface. Her eyes were black and restless. Her dress was a frock, of what stuff it would have been impossible to determine, scarcely reaching below her knees, and rent upward into an irregular fringe of ribbons that frostily fanned her little legs as she followed the happy couple, in a pair of shoes much too large for her, and already worn into such holes as to afford more refuge for the snow than for her feet. Her little knees were very black, and oh! those poor legs, caked and streaked with dirt, and the delicate skin of them thickened and cracked with frost and east winds and neglect! They could carry her through the snow satisfactorily, however—with considerable suffering to themselves, no doubt. But Poppie was not bound to be miserable because Poppie's legs were anything but comfortable; there is no selfishness in not being sorry for one's own legs. Her hair, which might have been expected to be quite black, was mingled with a reddish tinge from exposure to the hot sun of the preceding summer. It hung in tangled locks about her, without protection of any sort. How strange the snow must have looked upon it! No doubt she had been out in the storm. Her face peeped out from among it with the wild innocence of a gentle and shy but brave little animal of the forest. Purposely she followed Lucy's red cloak. But this was not the first time she had followed her; like a lost pup, she would go after this one and that one—generally a lady—for a whole day from place to place, obedient to some hidden drawing of the heart. She had often seen Lucy start from Guild Court, and had followed her to the railway; and, at length, by watching first one station and then another, had found out where she went every morning. Knowing then that she could find her when she pleased, she did not follow her more than twice a week or so, sometimes not once—just as the appetite woke in her for a little of her society. But my reader must see more of her before he or she will be interested enough in her either to please me or to care to hear more about the habits of this little wild animal of the stone forest of London. She had never seen Lucy with a gentleman before. I wonder if she had ever in her little life walked side by side with anybody herself; she was always trotting behind. This was the little girl whom Miss Matilda Kitely, her father's princess, called Poppie, and patronized, although she was at least two years older than herself, as near as could be guessed. Nor had she any other name; for no one knew where she had come from, or who were her parents, and she herself cared as little about the matter as anybody.

The lovers were some distance ahead of Poppie, as they had been all the way, when they entered the passage leading to the wax works. The instant she lost sight of them so suddenly, Poppie started in pursuit, lost one of her great shoes, and, instead of turning to pick it up, kicked the other after it— no great loss—and scampered at full barefooted speed over the snow, which was here well trodden. They could hardly have more than disappeared at the further end when she arrived at the entrance.

Poppie never thought about *might* or *might* not, but only about *could* or *could not*. So the way being open, and she happening to have no mind that morning to part with her company before she was compelled, she darted in to see whether she could not get another peep of the couple. Not only was the red cloak a fountain of warmth to Poppie's imagination, but the two seemed so happy together that she felt in most desirable society.

Thomas was in the act of paying for admission at the turnstile, when she caught sight of them again. The same moment that he admitted them, the man turned away from his post. In an instant Poppie had crept through underneath, dodged the man, and followed them, taking care, however, not to let them see her, for she had not the smallest desire to come to speech with them.

The gorgeousness about her did not produce much effect upon Poppie's imagination. What it might have produced was counteracted by a strange fancy that rose at once under the matted covering of that sunburnt hair. She had seen more than one dead man carried home upon a stretcher. She had seen the miserable funerals of the poor, and the desolate coffin put in the earth. But she knew that of human beings there were at least two very different breeds, of one of which she knew something of the habits and customs, while of the other she knew nothing, except that they lived in great houses, from which they were carried away in splendid black carriages, drawn by ever so many horses, with great black feathers growing out of their heads. What became of them after that she had not the smallest idea, for no doubt they would be disposed of in a manner very different from the funerals she had been allowed to be present at. When she entered the wax-work exhibition the question was solved. This was one of the places to which they carried the grand people after they were dead. Here they set them up, dressed in their very best, to stand there till—ah, till when, Poppie? That question she made no attempt to answer. She did not like the look of the dead people. She thought it a better way to put them in the earth and have done with them, for they had a queer look, as if they did not altogether like the affair themselves. And when one of them stared at her, she dodged its eyes, and had enough to do between them all and the showman; for though Poppie was not afraid of anybody, she had an instinctive knowledge that it was better to keep out of some people's way. She followed the sight of her friend, however, till the couple went into the "chamber of horrors," as if there was not horror enough in seeing humanity imitated so abominably in the outer room.

Yes, I am sorry to say it, Lucy went into that place, but she did not know what she was doing, and it was weeks before she recovered her self-respect after it. However, as Thomas seemed interested, she contrived to endure it for a little while—to endure, I do not mean the horror, for that was not very great—but the vulgarity of it all. Poppie lingered, not daring to follow them, and at length, seeing a large party arrive, began to look about for some place of refuge. In the art of vanishing she was an adept, with an extraordinary proclivity toward holes and comers. In fact, she could hardly see a hole big enough to admit her without darting into it at once to see if it would do—for what, she could not have specified—but for general purposes of refuge. She considered all such places handy, and she found one handy now.

Close to the entrance, in a recess, was a couch, and on this couch lay a man. He did not look like the rest of the dead people, for his eyes were closed. Then the dead people went to bed sometimes, and to sleep. Happy dead people—in a bed like this! For there was a black velvet cover thrown over the sleeping dead man, so that nothing but his face was visible; and to the eyes of Poppie this pall looked so soft, so comfortable, so enticing! It was a place to dream in. And could there be any better hiding-place than this? If the man was both dead and sleeping, he would hardly object to having her for a companion. But as she sent one parting peep round the corner of William Pitt or Dick Turpin, after her friends, ere she forsook them to lie down with the dead, one of the attendants caught sight of her, and advanced to expel the dangerous intruder. Poppie turned and fled, sprang into the recess, crept under the cover, like a hunted mouse, and lay still, the bed-fellow of no less illustrious a personage than the Duke of Wellington, and cold as he must have been, Poppie found him warmer than her own legs.

The man never thought of following her in that direction, and supposed that she had escaped as she had managed to intrude.

Poppie found the place so comfortable that she had no inclination to change her quarters in haste. True, it was not nice to feel the dead man when she put out foot or hand; but then she need not put out foot or hand. And Poppie was not used to feeling warm. It was a rare sensation, and she found it delightful. Every now and then she peeped from under the *mortcloth*—for the duke was supposed to be lying in state—to see whether Thomas and Lucy were coming. But at length, what with the mental and physical effects of warmth and comfort combined, she fell fast asleep, and dreamed she was in a place she had been in once before, though she had forgotten all about it. From the indefinite account she gave of it, I can only conjecture that it was the embodiment of the vaguest memory of a motherly bosom; that it was her own mother's bosom she recalled even thus faintly, I much doubt. But from this undefined bliss she was suddenly aroused by a rough hand and a rough voice loaded with a curse. Poppie was used to curses, and did not mind them a bit—somehow they never hurt her—but she was a little frightened at the face of indignant surprise and wrath which she saw bending over her when she awoke. It was that of one of the attendants, with a policeman beside him, for whom he had sent before he awoke the child, allowing her thus a few moments of unconscious blessedness, with the future hanging heavy in the near distance. But the duke had slept none the less soundly that she was by his side, and had lost none of the warmth that she had gained. It was well for Ruth that there were no police when she slept in Boaz's barn; still better that some of the clergymen, who serve God by reading her story on the Sunday, were not the magistrates before whom the police carried her. With a tight grasp on her arm, Poppie was walked away in a manner uncomfortable certainly to one who was accustomed to trot along at her own sweet will—and a sweet will it was, that for happiness was content to follow and keep within sight of some one that drew her, without longing for even a word of grace—to what she had learned to call *the jug*, namely, the police prison; but my reader must not spend too much of his stock of sympathy upon Poppie; for she did not mind it much. To be sure in such weather the jug was very cold, but she had the memories of the past to comfort her, the near past, spent in the society of the dead duke, warm and consoling. When she fell asleep on the hard floor of the *lock-up*, she dreamed that she was dead and buried, and trying to be warm and comfortable, as she ought to be in her grave, only somehow or another she could not get things to come right; the wind would blow through the chinks of her pauper's coffin; and she wished she had been a duke or a great person generally, to be so grandly buried as they were in the cemetery in Baker Street. But Poppie was far less to be pitied for the time, cold as she was, than Mary Boxall, lying half asleep and half awake and all dreaming in that comfortable room, with a blazing fire, and her own mother sitting beside it. True, likewise, Poppie heard a good many bad words and horrid speeches in the jug, but she did not heed them much. Indeed, they did not even distress her, she was so used to them; nor, upon occasion, was her own language the very pink of propriety. How could it be? The vocabulary in use in the houses she knew had ten vulgar words in it to one that Mattie, for instance, would hear. But whether Poppie, when speaking the worst language that ever crossed her lips, was lower, morally and spiritually considered, than the young lord in the nursery, who, speaking with articulation clear cut as his features, and in language every word of which is to be found in Johnson; refuses his brother a share of his tart and gobbles it up himself, there is to me, knowing that if Poppie could swear she could share, no question whatever. God looks after his children in the cellars as well as in the nurseries of London.

Of course she was liberated in the morning, for the police magistrates of London are not so cruel as some of those country clergymen who, not content with preaching about the justice of God from the pulpit, must seat themselves on the magistrate's bench to dispense the injustice of men. If she had been brought before some of them for sleeping under a hay-stack, and having no money in her pocket, as if the night sky, besides being a cold tester to lie under, were something wicked as well, she would have been sent to prison; for, instead of believing in the blessedness of the poor, they are of Miss Kilmansegg's opinion, "that people with nought are naughty." The poor little thing was only reprimanded for being where she had no business to be, and sent away. But it was no wonder if, after this adventure, she should know Thomas again when she saw him; nay, that she should sometimes trot after him for the length of a street or so. But he never noticed her.

CHAPTER VIII
MR. SIMON'S ATTEMPT

The next day the sun shone brilliantly upon the snow as Thomas walked to the counting-house. He was full of pleasant thoughts, crossed and shadowed by a few of a different kind. He was not naturally deceitful, and the sense of having a secret which must get him into trouble if it were discovered, and discovered it must be some day, could not fail to give him uneasiness notwithstanding the satisfaction which the romance of the secrecy of a love affair afforded him. Nothing, however, as it seemed to him, could be done, for he was never ready to do anything to which he was neither led nor driven. He could not generate action, or, rather, he had never yet begun to generate action.

As soon as he reached Bagot Street, he tapped at the glass door, and was admitted to Mr. Boxall's room. He found him with a look of anxiety upon a face not used to express that emotion.

"I hope Miss Mary—" Thomas began, with a little hesitation.

"She's very ill," said her father, "very ill, indeed. It was enough to be the death of her. Excessively imprudent."

Now Mary had been as much to blame, if there was any blame at all, for the present results of the Christmas morning, as Thomas; but he had still generosity enough left not to say so to her father.

"I am very sorry," he said. "We were caught in the snow, and lost our way."

"Yes, yes, I know. I oughtn't to be too hard upon young people," returned Mr. Boxall, remembering, perhaps, that he had his share of the blame in leaving them so much to themselves.

"I only hope she may get through it. But she's in a bad way. She was quite delirious last night."

Thomas was really concerned for a moment, and looked so. Mr. Boxall saw it, and spoke more kindly.

"I trust, however, that there is not any immediate danger. It's no use you coming to see her. She can't see anybody but the doctor."

This was a relief to Thomas. But it was rather alarming to find that Mr. Boxall clearly expected him to want to go to see her.

"I am very sorry," he said again; and that was all he could find to say.

"Well, well," returned his master, accepting the words as if they had been an apology. "We must do our work, anyhow. Business is the first thing, you know."

Thomas took this as a dismissal, and retired to the outer office, in a mood considerably different from that which Mr. Boxall attributed to him.

A clerk's duty is a hard one, and this ought to be acknowledged. Neither has he any personal interest in the result of the special labor to which he is for the time devoted, nor can this labor have much interest of its own beyond what comes of getting things square, and the sense of satisfaction which springs from activity, and the success of completion. And it is not often that a young man is fortunate enough to have a master who will not only appreciate his endeavors, but will let him know that he does appreciate them. There are reasons for the latter fact beyond disposition and temperament. The genial employer has so often found that a strange process comes into operation in young and old, which turns the honey of praise into the poison of self-conceit, rendering those to whom it is given disagreeable, and ere long insufferable, that he learns to be very chary in the administration of the said honey, lest subordinates think themselves indispensable, and even neglect the very virtues which earned them the praise. A man must do his duty, if he would be a free man, whether he likes it or not, and whether it is appreciated or not. But if he can regard it as the will of God, the work not fallen upon him by chance, but *given* him to do, understanding that every thing well done belongs to His kingdom, and every thing ill done to the kingdom of darkness, surely even the irksomeness of his work will be no longer insuperable. But Thomas had never been taught this. He did not know that his day's work had anything to do with the saving of his soul. Poor Mr. Simon gave him of what he had, like his namesake at the gate of the temple, but all he had served only to make a man creep; it could not make him stand up and walk. "A servant with this clause,"—that is the clause, "*for thy sake,*"—wrote George Herbert:

> "A servant with this clause
> Makes drudgery divine;
> Who sweeps a room, as for thy laws,
> Makes that and the action fine."

But Mr. Simon could not understand the half of this, and nothing at all of the essential sacredness of the work which God would not give a man to do if it were not sacred. Hence Thomas regarded his work only as drudgery; considered it beneath him; judged himself fitter for the army, and had hankerings after gold lace. He dabbled with the fancy that there was a mistake somewhere in the arrangement of mundane affairs, a serious one, for was he not fitted by nature to move in some showy orbit, instead of being doomed to rise in Highbury, shine in Bagot Street, and set yet again in Highbury? And so, although he did not absolutely neglect his work, for he hated to be found fault with, he just did it, not entering into it with any spirit; and as he was clever enough, things went on with tolerable smoothness.

That same evening, when he went home from his German lesson of a quarter of an hour, and his interview with Lucy of an hour and a quarter, he found Mr. Simon with his mother. Thomas would have left the room; for his conscience now made him wish to avoid Mr. Simon—who had pressed him so hard, with the stamp of religion that the place was painful, although the impression was fast disappearing.

"Thomas," said his mother, with even more than her usual solemnity, "Thomas, come here. We want to have some conversation with you."

"I have not had my tea yet, mother."

"You can have your tea afterward. I wish you to come here now."

Thomas obeyed, and threw himself with some attempt at nonchalance into a chair.

"Thomas, my friend," began Mr. Simon, with a tone—how am I to describe it? I could easily, if I chose to use a contemptuous word, but I do not wish to intrude on the region of the comic satirist, and must therefore use a periphrase—with the tone which corresponds to the long face some religions people assume the moment the conversation turns toward sacred things, and in which a certain element of the ludicrous, because affected, goes far to destroy the solemnity, "I am uneasy about you. Do not think me interfering, for I watch for your soul as one that must give an account. I have to give an account of you, for at one time you were the most promising seal of my ministry. But your zeal has grown cold; you are unfaithful to your first love; and when the Lord cometh as a thief in the night, you will be to him as one of the lukewarm, neither cold nor hot, my poor friend. He will spue you out of his mouth. And I may be to blame for this, though at present I know not how. Ah, Thomas! Thomas! Do not let me have shame of you at his appearing. The years are fleeting fast, and although he delay his coming, yet he *will* come; and he will slay his enemies with the two-edged sword that proceedeth out of his mouth."

Foolish as Mr. Simon was, he was better than Mr. Potter, if Mr. Kitely's account of him was correct; for he was in earnest, and acted upon his belief. But he knew nothing of human nature, and as Thomas grew older, days, even hours, had widened the gulf between them, till his poor feeble influences could no longer reach across it, save as unpleasant reminders of something that had been. Happy is the youth of whom a sensible, good clergyman has a firm hold—a firm human hold, I mean—not a priestly one, such as Mr. Simon's. But if the clergyman be feeble and foolish, the worst of it is, that the youth will transfer his growing contempt for the clergyman to the religion of which he is such a poor representative. I know another clergyman— perhaps my readers may know him too—who, instead of lecturing Thomas through the medium of a long string of Scripture phrases, which he would have had far too much reverence to use after such a fashion, would have taken him by the shoulder, and said, "Tom, my boy, you've got something on your mind. I hope it's nothing wrong. But whatever it is, mind you come to me if I can be of any use to you."

To such a man there would have been a chance of Tom's making a clean breast of it—not yet, though—not before he got into deep water. But Mr. Simon had not the shadow of a chance of making him confess. How could Thomas tell such a man that he was in love with one beautiful girl, and had foolishly got himself into a scrape with another?

By this direct attack upon him in the presence of his mother, the man had lost the last remnant of his influence over him, and, in fact, made him feel as if he should like to punch his head, if it were not that he could not bear to hurt the meek little sheep. He did not know that Mr. Simon had been rather a bruiser at college—small and meek as he was—only that was before his conversion. If he had cared to defend himself from such an attack, which I am certain he would not have doubled fist to do, Thomas could not have stood one minute before him.

"Why do you not speak, Thomas?" said his mother, gently.

"What do you want me to say, mother?" asked Thomas in return, with rising anger. He never could resist except his temper came to his aid.

"Say what you ought to say," returned Mrs. Worboise, more severely.

"What ought I to say, Mr. Simon?" said Thomas, with a tone of mock submission, not so marked, however, that Mr. Simon, who was not sensitive, detected it.

"Say, my young friend, that you will carry the matter to the throne of grace, and ask the aid—"

But I would rather not record sacred words which, whatever they might mean in Mr. Simon's use of them, mean so little in relation to my story.

Thomas, however, was not yet so much of a hypocrite as his training had hitherto tended to make him, and again he sat silent for a few moments, during which his mother and her friend sat silent likewise, giving him time for reflection. Then he spoke, anxious to get rid of the whole unpleasant affair.

"I will promise to think of what you have said, Mr. Simon."

"Yes, Thomas, but *how* will you think of it?" said his mother.

Mr. Simon, however, glad to have gained so much of a concession, spoke more genially. He would not drive the matter further at present.

"Do, dear friend; and may He guide you into the truth. Remember, Thomas, the world and the things of this world are passing away. You are a child no longer, and are herewith called upon to take your part, for God or against him—"

And so on, till Thomas grew weary as well as annoyed.

"Will you tell me what fault you have to find with me?" he said at last. "I am regular at the Sunday-school, I am sure."

"Yes, that we must allow, and heartily," answered Mr. Simon, turning to Mrs. Worboise as if to give her the initiative, for he thought her rather hard with her son; "only I would just suggest to you, Mr. Thomas—I don't ask you the question, but I would have you ask yourself—whether your energy is equal to what it has been? Take care lest, while you teach others, you yourself should be a castaway. Remember that nothing but faith in the merits—"

Thus started again, he went on, till Thomas was forced loose from all sympathy with things so unmercifully driven upon him, and vowed in his heart that he would stand it no longer.

Still speaking, Mr. Simon rose to take his leave. Thomas, naturally polite, and anxious to get out of the scrutiny of those cold blue eyes of his mother, went to open the door for him, and closed it behind him with a sigh of satisfaction. Then he had his tea and went to his own room, feeling wrong, and yet knowing quite well that he was going on to be and to do wrong. Saintship like his mother's and Mr. Simon's was out of his reach.

Perhaps it was. But there were other things essential to saintship that were within his reach—and equally essential to the manliness of a gentleman, which he would have been considerably annoyed to be told that he was in much danger of falling short of, if he did not in some way or other mend his ways, and take heed to his goings.

The next morning mother and pastor held a long and, my reader will believe, a dreary consultation over the state of Thomas. I will not afflict him with a recital of what was said and resaid a dozen times before they parted. If Mr. Worboise had overheard it, he would have laughed, not heartily, but with a perfection of contempt, for he despised all these things, and would have despised better things, too, if he had known them.

The sole result was that his mother watched Thomas with yet greater assiduity; and Thomas began to feel that her eyes were never off him, and to dislike them because he feared them. He felt them behind his back. They haunted him in Bagot Street. Happy with Lucy, even there those eyes followed him, as if searching to find out his secret; and a vague fear kept growing upon him that the discovery was at hand. Hence he became more and more cunning to conceal his visits. He dreaded what questions those questioning eyes might set the tongue asking. For he had not yet learned to lie. He prevaricated, no doubt; but lying may be a step yet further on the downward road.

One good thing only came out of it all: he grew more and more in love with Lucy. He almost loved her.

CHAPTER IX
BUSINESS

For some days Mr. Boxall was so uneasy about Mary that he forgot his appointment with Mr. Worboise. At length, however, when a thaw had set in, and she had began to improve, he went to call upon his old friend.

"Ah, Boxall! glad to see you. What a man you are to make an appointment with! Are you aware, sir, of the value of time in London, not to say in this life generally? Are you aware that bills are due at certain dates, and that the man who has not money at his banker's to meet them is dishonored— euphemistically shifted to the bill?"

Thus jocosely did Mr. Worboise play upon the well-known business habits of his friend, who would rather, or at least believed he would rather, go to the scaffold than allow a bill of his to be dishonored. But Mr. Boxall was in a good humor, too, this morning.

"At least, Worboise," he answered, "I trust when the said bill is dishonored, you may not be the holder."

"Thank you. I hope not. I don't like losing money."

"Oh, don't mistake me! I meant for my sake, not yours."

"Why?"

"Because you would skin the place before you took the pound of flesh. I know you!"

Mr. Worboise winced. Mr. Boxall thought he had gone too far, that is, had been rude. But Mr. Worboise laughed aloud.

"You flatter me, Boxall," he said. "I had no idea I was such a sharp practitioner. But you ought to know best. We'll take care, at all events, to have this will of yours right."

So saying, he went to a drawer to get it out. But Mr. Boxall still feared that his friend had thought him rude.

"The fact is," he said, "I have been so uneasy about Mary."

"Why? What's the matter?" interrupted Mr. Worboise, stopping on his way across the room.

"Don't you know?" returned Mr. Boxall, in some surprise. "She's never got over that Hampstead Heath affair. She's been in bed ever since."

"God bless me!" exclaimed the other. "I never heard a word of it. What was it?"

So Mr. Boxall told as much as he knew of the story, and any way there was not much to tell.

"Never heard a word of it!" repeated the lawyer.

The statement made Mr. Boxall more uneasy than he cared to show.

"But I must be going," he said; "so let's have this troublesome will signed and done with."

"Not in the least a troublesome one, I assure you. Rather too simple, I think. Here it is."

And Mr. Worboise began to read it over point by point to his client.

"All right," said the latter. "Mrs. Boxall to have everything to do with it as she pleases. It is the least I can say, for she has been a good wife to me."

"And will be for many years to come, I hope," said Mr. Worboise.

"I hope so. Well, go on."

Mr. Worboise went on.

"All right," said his client again. "Failing my wife, my daughters to have everything, as indeed they will whether my wife fails or not—at last, I mean, for she would leave it to them, of course."

"Well," said the lawyer, "and who comes next?"

"Nobody. Who do you think?"

"It's rather a short—doesn't read quite business-like. Put in any body, just for the chance—a poor one, ha! ha! with such a fine family as yours."

"Stick yourself in then, old fellow; and though it won't do you any good, it will be an expression of my long esteem and friendship for you."

"What a capital stroke!" thought Mr. Boxall. "I've surely got that nonsense out of his head now. He'll never think of it more. I *was* country-bred."

"Thank you, old friend," said Mr. Worboise, quietly, and entered his own name in succession.

The will was soon finished, signed, and witnessed by two of Mr. Worboise's clerks.

"Now what is to be done with it?" asked Mr. Worboise.

"Oh, you take care of it for me. You have more storage—for that kind of thing, I mean, than I have. I should never know where to find it."

"If you want to make any alteration in it, there's your box, you know."

"Why, what alteration could I want to make in it?"

"That's not for me to suppose. You might quarrel with me though, and want to strike out my name."

"True. I *might* quarrel with my wife too, mightn't I, and strike her name out?"

"It might happen."

"Yes; anything might happen. Meantime I am content with sufficient probabilities."

"By the way, how is that son of mine getting on?"

"Oh, pretty well. He's regular enough, and I hear no complaints of him from Stopper; and *he's* sharp enough, I assure you."

"But you're not over-satisfied with him yourself, eh?"

"Well, to speak the truth, between you and me, I don't think he's cut out for our business."

"That's much the same as saying he's of no use for business of any sort."

"I don't know. He does his work fairly well, as I say, but he don't seem to have any heart in it."

"Well, what do you think he is fit for now?"

"I'm sure I don't know. You could easily make a fine gentleman of him."

Mr. Boxall spoke rather bitterly, for he had already had flitting doubts in his mind whether Tom had been behaving well to Mary. It had become very evident since her illness that she was very much in love with Tom, and that he should be a hair's-breadth less in love with her was offense enough to rouse the indignation of a man like Mr. Boxall, good-natured as he was; and that he had never thought it worth while even to mention the fact of her illness to his father, was strange to a degree.

"But I can't afford to make a fine gentleman of him. I've got his sister to provide for as well as my fine gentleman. I don't mean to say that I could not leave him as much, perhaps more than you can to *each* of your daughters; but girls are so different from boys. Girls can live upon anything; fine gentlemen can't." And here Mr. Worboise swore.

"Well, it's no business of mine," said Mr. Boxall. "If there's anything I can do for him, of course, for your sake, Worboise—"

"The rascal has offended him somehow," said Mr. Worboise to himself. "It's that Hampstead business. Have patience with the young dog," he said, aloud. "That's all I ask you to do for him. Who knows what may come out of him yet?"

"That's easy to do. As I tell you, there's no fault to find with him," answered Mr. Boxall, afraid that he had exposed some feeling that had better have been hidden. "Only one must speak the truth."

With these words Mr. Boxall took his leave.

Mr. Worboise sat and cogitated.

"There's something in that rascal's head, now," he said to himself. "His mother and that Simon will make a spoon of him. I want to get some sense out of him before he's translated to kingdom-come. But how the deuce to get any sense out when there's so precious little in! I found seventeen volumes of Byron on his book-shelves last night. I'll have a talk to his mother about him. Not that that's of much use!"

To her husband Mrs. Worboise always wore a resigned air, believing herself unequally yoked to an unbeliever with a bond which she was not at liberty to break, because it was enjoined upon her to win her husband by her chaste conversation coupled with fear. Therefore when he went into her room that evening, she received him as usual with a look which might easily be mistaken, and not much mistaken either, as expressive of a sense of injury.

"Well, my dear," her husband began, in a conciliatory, indeed jocose, while yet complaining tone, "do you know what this precious son of ours has been about? Killing Mary Boxall in a snow-storm, and never telling me a word about it. I suppose you know the whole story, though? You *might* have told me."

"Indeed, Mr. Worboise, I am sorry to say I know nothing about Thomas nowadays. I can't understand him. He's quite changed. But if I were not laid on a couch of suffering—not that I complain of that—I should not come to *you* to ask what he was about. I should find out for myself."

"I wish to goodness you were able."

"Do not set your wish against *His* will," returned Mrs. Worboise, with a hopeless reproof in her tone, implying that it was of no use to say so, but she must bear her testimony notwithstanding.

"Oh! no, no," returned her husband; "nothing of the sort. Nothing further from my intention. But what is to be done about this affair? You know it would please you as well as me to see him married to Mary Boxall. She's a good girl, that you know."

"If I were sure that she was a changed character, there is nothing I should like better, I confess—that is, of worldly interest."

"Come, come, Mrs. Worboise. I don't think you're quite fair to the girl."

"What *do* you mean, Mr. Worboise?"

"I mean that just now you seemed in considerable doubt whether or not your son was a changed character, as you call it. And yet you say that if Mary Boxall were a changed character, you would not wish anything more—that is, of worldly interest—than to see him married to Mary Boxall. Is that fair to Mary Boxall? I put the question merely."

"There would be the more hope for him; for the Scripture says that the believing wife may save her husband."

Mr. Worboise winked inwardly to himself. Because his wife's religion was selfish, and therefore irreligious, therefore, religion was a humbug, and *therefore* his conduct might be as selfish as ever he chose to make it.

"But how about Mary? Why should you wish her, if she was a changed character, to lose her advantage by marrying one who is not so?"

"She might change him, Mr. Worboise, as I have said already," returned the lady, decisively; "for she might speak with authority to one who knew nothing about these things."

"Yes. But if Thomas were changed, and Mary not—what then?"

Mrs. Worboise murmured something not quite audible about "I and the children whom God hath given me."

"At the expense of the children he hasn't given you!" said Mr. Worboise, at a venture; and chuckled now, for he saw his victory in her face.

But Mr. Worboise's chuckle always made Mrs. Worboise *shut up*, and not another word could he get out of her that evening. She never took refuge in her illness, but in an absolute dogged silence, which she persuaded herself that she was suffering for the truth's sake.

Her husband's communication made her still more anxious about Thomas, and certain suspicions she had begun to entertain about the

German master became more decided. In her last interview with Mr. Simon, she had hinted to him that Thomas ought to be watched, that they might know whether he really went to his German lesson or went somewhere else. But Mr. Simon was too much of a gentleman not to recoil from the idea, and Mrs. Worboise did not venture to press it. When she saw him again, however, she suggested—I think I had better give the substance of the conversation, for it would not in itself be interesting to my readers—she suggested her fears that his German master had been mingling German theology, with his lessons, and so corrupting the soundness of his faith. This seemed to Mr. Simon very possible indeed, for he knew how insidious the teachers of such doctrines are, and, glad to do something definite for his suffering friend, he offered to call upon the man and see what sort of person he was. This offer Mrs. Worboise gladly accepted, without thinking that of all men to find out any insidious person, Mr. Simon, in his simplicity, was the least likely.

But now the difficulty arose that they knew neither his name nor where he lived, and they could not ask Thomas about him. So Mr. Simon undertook the task of finding the man by inquiry in the neighborhood of Bagot Street.

"My friend, he said, stepping the next morning into Mr. Kitely's shop,—he had a way of calling everybody his friend, thinking so to recommend the Gospel.

"At your service, sir," returned Mr. Kitely, brusquely, as he stepped from behind one of the partitions in the shop, and saw the little clerical apparition which had not even waited to see the form of the human being to whom he applied the sacred epithet.

"I only wanted to ask you," drawled Mr. Simon, in a drawl both of earnestness and unconscious affectation, "whether you happen to know of a German master somewhere in this neighborhood."

"Well, I don't know," returned Mr. Kitely, in a tone that indicated a balancing rather than pondering operation of the mind. For although he was far enough from being a Scotchman, he always liked to know why one asked a question, before he cared to answer it. "I don't know as I could recommend one over another."

"I am not in want of a master. I only wish to find out one that lives in this neighborhood."

"I know at least six of them within a radius of one-half mile, taking my shop here for the center of the circle," said Mr. Kitely, consequentially. "What's the man's name you want?"

"That is what I cannot tell you."

"Then how am I to tell you, sir?"

"If you will oblige me with the names and addresses of those six you mention, one of them will very likely be the man I want."

"I dare say the clergyman wants Mr. Moloch, father," said a voice from somewhere in the neighborhood of the floor, "the foreign gentleman that Mr. Worboise goes to see, up the court."

"That's the very man, my child," responded Mr. Simon. "Thank you very much. Where shall I find him?"

"I'll show you," returned Mattie.

"Why couldn't he have said so before?" remarked Mr. Kitely to himself with indignation. "But it's just like them."

By *them* he meant clergymen in general.

"What a fearful name—*Moloch!*" reflected Mr. Simon, as he followed Mattie up the court. He would have judged it a name of bad omen, had he not thought *omen* rather a wicked word. The fact was, the German's name was Molken, a very innocent one, far too innocent for its owner, for it means only *whey*.

Herr Molken was a *ne'er-do-weel* student of Heidelberg, a clever fellow, if not a scholar, whose bad habits came to be too well known at home for his being able to indulge them there any longer, and who had taken refuge in London from certain disagreeable consequences which not unfrequently follow aberrant efforts to procure the means of gambling and general dissipation. Thomas had as yet spent so little time in his company, never giving more than a quarter of an hour or so to his lesson, that Molken had had no opportunity of influencing him in any way. But he was one of those who, the moment they make a new acquaintance, begin examining him for the sake of discovering his weak points, that they may get some hold of him. He measured his own strength or weakness by the number of persons of whom at any given time he had a hold capable of being turned to advantage in some way or other in the course of events. Of all dupes, one with some intellect and no principle, weakened by the trammels of a religious system with which he is at strife, and which therefore hangs like a millstone about his neck, impedes his every motion, and gives him up to the mercy of his enemy, is the most thorough prey to the pigeon-plucker; for such a one has no recuperative power, and the misery of his conscience makes him abject. Molken saw that Tom was clever, and he seemed to have some money—if he could get this hold of him in any way, it might be "to the welfare of his advantage."

The next lesson fell on the evening after Mr. Simon's visit in Guild Court, and Mr. Molken gave Thomas a full account of the "beseek" he had had from "one soft ghostly," who wanted to find out something about Thomas, and how he had told him that Mr. Worboise was a most excellent and religious young man; that he worked very hard at his German, and that he never spent less (here Mr. Molken winked at Thomas) than an hour and a half over Krummacher or some other religious writer. All this Mr. Simon had faithfully reported to Mrs. Worboise, never questioning what Mr. Molken told him, though how any one could have looked at him without finding cause to doubt whatever he might say, I can hardly imagine. For Mr. Molken was a small, wiry man, about thirty, with brows overhanging his eyes like the eaves of a Swiss cottage, and rendering those black and wicked luminaries blacker and more wicked still. His hair was black, his beard was black, his skin was swarthy, his forehead was large; his nose looked as if it had been made of putty and dabbed on after the rest of his face was finished; his mouth was sensual; and, in short, one was inclined to put the question in the gospel—Whether hath sinned, this man or his parents? He could, notwithstanding, make himself so agreeable, had such a winning carriage and dignified deference, that he soon disarmed the suspicion caused by his appearance. He had, besides, many accomplishments, and seemed to know everything—at least to a lad like Thomas, who could not detect the assumption which not unfrequently took the place of knowledge. He manifested, also, a genuine appreciation of his country's poetry, and even the short lessons to which Thomas submitted had been enlivened by Herr Molken's enthusiasm for Goethe. If those of his poems which he read and explained to Thomas were not of the best, they were none the worse for his purposes. ￢

Now he believed he had got, by Mr. Simon's aid, the hold that he wanted. His one wink, parenthetically introduced above, revealed to Thomas that he was master of his secret, and Thomas felt that he was, to a considerable degree, in his hands. This, however, caused him no apprehension.

His mother, although in a measure relieved, still cherished suspicions of German theology which the mention of Krummacher had failed to remove. She would give her son a direct warning on the subject. So, when he came into her room that evening, she said:

"Mr. Simon has been making some friendly inquiries about you, Thomas. He was in the neighborhood, and thought he might call on Mr. Moloch—what a dreadful name! Why have you nothing to say to me about your studies? Mr. Simon says you are getting quite a scholar in German. But it is a dangerous language, Thomas, and full of errors. Beware of yielding too ready an ear to the seductions of human philosophy and the undermining attacks of will-worship."

Mrs. Worboise went on in this strain, intelligible neither to herself nor her son, seeing she had not more than the vaguest notion of what she meant by German theology, for at least five minutes, during which Thomas did not interrupt her once. By allowing the lies of his German master to pass thus uncontradicted, he took another long stride down the inclined plane of deceit.

After this he became naturally more familiar with Mr. Molken. The German abandoned books, and began to teach him fencing, in which he was an adept, talking to him in German all the while, and thus certainly increasing his knowledge of the language, though not in a direction that was likely within fifty years to lead him to the mastery of commercial correspondence in that tongue.

CHAPTER X
MOTHER AND DAUGHTER

Mr. Boxall, with some difficulty, arising from reluctance, made his wife acquainted with the annoyance occasioned him by the discovery of the fact that Tom Worboise had not even told his father that Mary was ill.

"I'm convinced," he said, "that the young rascal has only been amusing himself—flirting, I believe, you women call it."

"I'm none so sure of that, Richard," answered his wife. "You leave him to me."

"Now, my dear, I won't have you throwing our Mary in any fool's face. It's bad enough as it is. But I declare I would rather see her in her grave than scorned by any man."

"You may see her there without before long," answered his wife, with a sigh.

"Eh! What! She's not worse, is she?"

"No; but she hasn't much life left in her. I'm afraid it's settling on her lungs. Her cough is something dreadful to hear, and tears her to pieces."

"It's milder weather, though, now, and that will make a difference before long. Now, I know what you're thinking of, my dear, and I won't have it. I told the fellow she wasn't fit to see anybody."

"Were you always ready to talk about me to everyone that came in your way, Richard?" asked his wife, with a good-humored smile.

"I don't call a lad's father and mother any one that comes in the way— though, I dare say, fathers and mothers are in the way sometimes," he added, with a slight sigh.

"Would you have talked about me to your own father, Richard?"

"Well, you see, I wasn't in his neighborhood. But my father was a—a— stiff kind of man to deal with."

"Not worse than Mr. Worboise, depend upon it, my dear."

"But Worboise would like well enough to have our Mary for a daughter-in-law."

"I dare say. But that mightn't make it easier to talk to him about her—for Tom, I mean. For my part, I never did see two such parents as poor Tom has got. I declare it's quite a shame to sit upon that handsome young lad—and amiable—as they do. He can hardly call his nose his own. I wouldn't trust that Mr. Worboise, for my part, no, not if I was drowning."

"Why, wife!" exclaimed Mr. Boxall, both surprised and annoyed, "this *is* something new. How long—"

But his wife went on, regardless.

"And that mother of his! It's a queer kind of religion that freezes the life out of you the moment you come near her. How ever a young fellow could talk about his sweetheart to either of them is more than I can understand—or you either, my dear. So don't look so righteous over it."

Mrs. Boxall's good-natured audacity generally carried everything before it, even with more dangerous persons than her own husband. He could not help—I do not say smiling, but trying to smile; and though the smile was rather a failure, Mrs. Boxall chose to take it for one. Indeed, she generally put her husband into good humor by treating him as if he were in a far better humor than he really was in. It never does any good to tell a man that he is cross. If he is, it makes him no better, even though it should make him vexed with himself; and if he isn't cross, nothing is more certain to make him cross, without giving him a moment's time to consult the better part of him.

Within the next eight days, Mrs. Boxall wrote to Tom as follows:

"My Dear Mr. Thomas—Mary is much better, and you need not be at all uneasy about the consequences of your expedition to the North Pole on Christmas Day. I am very sorry I was so cross when you brought her home. Indeed, I believe I ought to beg your pardon. If you don't come and see us soon, I shall fancy that I have seriously offended you. But I knew she never could stand exposure to the weather, and I suppose that was what upset my temper. Mary will be pleased to see you.—I am, ever yours sincerely,

Jane Boxall."

Tom received this letter before he left for town in the morning. What was he to do? Of course he must go and *call* there, as he styled it, but he pronounced it a great bore. He was glad the poor girl was better; but he couldn't help it, and he had no fancy for being hunted up after that fashion. What made him yet more savage was, that Mr. Boxall was absolutely surly — he had never seen him so before — when he went into his room upon some message from Mr. Stopper. He did not go that day nor the next.

On the third evening he went; — but the embarrassment of feeling that he ought to have gone before was added to the dislike of going at all, and he was in no enviable condition of mind when he got off the Clapton omnibus. Add to this that an unrelenting east wind was blowing, and my reader will believe that Tom Worboise was more like a man going to the scaffold than one going to visit a convalescent girl.

There was something soothing, however, in the glow of warmth and comfort which the opening door revealed. The large hall, carpeted throughout, the stove burning in it most benevolently, the brightness of the thick stair-rods, like veins of gold in the broad crimson carpeting of the generously wide stair-case — all was consoling to Thomas, whose home was one of the new straight-up-and-down, stucco-faced abominations which can never be home-like except to those who have been born in them — and no thanks to them, for in that case a rabbit-hutch will be home-like. Mrs. Boxall was one of those nice, stout, kindly, middle-aged women who have a positive genius for comfort. Now there is no genius in liking to be comfortable; but there is some genius in making yourself comfortable, and a great deal more in making other people comfortable. This Mrs. Boxall possessed in perfection; and you felt it the moment you entered her house, which, like her person, summer and winter, was full of a certain autumnal richness — the bloom of peaches and winter apples. And what was remarkable was, that all this was gained without a breath of scolding to the maids. She would ring the bell ten times an hour for the same maid, if necessary. She would ring at once, no matter how slight the fault — a scrap of paper, a cornerful of dust, a roll of flue upon that same stair-carpet — but not even what might make an indulgent mistress savage — a used lucifer match — would upset the temper of Mrs. Boxall. Why do I linger on these trifles, do you ask, reader? Because I shall have to part with Mrs. Boxall soon; and — shall I confess it? — because it gives me a chance of reading a sly lecture to certain ladies whom I know, but who cannot complain when I weave it into a history. My only trouble about Mrs. Boxall is, to think in what condition she must have found herself when she was no longer in the midst of any of the circumstances of life — had neither house nor clothes, nor even the body she had been used to dress with such matronly taste, to look after.

It was with a certain tremor that Tom approached the door of Mary Boxall's room. But he had not time to indulge it, as I fear he might have done if he had had time, for, as I have said, he prized feelings, and had not begun even to think about actions.

What a change from the Mary of the snow-storm! She lay on a couch near the fire, pale and delicate, with thin white hands, and altogether an altered expression of being. But her appearance of health had always been somewhat boastful. Thomas felt that she was far lovelier than before, and approached her with some emotion. But Mary's illness had sharpened her perceptions. There was no light in the room but that of the fire, and it lightened and gloomed over her still face, as the clouds and the sun do over a landscape. As the waters shine out and darken again in the hollows, so her eyes gleamed and vanished, and in the shadow Thomas could not tell whether she was looking at him or not. But then Mary was reading his face like a book in a hard language, which yet she understood enough to read it. Very little was said between them, for Mary was sad and weak, and Thomas was sorrowful and perplexed. She had been reckoning on this first visit from Thomas ever since she had recovered enough to choose what she would think about; and now it was turning out all so different from what she had pictured to herself. Her poor heart sank away somewhere, and left a hollow place where it had used to be. Thomas sat there, but there was a chasm between them, not such as she any longer sought to cross, but which she would have wider still. She wished he would go. A few more commonplaces across the glimmering fire, and it sank, as if sympathetic, into a sullen gloom, and the face of neither was visible to the other. Then Thomas rose with the effort of one in a nightmare dream. Mary held out her hand to him. He took it in his, cold to the heart. The fire gave out one flame which flickered and died. In that light she looked at him—was it reproachfully? He thought so, and felt that her eyes were like those of one trying to see something at a great distance. One pressure of her hand, and he left her. He would gladly have shrunk into a nutshell. "Good-by, Thomas," "Good-by, Mary," were the last words that passed between them.

Outside the room he found Mrs. Boxall.

"Are you going already, Mr. Thomas?" she said, in an uncertain kind of tone.

"Yes, Mrs. Boxall," was all Tom had to reply with.

Mrs. Boxall went into her daughter's room, and shut the door. Thomas let himself out, and walked away.

She found Mary lying staring at the fire, with great dry eyes, lips pressed close together, and face even whiter than before.

"My darling child!" said the mother.

"It's no matter, mother. It's all my own foolish fault. Only bed again will be so dreary now."

The mother made some gesture, which the daughter understood.

"No, mother; don't say a word. I won't hear a word of that kind. I'm a good deal wiser already than I used to be. If I get better, I shall live for you and papa."

A dreadful fit of coughing interrupted her.

"Don't fancy I'm going to die for love," she said, with a faint attempt at a smile. "I'm not one of that sort. If I die, it'll be of a good honest cough, that's all. Dear mother, it's nothing, I declare."

Thomas never more crossed that threshold. And ever after, Mr. Boxall spoke to him as a paid clerk, and nothing more. So he had to carry some humiliation about with him. Mr. Stopper either knew something of the matter, or followed the tone of his principal. Even Charles Wither was short with him after awhile. I suppose Jane told him that he had behaved very badly to Mary. So Tom had no friend left but Lucy, and was driven nearer to Mr. Molken. He still contrived to keep his visits at Guild Court, except those to Mr. Molken, a secret at home. But I think Mr. Stopper had begun to suspect, if not to find him out.

I have not done with the Boxalls yet, though there is hence—forth an impassable gulf between Tom and them.

As the spring drew on, Mary grew a little better. With the first roses, Uncle John Boxall came home from the Chinese Sea, and took up his residence for six weeks or so with his brother. Mary was fond of Uncle John, and his appearance at this time was very opportune. A more rapid improvement was visible within a few days of his arrival. He gave himself up almost to the invalid; and as she was already getting over her fancy for Tom, her love for her uncle came in to aid her recovery.

"It's the smell of the salt water," said he, when they remarked how much good he had done her; "and more of it would do her more good yet."

They thought it better not to tell him anything about Tom. But one day after dinner, in a gush of old feelings, brought on by a succession of reminiscences of their childhood, Richard told John all about it, which was not much. John swore, and kept pondering the matter over.

CHAPTER XI
MATTIE FOR POPPIE

One bright morning, when the flags in the passage were hot to her feet, and the shoes she had lost in the snow-storm had not the smallest chance of recurring to the memory of Poppie, in this life at least, Mattie was seated with Mr. Spelt in his workshop, which seemed to the passer-by to be supported, like the roof of a chapter-house, upon the single pillar of Mr. Dolman, with his head for a capital—which did not, however, branch out in a great many directions. She was not dressing a doll now, for Lucy had set her to work upon some garments for the poor, Lucy's relation with whom I will explain by and by.

"I've been thinking, mother," she said—to Mr. Spelt, of course—"that I wonder how ever God made me. Did he cut me out of something else, and join me up, do you think? If he did, where did he get the stuff? And if he didn't, how did he do it?"

"Well, my dear, it would puzzle a wiser head than mine to answer that question," said Mr. Spelt, who plainly judged ignorance a safer refuge from Mattie than any knowledge he possessed upon the subject. Her question, however, occasioned the return, somehow or other, of an old suspicion which he had not by any means cherished, but which would force itself upon him now and then, that the splendid woman, Mrs. Spelt, "had once ought" to have had a baby, and, somehow, he never knew what had come of it. She got all right again, and the baby was nowhere.

"I wish I had thought to watch while God was a-making of me, and then I should have remembered how he did it," Mattie resumed. "Ah! but I couldn't," she added, checking herself, "for I wasn't made till I was finished, and so I couldn't remember."

This was rather too profound for Mr. Spelt to respond to in any way. Not that he had not a glimmering of Mattie's meaning, but that is a very different thing from knowing what to answer. So he said nothing, except what something might be comprised in a bare assent. Mattie, however, seemed bent on forcing conversation, and, finding him silent, presently tried another vein.

"Do you remember a conversation we had, in this very place"—that was not wonderful, anyhow—"some time ago—before my last birthday—about God being kinder to some people than to other people?" she asked.

"Yes, I do," answered Mr. Spelt, who had been thinking about the matter a good deal since. "Are you of the same mind still, Mattie?"

"Well, yes, and no," answered Mattie. "I think now there may be something in it I can't quite get at the bottom of. Do you know, mother, I remembered all at once, the other day, that when I was a little girl, I used to envy Poppie. Now, where ever was there a child that had more of the blessings of childhood than me?"

"What made you envy Poppie, then, Mattie?"

"Well, you see, my father's shop was rather an awful place, sometimes. I never told you, mother, what gained me the pleasure of your acquaintance. Ever since I can remember—and that is a very long time ago now—I used now and then to grow frightened at father's books. Sometimes, you know, they were all quiet enough. You would generally expect books to be quiet, now wouldn't you? But other times—well, they wouldn't be quiet. At least, they kept thinking all about me, till my poor head couldn't bear it any longer. That always was my weak point, you know."

Mr. Spelt looked with some anxiety at the pale face and great forehead of the old little woman, and said:

"Yes, yes, Mattie. But we've got over all that, I think, pretty well by now."

"Well, do you know, Mr. Spelt, I have not even yet got over my fancies about the books. Very often, as I am falling asleep, I hear them all thinking;—they can hardly help it, you know, with so much to think about inside them. I don't hear them exactly, you know, for the one thinks into the other's thinks—somehow, I can't tell—and they blot each other out like, and there is nothing but a confused kind of a jumble in my head till I fall asleep. Well, it was one day, very like this day—it was a hot summer forenoon, wasn't it, mother?—I was standing at that window over there. And Poppie was playing down in the court. And I thought what a happy little girl she was, to go where she pleased in the sunshine, and not need to put on any shoes. Father wouldn't let me go where I liked. And there was nothing but books everywhere. That was my nursery then. It was all round with books. And some of them had dreadful pictures in them. All at once the books began talking so loud as I had never heard them talk before. And I thought with myself—'I won't stand this any longer. I will go away with Poppie.'

"So I ran down stairs, but because I couldn't open the door into the court, I had to watch and dodge father among the book-shelves. And when I got out, Poppie was gone—and then, what next, mother?"

"Then my thread knotted, and that always puts me out of temper, because it stops my work. And I always look down into the court when I stop. Somehow that's the way my eyes do of themselves. And there I saw a tiny little maiden staring all about her as if she had lost somebody, and her face looked as if she was just going to cry. And I knew who she was, for I had seen her in the shop before. And so I called to her and she came. And I asked her what was the matter."

"Well, and I said, 'It's the books that will keep talking:' didn't I?"

"Yes. And I took you up beside me. But you was very ill after that, and it was long before you came back again after that first time."

This story had been gone over and over again between the pair; but every time that Mattie wanted to rehearse the one adventure of her life, she treated it as a memory that had just returned upon her. How much of it was an original impression and how much a rewriting by the tailor upon the blotted tablets of her memory, I cannot tell.

"Well, where was I?" said Mattie, after a pause, laying her hands on her lap and looking up at the tailor with eyes of inquiry.

"I'm sure I don't know, Mattie," answered Mr. Spelt.

"I was thinking, you know, that perhaps Poppie has her share of what's going on, after all."

"And don't you think," suggested her friend, "that perhaps God doesn't want to keep all the good-doing to himself, but leaves room for us to have a share in it? It's very nice work that you're at now—isn't it Mattie?"

"Well, it is."

"As good as dressing dolls?"

"Well, it's no end of better."

"Why?"

"Because the dolls don't feel a bit better for it, you know."

"And them that'll wear that flannel petticoat will feel better for it, won't they?"

"That they will, *I* know."

"But suppose everybody in the world was as well off as you and me, Mattie—you with your good father, and—"

"Well, my father ain't none so good, just. He swears sometimes."

"He's good to you, though, ain't he?"

"I don't know that either, mother: he spoils me," answered Mattie, who seemed to be in a more than usually contradictory humor this morning.

"Supposing, though, that everybody had a father that spoiled them, you wouldn't have any such clothes to make, you know."

"But they wouldn't want them."

"And you would be forced to go back to your dolls as have no father or mother and come across the sea in boxes."

"I see, I see, mother. Well, I suppose I must allow that it is good of God to give us a share in making people comfortable. You see he could do it himself, only he likes to give us a share. That's it, ain't, it mother?"

"That's what I mean, Mattie."

"Well, but you'll allow it does seem rather hard that I should have this to do now, and there's Poppie hasn't either the clothes to wear or to make."

"Can't you do something for Poppie, then?"

"Well, I'll think about it, and see what I can do."

Here Mattie laid aside her work, crept on all fours to the door, and peeped over into the passage below.

"Well, Poppie," she began, in the intellectually condescending tone which most grown people use to children, irritating some of them by it considerably,—"Well, Poppie, and how do *you* do?"

Poppie heard the voice, and looked all round, but not seeing where it came from, turned and scudded away under the arch. Though Mattie knew Poppie, Poppie did not know Mattie, did not know her voice at least. It was not that Poppie was frightened exactly—she hardly ever was frightened at anything, not even at a policeman, but she was given to scudding; and when anything happened she did not precisely know what to do with, she scudded: at least if there was no open drain or damaged hoarding at hand. But she did not run far this time. As soon as she got under the shelter of the arch, she turned behind a sort of buttress that leaned against the bookseller's house, and peeped back toward the court.

At that moment Lucy came out of the house. She came down the passage, and as Mattie was still leaning over the door, or the threshold, rather, of the workshop, she saw her, and stopped. Thereupon Poppie came out of her "coign of vantage," and slowly approached, just like a bird or a tame rabbit—only she was not by any means so tame as the latter.

"Are you getting on with that petticoat, Mattie?" said Lucy.

"Yes, miss, I am. Only not being used to anything but boys' clothes, I am afraid you won't like the tailor's stitch, miss."

"Never mind that. It will be a curiosity, that's all. But what do you think, Mattie? The kind lady who gives us this work to do for the poor people, has invited all of us to go and spend a day with her."

Mattie did not answer. Lucy thought she did not care to go. But she was such an oddity that she wanted very much to take her.

"She has such a beautiful garden, Mattie! And she's *so* kind."

Still Mattie made no reply. Lucy would try again.

"And it's such a beautiful house, too, Mattie! I'm sure you would like to see it. And," she added, almost reduced to her last resource, "she would give us such a nice dinner, *I* know!"

This at length burst the silence, but not as Lucy had expected.

"Now that's just what I'm determined I will not stand," said the little maid.

"What *do* you mean, Mattie?" exclaimed Lucy, surprised and bewildered.

"I'll tell you what I mean, and that soon enough," said Mattie. "It's all vēry kind of Mrs. Morgingturn to ask you and me, what are well-to-do people, and in comfortable circumstances, as people say, to go and spend this day or that with her. And do you know, Mr. Spelt"—here Mattie drew herself in and turned her face right round from Lucy to the tailor, for the side of her mouth which she used for speech was the left, and the furthest from Spelt—"it just comes into my head that this kind lady who gives me petticoats to make instead of doll's trousers, is doing the very thing you read about last night out of the New Testament before I went into bed. It's so nice now there's light enough to read a little before we part for the night! ain't it, mother?"

"I know, I know," said the tailor in a low voice, not wishing to intrude himself into the conversation.

"What did Mr. Spelt read to you, Mattie?" asked Lucy.

"He read about *somebody*—"

It was very remarkable how Mattie would use the name of God, never certainly with irreverence, but with a freedom that seemed to indicate that to her he was chiefly if not solely an object of metaphysical speculation or, possibly, of investigation; while she hardly ever uttered the name of the Saviour, but spoke of him as *Somebody*. And I find that I must yet further interrupt the child herself to tell an anecdote about her which will perhaps help my reader to account for the fact I am about to finish telling. She was not three years old when she asked her mother, a sweet, thoughtful woman, in many ways superior to her husband, though not intellectually his equal—who made the tree in Wood Street? Her mother answered, of course, "God made it, my pet;" for by instinct, she never spoke of her God without using some term of endearment to her child. Mattie answered—"I would like it better if a man made it"—a cry after the humanity of God—a longing in the heart of the three years' child for the Messiah of God. Her mother did not know well enough to tell her that a man, yes, *the* man did make them—"for by Him all things were made;"—but Mattie may have had some undefined glimmering of the fact, for, as I have said, she always substituted *Somebody* for any name of the Lord. I cannot help wishing that certain religious people of my acquaintance would, I do not say follow queer little Mattie's example, but take a lesson from queer little Mattie.

"He read about *somebody* saying you shouldn't ask your friends and neighbors who could do the same for you again, but you should ask them that couldn't, because they hadn't a house to ask you to, like Poppie there."

Lucy looked round and saw the most tattered little scarecrow—useless even as such in the streets of London, where there are only dusty little sparrows and an occasional raven—staring at—I cannot call it a group—well, it was a group vertically, if not laterally—and not knowing or caring what to make of it, only to look at Lucy, and satisfy her undefined and undefinable love by the beholding of its object. She loved what was lovely without in the least knowing that it was lovely, or what lovely meant. And while Lucy gazed at Poppie, with a vague impression that she had seen the child before, she could not help thinking of the contrast between the magnificent abode of the Morgensterns—for magnificent it was, even in London—and the lip of the nest from which the strange child preached down into the world the words "friends and neighbors."

But she could say nothing more to Mattie till she had told, word for word, the whole story to Mrs. Morgenstern, who, she knew, would heartily enjoy the humor of it. Nor was Lucy, who loved her Lord very truly, even more than she knew, though she was no theologian like Thomas, in the least deterred from speaking of *Somebody*, by the fact that Mrs. Morgenstern did not receive him as the Messiah of her nation. If he did not hesitate to show himself where he knew he would not be accepted, why should she hesitate to speak his name? And why should his name not be mentioned to those who, although they had often been persecuted in his name by those who did not understand his mind, might well be proud that the man who was conquering the world by his strong, beautiful will, was a Jew.

But from the rather severe indisposition of her grandmother, she was unable to tell the story to Mrs. Morgenstern till the very morning of the gathering.

CHAPTER XII
A COMPARISON

Can I hope to move my readers to any pitiful sympathy with Mrs. Worboise, the whole fabric of whose desires was thus sliding into an abyss? That she is not an interesting woman, I admit; but, at the same time, I venture to express a doubt whether our use of the word *uninteresting* really expresses anything more than our own ignorance. If we could look into the movements of any heart, I doubt very much whether that heart would be any longer uninteresting to us. Come with me, reader, while I endeavor, with some misgiving, I confess, to open a peep into the heart of this mother, which I have tried hard, though with scarcely satisfactory success, to understand.

Her chief faculty lay in negations. Her whole life was a kind of negation—a negation of warmth, a negation of impulse, a negation of beauty, a negation of health. When Thomas was a child, her chief communication with him was in negatives. "*You must not; you are not; do not;*" and so on. Her theory of the world was humanity deprived of God. Because of something awful in the past, something awful lay in the future. To escape from the consequences of a condition which you could not help, you must believe certain things after a certain fashion—hold, in fact, certain theories with regard to the most difficult questions, on which, too, you were incapable of thinking correctly. Him who held these theories you must regard as a fellow-favorite of heaven; who held them not you would do well to regard as a publican and a sinner, even if he should be the husband in your bosom. All the present had value only of reference to the future. All your strife must be to become something you are not at all now, to feel what you do not feel, to judge against your nature, to regard everything in you as opposed to your salvation, and God, who is far away from you, and whose ear is not always ready to hear, as your only deliverer from the consequences he has decreed; and this in virtue of no immediate relation to you, but from regard to another whose innocent suffering is to our guilt the only counterpoise weighty enough to satisfy his justice. All her anxiety for her son turned upon his final escape from punishment. She did not torment her soul, her nights were not sleepless with the fear that her boy should be unlike Christ, that he might do that which was mean, selfish, dishonest, cowardly, vile, but with the fear that he was or might be doomed to an eternal suffering.

Now, in so far as this idea had laid hold of the boy, it had aroused the instinct of self-preservation mingled with a repellent feeling in regard to God. All that was poor and common and selfish in him was stirred up on the side of religion; all that was noble (and of that there was far more than my reader will yet fancy) was stirred up against it. The latter, however, was put down by degrees, leaving the whole region, when the far outlook of selfishness should be dimmed by the near urgings of impulse, open to the inroads of the enemy, enfeebled and ungarrisoned. Ah! if she could have told the boy, every time his soul was lifted up within him by anything beautiful, or great, or true, "That, my boy, is God—God telling you that you must be beautiful, and great, and true, else you cannot be His child!" If, every time he uttered his delight in flower or bird, she had, instead of speaking of sin and shortcoming, spoken of love and aspiration toward the Father of Light, the God of Beauty! If she had been able to show him that what he admired in Byron's heroes, even, was the truth, courage, and honesty, hideously mingled, as it might be, with cruelty and conceit and lies! But almost everything except the Epistles seemed to her of the devil and not of God. She was even jealous of the Gospel of God, lest it should lead him astray from the interpretation she put upon it. She did not understand that nothing can convince of sin—but the vision of holiness; that to draw near to the Father is to leave self behind; that the Son of God appeared that by the sight of himself he might convince the world of sin. But then hers was a life that had never broken the shell, while through the shell the worm of suffering had eaten, and was boring into her soul. Have pity and not contempt, reader, who would not be like her. She did not believe in her own love, even, as from God, and therefore she restrained it before the lad. So he had no idea of how she loved him. If she had only thrown her arms about him, and let her heart out toward him, which surely it is right to do sometimes at least, how differently would he have listened to what she had to say! His heart was being withered on the side next his mother for lack of nourishment: there are many lives ruined because they have not had tenderness enough. Kindness is not tenderness. She could not represent God to the lad. If, instead of constantly referring to the hell that lies in the future, she had reminded him of the beginnings of that hell in his own bosom, appealing to himself whether there was not a faintness there that indicated something wrong, a dull pain that might grow to a burning agony, a consciousness of wrong-doing, thinking, and feeling, a sense of a fearful pit and a miry clay within his own being from which he would gladly escape, a failing even from the greatness of such grotesque ideals as he loved in poetry, a meanness, paltriness, and at best insignificance of motive and action,—and then told him that out of this was God stretching forth the hand to take and lift him, that he was waiting to exalt him to a higher ideal of manhood than anything which it had entered into his heart to conceive, that he would make him clean from the defilement which he was afraid to confess to himself because it lowered him in his own esteem,—then perhaps the words of his mother, convincing him that God was not against him but for him, on the side of his best feelings and against his worst, might have sunk into the heart of the weak youth, and he would straightway have put forth what strength he had, and so begun to be strong. For he who acts has strength, is strong, and will be stronger. But she could not tell him this: she did not know it herself. Her religion was something there, then; not here, now. She would give Mr. Simon a five-pound note for his Scripture-reading among the poor, and the moment after refuse the request of her needle-woman from the same district who begged her to raise her wages from eighteen pence to two shillings a day. Religion—the bond between man and God—had nothing to do with the earnings of a sister, whose pale face told of "penury and pine" a sadder story even than that written upon the countenance of the invalid, for to labor in weakness, longing for rest, is harder than to endure a good deal of pain upon a sofa. Until we begin to learn that the only way to *serve* God in any real sense of the word is to serve our neighbor, we may have knocked at the wicket-gate, but I doubt if we have got one foot across the threshold of the kingdom.

Add to this condition of mind a certain uncomfortable effect produced upon the mother by the son's constantly reminding her of the father whom she had quite given up trying to love, and I think my reader will be a little nearer to the understanding of the relation, if such it could well be called, between the two. The eyes of both were yet unopened to the poverty of their own condition. The mother especially said that she was "rich, and had need of nothing," when she was "wretched, and miserable, and poor, and blind, and naked." But she had a hard nature to begin with, and her pain occupied her all the more that she neither sought nor accepted sympathy. And although she was none the less a time-server and a worldly-minded woman that she decried worldliness, and popery, and gave herself to the saving of her soul, yet the God who makes them loves even such people and knows all about them; and it is well for them that he is their judge and not we.

Let us now turn to another woman—Mrs. Morgenstern. I will tell you what she was like. She was a Jewess and like a Jewess. But there is as much difference between Jewesses as there is between Englishwomen. Is there any justice in fixing upon the lowest as *the type*? How does the Scotchman like to have his nation represented: by the man outside the tobacco-shop, or by the cantankerous logician and theologian so well known to some of us? There is a Jewess that flaunts in gorgeous raiment and unclean linen; and there is a Jewess noble as a queen, and pure as a daisy—fit to belong to that nation of which Mary the mother was born. Mrs. Morgenstern was of the latter class—tall, graceful, even majestic in the fashion of her form and carriage. Every feature was Jewish, and yet she might have been English, or Spanish, or German, just as well. Her eyes were dark—black, I would say, if I had ever seen black eyes—and proud, yet with a dove-like veil over their fire. Sometimes there was even a trouble to be seen in them, as of a rainy mist amid the glow of a southern sky. I never could be quite sure what this trouble meant. She was rich, therefore she had no necessity; she was not avaricious, and therefore she had no fear of dying in the work-house. She had but one child, therefore she was neither wearied with motherhood, nor a sufferer from suppressed maternity, moved by which divine impulse so many women take to poodles instead of orphans. Her child was healthy and active, and gave her no anxiety. That she loved her husband, no one who saw those eastern eyes rest upon him for a moment could doubt. What, then, could be the cause of that slight restlessness, that gauzy change, that pensive shadow? I think that there was more love in her yet than knew how to get out of her. She would look round sometimes—it was a peculiar movement—just as if some child had been pulling at her skirts. She had lost a child, but I do not think that was the cause. And however this may be, I do believe that nothing but the love of God will satisfy the power of love in any woman's bosom. But did not Rebecca—they loved their old Jewish names, that family—did not Rebecca Morgenstern love God? Truly I think she did—but not enough to satisfy herself. And I venture to say more: I do not believe she could love him to the degree necessary for her own peace till she recognized the humanity in him. But she was more under the influences emanating from that story of the humanity of God than she knew herself. At all events she was a most human and lovely lady, full of grace and truth, like Mary before she was a Christian; and it took a good while, namely all her son's life and longer, to make *her* one. Rebecca Morgenstern never became a Christian. But she loved children, whether they were Christians or not. And she loved the poor, whether they were Christians or not; and, like Dorcas, made and caused to be made, coats and garments for them. And, for my part, I know, if I had the choice, whether I would appear before the Master in the train of the *unbelieving* Mrs. Morgenstern or that of the *believing* Mrs. Worboise. And as to self-righteousness, I think there is far less of that among those who regard the works of righteousness as the means of salvation, than among those by whom faith itself is degraded into a work of merit—a condition by fulfilling which they become fit for God's mercy; for such is the trick which the old Adam and the Enemy together are ready enough to play the most orthodox, in despite of the purity of their creed.

CHAPTER XIII
MATTIE'S MICROCOSM

Although Mrs. Boxall, senior, was still far from well, yet when the morning of Mrs. Morgenstern's gathering dawned, lovely even in the midst of London, and the first sun-rays, with green tinges and rosy odors hanging about their golden edges, stole into her room, reminding her of the old paddock and the feeding cows at Bucks Horton, in Buckingham, she resolved that Lucy should go to Mrs. Morgenstern's. So the good old lady set herself to feel better, in order that she might be better, and by the time Lucy, who had slept in the same room with her grandmother since her illness, awoke, she was prepared to persuade her that she was quite well enough to let her have a holiday.

"But how am I to leave you, grannie, all alone?" objected Lucy.

"Oh! I dare say that queer little Mattie of yours will come in and keep me company. Make haste and get your clothes on, and go and see."

Now Lucy had had hopes of inducing Mattie to go with her; as I indicated in a previous chapter; but she could not press the child after the reason she gave for not going. And now she might as well ask her to stay with her grandmother. So she went round the corner to Mr. Kitely's shop, glancing up at Mr. Spelt's nest in the wall as she passed, to see whether she was not there.

When she entered the wilderness of books she saw no one; but peeping round one of the many screens, she spied Mattie sitting with her back toward her and her head bent downward. Looking over her shoulder, she saw that she had a large folding plate of the funeral of Lord Nelson open before her, the black shapes of which, with their infernal horror of plumes—the hateful flowers that the buried seeds of ancient paganism still shoot up into the pleasant Christian fields—she was studying with an unaccountable absorption of interest.

"What *have* you got there Mattie?" asked Lucy.

"Well, I don't ezackly know, miss," answered the child, looking up, very white-faced and serious.

"Put the book away and come and see grannie. She wants you to take care of her to-day, while I go out."

"Well, miss, I would with pleasure; but you see father is gone out, and has left me to take care of the shop till he comes back."

"But he won't be gone a great while, will he?"

"No, miss. He knows I don't like to be left too long with the books. He'll be back before St. Jacob's strikes nine—that I know."

"Well, then, I'll go and get grannie made comfortable; and if you don't come to me by half-past nine, I'll come after you again."

"Do, miss, if you please; for if father ain't come by that time—my poor head—"

"You must put that ugly book away," said Lucy, "and take a better one."

"Well, miss, I know I oughtn't to have taken this book, for there's no summer in it; and it talks like the wind at night."

"Why did you take it, then?"

"Because Syne told me to take it. But that's just why I oughtn't to ha' taken it."

And she rose and put the book in one of the shelves over her head, moving her stool when she had done so, and turning her face toward the spot where the book now stood. Lucy watched her uneasily.

"What do you mean by saying that Syne told you?" she asked. "Who is Syne?"

"Don't you know Syne, miss? Syne is—you know 'Lord Syne was a miserly churl'—don't you?"

Then, before Lucy could reply, she looked up in her face, with a smile hovering about the one side of her mouth, and said:

"But it's all nonsense, miss, when you're standing there. There isn't no such person as Syne, when you're there. I don't believe there is any such person. But," she added with a sigh, "when you're gone away—I don't know. But I think he's up stairs in the nursery now," she said, putting her hand to her big forehead. "No, no; there's no such person."

And Mattie tried to laugh outright, but failed in the attempt, and the tears rose in her eyes.

"You've got a headache, dear," said Lucy.

"Well, no," answered Mattie. "I cannot say that I have just a headache, you know. But it does buzz a little. I hope Mr. Kitely won't be long now."

"I don't like leaving you, Mattie; but I must go to my grandmother," said Lucy, with reluctance.

"Never mind me, miss. I'm used to it. I used to be afraid of Lord Syne, for he watched me, ready to pounce out upon me with all his men at his back, and he laughed so loud to see me run. But I know better now. I never run from him now. I always frown at him, and take my own time and do as I like. I don't want him to see that I'm afraid, you know. And I do think I have taught him a lesson. Besides, if he's very troublesome, you know, miss, I can run to Mr. Spelt. But I never talk to him about Syne, because when I do he always looks so mournful. Perhaps he thinks it is wicked. He is so good himself, he has no idea how wicked a body can be."

Lucy thought it best to hurry away, that she might return the sooner; for she could not bear the child to be left alone in such a mood. And she was sure that the best thing for her would be to spend the day with her cheery old grandmother. But as she was leaving the shop, Mr. Kitely came in, his large, bold, sharp face fresh as a north wind without a touch of east in it. Lucy preferred her request about Mattie, and he granted it cordially.

"I'm afraid, Mr. Kitely," said Lucy, "the darling is not well. She has such strange fancies."

"Oh, I don't know," returned the bookseller, with mingled concern at the suggestion and refusal to entertain it. "She's always been a curious child. Her mother was like that, you see, and she takes after her. Perhaps she does want a little more change. I don't think she's been out of this street, now, all her life. But she'll shake it off as she gets older, I have no doubt."

So saying, he turned into his shop, and Lucy went home. In half an hour she went back for Mattie, and leaving the two together, of whom the child, in all her words and ways, seemed the older, set out for the West End, where Mrs. Morgenstern was anxiously hoping for her appearance, seeing she depended much upon her assistance, in the treat she was giving to certain poor people of her acquaintance. By any person but Mattie, Mrs. Morgenstern would have been supposed to be literally fulfilling the will of our Lord in asking only those who could not return her invitation.

CHAPTER XIV
THE JEWESS AND HER NEIGHBORS

Mrs. Morgenstern looked splendid as she moved about among the hot-house plants, arranging them in the hall, on the stairs, and in the drawing-rooms. She judged, and judged rightly, that one ought to be more anxious to show honor to poor neighbors by putting on her best attire, than to ordinary guests of her own rank. Therefore, although it was the morning, she had put on a dress of green silk, trimmed with brown silk and rows of garnet buttons, which set off her dark complexion and her rich black hair, plainly braided down her face, and loosely gathered behind. She was half a head taller than Lucy, who was by no means short. The two formed a beautiful contrast. Lucy was dark-haired and dark-eyed as well as Mrs. Morgenstern, but had a smaller face and features, regular to a rare degree. Her high, close-fitting dress of black silk, with a plain linen collar and cuffs, left her loveliness all to itself. Lucy was neither strikingly beautiful nor remarkably intellectual: when one came to understand what it was that attracted him so much, he found that it was the wonderful harmony in her. As Wordsworth prophesied for his Lucy that "beauty born of murmuring sound 'should' pass into her face," so it seemed as if the harmonies which flowed from her father's fingers had molded her form and face, her motions and thoughts, after their own fashion, even to a harmony which soothed before one knew that he was receiving it, and when he had discovered its source, made him ready to quote the words of Sir Philip Sidney—

> Just accord all music makes:
> In thee just accord excelleth.
> Where each part in such peace dwelleth,
> Each of other beauty takes.

I have often wondered how it was that Lucy was capable of so much; how it was, for instance, that, in the dispensing of Mrs. Morgenstern's bounty, she dared to make her way into places where no one but herself thought it could be safe for her to go, but where not even a rude word was ever directed against her or used with regard to her. If she had been as religious as she afterward became, I should not have wondered thus; for some who do not believe that God is anywhere in these dens of what looks to them all misery, will dare everything to rescue their fellow-creatures from impending fate. But Lucy had no theories to spur or to support her. She never taught them any religion; she was only, without knowing it, a religion to their eyes. I conclude, therefore, that at this time it was just the harmony of which I have spoken that led her, protected her, and, combined with a dim consciousness that she must be doing right in following out the loving impulses of her nature, supported her in the disagreeable circumstances into which she was sometimes brought.

While they were thus busy with the flowers, Miriam joined them. She had cast her neutral tints, and appeared in a frock of dark red, with a band of gold in her dusky hair, somberly rich. She was a strange-looking child, one of those whose coming beauty promises all the more that it has as yet reached only the stage of interesting ugliness. Splendid eyes, olive complexion, rounded cheeks, were accompanied by a very unfinished nose, and a large mouth, with thick though finely-modeled lips. She would be a glory some day. She flitted into the room, and flew from flower to flower like one of those black and red butterflies that Scotch children call witches. The sight of her brought to Lucy's mind by contrast the pale face and troubled brow of Mattie, and she told Mrs. Morgenstern about her endeavor to persuade the child to come, and how and why she had failed. Mrs. Morgenstern did not laugh much at the story, but she very nearly did something else.

"Oh! do go and bring little Mattie," said Miriam. "I will be very kind to her. I will give her my doll's house; for I shall be too big for it next year."

"But I left her taking care of my grandmother," said Lucy, to the truth of whose character it belonged to make no concealment of the simplicity of the household conditions of herself and her grandmother. "And," she added, "if she were to come I must stay, and she could not come without me."

"But I'll tell you what—couldn't you bring the other—the little Poppie she talks about? I should like to show Mattie that we're not quite so bad as she thinks us. Do you know this Poppie?" said Mrs. Morgenstern.

Then Lucy told her what she knew about Poppie. She had been making inquiries in the neighborhood, and though she had not traced the child to head-quarters anywhere, everybody in the poor places in which she had sought information knew something about her, though all they knew put together did not come to much. She slept at the top of a stair here, in the bottom of a cupboard there, coiling herself up in spaces of incredible smallness; but no one could say where her home was, or, indeed, if she had any home. Nor, if she wanted to find her, was it of much consequence whether she knew her home or not, for that would certainly be the last place where Poppie would be found.

"But," she concluded, "if you would really like to have her, I will go and try if I can find her. I could be back in an hour and half or so."

"You shall have the brougham."

"No, no," interrupted Lucy. "To go in a brougham to look for Poppie would be like putting salt on a bird's tail. Besides, I should not like the probable consequences of seating her in your carriage. But I should like to see how that wild little savage would do in such a place as this."

"Oh, do go," cried Miriam, clapping her hands. "It will be *such* fun!"

Lucy ran for her bonnet, with great doubts of success, yet willing to do her best to find the child. She did not know that Poppie had followed her almost to Mrs. Morgenstern's door that very morning.

Now what made Lucy sufficiently hopeful of finding Poppie to start in pursuit of her, was the fact that she had of late seen the child so often between Guild Court and a certain other court in the neighborhood of Shoreditch. But Lucy did not know that it was because she was there that Poppie was there. She had not for some time, as I have said, paid her usual visits at Mrs. Morgenstern's because of her grandmother's illness; and when she did go out she had gone only to the place I have just mentioned, where the chief part of her work among the poor lay. Poppie haunting her as she did, where Lucy was there she saw Poppie. And, indeed, if Poppie had any ties to one place more than a hundred others, that place happened to be Staines Court.

When Lucy came out of Mrs. Morgenstern's, if she had only gone the other way, she would have met Poppie coming round the next corner. After Lucy had vanished, Poppie had found a penny in the gutter, had bought a fresh roll with it and given the half of it to a child younger than herself, whom she met at the back of the Marylebone police station, and after contemplating the neighboring church-yard through the railings while they ate their roll together, and comparing this resting-place of the dead with the grand Baker Street Cemetery, she had judged it time to scamper back to the neighborhood of Wyvil Place, that she might have a chance of seeing the beautiful lady as she came out again. As she turned the corner she saw her walking away toward the station, and after following her till she entered it, scudded off for the city, and arrived in the neighborhood of Guild Court before the third train reached Farringdon Street, to which point only was the railway then available.

Lucy walked straight to Staines Court, where she was glad of the opportunity of doing some business of loving kindness at the same time that she sought Poppie. The first house she entered was in a dreadful condition of neglect. There were hardly more balusters in the stairs than served to keep the filthy hand-rail in its place; and doubtless, they would by and by follow the fate of the rest, and vanish as fire-wood. One or two of the stairs, even, were torn to pieces for the same purpose, and the cupboard doors of the room into which Lucy entered had vanished, with half the skirting board and some of the flooring, revealing the joists, and the ceiling, of the room below. All this dilapidation did not matter much in summer weather, but how would it be in the winter—except the police condemned the building before then, and because the wretched people who lived in it could get no better, decreed that so far they should have no shelter at all? Well, when the winter came, they would just go on making larger and larger holes to let in the wind, and fight the cold by burning their protection against it.

In this room there was nobody. Something shining in a dingy sunbeam that fell upon one of the holes in the floor, caught Lucy's eye. She stooped, and putting in her hand, drew out a bottle. At the same moment she let it fall back into the hole, and started with a sense of theft.

"Don't touch Mrs. Flanaghan's gin bottle, lady. She's a good 'un to swear, as you'd be frightened to hear her. She gives me the creepers sometimes, and I'm used to her. She says it's all she's got in the world, and she's ready to die for the 'ould bottle.'"

It was Poppie's pretty, dirty face and wild, black eyes that looked round the door-post.

Lucy felt considerably relieved. She replaced the bottle carefully, saying as she rose:

"I didn't mean to steal it, Poppie. I only saw it shining, and wanted to know what it was. Suppose I push it a little further in, that the sun mayn't be able to see it?"

Poppie thought this was fun, and showed her white teeth.

"But it was you I was looking for—not in that hole, you know," added Lucy, laughing.

"I think I could get into it, if I was to put my clothes off," said Poppie.

Lucy thought it would be a tight fit indeed, if her clothes made any difference.

"Will you come with me?" she said. "I want you."

"Yes, lady," answered Poppie, looking, though, as if she would bolt in a moment.

"Come, then," said Lucy, approaching her where she stood still in the doorway.

But before she reached her, Poppie scudded, and was at the bottom of the stair before Lucy recovered from the surprise of her sudden flight. She saw at once that it would not do to make persistent advances, or show the least desire to get a hold of her.

When she got to the last landing-place on the way down, there was Poppie's face waiting for her in the door below. Careful as one who fears to startle a half-tamed creature with wings, Lucy again approached her; but she vanished again, and she saw no more of her till she was at the mouth of the court. There was Poppie once more, to vanish yet again. In some unaccountable way she seemed to divine where Lucy was going, and with endless evanishments still reappeared in front of her, till she reached the railway station. And there was no Poppie.

For a moment Lucy was dreadfully disappointed. She had not yet had a chance of trying her powers of persuasion upon the child; she had not been within arm's length of her. And she stood at the station door, hot, tired, and disappointed — with all the holiday feeling gone out of her.

Poppie had left her, because she had no magic word by which to gain access to the subterranean regions of the guarded railway. She thought Lucy was going back to the great house in Wyvil Place; but whether Poppie left her to perform the same journey on foot, I do not know. She had scarcely lost sight of Lucy, however, before she caught sight of Thomas Worboise, turning the corner of a street a hundred yards off. She darted after him, and caught him by the tail of his coat. He turned on her angrily, and shook her off.

"The lady," gasped Poppie; but Thomas would not listen, and went on his way. Poppie in her turn was disappointed, and stood "like one forbid." But at that very moment her eye fell on something in the kennel. She was always finding things, though they were generally the veriest trifles. The penny of that morning was something almost awful in its importance. This time it was a bit of red glass. Now Poppie had quite as much delight in colored glass as Lord Bacon had, who advised that hedges in great gardens should be adorned on the top here and there "with broad plates of round, colored glass, gilt, for the sun to play upon," only as she had less of the ways and means of procuring what she valued, she valued what she could lay her hands upon so much the more. She darted at the red shine, wiped it on her frock, sucked it clean in her mouth, as clean as her bright ivories, and polished it up with her hands, scudding all the time, in the hope that Lucy might be at the station still. Poppie did not seek to analyze her feelings in doing as she did; but what she wanted was to give Lucy her treasure-trove. She never doubted that what was valuable to her would be valuable to a beautiful lady. As little did she imagine how much value, as the gift of a ragged little personage like herself, that which was all but worthless would acquire in the eyes of a lady beautiful as Lucy was beautiful, with the beauty of a tender human heart.

Lucy was sitting in the open waiting-room, so weary and disappointed that little would have made her cry. She had let one train go on the vague chance that the erratic little maiden might yet show herself, but her last hope was almost gone when, to her great delight, once more she spied the odd creature peeping round the side of the door. She had presence of mind enough not to rise, lest she should startle the human lapwing, and made her a sign instead to come to her. This being just what Poppie wished at the moment, she obeyed. She darted up to Lucy, put the piece of red glass into her hand, and would have been off again like a low-flying swallow, had not Lucy caught her by the arm. Once caught, Poppie never attempted to struggle. On this occasion she only showed her teeth in a rather constrained smile, and stood still. Lucy, however, did not take her hand from her arm, for she felt that the little phenomenon would disappear at once if she did.

"Poppie," she said, "I want you to come with me."

Poppie only grinned again. So Lucy rose, still holding her by the arm, and went to the ticket-window and got two second-class tickets. Poppie went on grinning, and accompanied her down the stairs without one obstructive motion.

When they were fairly seated in the carriage, and there was no longer any danger of her prisoner attempting to escape, Lucy thought of the something Poppie had given her, at which she had not even looked, so anxious was she to secure her bird. When she saw it, she comprehended it at once—the sign of love, the appeal of a half-savage sister to one of her own kind, in whom she dimly recognized her far-off ideal; even then not seeking love from the higher, only tendering the richest human gift, simple love, unsought, unbought. Thus a fragment dropped by some glazier as he went to mend the glass door leading into a garden, and picked out of the gutter by a beggar girl, who had never yet thought whether she had had a father or a mother, became in that same girl's hands a something which the Lord himself, however some of his interpreters might be shocked at the statement, would have recognized as partaking of the character of his own eucharist. And as such, though without thinking of it after that fashion, it was received by the beautiful lady. The tears came into her eyes. Poppie thought she half offended or disappointed her, and looked very grave. Lucy saw she had misunderstood her. There was no one in the carriage with them. She stooped and kissed her. Then the same tears came, almost for the first time since she had been an infant, into Poppie's eyes. But just then the train moved off, and although the child by no remark and no motion evinced astonishment any more than fear, she watched everything with the intensity of an animal which in new circumstances cannot afford to lose one moment of circumspection, seeing a true knowledge of the whole may be indispensable to the retention of its liberty; and before they reached King's Cross, her eyes were clear, and only a channel on each cheek, ending in a little mud-bank, showed that just two tears had flowed half way down her cheeks and dried there undisturbed in the absorption of her interest.

Before they reached Baker Street station, Lucy had begun to be anxious as to how she should get her charge through the streets. But no sooner were they upon the stairs, than Lucy perceived by the way in which Poppie walked, and the way in which she now and then looked up at her, that there was no longer any likelihood that she would run away from her. When they reached the top, she took her by the hand, and, without showing the slightest inclination to bolt, Poppie trotted alongside of her to Mrs. Morgenstern's door. Having gained her purpose, Lucy's weariness had quite left her, and her eyes shone with triumph. They made a strange couple, that graceful lady and that ragged, bizarre child, who would, however, have shown herself lovely to any eyes keen enough to see through the dirt which came and went according to laws as unknown to Poppie as if it had been a London fog.

Lucy knocked at the door. It was opened by a huge porter in a rich livery, and shoulder-knots like the cords of a coffin, as if he were about to be lowered into his grave standing. He started at sight of the little city Bedouin, but stood aside to let them enter, with all the respect which, like the rest of his class, he ever condescended to show to those who, like Miss Burton, came to instruct Miss Morgenstern, and gave him, so much their superior, the trouble of opening the door to them. The pride of the proudest nobleman or parvenu-millionaire is entirely cast in the shade by the pride of his servants, justifying the representation of Spenser, that although Orgoglio is the son of Terra by Æolus, he cannot be raised to his full giantship without the aid of his foster-father Ignaro. Lucy, however, cared as little for this form of contempt as impervious little Poppie by her side, who trotted as unconcerned over the black and white lozenges of the marble floor as over the ordinary slabs of Guild Court, or the round stones of Staines Court, and looked up the splendid stair-case which rose from the middle of the round hall till it reached its side, and then branched into two that ran circling and ascending the wall to the floor above, its hand-rails and balusters shining with gold, and its steps covered with a carpet two yards wide, in which the foot sank as if in grass, with as much indifference as if it were the breakneck stair-case I have already described as leading to the abode of Mistress Flanaghan. But little bare feet were not destined to press such a luxurious support; better things awaited them, namely, the grass itself; for the resplendent creature whose head and legs were equally indebted to the skill of the cunning workman, strode on before them, and through a glass door at the back, to a lawn behind, such as few London dwellings have to show. They might have thought that they had been transported by enchantment to some country palace, so skillfully were the neighboring houses hidden by the trees that encircled the garden. Mrs. Morgenstern, with a little company of her friends, was standing in the middle of the lawn, while many of her poorer *neighbors* were wandering about the place enjoying the flowers, and what to them was indeed fresh air, when Lucy came out with the dirty, bare-legged child in her hand. All eyes turned upon her, and a lovelier girl doing lovelier deed would have taken more than that summer morning to discover.

But Lucy had the bit of red glass in her mind, and, without heeding hostess or friends for the moment, led Poppie straight toward a lovely rose-tree that stood in full blossom on one side of the lawn. How cool that kindly humble grass must have felt to the hot feet of the darling! But she had no time to think about it. For as she drew near the rose-tree, her gaze became more and more fixed upon it; when at length she stood before it, and beheld it in all its glory, she burst into a very passion of weeping. The eyes of the daughter of man became rivers, and her head a fountain of waters, filled and glorified by the presence of a rose-tree. All that were near gathered about, till Lucy, Poppie, and the rose-tree were the center of a group. Lucy made no attempt to stay the flow of Poppie's tears, for her own heart swelled and swelled at the sight of the child's feelings. Surely it was the presence of God that so moved her: if ever bush burned with fire and was not consumed, that rose-bush burned with the presence of God. Poppie had no handkerchief; nor was there continuity of space enough in her garments to hold a pocket: she generally carried things in her mouth when they were small enough to go in. And she did not even put her hands to her face to hide her emotion. She let her tears run down her stained cheeks, and let sob follow sob unchecked, gazing ever through the storm of her little world at the marvel in front of her. She had seen a rose before, but had never seen a rose-tree full of roses. At last Lucy drew her handkerchief from her pocket, and for the first time in her life Poppie had tears wiped from her face by a loving hand.

There was one man, and only one, in the company—Mr. Sargent, a young barrister. He was the first to speak. He drew near to Lucy and said, in a half whisper:

"Where did you find the little creature, Miss Burton?"

"That would be hard to say," answered Lucy, with a smile. "Isn't she a darling?"

"You are a darling, anyhow," said Mr. Sargent, but neither to Lucy nor to any one but himself. He had been like one of the family for many years, for his father and Mr. Morgenstern had been intimate, and he had admired Lucy ever since she went first to the house; but he had never seen her look so lovely as she looked that morning.

Certain harmonious circumstances are always necessary to bring out the peculiar beauty both of persons and things—a truth recognized by Emerson in his lovely poem called "Each and All," but recognized imperfectly, inasmuch as he seems to represent the beauty of each as dependent on the all not merely for its full manifestation, but for its actual being; a truth likewise recognized by Shakespeare, but by him with absolute truth of vision—

> The nightingale, if she should sing by day,
> When every goose is cackling, would be thought
> No better a musician than the wren.
> *How many things by season seasoned are*
> *To their right praise and true perfection!*

It was to the praise of Lucy's beauty, that in this group she should thus look more beautiful. The rose-tree and the splendor of Mrs. Morgenstern did not eclipse her, because her beauty was of another sort, which made a lovely harmony of difference with theirs. Or perhaps, after all, it was the ragged child in her hand that gave a tender glow to her presence unseen before.

Little Miriam pulled at her mamma's skirt. She stooped to the child.

"Somebody has lost that one," said Miriam, pointing shyly to Poppie. "She looks like it."

"Perhaps," said her mother. But the answer did not satisfy Miriam.

"You told me you had lost a little girl once," she said.

Mrs. Morgenstern had never yet uttered the word *death* in her hearing. As to the little dead daughter, she had to the sister said only that she had lost her. Miriam had to interpret the phrase for herself.

"Yes, dear child," answered her mother, not yet seeing what she was driving at.

"Don't you think, mamma," pursued Miriam, with the tears rising in her great black eyes, "that that's her? I do. I am sure it is my little sister."

Mrs. Morgenstern had the tenderest memories of her lost darling, and turned away to hide her feelings. Meantime a little conversation had arisen in the group. Lucy had let go her hold of Poppie, whose tears had now ceased. Miriam drew near, shyly, and possessed herself of the hand of the vagrant. Her mother turned and saw her, and motherhood spoke aloud in her heart. How did it manifest itself? In drawing her child away from the dirt that divided their hands? That might have proved her a dam, but would have gone far to disprove her motherhood.

"What shall we do with her, Miriam?" she said.

"Ask nurse to wash her in the bath, and put one of my frocks on her."

Poppie snatched her hand from Miriam's, and began to look about her with wild-eyed search after a hole to run into. Mrs. Morgenstern saw that she was frightened, and turned away to Lucy, who was on the other side of the rose-tree, talking to Mr. Sargent.

"Couldn't we do something to make the child tidy, Lucy?" she said.

Lucy gave her shoulders a little shrug, as much as to say she feared it would not be of much use. She was wrong there, for if the child should never be clean again in her life, no one could tell how the growth of moral feeling might be aided in her by her once knowing what it was to have a clean skin and clean garments. It might serve hereafter, in her consciousness, as a type of something better still than personal cleanliness, might work in aid of her consciousness as a vague reminder of ideal parity—not altogether pleasant to her ignorant fancy, and yet to be—faintly and fearingly—desired. But although Lucy did not see much use in washing her, she could not help wondering what she would look like if she were clean. And she proceeded to carry out her friend's wishes.

Poppie was getting bored already with the unrealized world of grandeur around her. The magic of the roses was all gone, and she was only looking out for a chance of scudding. Yet when Lucy spoke to her she willingly yielded her hand, perhaps in the hope that she was, like Peter's angel, about to open the prison-doors, and lead her out of her prison.

Lucy gave an amusing account of how Poppie looked askance, with a mingling of terror and repugnance, at the great bath, half full of water, into which she was about to be plunged. But the door was shut, and there was not even a chimney for her to run up, and she submitted. She looked even pleased when she was at length in the midst of the water. But Lucy found that she had undertaken a far more difficult task than she had expected—especially when she came to her hair. It was nearly two hours, notwithstanding repeated messages from Mrs. Morgenstern and tappings at the door of the bath-room by Miriam, before she was able to reproduce the little savage on whom she had been bestowing this baptism of love.

When she came down at last, the company, consisting of some of Mrs. Morgenstern's more intimate friends, and a goodly number of *clients* if not exactly dependents, was seated at luncheon in the large dining-room. Poppie attracted all eyes once more. She was dressed in a last year's summer frock of Miriam's, and her hair was reduced to order; but she had begun to cry so piteously when Lucy began to put stockings upon her, that she gave it up at once, and her legs were still bare. I presume she saw the last remnants of her freedom vanishing in those gyves and fetters. But nice and clean as she looked, she certainly had lost something by her decent garments. Poppie must have been made for rags and rags for Poppie—they went so admirably together. And there is nothing wicked in rags or in poverty. It is possible to go in rags and keep the Ten Commandments, and it is possible to ride in purple and fine linen and break every one of them. Nothing, however, could spoil the wildness of those honestly furtive eyes.

Seated beside Lucy at the table, she did nothing but first stare, then dart her eyes from one to another of the company with the scared expression of a creature caught in a trap, and then stare again. She was evidently anything but comfortable. When Lucy spoke to her she did not reply, but gazed appealingly, and on the point of crying, into her eyes, as if to say, "What *have* I done to be punished in this dreadful manner?" Lucy tried hard to make her eat, but she sat and stared and would touch nothing. Her plate, with the wing of a chicken on it, stood before her unregarded. But all at once she darted out her hand like the paw of a wild beast, caught something, slipped from her chair, and disappeared under the table. Peeping down after her, Lucy saw her seated on the floor, devouring the roll which had been put by the side of her plate. Judging it best not to disturb her, she took no more notice of her for some time, during which Poppie, having discovered a long row of resplendent buttons down the front of her dress, twisted them all off with a purpose manifested as soon as the luncheon was over. When the company rose from their seats, she crawled out from under the table and ran to Miriam, holding out both her hands. Miriam held out her hands to meet Poppie's, and received them full of the buttons off her own old frock.

"Oh! you naughty Poppie," said Lucy, who had watched her. "Why did you cut off the buttons? Don't you like them?"

"Oh! golly! don't I just? And so does *she*. Tuck me up if she don't!"

Poppie had no idea that she had done anything improper. It was not as buttons, but *per se*, as pretty things, that she admired the knobs, and therefore she gave them to Miriam. Having said thus, she caught at another *tommy*, as she would have called it, dived under the table again, and devoured it at her ease, keeping, however, a sharp eye upon her opportunity. Finding one when Lucy, who had remained in the room to look after her, was paying more attention to the party in the garden, she crawled out at the door, left open during the process of *taking away*, and with her hand on the ponderous lock of the street door, found herself seized from behind by the porter. She had been too long a pupil of the London streets not to know the real position of the liveried in the social scale, and for them she had as little respect as any of her tribe. She therefore assailed him with such a torrent of bad language, scarcely understanding a word that she used, that he declared it made his "'air stand on hend," although he was tolerably familiar with such at the Spotted Dog round the corner. Finding, however, that this discharge of cuttle-fish ink had no effect upon the enemy, she tried another mode—and, with a yell of pain, the man fell back, shaking his hand, which bore the marks of four sharp incisors. In one moment Poppie was free, and scudding. Thus ended her introduction to civilized life.

Poppie did not find it nice. She preferred all London to the biggest house and garden in it. True, there was that marvelous rose-tree. But free-born creatures cannot live upon the contemplation of roses. After all, the thing she had been brought up to—the streets, the kennels with their occasional crusts, pennies, and bits of glass, the holes to creep into, and the endless room for scudding—was better. And her unsuitable dress, which did attract the eyes of the passers—being such as was seldom seen in connection with bare hair and legs—would soon accommodate itself to circumstances, taking the form of rags before a week was over, to which change of condition no care of Poppie's would interpose an obstacle. For, like the birds of the air and the lilies of the field, she had no care. She did not know what it meant. And possibly the great One who made her may have different ideas about respectability from those of dining aldermen and members of Parliament from certain boroughs that might be named.

At the porter's cry Lucy started, and found to her dismay that her charge was gone. She could not, however, help a certain somewhat malicious pleasure at the man's discomfiture and the baby-like way in which he lamented over his bitten finger. He forgot himself so far as to call her "the little devil"—which was quite in accordance with his respectable way of thinking. Both Mrs. Morgenstern and Lucy, after the first disappointment and vexation were over, laughed heartily at the affair, and even Miriam was worked up to a smile at last. But she continued very mournful, notwithstanding, over the loss of her sister, as she would call her.

Mr. Sargent did his best to enliven the party. He was a man of good feeling, and of more than ordinary love for the right. This, however, from a dread of what he would have called *sentimentality*, he persisted in regarding as a mere peculiarity, possibly a weakness. If he made up his mind to help any one who was wronged, for which it must be confessed he had more time than he would have cared to acknowledge, he would say that he had "taken an *interest* in such or such a case;" or that the case involved "points of *interest*," which he was "willing to see settled." He never said that he wanted to see right done: that would have been enthusiastic, and unworthy of the cold dignity of a lawyer. So he was one of those false men, alas too few! who always represent themselves as inferior to what they are. Many and various were the jokes he made upon Poppie and Jeames, ever, it must be confessed, with an eye to the approbation of Miss Burton. He declared, for instance, that the Armageddon of class-legislature would be fought between those of whom the porter and Poppie were the representatives, and rejoiced that, as in the case of the small quarrel between Fitz James and Roderick Dhu, Poppie had drawn the first blood, and gained thereby a good omen. And Lucy was pleased with him, it must be confessed. She never thought of comparing him with Thomas, which was well for Thomas. But she did think he was a very clever, gentlemanly fellow, and knew how to make himself agreeable.

He offered to see her home, which she declined, not even permitting him to walk with her to the railway.

CHAPTER XV
THE TWO OLD WOMEN

She found the two old women, of whom Mattie still seemed the older, seated together at their tea. Not a ray of the afternoon sun could find its way into the room. It was dusky and sultry, with a smell of roses. This, and its strange mingling of furniture, made it like a room over a broker's in some country town.

"Well, Miss Burton, here you are at last!" said Mattie, with a half smile on the half of her mouth.

"Yes, Mattie, here I am. Has grandmother been good to you?"

"Of course she has—very good. Everybody is good to *me*. I am a very fortunate child, as my father says, though he never seems to mean it."

"And how do you think your patient is?" asked Lucy, while Mrs. Boxall sat silent, careful not to obstruct the amusement which the child's answers must give them.

"Well, I do not think Mrs. Boxall is worse. She has been very good, and has done everything I found myself obliged to recommend. I would not let her get up so soon as she wanted to."

"And what did you do to keep her in bed?" asked Lucy.

"Well, I could not think of a story to tell her just then, so I got the big Bible out of the book-case, and began to show her the pictures. But she did not care about that. I think it was my fault, though, because I was not able to hold the book so that she could see them properly. So I read a story to her, but I do not think I chose a very nice one."

Mrs. Boxall made a deprecating motion with her head and hands, accompanied by the words—

"She *will* say what she thinks—Bible or Prayer-book."

"Well, and where's the harm, when I mean none? Who's to be angry at that? I *will* say," Mattie went on, "that it was an ugly trick of that woman to serve a person that never did *her* any harm; and I wonder at two sensible women like Mrs. Boxall and Deborah sticking up for her."

"Is it Jael she means, grannie?" asked Lucy, very softly.

"Yes, it is Jael she means," answered Mattie for herself, with some defiance in her tone.

"For my part," she continued, "I think it was just like one of Syne's tricks."

"Have you seen Mr. Spelt to-day, Mattie?" asked Lucy, desirous of changing the subject, because of the direction the child's thoughts had taken.

"Well, I haven't," answered Mattie, "and I will go and see now whether he's gone or not. But don't you fancy that I don't see through it for all that, Miss Burton," she continued. "I shouldn't have been in the way, though — not much, for I like to see young people enjoying themselves."

"What *do* you mean, Mattie?" asked Lucy with a bewilderment occasioned rather by the quarter whence the words proceeded than by the words themselves; for she did expect to see Thomas that evening.

Mattie vouchsafed no reply to the question, but bade them good-night, the one and the other, with an evident expression of *hauteur*, and marched solemnly down the stairs, holding carefully by the balusters, for she was too small to use the hand-rail comfortably.

Mr. Spelt's roost was shut up for the night: he had gone to take some work home. Mattie therefore turned toward her father's shop.

In the archway she ran against Thomas, or, more properly, Thomas ran against her, for Mattie never ran at all, so that he had to clasp her to prevent her from falling.

"Well, you needn't be in such a hurry, Mr. Thomas, though she is a-waiting for you. She won't go till you come, *I* know."

"You're a cheeky little monkey," said Thomas, good naturedly. But the words were altogether out of tune with the idea of Mattie, who again felt her dignity invaded, and walked into the shop with her chin projecting more than usual.

"Come, my princess," said her father, seating himself in an old chair, and taking the child on his knee. "I haven't seen my princess all day. — How's your royal highness this night?"

Mattie laid her head on his shoulder, and burst into tears.

"What's the matter with my pet?" said her father, fondling and soothing her with much concern. "Has anybody been unkind to you?"

"No, Mr. Kitely," said the child, "but I feel that lonely! I wish you would read to me a bit, for Mr. Spelt ain't there, and I read something in the Bible this morning that ain't done me no good."

"You shouldn't read such things, Mattie," said the bookseller. "They ain't no good. I'll go and get a candle. Sit you there till I come back."

"No, no, father. Don't leave me here. I don't like the books to-night. Take me with you. Carry me."

The father obeyed at once, took his child on his arm, got a candle from the back room, for the place was very dusky—he did not care to light the gas this time of the year—and sat down with Mattie in a part of the shop which was screened from the door, where he could yet hear every footstep that passed.

"What shall I read now, my precious?" he asked.

"Well, I don't think I care for anything but the New Testament to-night, father."

"Why, you've just been saying it disagreed with you this very morning," objected Mr. Kitely.

"No, father. It wasn't the New Testament at all. It was the very old Testament, I believe; for it was near the beginning of it, and told all about a horrid murder. I do believe," she added, reflectively, "that that book grows better as it gets older—younger, I mean."

The poor child wanted some one to help her out of her Bible difficulties, and her father certainly was not the man to do so, for he believed nothing about or in it. Like many other children far more carefully taught of man, she was laboring under the misery of the fancy that everything related in the Old Testament without remark of disapprobation is sanctioned by the divine will. If parents do not encourage their children to speak their minds about what they read generally, and especially in the Bible, they will one day be dismayed to find that they have not merely the strangest but the most deadly notions of what is contained in that book—as, for instance, besides the one in hand, that God approved of all the sly tricks of Jacob— for was not he the religious one of the brothers, and did not all his tricks succeed? They are not able without help to regard the history broadly, and see that just because of this bad that was in him, he had to pass through a life of varied and severe suffering, punished in the vices which his children inherited from himself, in order that the noble part of his nature might be burned clean of the filth that clung to it.

Such was Mr. Kitely's tenderness over his daughter, increased by some signs he had begun to see of the return of an affection of the brain from which he had been on the point of losing her some years before, that he made no further opposition, but, rising again, brought an old "breeches Bible" from a shelf, and, taking her once more on his knee, supported her with one hand and held the book with the other.

"Well, I don't know one chapter from another," reflected Mr. Kitely aloud. "I wonder where the child would like me to read. I'm sure I can't tell what to read."

"Read about *Somebody*," said Mattie.

From the peculiar expression she gave to the word, her father guessed at her meaning, and opening the gospel part of the book at random, began to read.

He read, from the Gospel by St. Matthew, the story of the Transfiguration, to which Mattie listened without word or motion. He then went on to the following story of the lunatic and apparently epileptic, boy. As soon as he began to read the account of how the child was vexed, Mattie said conclusively:

"That was Syne. *I* know him. He's been at it for a long time."

"'And Jesus rebuked the devil; and he departed out of him; and the child was cured from that very hour,'" the bookseller went on reading in a subdued voice, partly because he sat in his shop with the door open, partly because not even he could read "the ancient story, ever new" without feeling a something he could not have quite accounted for if he had thought of trying. But the moment he had read those words, Mattie cried:

"There, I knew it!"

It must be remembered that Mattie had not read much of the New Testament. Mr. Spelt alone had led her to read any. Everything came new to her, therefore; every word was like the rod of Moses that drew the waters of response.

"What did you know, princess?" asked her father.

"I knew that Somebody would make him mind what he was about—I did. I wonder if he let a flash of that light out on him that he shut up inside him again. I shouldn't wonder if that was it. I know Syne couldn't stand that—no, not for a moment. I think I'll go to bed, Mr. Kitely."

CHAPTER XVI
ON THE RIVER

Notwithstanding the good-humored answer Thomas had made to Mattie, her words stuck to him and occasioned him a little discomfort. For if the bookseller's daughter, whose shop lay between the counting-house and the court, knew so well of his visits to Lucy, how could he hope that they would long remain concealed from other and far more dangerous eyes. This thought oppressed him so much, that instead of paying his usual visit to Mr. Molken, he went to Mrs. Boxall's at once. There, after greetings, he threw himself on the cushions of the old settle, and was gloomy. Lucy looked at him with some concern. Mrs. Boxall murmured something about his being in the doldrums—a phrase she had learned from her son John.

"Let's go out, Lucy," said Thomas; "it is so sultry."

Lucy was quite ready in herself to comply. For one reason, she had something upon her mind about which she wanted to talk to him. But she objected.

"My grandmother is not fit to be left alone, Thomas," she said, regretfully.

"Oh! ah!" said Thomas.

"Never mind me, child," interposed the old woman. "You'll make me wish myself in my grave, if you make me come between young people. You go, my dear, and never mind me. You needn't be gone a great while, you know."

"Oh, no, grannie; I'll be back in an hour, or less, if you like," said Lucy, hastening to put on her bonnet.

"No, no, my dear. An hour's in reason. Anything in reason, you know."

So Lucy made the old lady comfortable in her arm-chair, and went out with Thomas.

The roar of the city had relaxed. There would be no more blocks in Gracechurch Street that night. There was little smoke in the air, only enough to clothe the dome of St. Paul's in a faintly rosy garment, tinged from the west, where the sun was under a cloud. The huge mass looked ethereal, melted away as to a shell of thicker air against a background of slate-color, where a wind was gathering to flow at sunset through the streets and lanes, cooling them from the heat of the day, of the friction of iron and granite, of human effort, and the thousand fires that prepared the food of the city-dining population. Crossing the chief thoroughfares, they went down the lanes leading to the river. Here they passed through a sultry region of aromatic fragrance, where the very hooks that hung from cranes in doorways high above the ground, seemed to retain something of the odor of the bales they had lifted from the wagons below during the hot sunshine that drew out their imprisoned essences. By yet closer ways they went toward the river, descending still, and at length, by a short wooden stair, and a long wooden way, they came on a floating pier. There the wind blew sweet and cooling and very grateful, for the summer was early and fervid. Down into the east the river swept away, somber and sullen, to gurgle blindly through the jungle of masts that lay below the bridge and crossed the horizontal lines of the sky with their delicate spars, and yet more delicate cordage. Little did Thomas think that one of those masts rose from a vessel laden, one might say, with his near, though not his final fate—a fate that truth might have averted, but which the very absence of truth made needful and salutary. A boat was just starting up the river toward the light.

"Let's have a blow," said Thomas.

"That will be delightful," answered Lucy, and they went on board. First one wheel, then the other, then both together, dashed the Stygian waters of the Thames into a white fury, and they were moving up the stream. They went forward into the bows of the boat to get clear of the smoke, and sat down. There were so few on board that they could talk without being overheard. But they sat silent for some time; the stillness of the sky seemed to have sunk into their hearts. For that was as pure over their heads as if there had been no filthy Thames beneath their feet; and its light and color illuminated the surface of the river, which was not yet so vile that it could not reflect the glory that fell upon its face. The tide was against them, and with all the struggles of the little steamer they made but slow way up the dark, hurrying water. Lucy sat gazing at the banks of the river, where the mighty city on either hand has declined into sordid meanness, skeleton exposure; where the struggles of manufacture and commerce are content to abjure their own decencies for the sake of the greater gain. Save where the long line of Somerset House, and the garden of the Temple asserted the ancient dignity of order and cleanliness, the whole looked like a mean, tattered, draggled fringe upon a rich garment. Then she turned her gaze down on the river, which, as if ashamed of the condition into which it had fallen from its first estate, crawled fiercely away to hide itself in the sea.

"How different," she said, looking up at Thomas, who had been sitting gazing at her all the time that she contemplated the shore and the river— "How different things would be if they were only clean!"

"Yes, indeed," returned Thomas. "Think what it would be to see the fishes—the salmon, say—shooting about in clear water under us, like so many silver fishes in a crystal globe! If people were as fond of the cleanliness you want as they are of money, things would look very different indeed!"

I have said that Thomas loved Lucy more and more. Partly a cause, partly a consequence of this, he had begun to find out that there was a poetic element in her, and he flattered himself that he had developed it. No doubt he had had a share in its development, but it was of a deeper, truer, simpler kind than his own, and would never have been what it was, in rapport always with the facts of nature and life, if it had been only a feminine response to his. Men like women to reflect them, no doubt; but the woman who can only reflect a man, and is nothing in herself, will never be of much service to him. The woman who cannot stand alone is not likely to make either a good wife or mother. She may be a pleasant companion so far as the intercourse of love-making goes, no doubt—scarcely more; save, indeed, the trials that ensue upon marriage bring out the power latent in her. But the remark with which Thomas responded to Lucy was quite beyond his usual strain. He had a far finer nature underneath than his *education* had allowed to manifest itself, and the circumstances in which he was at the moment were especially favorable to his best. Casca, on his first appearance in *Julius Cæsar*, talks blunt and snarling prose: in the very next scene, which is a fearfully magnificent thunder-storm, he speaks poetry. "He was quick mettle when he went to school," and the circumstances brought it out.

"I wish the world was clean, Thomas, all through," said Lucy.

Thomas did not reply. His heart smote him. Those few words went deeper than all Mr. Simon's sermons, public and private. For a long time he had not spoken a word about religion to Lucy. Nor had what he said ever taken any hold upon her intellect, although it had upon her conscience; for, not having been brought up to his vocabulary, and what might be called the technical phrases if not *slang* of his religion, it had been to her but a vague sound, which yet she received as a reminder of duty. Some healthy religious teaching would be of the greatest value to her now. But Mr. Potter provided no food beyond the established fare; and whatever may be said about the sufficiency of the church-service, and the uselessness of preaching, I for one believe that a dumb ass, if the Lord only opens his mouth, may rebuke much madness of prophets, and priests too. But where there is neither honesty nor earnestness, as in the case of Mr. Potter, the man is too much of an ass for even the Lord to open his mouth to any useful purpose. His heart has to be opened first, and that takes time and trouble.

Finding that Thomas remained silent, Lucy looked into his face, and saw that he was troubled. This brought to the point of speech the dissatisfaction with himself which had long been moving restlessly and painfully in his heart, and of which the quiet about him, the peace of the sky, and that sense of decline and coming repose, which invades even the heart of London with the sinking sun, had made him more conscious than he had yet been.

"Oh, Lucy," he said, "I wish you would help me to be good."

To no other could he have said so. Mr. Simon, for instance, aroused all that was most contrarious in him. But Lucy at this moment seemed so near to him that before her he could be humble without humiliation, and could even enjoy the confession of weakness implied in his appeal to her for aid.

She looked at him with a wise kind of wonder in her look. For a moment she was silent.

"I do not know how I can help you, Thomas, for you know better about all such things than I do. But there is one thing I want very much to speak to you about, because it makes me unhappy—rather—not *very*, you know."

She laid his hand upon his. He looked at her lovingly. She was encouraged, and continued:

"I don't like this way of going on, Thomas. I never quite liked it, but I've been thinking more about it, lately. I thought you must know best, but I am not satisfied with myself at all about it."

"What do you mean, Lucy?" asked Thomas, his heart beginning already to harden at the approach of definite blame. It was all very well for him to speak as if he might be improved—it was another thing for Lucy to do so.

"Do not be vexed with me, Thomas. You must know what I mean. I wish your mother knew all about it," she added, hastily, after a pause. And then her face flushed red as a sunset.

"She'll know all about it in good time," returned Thomas, testily; adding, in an undertone, as if he did not mean to press the remark, although he wanted her to hear it: "You do not know my mother, or you would not be so anxious for her to know all about it."

"Couldn't you get your father to tell her, then, and make it easier for you?"

"My father," answered Thomas, coolly, "would turn me out of the house if I didn't give you up; and as I don't mean to do that, and don't want to be turned out of the house just at present, when I have nowhere else to go, I don't want to tell him."

"I *can't* go on in this way, then. Besides, they are sure to hear of it, somehow."

"Oh, no, they won't. Who's to tell them?"

"Don't suppose I've been listening, Tom, because I heard your last words," said a voice behind them—that of Mr. Wither. "I haven't been watching you, but I have been watching for an opportunity of telling you that Stopper is keeping far too sharp a lookout on you to mean you any good by it. I beg your pardon, Miss Boxall," he resumed, taking off his hat. "I fear I have been rude; but, as I say, I was anxious to tell Mr. Worboise to be cautious. I don't see why a fellow should get into a scrape for want of a hint."

The manner with which Wither spoke to her made poor Lucy feel that there was not merely something unfitting, but something even disreputable, in the way her relation to Thomas was kept up. She grew as pale as death, rose, and turned to the side of the vessel, and drew her veil nervously over her face.

"It's no business of mine, of course, Tom. But what I tell you is true. Though if you take my advice," said Wither, and here he dropped his voice to a whisper, "this connection is quite as fit a one to cut as the last; and the sooner you do it the better, for it'll make a devil of a row with old Boxall. You ought to think of the girl, you know. Your own governor's your own lookout. There's none of it any business of mine, you know."

He turned with a nod and went aft; for the steamer was just drawing in to the Hungerford pier, where he had to go ashore.

For a few minutes not a word passed between Thomas and Lucy. A sudden cloud had fallen upon them. They must not go on this way, but what other way were they to take? They stood side by side, looking into the water, Thomas humiliated and Lucy disgraced. There was no comfort to be got out of that rushing blackness, and the mud banks grew wider and wider.

Lucy was the first to speak, for she was far more capable than Tom.

"We must go ashore at the next pier," she said.

"Very well," said Tom, as if he had been stunned into sullenness. "If you want to get rid of me because of what that fellow said—"

"Oh, Tom!" said Lucy, and burst out crying.

"Well, what *do* you want, Lucy?"

"We *must* part, Tom," sobbed Lucy.

"Nonsense!" said Tom, nearly crying himself, for a great, painful lump had risen in his throat.

"We can love each other all the same," said Lucy, still sobbing; "only you must not come to see me any more—that is—I do not mean—never any more at all—but till you have told them—all about it. I don't mean now, but some time, you know. When will you be of age, Tom?"

"Oh, that makes no difference. As long's I'm dependent, it's all the same. I wish I was my own master. I should soon let them see I didn't care what they said."

Silence again followed, during which Lucy tried in vain to stop her tears by wiping them away. A wretched feeling awoke in her that Thomas was not manly, could not resolve—or rather, could not help her when she would do the right thing. She would have borne anything rather than that. It put her heart in a vise.

The boat stopped at the Westminster pier. They went on shore. The sun was down, and the fresh breeze that blew, while it pleasantly cooled the hot faces that moved westward from their day's work, made Lucy almost shiver with cold. For loss had laid hold of her heart. They walked up Parliament Street. Thomas felt that he must say something, but what he should say he could not think. He always thought what he should say—never what he should do.

"Lucy, dear," he said at last, "we won't make up our minds to-night. Wait till I see you next. I shall have time to think about it before then. I will be a match for that sneaking rascal, Stopper, yet."

Lucy felt inclined to say that to sneak was no way to give sneaking its own. But she said neither that nor anything else.

They got into an omnibus at Charing Cross, and returned—deafened, stupefied, and despondent—into the city. They parted at Lucy's door, and Thomas went home, already much later than usual.

What should he do? He resolved upon nothing, and did the worst thing he could have done. He lied.

"You are very late to-night, Thomas," said his mother. "Have you been all this time with Mr. Moloch?"

"Yes, mother," answered Thomas.

And when he was in bed he comforted himself by saying there was no such person as Mr. Moloch.

When Lucy went to bed, she prayed to God in sobs and cries of pain. Hitherto she had believed in Thomas without a question crossing the disk of her faith; but now she had begun to doubt, and the very fact that she could doubt was enough to make her miserable, even if there had been no ground for the doubt. My readers must remember that no one had attempted to let her into the secrets of his character as I have done with them. His beautiful face, pleasant manners, self-confidence, and, above all, her love, had blinded her to his faults. For, although I do not in the least believe that Love is blind, yet I must confess that, like kittens and some other animals, he has his blindness nine days or more, as it may be, from his birth. But once she had begun to suspect, she found ground for suspicion enough. She had never known grief before—not even when her mother died—for death has not anything despicable, and Thomas had.

What Charles Wither had told Thomas was true enough. Mr. Stopper was after him. Ever since that dinner-party at Mr. Boxall's he had hated him, and bided his time.

Mr. Stopper was a man of forty, in whose pine-apple whiskers and bristly hair the first white streaks of autumn had begun to show themselves. He had entered the service of Messrs. Blunt & Baker some five-and-twenty years before, and had gradually risen through all the intervening positions to his present post. Within the last year, moved by prudential considerations, he had begun to regard the daughters of his principal against the background of possible marriage; and as he had hitherto, from motives of the same class, resisted all inclinations in that direction, with so much the more force did his nature rush into the channel which the consent of his selfishness opened for the indulgence of his affections. For the moment he saw Mary Boxall with this object in view, he fell in love with her after the fashion of such a man, beginning instantly to build, not castles, but square houses in the air in the dining-rooms especially of which her form appeared in gorgeous and somewhat matronly garments amid ponderous mahogany, seated behind the obscuration of tropical plants at a table set out *à la Russe*. His indignation, when he entered the drawing-room after Mr. Boxall's dinner, and saw Thomas in the act of committing the indiscretion recorded in that part of my story, passed into silent hatred when he found that while his attentions were slighted, those of Thomas, in his eyes a mere upstart—for he judged everything in relation to the horizon of Messrs. Blunt & Baker, and every man in relation to himself, seated upon the loftiest summit within the circle of that horizon—not even offered, but only dropped at her feet in passing, were yet accepted.

Among men Mr. Stopper was of the bull-dog breed, sagacious, keen-scented, vulgar, and inexorable; capable of much within the range of things illuminated by his own interests, capable of nothing beyond it. And now one of his main objects was to catch some scent—for the bull-dog has an excellent nose—of Thomas's faults or failings, and follow such up the wind of his prosperity, till he should have a chance of pulling him down at last. His first inclination toward this revenge was strengthened and elevated into an imagined execution of justice when Mary fell ill, and it oozed out that her illness had not a little to do with some behavior of Thomas's. Hence it came that, both consciously and unconsciously, Mr. Stopper was watching the unfortunate youth, though so cautious was Thomas that he had not yet discovered anything of which he could make a definite use. Nor did he want to interrupt Thomas's projects before he found that they put him in his power.

So here was a weak and conceited youth of fine faculties and fine impulses, between the malign aspects of two opposite stars—watched, that is, and speculated upon by two able and unprincipled men; the one, Mr. Molken, searching him and ingratiating himself with him, "to the end to know how to worke him, or winde him, or governe him," which, Lord Bacon goes on to say, "proceedeth from a heart that is double and cloven, and not entyre and ingenuous;" the other, Mr. Stopper, watching his conduct, not for the sake of procuring advantage to himself, but injury to Thomas. The one sought to lead him astray, that he might rob him in the dark; the other sought a chance of knocking him down, that he might leave him lying in the ditch. And they soon began to play into each other's hands.

CHAPTER XVII
CAPTAIN BOXALL'S PROPOSAL

About three weeks before the occurrences last recorded, the following conversation took place between Richard and John Boxall over their wine:

"I tell you what, brother," said the captain, "you're addling good brains with overwork. You won't make half so much money if you're too greedy after it. You don't look the same fellow you used to."

"I hope I'm not too greedy after money, John. But it's my business, as your's is to sail your ship."

"Yes, yes. I can't sail my ship too well, nor you attend to your business too well. But if I was to sail two ships instead of one, or if I was to be on deck instead of down at my dinner when she was going before the wind in the middle of the Atlantic, I shouldn't do my best when it came on to blow hard in the night."

"That's all very true. But I don't think it applies to me. I never miss my dinner, by any chance."

"Don't you turn your blind eye on my signal, Dick. You know what I mean well enough. I've got a proposal to make—the jolliest thing in the world."

"Go on. I'm listening."

"Mary ain't quite so well again—is she now?"

"Well, I don't think she's been getting on so fast. I suppose it's the spring weather."

"Why, you may call it summer now. But she ain't as I should like to see her, the darling."

"Well, no. I must confess I'm sometimes rather uneasy about her."

"And there's Jane. She don't look at home, somehow."

For some time Richard had been growing more and more uneasy as the evidence of his daughter's attachment to Charles Wither became plainer. Both he and his wife did the best they could to prevent their meeting, but having learned a little wisdom from the history of his father's family, and knowing well the hastiness of his own temper, he had as yet managed to avoid any open conflict with his daughter, who he knew had inherited his own stubbornness. He had told his brother nothing of this second and now principal source of family apprehension; and the fact that John saw that all was not right with Jane, greatly increased his feeling of how much things were going wrong. He made no reply, however, but sat waiting what was to follow. Accumulating his arguments the captain went on.

"And there's your wife; she's had a headache almost every day since I came to the house."

"Well, what are you driving at, John?" said his brother, with the more impatience that he knew all John said was true.

"What I'm driving at is this," answered the captain, *bringing-to* suddenly. "You must all make this next voyage in my clipper. It'll do you all a world o' good, and me too."

"Nonsense, John," said Richard, feeling however that a faint light dawned through the proposal.

"Don't call it nonsense till you've slept upon it, Dick. The ship's part mine, and I can make it easy for you. You'll have to pay a little passage-money, just to keep me right with the rest of the owners; but that won't be much, and you're no screw, though I did say you were too greedy after the money. I believe it's not the money so much as the making of it that fills your head."

"Still, you wouldn't have me let the business go to the dogs?"

"No fear of that, with Stopper at the head of affairs. I'll tell you what you must do. You must take him in."

"Into partnership, do you mean?" said Richard, his tone expressing no surprise, for he had thought of this before.

"Yes, I do. You'll have to do it some day, and the sooner the better. If you don't, you'll lose him, and that you'll find won't be a mere loss. That man'll make a dangerous enemy. Where he bites he'll hold. And now's a good time to serve yourself and him too."

"Perhaps you're right, brother," answered the merchant, emptying his glass of claret and filling it again instantly, an action indicating a certain perturbed hesitation not in the least common to him. "I'll turn it over in my mind. I certainly should not be sorry to have a short holiday. I haven't had one to speak of for nearly twenty years, I do believe."

John judged it better not to press him. He believed from what he knew of himself and his brother too that good advice was best let alone to work its own effects. He turned the conversation to something indifferent.

But after this many talks followed. Mrs. Boxall, of course, was consulted. Although she shrunk from the thought of a sea voyage, she yet saw in the proposal a way out of many difficulties, especially as giving room for time to work one of his especial works—that of effacement. So between the three the whole was arranged before either of the young people was spoken to on the subject. Jane heard it with a rush of blood to her heart that left her dark face almost livid. Mary received the news gladly, even merrily, though a slight paleness followed and just indicated that she regarded the journey as the symbol and sign of severed bonds. Julia, a plump child of six, upon whose condition no argument for the voyage could be founded, danced with joy at the idea of going in Uncle John's ship. Mr. Stopper threw no difficulty in the way of accepting a partnership in the concern, and thus matters were arranged.

John Boxall had repeatedly visited his mother during the six weeks he spent at his brother's house. He seldom saw Lucy, however, because of her engagement at the Morgensterns', until her grandmother's sickness kept her more at home. Then, whether it was that Lucy expected her uncle to be prejudiced against her, or that he really was so prejudiced, I do not know, but the two did not take much to each other. Lucy considered her uncle a common and rough-looking sailor; John Boxall called his niece a fine lady. And so they parted.

On the same day on which Thomas and Lucy *had their blow* on the river, the *Ningpo* had cleared out of St. Katharine's Dock, and was lying in the Upper Pool, all but ready to drop down with the next tide to Gravesend, where she was to take her passengers on board.

CHAPTER XVIII
THE TEMPTER

The next day, Thomas had made up his mind not to go near Guild Court; but in the afternoon Mr. Stopper himself sent him to bring an old ledger from the floor above Mrs. Boxall's. As he got down from his perch, and proceeded to get his hat—

"There's no use in going round such a way," said Mr. Stopper. "Mr. Boxall's not in; you can go through his room. Here's the key of the door. Only mind you lock it when you come back."

The key used to lie in Mr. Boxall's drawer, but now Mr. Stopper took it from his own. Thomas was not altogether pleased at the change of approach, though why, he would hardly have been able to tell. Probably he felt something as a miser would feel, into whose treasure-cave the new gallery of a neighboring mine threatened to break. He was, as it were, exposed upon the flank. Annoyance instantly clouded the expression of eagerness which he had not been able to conceal; and neither the light nor the following cloud escaped Mr. Stopper, who, although the region of other men's thoughts was dark as pitch to him in the usual relation he bore to them, yet the moment his interests or—rare case—his feelings brought him into the contact of opposition with any man, all the man's pregnable points lay bare before him.

Thomas had nothing to do but take the key and go. He had now no opportunity of spending more than one moment with Lucy. When the distance was of some length, he could cut both ways, and pocket the time gained; now there was nothing to save upon. Nevertheless, he sped up the stairs as if he would overtake old Time himself.

Rendered prudent, or cunning, by his affections, he secured the ordered chaos of vellum before he knocked at Mrs. Boxall's door, which he then opened without waiting for the response to his appeal.

"Lucy! Lucy!" he said; "I have but one half minute, and hardly that."

Lucy appeared with the rim of a rainy sunset about her eyes. The rest of her face was still as a day that belonged to not one of the four seasons—that had nothing to do.

"If you have forgotten yesterday, Thomas, I have not," she said.

"Oh! never mind yesterday," he said. "I'm coming in to-night; and I can stay as long as I please. My father and mother are gone to Folkestone, and there's nobody to know when I go home. Isn't it jolly?"

And without waiting for an answer, he scudded like Poppie. But what in Poppie might be graceful, was not dignified in Thomas; and I fear Lucy felt this, when he turned the corner to the stair-case with the huge ledger under his arm, and his coat flying out behind him. But she would not have felt it had she not had on the preceding evening, for the first time, a peep into his character.

As he reëntered the counting-house he was aware of the keen glance cast at him by Stopper, and felt that he reddened. But he laid the ledger on the desk before him, and perched again with as much indifference as he could assume.

Wearily the hours passed. How could they otherwise pass with figures, figures everywhere, Stopper right before him at the double desk, and Lucy one story removed and inaccessible? Some men would work all the better for knowing their treasure so near, but Thomas had not yet reached such a repose. Indeed, he did not yet love Lucy well enough for that. People talk about loving too much; for my part, I think all the mischief comes of loving too little.

The dinner-hour at length arrived. Thomas, however, was not in the way of attempting to see Lucy at that time. He would have said that there was too much coming and going of the clerks about that hour: I venture to imagine that a quiet enjoyment of his dinner had something to do with it. Now, although I can well enough understand a young fellow in love being as hungry as a hawk, I cannot quite understand his spending an hour over his dinner when the quarter of it would be enough, and the rest might give him if but one chance of one peep at the lady. On the present occasion, however, seeing he had the whole evening in prospect, Thomas may have been quite right to devote himself to his dinner, the newspaper, and anticipation. At all events, he betook himself to one of the courts off Cornhill, and ascended to one of those eating-houses which abound in London city, where a man may generally dine well, and always at moderate expense.

Now this was one of the days on which Thomas usually visited Mr. Molken. But as he had missed two lessons, the spider had become a little anxious about his fly, and knowing that Thomas went to dine at this hour, and knowing also where he went, he was there before him, and on the outlook for his entrance. This was not the sort of place the German generally frequented. He was more likely to go prowling about Thames Street for his dinner; but when Thomas entered, there he was, signaling to him to take his place beside him.

Thomas did not see that in the dark corner of an opposite box sat Mr. Stopper. He obeyed the signal, and a steak was presently broiling for him upon the gridiron at the other end of the room.

"You vas not come fore your lesson de letst time, Mistare Verbose," said Molken.

"No," answered Thomas, who had not yet made a confidant of Mr. Molken. "I was otherwise engaged."

He spoke quite carelessly.

"Ah! I yes. Oddervise," said Molken, and said no more.

Presently he broke into a suppressed laugh, which caused Thomas, who was very sensitive as to his personal dignity, to choke over his tankard of bitter ale, with which he was consoling himself for the delay of his steak.

"What is it you find so amusing, Mr. Molken?" he asked.

"I beg your pardon," returned Molken. "It was very rude; but I could not help it. I will tell you one story I did see last night. I am a man of de vorld, as you know, Mr. Verbose."

My reader must excuse me if I do not keep to the representation of the fellow's German-English. It is hardly worth doing, and I am doubtful, besides, whether I can do it well.

"I am a man of the world," said Molken, "and I was last night in one of those shops, what you call them—paradise; no, the other thing—hell— where they have the spinning thing—the Roulette—and the Rouge et Noir, and *cætera*. I do not mean to say that I was gambling. Oh, no! I was at the bar having a glass of Judenlip, when lo! and behold! down through the green door, with a burst, comes a young man I knew. He was like yourself, Mr. Worboise, a clerk in a counting-house."

Thomas winced, but said nothing. He regarded his business as he ought to have regarded himself, namely, as something to be ashamed of.

"Well, he comes up to me, and he says, 'Herr Molken, we are old friends; will you lend me a sovereign?' 'No,' I said, 'Mr.—,'—I forget the young man's name, but I did know him—' I never lend money for gambling purposes. Get the man who won your last sovereign to lend you another. For my own part, I've had enough of that sort of thing,' For you see, Mr. Thomas, I *have* gambled in my time—yes, and made money by it, though

I spent it as foolishly as I got it. You don't think I would spend my time in teaching *Ich habe, Du hast*, if I hadn't given up gambling. But university men, you know, learn bad habits."

"What did he say to that?" asked Thomas.

"He swore and turned away as if he was choking. But the fact was, Mr. Verbose, I hadn't a sovereign in my possession. I wasn't going to tell him that. But if I had had one, he should have had it; for I can't forget the glorious excitement it used to be to see the gold lying like a yellow mole-hill on the table, and to think that one fortunate turn might send it all into your own pockets."

"But he didn't choke, did he?" said Thomas, weakly trying to be clever.

"No. And I will tell you how it was that he didn't. 'By Jove!' he cried. Now I had seen him fumbling about his waistcoat as if he would tear his heart out, and all at once dive his two forefingers into a little pocket that was meant to hold a watch, only the watch had gone up the spout long ago. 'By Jove!' he said—that's the right swear, isn't it, Mr. Verbose?—and then he rushed through the green door again. I followed him, for I wanted to see what he was after. In half an hour he had broken the bank. He had found a sovereign in that little pocket. How it got there the devil only knew. He swept his money into his pockets and turned to go. I saw the people of the house getting between him and the door, and I saw one of the fellows—I knew him—who had lost money all the evening, going to pick a quarrel with him. For those gamblers have no honor in them. So I opened the door as if to leave the room, and pretending to hesitate as if I had left something, kept it open, and made a sign to him to bolt, which he understood at once, and was down-stairs in a moment, and I after him. Now let me tell you a secret," continued Molken, leaning across the table, and speaking very low and impressively—"that young man confessed to me that same evening, that when I refused him the sovereign, he had just lost the last of two hundred pounds of his master's money. To-day I hope he has replaced it honestly, as he ought; for his winnings that night came to more than seven hundred."

"But he was a thief," said Thomas, bluntly.

"Well, so he was; but no more a thief than many a respectable man who secures his own and goes on risking other people's money. It's the way of the world. However, as I told you, *I* gave it up long ago. There *was* a time in my life when I used to live by it."

"How did you manage that?"

"There are certain rules to be observed, that's all. Only you must stick to them. For one thing, you must make up your mind never to lose more than a certain fixed sum any night you play. If you stick to that, you will find your winnings always in excess of your losses."

"How can that be?"

"Oh, I don't pretend to account for it. Gaming has its laws as well as the universe generally. Everything goes by laws, you know-laws that cannot be round out except by experiment; and that, as I say, is one of the laws of gambling."

All this time Mr. Stopper had been reading Mr. Molken's face. Suddenly Tom caught sight of his superior; the warning of Wither rushed back on his mind, and he grew pale as death. Molken perceiving the change, sought for its cause, but saw nothing save a stony gentleman in the opposite box sipping sherry, and picking the ripest pieces out of a Stilton.

"Don't look that way, Molken," said Tom, in an undertone. "That's our Mr. Stopper."

"Well, haven't we as good a right to be here as Mr. Stopper?" returned Molken, in a voice equally inaudible beyond the table, but taking piercing eyeshots at the cause of Tom's discomposure.

The two men very soon had something like each other's measure. They could each understand his neighbor's rascality, while his own seemed to each only a law of nature.

"You generally pay, don't you?" added Molken.

Tom laughed.

"Yes, I do generally, and a penny to the cook besides, which, I will be bound, he does not. But that's nothing to the point. He hates me, though why, I'm sure I don't—I can only guess."

"Some girl, I suppose," said Molken, coolly.

Thomas felt too much flattered to endeavor even to dilute the insinuation; and Molken went on:

"Well, but how can the fellow bear malice? Of course, he must have seen from the first that he had no chance with you. I'll tell you what, Worboise; I have had a good deal of experience, and it is my conviction, from what I have seen of you, that you are one of the lucky ones—one of the elect, you know-born to it, and can't help yourself."

Tom pulled out his watch.

"Half an hour to spare yet," he said. "Come up to the smoking-room."

Having ordered a bottle of Rhine wine, Tom turned to Molken, and said:

"What did you mean by saying that I was one of the lucky ones?"

"Oh, don't you know there are some men born under a lucky star—as they would have said in old times? What the cause is, of course I don't know, except it be that Heaven must have some favorites, if only for the sake of variety. At all events, there is no denying that some men are born to luck. They are lucky in everything they put their hands to. Did you ever try your luck in a lottery, now?"

"I did in a raffle, once."

"Well?"

"I won a picture."

"I told you so! And it would be just the same whatever you tried. You are cut out for it. You have the luck-mark on you. I was sure of it."

"How can you tell that?" asked Tom, lingering like a fly over the sweet poison, and ready to swallow almost any absurdity that represented him as something different from the ran of ordinary mortals, of whom he was, as yet at least, a very ordinary specimen.

"Never you mind how I can tell. But I will tell you this much, that I have experience; and your own Bacon says that the laws of everything are to be found out by observation and experiment. I have observed, and I have experimented, and I tell you you are a lucky one."

Tom stroked the faintest neutrality of a coming mustache, ponderingly and pleasedly, and said nothing.

"By the by, are you coming to me to-night?" asked Molken.

"No—o," answered Tom, still stroking his upper lip with the thumb and forefinger of his left hand, "I think not. I believe I have an engagement to-night, somewhere or other."

He took out his pocket-book, and pretended to look.

"Yes. I can't have my lesson to-night."

"Then I needn't stop at home for you. By the way, have you a sovereign about you? I wouldn't trouble you, you know, only, as I told you, I haven't got one. I believe your quarter is out to-night."

"Oh, I beg your pardon; I ought to have thought of that. I have two half-sovereigns in my pocket, and no more, I am sorry to say. Will one of them do for to-night? You shall have more to-morrow."

"Oh, thank you; it's of no consequence. Well, I don't know—I think I *will* take the ten shillings, for I want to go out this evening. Yes. Thank you. Never mind to-morrow, *except* it be convenient."

Tom settled the bill, and put the change of the other half-sovereign in his pocket. Molken left him at the door of the tavern, and he went back to the counting-house.

"Who was that with you at the Golden Fleece, Tom?" asked Mr. Stopper, as he entered; for he took advantage of his position to be as rude as he found convenient.

Taken by surprise, Tom answered at once:

"Mr. Molken."

"And who is he?" asked Stopper, again.

"My German master," answered Tom.

The next moment he could have knocked his head against the wall with indignation at himself. For, always behindhand when left to himself, he was ready enough when played upon by another to respond and repent.

"He's got a hangdog phiz of his own," said Mr. Stopper, as he plunged again into the business before him, writing away as deliberately as if it had been on parchment instead of foolscap; for Stopper was never in a hurry, and never behind.

Tom's face flushed red with wrath.

"I'll thank you to be civil in your remarks on my friends, Mr. Stopper."

Mr. Stopper answered with a small puff of windy breath from distended lips. He blew, in short. Tom felt his eyes waver. He grew almost blind with rage. If he had followed his inclination, he would have brought the ruler beside him down, with a terrible crack, on the head, before him. "Why didn't he?" does my reader inquire? Just because of his incapacity for action of any sort. He did not refrain in the pity that disarms some men in the midst of their wrath, nor yet from the sense that vengeance is God's business, and will be carried out in a mode rather different from that in which man would prosecute his.

CHAPTER XIX
HOW TOM SPENT THE EVENING

When Tom left the office he walked into Mr. Kitely's shop, for he was afraid lest Mr. Stopper should see him turn up to Guild Court. He had almost forgotten Mr. Kitely's behavior about the book he would not keep for him, and his resentment was gone quite. There was nobody in the shop but Mattie.

"Well, chick," said Thomas, kindly, but more condescendingly than suited Miss Matilda's tastes.

"Neither chick nor child," she answered promptly; though where she got the phrase is a mystery, as indeed is the case with almost all the sayings of such children.

"What are you, then? A fairy?"

"If I was, I know what I would do. Oh, wouldn't I just! I should think I would!"

"Well, what would you do, little Miss What's-your-name?"

"My name is Miss Kitely; but that's neither here nor there. Oh, no! it's not me! Wouldn't I just!"

"Well, Miss Kitely, I want to know what you would do if you were a fairy?"

"I would turn your eyes into gooseberries, and your tongue into a bit of leather a foot long; and every time you tried to speak your long tongue would slap your blind eyes and make you cry."

"What a terrible doom!" returned Thomas, offended at the child's dislike to him, but willing to carry it off. "Why?"

"Because you've made Miss Burton's eyes red, you naughty man! I know you. It must be you. Nobody else could make her eyes red but you, and you go and do it."

Thomas's first movement was of anger; for he felt, as all who have concealments are ready to feel, that he was being uncomfortably exposed.

He turned his back on the child, and proceeded to examine the books on a level with his face. While he was thus engaged, Mr. Kitely entered.

"How do you do, Mr. Worboise?" he said. "I've got another copy of that book you and I fell out about some time ago. I can let you have this one at half the price."

It was evident that the bookseller wanted to be conciliatory. Thomas, in his present mood was inclined to repel his advances, but he shrank from contention, and said:

"Thank you. I shall be glad to have it. How much is it?"

Mr. Kitely named the amount, and, ashamed to appear again unable, even at the reduced price, to pay for it, Thomas pulled out the last farthing of the money in his pocket, which came to the exact sum required, and pocketed the volume.

"If you would excuse a man who has seen something of the world—more than was good for him at one time of his life—Mr. Worboise," said Mr. Kitely, as he pocketed the money, "I would give you a hint about that German up the court. He's a clever fellow enough, I dare say—perhaps too clever. Don't you have anything to do with him beyond the German. Take my advice. I don't sit here all day at the mouth of the court for nothing. I can see what comes in my way as well as another man."

"What is there to say against him, Mr. Kitely? I haven't seen any harm in him."

"I'm not going to commit myself in warning you, Mr. Worboise. But I do warn you. Look out, and don't let him lead you into mischief."

"I hope I am able to take care of myself, Mr. Kitely," said Thomas, with a touch of offense.

"I hope you are, Mr. Worboise," returned the bookseller, dryly; "but there's no offense meant in giving you the hint."

At this moment Mr. Stopper passed the window. Thomas listened for the echo of his steps up the archway, and as none came, he knew that he had gone along the street. He waited, therefore, till he thought he must be out of sight, and then sped uneasily from the shop, round the corner, and up to Mrs. Boxall's door, which the old lady herself opened for him, not looking so pleased as usual to see him. Mr. Molken was watching from the opposite ground-floor window. A few minutes after, Mr. Stopper re-passed the window of Mr. Kitely's shop, and went into the counting-house with a pass-key.

Thomas left Mrs. Boxall to shut the door, and rushed eagerly up the stairs, and into the sitting-room. There he found the red eyes of which Mattie had spoken. Lucy rose and held out her hand, but her manner was constrained, and her lips trembled as if she were going to cry. Thomas would have put his arm round her and drawn her to him, but she gently pushed his arm away, and he felt as many a man has felt, and every man, perhaps, ought to feel, that in the gentlest repulse of the woman he loves there is something terribly imperative and absolute.

"Why, Lucy!" he said, in a tone of hurt; "what have I done?"

"If you can forget so soon, Thomas," answered Lucy, "I cannot. Since yesterday I see things in a different light altogether. I cannot, for your sake any more than my own, allow things to go on in this doubtful way."

"Oh I but, Lucy, I was taken unawares yesterday; and to-day, now I have slept upon it, I don't see there is any such danger. I ought to be a match for that brute Stopper, anyhow."

Yet the brute Stopper had outreached him, or, at least, "served him out," three or four times that very day, and he had refused to acknowledge it to himself, which was all his defense, poor wretch.

"But that is not all the question, Thomas. It is not right. At least, it seems to me that it is not right to go on like this. People's friends ought to know. I would not have done it if grannie hadn't been to know. But then I ought to have thought of your friends as well as my own."

"But there would be no difficulty if I had only a grandmother," urged Thomas, "and one as good as yours. I shouldn't have thought of not telling."

"I don't think the difficulty of doing right makes it unnecessary to do it," said Lucy.

"I think you might trust that to me, Lucy," said Thomas, falling back upon his old attempted relation of religious instructor to his friend.

Lucy was silent for a moment; but after what she had gone through in the night, she knew that the time had come for altering their relative position if not the relation itself.

"No, Thomas," said she; "I must take my own duty into my own hands. I *will* not go on this way."

"Do you think then, Lucy, that in affairs of this kind a fellow ought to do just what his parents want?"

"No, Thomas. But I do think he ought not to keep such things secret from them."

"Not even if they are unreasonable and tyrannical?"

"No. A man who will not take the consequences of loving cannot be much of a lover."

"Lucy!" cried Thomas, now stung to the heart.

"I can't help it, Thomas," said Lucy, bursting into tears; "I *must* speak the truth, and if you cannot bear it, the worse for me—and for you, too, Thomas."

"Then you mean to give me up?" said Thomas, pathetically, without, however, any real fear of such an unthinkable catastrophe.

"If it be giving you up to say I will not marry a man who is too much afraid of his father and mother to let them know what he is about, then I do give you up. But it will be you who give me up if you refuse to acknowledge me as you ought."

Lucy could not have talked like this ever before in her life. She had gone through an eternity of suffering in the night. She was a woman now. She had been but a girl before. Now she stood high above Thomas. He was but a boy still, and not beautiful as such. She was all at once old enough to be his mother. There was no escape from the course she took; no *dodging* was possible. This must be. But she was and would be gentle with poor Thomas.

"You do not love me, Lucy," he cried.

"My poor Thomas, I do love you; love you so dearly that I trust and pray you may be worthy of my love. Go and do as you ought, and come back to me—like one of the old knights you talk about," she added, with the glimmer of a hopeful smile, "bringing victory to his lady."

"I will, I will," said Thomas, overcome by her solemn beauty and dignified words. It was as if she had cast the husk of the girl, and had come out a saving angel. But the perception of this was little more to him yet than a poetic sense of painful pleasure.

"I will, I will," he said. "But I cannot to-night, for my father and mother are both at Folkestone. But I will write to them—that will be best."

"Any way you like, Thomas. I don't care how you do it, so it is done."

All this time the old lady, having seen that something was wrong, had discreetly kept out of the way, for she knew that the quarrels of lovers at least are most easily settled between themselves. Thomas now considered it all over and done with, and Lucy, overjoyed at her victory, leaned into his arms, and let him kiss her ten times. Such a man, she ought not, perhaps— only she did not know better—to have allowed to touch her till he had done what he had promised. To some people the promise is the difficult part, to others the performance. To Thomas, unhappily, the promising was easy.

They did not hear the door open. It was now getting dark, but the two were full in the light of the window, and visible enough to the person who entered. He stood still for one moment, during which the lovers unwound their arms. Only when parting, they became aware that a man was in the room. He came forward with hasty step. It was Richard Boxall. Thomas looked about for his hat. Lucy stood firm and quiet, waiting.

"Lucy, where is your grandmother?"

"Up stairs, uncle, I believe."

"Is she aware of that fellow's presence?"

"You are not very polite, uncle," said Lucy, with dignity. "This is my friend, Mr. Worboise, whom I believe you know. Of course I do not receive visitors without my grandmother's knowledge."

Mr. Boxall choked an oath in his throat, or rather the oath nearly choked him. He turned and went down the stair again; but neither of them heard the outer door close. Thomas and Lucy stared at each other in dismay.

The facts of the case were these, as near as I can guess. The *Ningpo* had dropped down to Gravesend, and the Boxalls had joined her there. But some delay had arisen, and she was not to sail till the next morning. Mr. Boxall had resolved to make use of the time thus gained or lost, and had come up to town. I cannot help believing that it was by contrivance of Mr. Stopper, who had watched Tom and seen him go up the court, that he went through the door from his private room, instead of going round, which would have given warning to the lovers. Possibly he returned intending to see his mother; but after the discovery he made, avoided her, partly because he was angry and would not quarrel with her the last thing before his voyage. Upon maturer consideration, he must have seen that he had no ground for quarreling with her at all, for she could have known nothing about Tom in relation to Mary, except Tom had told her, which was not at all likely. But before he had had time to see this, he was on his way to Gravesend again. He was so touchy as well as obstinate about everything wherein his family was concerned, that the sight of Tom with his Mary's cousin was enough to drive all reflection out of him for an hour at least.

Thomas and Lucy stood and stared at each other. Thomas stared from consternation; Lucy only stared at Tom.

"Well, Thomas," she said at last, with a sweet, watery smile; for she had her lover, and she had lost her idol. She had got behind the scenes, and could worship no more; but Dagon was a fine idea, notwithstanding his fall, and if she could not set him up on his pedestal again, she would at least try to give him an arm-chair. Fish-tailed Dagon is an unfortunate choice for the simile, I know, critical reader; but let it pass, and the idea that it illustrates being by no means original, let the figure at least have some claim to the distinction.

"Now he'll go and tell my father," said Tom; "and I wish you knew what a row my mother and he will make between them."

"But why, Tom? Have they any prejudice against me? Do they know there is such a person?"

"I don't know. They may have heard of you at your uncle's."

"My father because you have no money, and my mother because you have no grace."

"No grace, Tom? Am I so very clumsy?"

Thomas burst out laughing.

"I forgot," he said. "You were not brought up to my mother's slang. She and her set use Bible words till they make you hate them."

"But you shouldn't hate them. They are good in themselves, though they be wrong used."

"That's all very well. Only if you had been tried with them as I have been, I am afraid you would have had to give in to hating them, as well as me, Lucy. I never did like that kind of slang. But what am I to do with old Boxall—I beg your pardon—with your uncle Richard? He'll be sure to write to my father before he sails. They're friends, you know."

"Well, but you will be beforehand with him, and then it won't matter. You were going to do it at any rate, and the thing now is to have the start of him," said Lucy, perhaps not sorry to have in the occurrence an additional spur to prick the sides of Thomas's intent.

"Yes, yes; that's all very well," returned Thomas, dubiously, as if there was a whole world behind it.

"Now, dear Tom, do go home at once, and write. You will save the last post if you do," said Lucy, decidedly; for she saw more and more the necessity, for Thomas's own sake, of urging him to action.

"So, instead of giving me a happy evening, you are going to send me home to an empty house!"

"You see the thing must be done, or my uncle will be before you," said Lucy, beginning to be vexed with him for his utter want of decision, and with herself for pushing him toward such an act. Indeed, she felt all at once that perhaps she had been unmaidenly. But there was no choice except to do it, or break off the engagement.

Now, whether it was that her irritation influenced her tone and infected Tom with like irritation, or that he could not bear being thus driven to do what he so much disliked, while on the whole he would have preferred that Mr. Boxall should tell his father and so save him from the immediate difficulty, the evil spirit in him arose once more in rebellion, and, like the mule that he was, he made an effort to unseat the gentle power that would have urged him along the only safe path on the mountain-side.

"Lucy, I will not be badgered in this way. If you can't trust me, you won't get anything that way."

Lucy drew back a step and looked at him for one moment; then turned and left the room. Thomas waited for a minute; then, choosing to arouse a great sense of injury in his bosom, took his hat, and went out, banging the door behind him.

Just as he banged Lucy's door, out came Mr. Molken from his. It was as if the devil had told a hawk to wait, and he would fetch him a pigeon.

"Coming to have your lesson after all?" he asked, as Thomas, from very indecision, made a step or two toward him.

"No; I don't feel inclined for a lesson to-night."

"Where are you going, then?"

"Oh, I don't know," answered Tom; trying to look nohow in particular.

"Come along with me, then. I'll show you something of life after dark."

"But where are you going?"

"You'll see that when we get there. You're not afraid, are you?"

"Not I," answered Tom; "only a fellow likes to know where he's going. That's all."

"Well, where would you like to go? A young fellow like you really ought to know something of the world he lives in. You are clever enough, in all conscience, if you only knew a little more."

"Go on, then. I don't care. It's nothing to me where I go. Only," Tom added, "I have no money in my pocket. I spent my last shilling on this copy of Goethe's poems."

"Ah, you never spent your money better! There was a man, now, that never contented himself with hearsay! He would know all the ways of life for himself—else how was he to judge of them all? He would taste of everything, that he might know the taste of it. Why should a man be ignorant of anything that can be known. Come along. I will take care of you. See if I don't!"

"But you can't be going anywhere in London for nothing. And I tell you I haven't got a farthing in my purse."

"Never mind that. It shan't cost you anything. Now I am going to make a clean breast of it, as you English call it; though why there should be anything dirty in keeping your own secrets I don't know. I want to make an experiment with you."

"Give me chloroform, and cut me up?" said Tom, reviving as his quarrel with Lucy withdrew a little into the background.

"Not quite that. You shall neither take chloroform, nor have your eyes bandaged, nor be tied to the table. You can go the moment you have had enough of it. It is merely for the sake of my theory. Entirely an experiment."

"Perhaps, if you told me your theory, I might judge of the nature of the experiment."

"I told you all about it the other day. You are one of those fortunate mortals doomed to be lucky. Why, I knew one—not a gambler, I don't mean that—whose friends at last would have nothing to do with him where any chance was concerned. If it was only sixpenny points, they wouldn't play a single rubber of whist with him except he was their partner. In fact, the poor wretch was reduced to play only with strangers,—comparative strangers I mean, of course. He won everything."

"Then what do you want with me? Out with it."

"I only want to back you. You don't understand the thing. You shan't spend a farthing. I have plenty." Here Molken pulled a few sovereigns from his pocket as he went on, and it never occurred to Tom to ask how he had them, seeing he was so hard-up at dinner-time. "It's all for my theory of luck, I assure you. I have given up practical gambling, as I told you, long ago. It's not right. I *have* known enough about it, I confess to you—you know *we* understand each other; but I confess too—my theory—I *am* anxious about that."

All this time they had been walking along, Thomas paying no heed to the way they went. He would have known little about it, however, well as he thought he knew London, for they had entered a region entirely unknown to him.

"But you haven't told me, after all," he said, "where you are going."

"Here," answered Molken, pushing open the swing-door of a public-house.

The next morning Thomas made his appearance in the office at the usual hour, but his face was pale and his eyes were red. His shirt-front was tumbled and dirty, and he had nearly forty shillings in his pocket. He never looked up from his work, and now and then pressed his hand to his head. This Mr. Stopper saw and enjoyed.

CHAPTER XX
HOW LUCY SPENT THE NIGHT

When Lucy left the room, with her lover—if lover he could be called—alone in it, her throat felt as if it would burst with the swelling of something like bodily grief. She did not know what it was, for she had never felt anything like it before. She thought she was going to die. Her grandmother could have told her that she would be a happy woman if she did not have such a swelling in her throat a good many times without dying of it; but Lucy strove desperately to hide it from her. She went to her own room and threw herself on her bed, but started up again when she heard the door bang, flew to the window, and saw all that passed between Molken and Thomas till they left the court together. She had never seen Molken so full in the face before; and whether it was from this full view, or that his face wore more of the spider expression upon this occasion, I do not know—I incline to the latter, for I think that an on-looker can read the expression of two countenances better, sometimes, than those engaged in conversation can read each other's—however it was, she felt a dreadful repugnance to Molken from that moment, and became certain that he was trying in some way or other to make his own out of Thomas. With this new distress was mingled the kind but mistaken self-reproach that she had driven him to it. Why should she not have borne with the poor boy, who was worried to death between his father and mother and Mr. Stopper and that demon down there? He would be all right if they would only leave him alone. He was but a poor boy, and, alas! she had driven him away from his only friend—for such she was sure she was. She threw herself on her bed, but she could not rest. All the things in the room seemed pressing upon her, as if they had staring eyes in their heads; and there was no heart anywhere.

Her grandmother heard the door bang, and came in search of her.

"What's the matter, my pet?" she asked, as she entered the room and found her lying on the bed.

"Oh, nothing, grannie," answered Lucy, hardly knowing what she said.

"You've quarrelled with that shilly-shally beau of yours, I suppose. Well, let him go—*he's* not much."

Lucy made no reply, but turned her face toward the wall, as mourners did ages before the birth of King Hezekiah. Grannie had learned a little wisdom in her long life, and left her. She would get a cup of tea ready, for she had great faith in bodily cures for mental aches. But before the tea was well in the tea-pot Lucy came down in her bonnet and shawl.

She could not rest. She tossed and turned. What could Thomas be about with that man? What mischief might he not take him into? Good women, in their supposed ignorance of men's wickedness, are not unfrequently like the angels, in that they understand it perfectly, without the knowledge soiling one feather of their wings. They see it clearly—even from afar. Now, although Lucy could not know so much of it as many are compelled to know, she had some acquaintance with the lowest castes of humanity, and the vice of the highest is much the same as the vice of the lowest, only in general worse—more refined, and more detestable. So, by a natural process, without knowing how, she understood something of the kind of gulf into which a man like Molken might lead Thomas, and she could not bear the thoughts that sprung out of this understanding. Hardly knowing what she did, she got up and put on her bonnet and shawl, and went down stairs.

"Where on earth are you going, Lucy?" asked her grandmother, in some alarm.

Lucy did not know in the least what she meant to do. She had had a vague notion of setting out to find Thomas somewhere, and rescue him from the grasp of Moloch, but, save for the restlessness with which her misery filled her, she could never have entertained the fancy. The moment her grandmother asked her the question, she saw how absurd it would be. Still she could not rest. So she invented an answer, and ordered her way according to her word.

"I'm going to see little Mattie," she said. "The child is lonely, and so am I. I will take her out for a walk."

"Do then, my dear. It will do you both good," said the grandmother. "Only you must have a cup of tea first."

Lucy drank her cup of tea, then rose, and went to the book-shop. Mr. Kitely was there alone.

"How's Mattie to-night, Mr. Kitely? Is she any better, do you think?" she asked.

"She's in the back room there. I'll call her," said the bookseller, without answering either of Lucy's questions.

"Oh! I'll just go in to her. You wouldn't mind me taking her out for a little walk, would you?"

"Much obliged to you, miss," returned the bookseller, heartily. "It's not much amusement the poor child has. I'm always meaning to do better for her, but I'm so tied with the shop that—I don't know hardly how it is, but somehow we go on the same old way. She'll be delighted."

Lucy went into the back parlor, and there sat Mattie, with her legs curled up beneath her on the window-sill, reading a little book, thumbed and worn at the edges, and brown with dust and use.

"Well, Miss Burton," she cried, before Lucy had time to speak, "I've found something here. I think it's what people call poetry. I'm not sure; but I'm sure it's good, whatever it is. Only I can't read it very well. Will you read it to me, please, miss? I do like to be read to."

"I want you to come out for a walk with me, Mattie," said Lucy, who was in no humor for reading.

Wise Mattie glanced up in her face. She had recognized the sadness in her tone.

"Read this first, please, Miss Burton," she said. "I think it will do you good. Things *will* go wrong. I'm sure it's very sad. And I don't know what's to be done with the world. It's always going wrong. It's just like father's watch. He's always saying there's something out of order in its inside, and he's always a-taking of it to the doctor, as he calls the watchmaker to amuse me. Only I'm not very easy to amuse," reflected Mattie, with a sigh. "But," she resumed, "I wish I knew the doctor to set the world right. The clock o' St. Jacob's goes all right, but I'm sure Mr. Potter ain't the doctor to set the world right, any more than Mr. Deny is for Mr. Kitely's watch."

The associations in Mattie's mind wĕre not always very clear either to herself or other people; they were generally just, notwithstanding.

"But you have never been to Mr. Potter's church to know, Mattie."

"Oh! haven't I, just? Times and times. Mr. Spelt has been a-taking of me. I do believe mother thinks I am going to die, and wants to get me ready. I wonder what it all means?"

"Nonsense, Mattie!" said Lucy, already tamed a little aside from her own sorrow by the words of the child. "You must put on your hat and come out with me."

"My bonnet, miss. Hats are only fit for very little girls. And I won't go till you read this poetry to me—if it be poetry."

Lucy took the book, and read. The verses were as follows:

As Christ went into Jericho town,
'Twas darkness all, from toe to crown,
About blind Bartimeus.
He said, Our eyes are more than dim,
And so, of course, we don't see Him,
But David's Son can see us.

Cry out, cry out, blind brother, cry;
Let not salvation dear go by;
Have mercy, Son of David.
Though they were blind, they both could hear —
They heard, and cried, and he drew near;
And so the blind were saved.

O Jesus Christ! I'm deaf and blind,
Nothing comes through into my mind,
I only am not dumb.
Although I see thee not, nor hear,
I cry because thou may'st be near;
O Son of David, come.

A finger comes into my ear;
A voice comes through the deafness drear;
Poor eyes, no more be dim.
A hand is laid upon mine eyes;
I hear, I feel, I see, I rise —
'Tis He, I follow Him.

Before Lucy had finished reading the not very poetic lines, they had somehow or other reached her heart. For they had one quality belonging to most good poetry — that of directness or simplicity; and never does a mind like hers — like hers, I mean, in truthfulness — turn more readily toward the unseen, the region out of which even that which is seen comes, than when a rain-cloud enwraps and hides the world around it, leaving thus, as it were, only the passage upward open. She closed the little book gently, laid it down, got Mattie's bonnet, and, heedless of the remarks of the child upon the poem, put it on her, and led her out. Her heart was too full to speak. As they went through the shop —

"A pleasant walk to you, ladies," said the bookseller.

"Thank you, Mr. Kitely," returned his daughter, for Lucy could not yet speak.

They had left Bagot Street, and were in one of the principal thoroughfares, before Lucy had got the lump in her throat sufficiently swallowed to be able to speak. She had not yet begun to consider where they should go. When they came out into the wider street, the sun, now near the going down, was shining golden through a rosy fog. Long shadows lay or flitted about over the level street. Lucy had never before taken any notice of the long shadows of evening. Although she was a town girl, and had therefore had comparatively few chances, yet in such wide streets as she had sometimes to traverse they were not a rare sight. In the city, to be sure, they are much rarer. But the reason she saw them now was that her sorrowful heart saw the sorrowfulness of the long shadows out of the rosy mist, and made her mind observe them. The sight brought the tears again into her eyes, and yet soothed her. They looked so strange upon that wood-paved street, that they seemed to have wandered from some heathy moor and lost themselves in the labyrinth of the city. Even more than the scent of the hay in the early morning, floating into the silent streets from the fields round London, are these long shadows to the lover of nature, convincing him that what seems the unnatural Babylon of artifice and untruth, is yet at least within the region of nature, contained in her bosom and subjected to her lovely laws; is on the earth as truly as the grassy field upon which the child sees with delighted awe his very own shadow stretch out to such important, yea, portentous, length. Even hither come the marvels of Nature's magic. Not all the commonplaces of ugly dwellings, and cheating shops that look churches in the face and are not ashamed, can shut out that which gives mystery to the glen far withdrawn, and loveliness to the mountain-side. From this moment Lucy began to see and feel things as she had never seen or felt them before. Her weeping had made way for a deeper spring in her nature to flow—a gain far more than sufficient to repay the loss of such a lover as Thomas, if indeed she must lose him.

But Mattie saw the shadows too.

"Well, miss, who'd have thought of such a place as this! I declare it bewilders my poor head. I feel every time a horse puts his foot on my shadow as if I must cry out. Isn't it silly? It's all my big head—it's not me; you know, miss."

Lucy could not yet make the remark, and therefore I make it for her— how often we cry out when something steps on our shadow, passing yards away from ourselves! There is not a phenomenon of disease—not even of insanity—that has not its counterpart in our moral miseries, all springing from want of faith in God. At least, so it seems to me. That will account for it all, or looks as if it would; and nothing else does.

It seems to me, too, that in thinking of the miseries and wretchedness in the world we seldom think of the other side. We hear of an event in association with some certain individual, and we say—"How dreadful! How miserable!" And perhaps we say—"Is there—can there be a God in the earth when such a thing can take place?" But we do not see into the region of actual suffering or conflict. We do not see the heart where the shock falls. We neither see the proud bracing of energies to meet the ruin that threatens, nor the gracious faint in which the weak escape from writhing. We do not see the abatement of pain which is Paradise to the tortured; we do not see the gentle upholding in sorrow that comes even from the ministrations of nature—not to speak of human nature—to delicate souls. In a word, we do not see, and the sufferer himself does not understand, how God is present every moment, comforting, upholding, heeding that the pain shall not be more than can be borne, making the thing possible and not hideous. I say nothing of the peaceable fruits that are to spring therefrom; and who shall dare to say where they shall not follow upon such tearing up of the soil? Even those long shadows gave Lucy some unknown comfort, flowing from Nature's recognition of the loss of her lover; and she clasped the little hand more tenderly, as if she would thus return her thanks to Nature for the kindness received.

To get out of the crowd on the pavement Lucy turned aside into a lane. She had got half way down it before she discovered that it was one of those through which she had passed the night before, when she went with Thomas to the river. She turned at once to leave it. As she turned, right before her stood an open church door. It was one of those sepulchral city churches, where the voice of the clergyman sounds ghostly, and it seems as if the dead below were more real in their presence than the half dozen worshipers scattered among the pews.

On this occasion, however, there were seven present when Lucy and Mattie entered and changed the mystical number to the magical.

It was a church named outlandishly after a Scandinavian saint. Some worthy had endowed a week-evening sermon there after better fashion than another had endowed the poor of the parish. The name of the latter was recorded in golden letters upon a black tablet in the vestibule, as the donor of £200, with the addition in letters equally golden, *None of which was ever paid by his trustees.*

I will tell you who the worshipers were. There was the housekeeper in a neighboring warehouse, who had been in a tumult all the day, and at night-fall thought of the kine-browsed fields of her childhood, and went to church. There was an old man who had once been manager of a bank, and had managed it ill both for himself and his company; and having been dismissed in consequence, had first got weak in the brain, and then begun to lay up treasure in heaven. Then came a brother and two sisters, none of them under seventy. The former kept shifting his brown wig and taking snuff the whole of the service, and the latter two wiping, with yellow silk handkerchiefs, brown faces inlaid with coal-dust. They could not agree well enough to live together, for their fathers will was the subject of constant quarrel. They therefore lived in three lodgings at considerable distances apart. But every night in the week they met at this or that church similarly endowed, sat or knelt or stood in holy silence or sacred speech for an hour and a half, walked together to the end of the lane discussing the sermon, and then separated till the following evening. Thus the better parts in them made a refuge of the house of God, where they came near to each other, and the destroyer kept a little aloof for the season. These, with the beadle and his wife, and Lucy and Mattie, made up the congregation.

Now, when they left the lane there was no sun to be seen; but when they entered the church, there he was—his last rays pouring in through a richly stained window, the only beauty of the building. This window—a memorial one—was placed in the northern side of the chancel, whence a passage through houses, chimneys, and churches led straight to the sunset, down which the last rays I speak of came speeding for one brief moment ere all was gone, and the memorial as faded and gray as the memory of the man to whom it was dedicated.

This change from the dark lane to the sun-lighted church laid hold of Lucy's feelings. She did not know what it made her feel, but it aroused her with some vague sense of that sphere of glory which enwraps all our lower spheres, and she bowed her knees and her head, and her being worshiped, if her thoughts were too troubled to go upward. The prayers had commenced, and she kneeled, the words "He pardoneth and absolveth," were the first that found luminous entrance into her soul; and with them came the picture of Thomas as he left the court with the man of the bad countenance. Of him, and what he might be about, her mind was full; but every now and then a flash of light, in the shape of words, broke through the mist of her troubled thoughts, and testified of the glory-sphere beyond; till at length her mind was so far calmed that she became capable of listening a little to the discourse of the preacher.

He was not a man of the type of Mr. Potter of St. Jacob's, who considered himself possessed of worldly privileges in virtue of a heavenly office not one of whose duties he fulfilled in a heavenly fashion. Some people considered Mr. Fuller very silly for believing that he might do good in a church like this, with a congregation like this, by speaking that which he knew, and testifying that which he had seen. But he did actually believe it. Somehow or other—I think because he was so much in the habit of looking up to the Father—the prayers took a hold of him once more every time he read them; and he so delighted in the truths he saw that he rejoiced to set them forth—was actually glad to *talk* about them to any one who would listen. When he confessed his feeling about congregations, he said that he preferred twelve people to a thousand. This he considered a weakness, however; except that he could more easily let his heart out to the twelve.

He took for his text the words of our Lord, "Come unto me, all ye that labor and are heavy laden." He could not see the strangers, for they sat behind a pillar, and therefore he had no means for discovering that each of them had a heavy-laden heart; Lucy was not alone in trouble, for Syne had been hard upon Mattie that day. He addressed himself especially to the two old women before him, of whose story he knew nothing, though their faces were as well known to him as the pillars of the church. But the basin into which the fountain of his speech flowed was the heart of those girls.

No doubt presented itself as to the truth of what the preacher was saying; nor could either of them have given a single argument from history or criticism for the reality of the message upon which the preacher founded his exhortation. The truth is not dependent upon proof for its working. Its relation to the human being is essential, is in the nature of things; so that if it be but received in faith—that is, acted upon—it works its own work, and needs the buttressing of no arguments any more than the true operation of a healing plant is dependent upon a knowledge of Dioscorides. My reader must not, therefore, suppose that I consider doubt an unholy thing; on the contrary, I consider spiritual doubt a far more precious thing than intellectual conviction, for it springs from the awaking of a deeper necessity than any that can be satisfied from the region of logic. But when the truth has begun to work its own influence in any heart, that heart has begun to rise out of the region of doubt.

When they came from the church, Lucy and Mattie walked hand in hand after the sisters and brother, and heard them talk.

"He's a young one, that!" said the old man. "He'll know a little better by the time he's as old as I am."

"Well, I did think he went a little too far when he said a body might be as happy in the work'us as with thousands of pounds in the Bank of England."

"I don't know," interposed the other sister. "He said it depended on what you'd got inside you. Now, if you've got a bad temper inside you, all you've got won't make you happy."

"Thank you, sister. You're very polite, *as usual*. But, after all, where should we have been but for the trifle we've got in the bank?"

"You two might ha' been living together like sisters, instead of quarreling like two cats, if the money had gone as it ought to," said the old man, who considered that the whole property belonged of right to him.

By this time they had reached the end of the lane, and, without a word to each other, they separated.

"Syne," said Mattie, significantly. Syne was evidently her evil incarnation. Lucy did not reply, but hastened home with her, anxious to be alone. She did not leave the child, however, before she had put her to bed, and read again the hymn that had taken her fancy before they went out.

I will now show my reader how much of the sermon remained upon Lucy's mind. She sat a few minutes with her grandmother, and then told her that she felt better, but would like to go to bed. So she took her candle and went. As soon as she had closed the door, she knelt down by her bedside, and said something like this—more broken, and with long pauses between—but like this:

"O Jesus Christ, I come. I don't know any other way to come. I speak to thee. Oh, hear me. I am weary and heavy laden. Give me rest. Help me to put on the yoke of thy meekness and thy lowliness of heart, which thou sayest will give rest to our souls. I cannot do it without thy help. Thou couldst do it without help. I cannot. Teach me. Give me thy rest. How am I to begin? How am I to take thy yoke on me? I must be meek. I am very troubled and vexed. Am I angry? Am I unforgiving? Poor Thomas! Lord Jesus, have mercy upon Thomas. He does not know what he is doing. I will be very patient. I will sit with my hands folded, and bear all my sorrow, and not vex Grannie with it; and I won't say an angry word to Thomas. But, O Lord, have mercy upon him, and make him meek and lowly of heart. I have not been sitting at thy feet and learning of thee. Thou canst take all my trouble away by making Thomas good. I ought to have tried hard to keep him in the way his mother taught him, and I have been idle and self-indulgent, and taken up with my music and dresses. I have not looked to my heart to see whether it was meek and lowly like thine. O Lord, thou hast given me everything, and I have not thought about thee. I thank thee that thou hast made me miserable, for now I shall be thy child. Thou canst bring Thomas home again to thee. Thou canst make him meek and lowly of heart, and give rest to his soul. Amen."

Is it any wonder that she should have risen from her knees comforted? I think not. She was already—gentle and good as she had always been— more meek and lowly. She had begun to regard this meekness as the yoke of Jesus, and therefore to will it. Already, in a measure, she was a partaker of his peace.

Worn out by her suffering, and soothed by her prayer, she fell asleep the moment she laid her head upon the pillow. And thus Lucy passed the night.

CHAPTER XXI
MORE SHUFFLING

Tom went home the next night with a racking headache. Gladly would he have gone to Lucy to comfort him, but he was too much ashamed of his behavior to her the night before, and too uneasy in his conscience. He was, indeed, in an abject condition of body, intellect, and morals. He went at once to his own room and to bed; fell asleep; woke in the middle of the night miserably gnawed by "Don Worm, the conscience;" tried to pray, and found it did him no good; turned his thoughts to Lucy, and burst into tears at the recollection of how he had treated her, imagining over and over twenty scenes in which he begged her forgiveness, till he fell asleep at last, dreamed that she turned her back upon him, and refused to hear him, and woke in the morning with the resolution of going to see her that night and confessing everything.

His father had come home after he went to bed, and it was with great trepidation that he went down to breakfast, almost expecting to find that he knew already of his relation to Lucy. But Richard Boxall was above that kind of thing, and Mr. Worboise was evidently free from any suspicion of the case.

He greeted his son kindly, or rather frankly, and seemed to be in good spirits.

"Our friends are well down the Channel by this time, with such a fair wind," he said. "Boxall's a lucky man to be able to get away from business like that. I wish you had taken a fancy to Mary, Tom. She's sure to get engaged before she comes back. Shipboard's a great place for getting engaged. Some hungry fellow, with a red coat and an empty breeches-pocket, is sure to pick her up. You might have had her if you had liked. However, you may do as well yet; and you needn't be in a hurry now. It's not enough that there's as good fish in the sea: they must come to your net, you know."

Tom laughed it off, went to his office, worked the weary day through, and ran round to Guild Court the moment he left business.

Lucy had waked in the night as well as Tom; but she had waked to the hope that there was a power somewhere—a power working good, and ·

upholding them that love it; to the hope that a thought lived all through the dark, and would one day make the darkness light about her; to the hope that a heart of love and help was at the heart of things, and would show itself for her need. When, therefore, Tom knocked—timidly almost—at the door, and opened it inquiringly, she met him with a strange light in her pale face, and a smile flickering about a lip that trembled in sympathy with her rain-clouded eyes. She held out her hand to him cordially, but neither offered to embrace—Thomas from shame, and Lucy from a feeling of something between that had to be removed before things could be as they were-or rather before their outward behavior to each other could be the same, for things could not to all eternity be the same again: they must be infinitely better and more beautiful, or cease altogether.

Thomas gave a look for one moment full in Lucy's eyes, and then dropped his own, holding her still by the consenting hand.

"Will you forgive me, Lucy?" he said, in a voice partly choked by feeling, and partly by the presence of Mrs. Boxall, who, however, could not hear what passed between them, for she sat knitting at the other end of the large room.

"Oh, Tom!" answered Lucy, with a gentle pressure of his hand.

Now, as all that Tom wanted was to be reinstated in her favor, he took the words as the seal of the desired reconciliation, and went no further with any confession. The words, however, meaning simply that she loved him and wanted to love him, ought to have made Tom the more anxious to confess all—not merely the rudeness of which he had been guilty and which had driven her from the room, but the wrong he had done her in spending the evening in such company; for surely it was a grievous wrong to a pure girl like Lucy to spend the space between the last and the next pressure of her hand in an atmosphere of vice. But the cloud cleared from his brow, and, with a sudden reaction of spirits, he began to be merry. To this change, however, Lucy did not respond. The cloud seemed rather to fall more heavily over her countenance. She turned from him, and went to a chair opposite her grandmother. Tom followed, and sat down beside her. He was sympathetic enough to see that things were not right between them after all. But he referred it entirely to her uneasiness at his parents' ignorance of their engagement.

Some of my readers may think that Lucy, too, was to blame for want of decision; that she ought to have refused to see Thomas even once again, till he had made his parents aware of their relation to each other. But knowing how little sympathy and help he had from those parents, she felt that to be severe upon him thus would be like turning him out into a snow-storm to find his way home across a desolate moor; and her success by persuasion would be a better thing for Thomas than her success by compulsion. No doubt, if her rights alone had to be considered, and not the necessities of Thomas's moral nature, the plan she did not adopt would have been the best. But no one liveth to himself—not even a woman whose dignity is in danger—and Lucy did not think of herself alone. Yet, for the sake of both, she remained perfectly firm in her purpose that Thomas should do something.

"Your uncle has said nothing about that unfortunate rencontre, Lucy," said Tom, hoping that what had relieved him would relieve her. "My father came home last night, and the paternal brow is all serene."

"Then I suppose you said something about it, Tom?" said Lucy, with a faint hope dawning in her heart.

"Oh! there's time enough for that. I've been thinking about it, you see, and I'll soon convince you," he added, hurriedly, seeing the cloud grow deeper on Lucy's face. "I must tell you something which I would rather not have mentioned."

"Don't tell me, if you ought not to tell me, Tom," said Lucy, whose conscience had grown more delicate than ever, both from the turning of her own face toward the light, and from the growing feeling that Tom was not to be trusted as a guide.

"There's no reason why I shouldn't," returned Tom. "It's only this— that my father is vexed with me because I wouldn't make love to your cousin Mary, and that I have let her slip out of my reach now; for, as he says, somebody will be sure to snap her up before she comes back. So it's just the worst time possible to tell him anything unpleasant, you know. I really had far better wait till the poor girl is well out to sea, and off my father's mind; for I assure you, Lucy, it will be no joke when he does know. He's not in any mood for the news just now, I can tell you. And then my mother's away, too, and there's nobody to stand between me and him."

Lucy made no reply to his speech, uttered in the eagerness with which a man, seeking to defend a bad position, sends one weak word after another, as if the accumulation of poor arguments would make up for the lack of a good one. She sat for a long minute looking down on a spot in the carpet— the sight of which ever after was the signal for a pain-throb; then, in a hopeless tone, said, with a great sigh:

"I've done all I can."

The indefiniteness of the words frightened Thomas, and he began again to make his position good.

"I tell you what, Lucy," he said; "I give you my promise that before another month is over—that is to give my father time to get over his vexation—I will tell him all about it, and take the consequences."

Lucy sighed once more, and looked dissatisfied. But again it passed through her mind that if she were to insist further, and refuse to see Thomas until he had complied with her just desire, she would most likely so far weaken, if not break, the bond between them, as to take from him the only influence that might yet work on him for good, and expose him entirely to such influences as she most feared. Therefore she said no more. But she could not throw the weight off her, or behave to Thomas as she had behaved hitherto. They sat silent for some time—Thomas troubled before Lucy, Lucy troubled about Thomas. Then, with another sigh, Lucy rose and went to the piano. She had never done so before when Thomas was with her, for he did not care much about her music. Now she thought of it as the only way of breaking the silence. But what should she play?

Then came into her memory a stately, sweet song her father used to sing. She did not know where he got either the words or the music of it. I know that the words are from Petrarch. Probably her father had translated them, for he had been much in Italy, and was a delicately gifted man. But whose was the music, except it was his own, I do not know. And as she sang the words, Lucy perceived for the first time how much they meant, and how they belonged to her; for in singing them she prayed both for herself and for Thomas.

> I am so weary with the burden old
> Of foregone faults, and power of custom base,
> That much I fear to perish from the ways,
> And fall into my enemy's grim hold.
> A mighty friend, to free me, though self-sold
> Came, of his own ineffable high grace,
> Then went, and from my vision took his face.
> Him now in vain I weary to behold.
> But still his voice comes echoing below:
> O ye that labor! see, here is the gate!
> Come unto me—the way all open lies!
> What heavenly grace will—what love—or what fate—
> The glad wings of a dove on me bestow,
> That I may rest, and from the earth arise?[1]

[1] Petrarch's sixtieth Sonnet.

Her sweet tones, the earnest music, and the few phrases he could catch here and there, all had their influence upon Tom. They made him feel. And with that, as usual, he was content. Lucy herself had felt as she had never felt before, and, therefore, sung as she had never sung before. And Tom was astonished to find that her voice had such power over him, and began to wonder how it was that he had not found it out before. He went home more solemn and thoughtful than he had ever been.

Still he did nothing.

CHAPTER XXII
A COMING EVENT

Thus things went on for the space of about three weeks. Tom went to see Lucy almost every night, and sometimes stayed late; for his mother was still from home, and his father was careless about his hours so long as they were decent. Lucy's face continued grave, but lost a little of its trouble; for Tom often asked her to sing to him now, and she thought she was gaining more of the influence over him which she so honestly wished to possess. As the month drew toward a close, however, the look of anxiety began to deepen upon her countenance.

One evening, still and sultry, they were together as usual. Lucy was sitting at the piano, where she had just been singing, and Tom stood beside her. The evening, as the Italian poets would say, had grown brown, and Mrs. Boxall was just going to light the candles, when Tom interposed a request for continued twilight.

"Please, grannie," he said—for he too called her grannie—"do not light the candles yet. It is so sweet and dusky—just like Lucy here."

"All very well for you," said Mrs. Boxall; "but what is to become of me? My love-making was over long ago, and I want to see what I'm about now. Ah! young people, your time will come next. Make hay while the sun shines."

"While the candle's out, you mean, grannie," said Tom, stealing a kiss from Lucy.

"I hear more than you think for," said the cheery old woman. "I'll give you just five minutes' grace, and then I mean to have my own way. I am not so fond of darkness, I can tell you."

"How close it is!" said Lucy. "Will you open the window a little wider, Tom. Mind the flowers."

She came near the window, which looked down on the little stony desert of Guild Court, and sank into a high-backed chair that stood beside it.

"I can hardly drag one foot after another," she said, "I feel so oppressed and weary."

"And I," said Tom, who had taken his place behind her, leaning on the back of her chair, "am as happy as if I were in Paradise."

"There must be thunder in the air," said Lucy. "I fancy I smell the lightning already. Oh, dear!"

"Are you afraid of lightning, then?" asked Thomas.

"I do not think I am exactly; but it shakes me so! I can't explain what I mean. It affects me like a false tone on the violin. No, that's not it. I can't tell what it is like."

A fierce flash broke in upon her words. Mrs. Boxall gave a scream.

"The Lord be about us from harm!" she cried.

Lucy sat trembling.

Thomas did not know how much she had to make her tremble. It is wonderful what can be seen in a single moment under an intense light. In that one flash Lucy had seen Mr. Molken and another man seated at a table, casting dice, with the eagerness of hungry fiends upon both their faces.

A few moments after the first flash, the wind began to rise, and as flash followed flash, with less and less of an interval, the wind rose till it blew a hurricane, roaring in the chimney and through the archway as if it were a wild beast caged in Guild Court, and wanting to get out.

When the second flash came, Lucy saw that the blind of Mr. Molken's window was drawn down.

All night long the storm raved about London. Chimney-pots clashed on the opposite pavements. One crazy old house, and one yet more crazy new one, were blown down. Even the thieves and burglars retreated to their dens. But before it had reached its worst Thomas had gone home. He lay awake for some time listening to the tumult and rejoicing in it, for it roused his imagination and the delight that comes of beholding danger from a far-removed safety—a selfish pleasure, and ready to pass from a sense of our own comfort into a complacent satisfaction in the suffering of others.

Lucy lay awake for hours. There was no more lightning, but the howling of the wind tortured her—that is, drew discords from the slackened strings of the human instrument—her nerves; made "broken music in her sides." She reaped this benefit, however, that such winds always drove her to her prayers. On the wings of the wind itself, she hastened her escape "from the windy storm and tempest." When at last she fell asleep, it was to dream that another flash of lightning—when or where appearing she did not know—revealed Thomas casting dice with Molken, and then left them lapt in the darkness of a godless world. She woke weeping, fell asleep again, and dreamed that she stood in the darkness once more, and that somewhere near Thomas was casting dice with the devil for his soul, but she could neither see him nor cry to him, for the darkness choked both voice and eyes. Then a hand was laid upon her head, and she heard the words—not in her ears, but in her heart—"Be of good cheer, my daughter." It was only a dream; but I doubt if even—I must not name names, lest I should be interpreted widely from my meaning—the greatest positivist alive could have helped waking with some comfort from that dream, nay, could have helped deriving a faint satisfaction from it, if it happened to return upon him during the day. "But in no such man would such a dream arise," my reader may object. "Ah, well," I answer, because I have nothing more to say. And perhaps even in what I have written I may have been doing or hinting some wrong to some of the class. It is dreadfully difficult to be just. It is far easier to be kind than to be fair.

It was not in London or the Empire only that that storm raged that night. From all points of the compass came reports of its havoc. Whether it was the same storm, however, or another on the same night, I cannot tell; but on the next morning save one, a vessel passing one of the rocky islets belonging to the Cape Verde group, found the fragments of a wreck floating on the water. The bark had parted amidships, for, on sending a boat to the island, they found her stem lying on a reef, round which little innocent waves were talking like human children. And on her stem they read her name, *Ningpo, London*. On the narrow strand they found three bodies: one, that of a young woman, vestureless and broken. They buried them as they could.

CHAPTER XXIII
MATTIE'S ILLNESS

The storm of that night beat furiously against poor Mattie's window, and made a dreadful tumult in her big head. When her father went into her little room, as was his custom every morning when she did not first appear in his, he found her lying awake, with wide eyes, seemingly unaware of what was before them. Her head and her hand were both hot; and when her father at length succeeded in gaining some notice from her, the words she spoke, although in themselves intelligible enough, had reference to what she had been going through in the night, in regions far withdrawn, and conveyed to him no understanding of her condition further than that she was wandering. In great alarm he sent the charwoman (whose morning visits were Mattie's sole assistance in the house, for they always had their dinner from a neighboring cook-shop) to fetch the doctor, while he went up the court to ask Lucy to come and see her.

Lucy was tossing in a troubled dream when she woke to hear the knock at the door. Possibly the whole dream passed between the first and second summons of the bookseller, who was too anxious and eager to shrink from rousing the little household. She thought she was one of the ten virgins; but whether one of the wise or foolish she did not know. She had knocked at a door, and as it opened, her lamp went out in the wind it made. But a hand laid hold of hers in the dark, and would have drawn her into the house. Then she knew that she was holding another hand, which at first she took to be that of one of her sisters, but found to be Thomas's. She clung to it, and would have drawn him into the house with her, but she could not move him. And still the other hand kept drawing her in. She woke in an agony just as she was losing her hold of Thomas, and heard Mr. Kitely's knock. She was out of bed in a moment, put on her dressing-gown and her shoes, and ran down stairs.

On learning what was the matter she made haste to dress, and in a few minutes stood by Mattie's bedside. But the child did not know her. When the doctor came, he shook his head, though he was one of the most undemonstrative of his profession; and after prescribing for her, said she must be watched with the greatest care, and gave Lucy urgent directions about her treatment. Lucy resolved that she would not leave her, and began at once to make what preparations were necessary for carrying out the doctor's instructions. Mattie took the medicine he sent; and in a little while the big eyes began to close, sunk and opened again, half closed and then started wide open, to settle their long lashes at last, after many slow flutterings, upon the pale cheek below them. Then Lucy wrote a note to Mrs. Morgenstern, and left her patient to run across to her grandmother to consult with her how she should send it. But when she opened the door into the court, there was Poppie, who of course flitted the moment she saw her, but only a little way off, like a bold bird.

"Poppie, dear Poppie!" cried Lucy, earnestly, "do come here. I want you."

"Blowed if I go there again, lady!" said Poppie, without moving in either direction.

"Come here, Poppie. I won't touch you—I promise you. I wouldn't tell you a lie, Poppie," she added, seeing that she made no impression on the child.

To judge by the way Poppie came a yard nearer, she did not seem at all satisfied by the assurance.

"Look here, Poppie. There's a little girl—you know her—Mattie—she's lying very ill here, and I can't leave her. Will you take this letter for me—to that big house in Wyvil Place—to tell them I can't come to-day?"

"They'll wash me," said Poppie, decisively.

"Oh, no, they won't again, Poppie. They know now that you don't like it."

"They'll be giving me something I don't want, then. I know the sort of them."

"You needn't go into the house at all. Just ring the bell, and give the letter to the servant."

Poppie came close up to Lucy.

"I'll tell you what, lady: I'm not afraid of *him*. *He* won't touch me again. If he do, I'll bite worser next time. But I won't run errands for nothink. Nobody does, miss. You ain't forgotten what you guv me last time? Do it again, and I'm off."

"A good wash, Poppie—that's what I gave you last time."

"No, miss," returned the child, looking up in her face beseechingly. "You know as well as me." And she held up her pretty grimy mouth, so that her meaning could not be mistaken. "Old Mother Flanaghan gave me a kiss once. You remember her gin-bottle, don't you, miss?" she added, still holding up her mouth.

For a moment Lucy did hesitate, but from no yielding to the repugnance she naturally felt at dirt. She hesitated, thinking to make a stipulation on her side, for the child's good.

"I tell you what, Poppie," she said; "I will kiss you every time you come to me with a clean face, as often as you like."

Poppie's dirty face fell. She put out her hand, took the letter, turned, and went away slowly.

Lucy could not bear it. She darted after her, caught her, and kissed her. The child, without looking round, instantly scudded.

Lucy could hardly believe her eyes, when, going down at Mr. Kitely's call, some time after, she found Poppie in the shop.

"She says she wants to see you, miss," said Kitely. "I don't know what she wants. Begging, I suppose."

And so she was. But all her begging lay in the cleanness and brightness of her countenance. She might have been a little saint but for the fact that her aureole was all in her face, and around it lay a border of darkness that might be felt.

"Back already!" said Lucy, in astonishment.

"Yes, lady. I didn't bite him. I throwed the letter at him, and he throwed it out again; and says I, pickin' of it up, 'You'll hear o' this to-morrow, Plush.' And says he, 'Give me that letter, you wagabones.' And I throwed it at him again, and he took it up and looked at it, and took it in. And here I am, lady," added Poppie, making a display of her clean face.

Lucy kissed her once more, and she was gone in a moment.

While Mattie was asleep Lucy did all she could to change the aspect of the place.

"She shan't think of Syne the first thing when she comes to herself," she said.

With the bookseller's concurrence, who saw the reason for it the moment she uttered it, she removed all the old black volumes within sight of her bed, and replaced them with the brightest bindings to be found in the shop. She would rather have got rid of the books altogether; but there was no time for that now. Then she ventured, finding her sleep still endure, to take down the dingy old chintz curtains from her tent bed, and replace them with her own white dimity. These she then drew close round the bed, and set about cleaning the window, inside and out. Her fair hands were perfectly fit for such work, or any other labor that love chose to require of them. "Entire affection hateth nicer hands," is one of the profoundest lines in all Spenser's profound allegory. But she soon found that the light would be far too much for her little patient, especially as she had now only white curtains to screen her. So the next thing was to get a green blind for the window. Not before that was up did Mattie awake, and then only to stare about her, take her medicine, and fall asleep again; or, at least, into some state resembling sleep.

She was suffering from congestion of the brain. For a week she continued in nearly the same condition, during which time Lucy scarcely left her bedside. And it was a great help to her in her own trouble to have such a charge to fulfill.

At length one morning, when the sun was shining clear and dewy through a gap between the houses of the court, and Lucy was rising early according to her custom—she lay on a sofa in Mattie's room—the child opened her eyes and saw. Then she closed them again, and Lucy heard her murmuring to herself:

"Yes, I thought so. I'm dead. And it is so nice; I've got white clouds to my bed. And there's Syne cutting away with all his men—just like a black cloud—away out of the world. Ah! I see you, Syne; you ought to be ashamed of yourself for worrying me as you've been doing all this time. You see it's no use. You ought really to give it up. He's too much for you, anyhow."

This she said brokenly and at intervals. The whole week had been filled with visions of conflict with the enemy, and the Son of Man had been with her in those visions. The spiritual struggles of them that are whole are the same in kind as those of this brain-sick child. They are tempted and driven to faithlessness, to self-indulgence, to denial of God and of his Christ, to give in—for the sake of peace, as they think. And I, believing that the very hairs of our heads are all numbered, and that not a sparrow can fall to the ground without our Father, believe that the Lord Christ—I know not how, because such knowledge is too wonderful for me—is present in the soul of such a child, as certainly as in his Church, or in the spirit of a saint who, in his name, stands against the whole world. There are two ways in which He can be present in the Church, one in the ordering of the confluence and working of men's deeds, the other in judgment: but he can be present in the weakest child's heart, in the heart of any of his disciples, in an infinitely deeper way than those, and without this deeper presence, he would not care for the outside presence of the other modes. It is in the individual soul that the Spirit works, and out of which he sends forth fresh influences. And

I believe that the good fight may be fought amid the wildest visions of a St. Anthony, or even in the hardest confinement of Bedlam. It was such a fight, perhaps, that brought the maniacs of old time to the feet of the Saviour, who gave them back their right mind. Let those be thankful who have it to fight amid their brothers and sisters, who can return look for look and word for word, and not among the awful visions of a tormented brain.

> "As thick and numberless
> As the gay motes that people the sunbeams."

Lucy did not venture to show herself for a little while, but at length she peeped within the curtain, and saw the child praying with folded hands. Ere she could withdraw, she opened her eyes and saw her.

"I thought I was in heaven!" she said; "but I don't mind, if you're there, miss. I've been seeing you all through it. But it's all over now," she added, with a sigh of relief.

"You must be very still, dear Mattie," said Lucy. "You are not well enough to talk yet."

"I am quite well, miss; only sleepy, I think." And before Lucy could answer, she was indeed asleep once more.

It was quite another fortnight before Lucy ventured to give up her place to her grandmother. During this time, she saw very little of Thomas—only for a few minutes every evening as he left the place—and somehow she found it a relief not to see more of him.

All the time of Mattie's illness, Mr. Spelt kept coming to inquire after her. He was in great concern about her, but he never asked to see her. He had a great gift in waiting, the little man. Possibly he fared the better, like Zaccheus, who wanted only to see, and *was seen*. But perhaps his quietness might be partly attributed to another cause—namely, that since Mattie's illness he had brooded more upon the suspicion that his wife had had a child. I cannot in the least determine whether this suspicion was a mere fancy or not; but I know that the tailor thought he had good grounds for it; and it does not require a very lawless imagination to presume the thing possible.

Every day of those three weeks, most days more than once or twice even, Poppie was to be seen at one hour or other in Guild Court, prowling about—with a clean face, the only part of her, I am all but certain, that was clean—for the chance of seeing Lucy. From what I know of Poppie, I cannot think that it was anxiety about Mattie that brought her there. I do not doubt that she was selfish—prowling about after a kiss from Lucy. And as often as Lucy saw her she had what she wanted.

But if Lucy did not see her sometimes, at least there was one who always did see her from his nest in the—rock, I was going to say, but it was only the wall. I mean, of course, Mr. Spelt. He saw her, and watched her, until at length, as he plied his needle, the fancy which already occupied his brain began to develop itself, and he wondered whether that Poppie might not be his very lost child. Nor had the supposition lasted more than five minutes before he passionately believed, or at least passionately desired to believe it, and began to devise how to prove it, or at least to act upon it.

CHAPTER XXIV
FISHING FOR A DAUGHTER

Mr. Spelt sat in his watch-tower, over the head of patiently cobbling Mr. Dolman, reflecting. He too was trying to cobble—things in general, in that active head of his beneath its covering of heathery hair. But he did not confine his efforts to things in general—one very particular thing had its share in the motions of his spirit—how to prove that Poppie was indeed his own child. He had missed his little Mattie much, and his child-like spirit was longing greatly after some child-like companionship. This, in Mattie's case, he had found did him good, cleared his inward sight, helped him to cobble things even when her questions showed him the need of fresh patching in many a place where he had not before perceived the rent or the thin-worn threads of the common argument or belief. And the thought had come to him that perhaps Mattie was taken away from him to teach him that he ought not, as Mattie had said with regard to Mrs. Morgenstern, to cultivate friendship only where he got good from it. The very possibility that he had a child somewhere in London seemed at length to make it his first duty to rescue some child or other from the abyss around him, and they were not a few swimming in the vast vortex.

Having found out that Mrs. Flanaghan knew more about Poppie than anyone else, and that she crept oftener into the bottom of an empty cupboard in her room than anywhere else, he went one morning to see whether he could not learn something from the old Irishwoman. The place looked very different then from the appearance it presented to Lucy the day she found it inhabited by nobody, and furnished with nothing but the gin-bottle.

When the tailor opened the door, he found the room swarming with children. Though it was hot summer weather, a brisk fire burned in the grate; and the place smelt strongly of *reesty* bacon. There were three different groups of children in three of the corners: one of them laying out the dead body of a terribly mutilated doll; another, the tangle-haired members of which had certainly had no share in the bacon but the smell of it, sitting listlessly on the floor, leaning their backs against the wall, apparently without hope and without God in the world; one of the third group searching for possible crumbs where she had just had her breakfast, the other two lying ill of the measles on a heap of rags. Mrs. Flanaghan was in the act of pouring a little gin into her tea. The tailor was quick-eyed, and took in the most of this at a glance. But he thought he saw something more, namely, the sharp eyes of Poppie peeping through the crack of the cupboard. He therefore thought of nothing more but a hasty retreat, for Poppie must not know he came after her.

"Good-morning to you, Mrs. Flanaghan," he said, with almost Irish politeness. Then, at a loss for anything more, he ventured to add—"Don't you think, ma'am, you'll have too much on your hands if all them children takes after the two in the corner? They've got the measles, ain't they, ma'am?"

"True for you, sir," returned Mrs. Flanaghan, whom the gin had soothed after the night's abstinence. "But we'll soon get rid o' the varmint," she said, rising from her seat. "Praise God the Father! we'll soon get rid o' them. Get out wid ye!" she went on, stamping with her foot on the broken floor. "Get out! What are ye doin' i' the house when ye ought to be enjoyin' yerselves in the fresh air? Glory be to God!—there they go, as I tould you. And now what'll I do for yerself this blessed marnin'?"

By this time the tailor had made up his mind to inquire after a certain Irishman, for whom he had made a garment of fustian, but who had never appeared to claim it. He did not expect her to know anything of the man, for he was considerably above Mrs. Flanaghan's level, but it afforded a decent pretext. Mrs. Flanaghan, however, claimed acquaintance with him, and begged that the garment in question might be delivered into her hands in order to reach him, which the tailor, having respect both to his word and his work, took care not to promise.

But as he went to his workshop, he thought what a gulf he had escaped. For suppose that Mrs. Flanaghan had been communicative, and had proved to his dissatisfaction that the girl was none of his! Why, the whole remaining romance of his life would have been gone. It was far better to think that she was or might be his child, than to know that she was not. And, after all, what did it matter whether she was or was not?—thus the process of thinking went on in the tailor's brain—was she not a child? What matter whether his own or someone else's? God must have made her all the same. And if he were to find his own child at last, neglected and ignorant and vicious, could he not pray better for her if he had helped the one he could help? Might he not then say, "O Lord, they took her from me, and I had no chance with *her*, but I did what I could—I caught a wild thing, and I tried to make something of her, and she's none the worse for it—do Thou help my poor child, for I could not, and Thou canst. I give thee back thine, help mine." Before he had reached his perch, he had resolved that he would make no further inquiry whatever about Poppie, but try to get a hold of her, and do for her what he could. For whether he was her father or not, neither case could alter the facts, that she was worth helping, and that it would be very hard to get a hold of her. All that Poppie could know of fathers would only make her more unwilling to be caught if she had a suspicion that Mr. Spelt laid such a claim to her; and he would therefore scheme as if their nearest common relations were "the grand old gardener and his wife," and with the care which the shy *startling* nature of Poppie, to use a Chaucerian word, rendered necessary. Tailors have time to think about things; and no circumstances are more favorable to true thought than those of any work which, employing the hands, leaves the head free. Before another day had passed Mr. Spelt had devised his bait.

The next morning came—a lovely morning for such fishing as he contemplated. Poppie appeared in the court, prowling as usual in the hope of seeing Lucy. But the tailor appeared to take no notice of her. Poppie's keen eyes went roving about as usual, wide awake to the chance of finding something. Suddenly she darted at a small object lying near the gutter, picked it up, put it in her mouth, and sucked it with evident pleasure. The tailor was as one who seeing sees not. Only he plied his needle and thread more busily, casting down sidelong glances in the drawing of the same. And there was no little triumph, for it was the triumph of confidence for the future, as well as of success for the present, in each of those glances. Suddenly Poppie ran away.

The morning after she was there again. Half involuntarily, I suppose, her eyes returned to the spot where she had found the bull's-eye. There, to the astonishment even of Poppie, who was very seldom astonished at anything, lay another—a larger one, as she saw at a glance, than the one she had found yesterday. It was in her mouth in a moment. But she gave a hurried glance round the court, and scudded at once. Like the cherub that sat aloft and saw what was going to come of it all, the little tailor drew his shortening thread, and smiled somewhere inside his impassive face, as he watched the little human butterfly, with its torn wings, lighting and flitting as in one and the same motion.

The next morning there again sat Mr. Spelt at his work—working and watching. With the queerest look of inquiry and doubtful expectation, Poppie appeared from under the archway, with her head already turned toward El Dorado—namely, the flag-stone upon which the gifts of Providence had been set forth on other mornings. There—could she, might she, believe her eyes?—lay a splendid polyhedral lump of rock; white as snow, and veined with lovely red. It was not quartz and porphyry, reader, but the most melting compound of sugar and lemon-juice that the sweet inventing Genius—why should she not have the name of a tenth muse? Polyhedia, let us call her—had ever hatched in her brooding brain, as she bent over melting sugar or dark treacle, "in linked sweetness long drawn out." This time Poppie hesitated a little, and glanced up and around. She saw nobody but the tailor, and he was too cunning even for her. Busy as a bee, he toiled away lightly and earnestly. Then, as if the sweetmeat had been a bird for which she was laying snares, as her would-be father was laying them for her, she took two steps nearer on tiptoe, then stopped and gazed again. It was not that she thought of stealing, any more than the birds who take what they find in the fields and on the hedges; it was only from a sort of fear that it was too good fortune for her, and that there must be something evanescent about it—wings somewhere. Or perhaps she vaguely fancied there must be some unfathomable design in it, awful and inscrutable, and therefore glanced around her once more—this time all but surprising the tailor, with uplifted head and the eager eyes of a fowler. But the temptation soon overcame any suspicion she might have. She made one bound upon the prize, and scudded as she had never scudded before. Mr. Spelt ran his needle in under the nail of his left thumb, and so overcame his delight in time to save his senses.

And now came a part of the design which Mr. Spelt regarded as a very triumph of cunning invention. That evening he drove two tiny staples of wire—one into Mr. Dolman's door-post close to the ground; the other into his own. The next morning, as soon as he arrived, he chose a thread as near the color of the flag-stones that paved the passage as he could find, fastened one end with a plug of toffee into a hole he bored with his scissors in another splendor of rock, laid the bait in the usual place, drew the long thread through the two eyes of the staples, and sat down in his lair with the end attached to the little finger of his left hand.

The time arrived about which Poppie usually appeared. Mr. Spelt got anxious—nervously anxious. She was later than usual, and he almost despaired; but at length, there she was, peeping cautiously round the corner toward the trap. She saw the bait—was now so accustomed to it that she saw it almost without surprise. She had begun to regard it as most people regard the operations of nature—namely, as that which always was so and always will be so, and therefore has no reason in it at all. But this time a variety in the phenomenon shook the couch of habitude upon which her mind was settling itself in regard to the saccharine bowlders; for, just as she stooped to snatch it to herself and make it her own, away it went as if in terror of her approaching fingers—but only to the distance of half a yard or so. Eager as the tailor was—far more eager to catch Poppie than

Poppie was to catch the lollypop—he could scarcely keep his countenance when he saw the blank astonishment that came over Poppie's pretty brown face. Certainly she had never seen a living lollypop, yet motion is a chief sign of life, and the lollypop certainly moved. Perhaps it would have been wiser to doubt her senses first, but Poppie had never yet found her senses in the wrong, and therefore had not learned to doubt them. Had she been a child of weak nerves, she might have recoiled for a moment from a second attempt, but instead of that she pounced upon it again so suddenly that the Archimago of the plot was unprepared. He gave his string a tug only just as she seized it, and, fortunately, the string came out of the plugged hole. Poppie held the bait, and the fisherman drew in his line as fast as possible, that his fish might not see it.

The motions of Poppie's mind were as impossible to analyze as those of a field-mouse or hedge-sparrow. This time she began at once to gnaw the sugar, staring about her as she did so, and apparently in no hurry to go. Possibly she was mentally stunned by the marvel of the phenomenon, but I do not think so. Poppie never could be much surprised at anything. Why should anything be surprising? To such a child everything was interesting— nothing overwhelming. She seemed constantly shielded by the divine buckler of her own exposure and helplessness. You could have thought that God had said to her, as to his people of old, "Fear not thou, O Poppie," and therefore Poppie did not fear, and found it answer. It is a terrible doctrine that would confine the tender care of the Father to those that know and acknowledge it. He carries the lambs in his bosom, and who shall say when they cease to be innocent lambs and become naughty sheep? Even then he goes into the mountains, and searches till he finds.

Not yet would the father aspirant show his craft. When he saw her stand there gnawing his innocent bait, he was sorely tempted to call, in the gentlest voice, "Poppie, dear;" but, like a fearful and wise lover, who dreads startling the maiden he loves, he must yet dig his parallels and approach with guile. He would even refine upon his own cunning. The next morning his bait had only a moral hook inside, that is, there was no string attached. But now that happened which he had all along feared. A child of the court— in which there were not more than two, I think—whom Mr. Spelt regarded, of course, as a stray interloper, for had she not enough of the good things already?—spied the sweetmeat, and following the impulses of her depraved humanity, gobbled it up without ever saying, like heathen Cassius, "By your leave, gods." Presently after Poppie appeared, looked, stared—actually astonished now—and, with fallen face, turned and went away. Whether she or her cunning enemy overhead was the more disappointed, I will not venture to determine, but Mr. Spelt could almost have cried. Four-and-twenty long tedious hours of needle and thread must pass before another chance would arrive—and the water so favorable, with the wind from the right quarter just clouding its surface, and the fly so taking!—it was hard to bear. He comforted himself, however, by falling back upon a kind of divine fatalism with which God had endowed him, saying to himself, "Well, it's all for the best,"—a phrase not by any means uncommon among people devoutly inclined; only there was this difference between most of us and Mr. Spelt, that we follow the special aphorism with a sigh, while he invariably smiled and brightened up for the next thing he had to do. To say things are all right and yet gloom does seem rather illogical in you and me, reader, does it not? Logical or illogical, it was not Spelt's way anyhow. He began to whistle, which he never did save upon such occasions when the faithful part of him set itself to conquer the faithless.

But he would try the bait without the line once more. Am I wearying my reader with the process? I would not willingly do so, of course. But I fancy he would listen to this much about a salmon any day, so I will go on with my child. Poppie came the next morning, notwithstanding her last disappointment, found the bull's-eye, for such I think it was this time, took it, and sucked it to nothing upon the spot—did it leisurely, and kept looking about—let us hope for Lucy, and that Poppie considered a kiss a lovelier thing still than a lollypop.

The next morning Mr. Spelt tried the string again, watched it better, and by a succession of jerks, not slow movements, lest, notwithstanding the cunning of the color, she should see the string, drew her step by step in the eagerness of wonder; as well as of that appetite which is neither hunger nor thirst, and yet concerned with the same organs, but for which we have, so far as I am aware, no word, I mean the love of sweets, to the very foot of his eyrie. When she laid hold of the object desired at the door-post, he released it by a final tug against the eye of the staple. Before she could look up from securing it, another lump of rock fell at her feet. Then she did look up, and saw the smiling face of the tailor looking out (once more like an angel over a cloudy beam) over the threshold, if threshold it could properly be called, of his elevated and stairless door. She gave back a genuine whole-faced smile, and turned and scudded. The tailor's right hand shuttled with increased vigor all the rest of that day.

CHAPTER XXV
MR. FULLER

One evening Lucy was sitting as usual with Mattie, for the child had no friends but her and grannie; her only near relative was a widowed sister of her father, whom she did not like. She was scarcely so well as she had been for the last few days, and had therefore gone early to bed, and Lucy sat beside her to comfort her. By this time she had got the room quite transformed in appearance—all the books out of it, a nice clean paper up on the walls, a few colored prints from the *Illustrated London News* here and there, and, in fact, the whole made fit for the abode of a delicate and sensitive child.

"What shall I read to-night, Mattie?" she asked. For Mattie must always have something read to her out of the New Testament before she went to sleep; Mr. Spelt had inaugurated the custom.

"Oh, read about the man that sat in his Sunday clothes," said Mattie.

"I don't know that story," returned Lucy.

"I wish dear mother was here," said Mattie, with the pettishness of an invalid. "He would know what story I mean—that he would."

"Would you like to see Mr. Spelt?" suggested Lucy. "He was asking about you not an hour ago."

"Why didn't he come up, then? I wonder he never comes to see me."

"I was afraid you weren't strong enough for it, Mattie. But I will run and fetch him now, if he's not gone."

"Oh, yes; do, please. I know he's not gone, for I have not heard his step yet. I always watch him out of the court when I'm in bed. He goes right under me."

Lucy went, and Mr. Spelt came gladly.

"Well, mother," said Mattie, holding out a worn little cloud of a hand, "how do you do?"

Mr. Spelt could hardly answer for emotion. He took the little hand in his, and it seemed to melt away in his grasp, till he could hardly feel it.

"Don't cry, mother. I am very happy. I do believe I've seen the last of old Syne. I feel just like the man that had got his Sunday clothes on, you know. You see what a pretty room Miss Burton has made, instead of all those ugly books that Syne was so fond of: well, my poor head feels just like this room, and I'm ready to listen to anything about Somebody. Read about the man in his Sunday clothes."

But Mr. Spelt, no less than Lucy, was puzzled as to what the child meant.

"I wish that good clergyman that talked about Somebody's burden being easy to carry, would come and see me," she said. "I know he would tell me the story. He knows all about Somebody."

"Shall I ask Mr. Potter to come and see you?" said Spelt, who had never heard of Mr. Fuller by name, or indeed anything about him, but what Mattie had told him before she was taken ill.

"I don't mean Mr. Potter—you know well enough. He's always pottering," said the child, with a laugh.

She had not yet learned to give honor where honor is not due; or, rather, she had never been young enough to take seeming for being, or place for character. The consequence was that her manners and her modesty had suffered—not her reverence or her heart.

"THE LITTLE TAILOR WAS VERY SHY OF READING BEFORE LUCY."

"I want to see the gentleman that really thinks it's all about something," she resumed. "Do you know where he lives, Miss Burton?"

"No," answered Lucy, "but I will find out to-morrow, and ask him to come and see you."

"Well, that will be nice," returned Mattie. "Read to me, Mr. Spelt—anything you like."

The little tailor was very shy of reading before Lucy, but Mattie would hear of nothing else, for she would neither allow Lucy to read, nor yet to go away.

"Don't mind me, Mr. Spelt," said Lucy, beseechingly. "We are all friends, you know. If we belong to the Somebody Mattie speaks about we needn't be shy of each other."

Thus encouraged, Mr. Spelt could refuse no longer. He read about the daughter of Jairus being made alive again.

"Oh, dear me!" said Mattie. "And if I had gone dead when Syne was tormenting of me, He could have come into the room, and taken me by the hand and said, 'Daughter, get up.' How strange it would be if He said, 'Daughter' to me, for then He would be my father, you know. And they say He's a king. I wonder if that's why Mr. Kitely calls me *princess*. To have Mr. Kitely and Somebody," she went on musingly, "both for fathers is more than I can understand. There's something about godfathers and godmothers in the Catechism, ain't there, Miss Burton?" Then, without, waiting for a reply, she went on, "I wish my father would go and hear what that nice gentleman—not Mr. Potter—has got to say about it. Miss Burton, read the hymn about blind Bartimeus, and that'll do mother good, and then I'll go to sleep."

The next day, after she came from the Morgensterns', Lucy went to find Mr. Fuller. She had been to the week-evening service twice since Mattie began to recover, but she had no idea where Mr. Fuller lived, and the only way she could think of for finding him was to ask at the warehouses about the church. She tried one after another, but nobody even knew that there was any service there—not to say where the evening preacher lived. With its closed, tomb-like doors, and the utter ignorance of its concerns manifested by the people of the neighborhood, the great ugly building stood like some mausoleum built in honor of a custom buried beneath it, a monument of the time when men could buy and sell and worship God. So Lucy put off further inquiry till the next week-evening service, for she had found already that Mr. Fuller had nothing to do with the Sunday services in that church.

How she wished that she could take Thomas with her the next time she went to receive Mr. Fuller's teaching! She had seen very little of Thomas, as I have said, and had been so much occupied with Mattie, that she did not even know whether he had fulfilled his promise about telling his father. I suspect, however, that she had been afraid to ask him, foreboding the truth that he had in fact let his promise lapse in time, and was yet no nearer toward its half redemption in act, which was all that remained possible now. And, alas! what likelihood was there of the good seed taking good root in a heart where there was so little earth?

Finding Mr. Kitely in his shop door, Lucy stopped to ask after Mattie, for she had not seen her that morning. And then she told him what she had been about, and her want of success.

"What does the child want a clergyman for?" asked Mr. Kitely, with some tone of dissatisfaction. "I'm sure you're better than the whole lot of them, miss. Now I could listen to you—"

"How do you know that?" retorted Lucy, smiling; for she wanted to stop the eulogium upon herself.

"Because I've listened to you outside the door, Miss Burton, when you was a-talking to Mattie inside."

"That wasn't fair, Mr. Kitely."

"No more it wasn't, but it's done me no harm, nor you neither. But for them parsons!—they're neither men nor women. I beg their pardons—they *are* old wives."

"But are you sure that you know quite what you are talking about? I think there must be all sorts of them as well as of other people. I wish you would come and hear Mr. Fuller some evening with Mattie and me when she's better. You would allow that he talks sense, anyhow."

"I ain't over hopeful, miss. And to tell the truth, I don't much care. I don't think there can be much in it. It's all an affair of the priests. To get the upper hand of people they work on their fears and their superstitions. But I don't doubt some of them may succeed in taking themselves in, and so go on like the fox that had lost his tail, trying to make others cut off theirs too."

Lucy, did not reply, because she had nothing at hand to say. The bookseller feared he had hurt her.

"And so you couldn't find this Mr. Fuller? Well, you leave it to me. I'll find him, and let you know in the afternoon."

"Thank you, Mr. Kitely. Just tell Mattie, will you? I must run home now, but I'll come in in the afternoon to hear how you have succeeded."

About six o'clock, Lucy reëntered Mr. Kitely's shop, received the necessary directions to find the "parson," ran up to tell Mattie that she was going, for the child had not come down stairs, and then set out.

To succeed she had to attend to Mr. Kitely's rather minute instructions; for although the parsonage lay upon the bank of one of the main torrents of city traffic, it was withdrawn and hidden behind shops and among offices, taverns, and warehouses. After missing the most direct way, she arrived at last, through lanes and courts, much to her surprise, at the border of a green lawn on the opposite side of which rose a tree that spread fair branches across a blue sky filled with pearly light, and blotted here and there with spongy clouds that had filled themselves as full of light as they could hold. The other half of the branches of the same tree spread themselves across the inside of a gable, all that remained of a tavern that was being pulled down. The gable was variegated with the incongruous papers of many small rooms, and marked with the courses of stairs and the holes for the joints of the floors; and this dreariness was the background for the leaves of the solitary tree. On the same side was the parsonage, a long, rather low, and country-looking house, from the door of which Lucy would not have been surprised to see a troop of children burst with shouts and laughter, to tumble each other about upon the lawn, as smooth, at least, if not as green, as any of the most velvety of its kind. One side of the square was formed by a vague, commonplace mass of dirty and expressionless London houses—what they might be used for no one could tell—one of them, probably, an eating-house—mere walls with holes to let in the little light that was to be had. The other side was of much the same character, only a little better; and the remaining side was formed by the long barn-like wall of the church, broken at regular intervals by the ugly windows, with their straight sides filled with parallelograms, and their half-circle heads filled with trapeziums—the ugliest window that can be made, except it be redeemed with stained glass, the window that makes the whole grand stretch of St. Paul's absolutely a pain. The church was built of brick, nearly black below, but retaining in the upper part of the square tower something of its original red. All this Lucy took in at a glance as she went up to the door of the parsonage.

She was shown into a small study, where Mr. Fuller sat. She told him her name, that she had been to his week-evening service with Mattie, and that the child was ill and wanted to see him.

"Thank you very much," said Mr. Fuller. "Some of the city clergymen have so little opportunity of being useful! I am truly grateful to you for coming to me. A child in my parish is quite a godsend to me—I do not use the word irreverently—I mean it. You lighten my labor by the news.

Perhaps I ought to say I am sorry she is ill. I dare say I shall be sorry when I see her. But meantime, I am very glad to be useful."

He promised to call the next day; and, after a little more talk, Lucy took her leave.

Mr. Fuller was a middle-aged man, who all his conscious years had been trying to get nearer to his brethren, moved thereto by the love he bore to the Father. The more anxious he was to come near to God, the more he felt that the high-road to God lay through the forest of humanity. And he had learned that love is not a feeling to be called up at will in the heart, but the reward as the result of an active exercise of the privileges of a neighbor.

Like the poor parson loved of Chaucer, "he waited after no pomp ne reverence;" and there was no chance of preferment coming in search of him. He was only a curate still. But the incumbent of St. Amos, an old man, with a grown-up family, almost unfit for duty, and greatly preferring his little estate in Kent to the city parsonage, left everything to him, with much the same confidence he would have had if Mr. Fuller had been exactly the opposite of what he was, paying him enough to live upon—indeed, paying him well for a curate. It was not enough to marry upon, as the phrase is, but Mr. Fuller did not mind that, for the only lady he had loved, or ever would love in that way, was dead; and all his thoughts for this life were bent upon such realizing of divine theory about human beings, and their relation to God and to each other, as might make life a truth and a gladness. It was therefore painful to him to think that he was but a *city* curate, a being whose thirst after the relations of his calling among his fellows reminded himself of that of the becalmed mariner, with "water, water everywhere, but water none to drink." He seemed to have nothing to do with them, nor they with him. Perhaps not one individual of the crowds that passed his church every hour in the week would be within miles of it on the Sunday; for even of those few who resided near it, most forsook the place on the day of rest, especially in the summer; and few indeed were the souls to whom he could offer the bread of life. He seemed to himself to be greatly overpaid for the work he had it in his power to do—in his own parish, that is. He had not even any poor to minister to. He made up for this by doing his best to help the clergyman of a neighboring parish, who had none but poor; but his heart at times burned within him to speak the words he loved best to speak to such as he could hope had the ears to hear them; for among the twelve people—a congregation he did not always have—that he said he preferred to the thousand, he could sometimes hardly believe that there was one who heard and understood. More of his reflections and resolutions, in regard to this state of affairs, we shall fall in with by and by. Meantime, my reader will believe that this visit of Lucy gave him pleasure and hope of usefulness.

The next morning he was in Mr. Kitely's shop as early as he thought the little invalid would be able to see him.

"Good-morning, sir," said Mr. Kitely, brusquely. "What can I do for you this morning?"

If Mr. Fuller had begun looking at his books, Kitely would have taken no notice of him. He might have stayed hours, and the bookseller would never have even put a book in his way; but he looked as if he wanted something in particular, and therefore Mr. Kitely spoke.

"You have a little girl that's not well, haven't you?" returned Mr. Fuller.

"Oh! you're the gentleman she wanted to see. She's been asking ever so often whether you wasn't come yet. She's quite impatient to see you, poor lamb!"

While he spoke, Kitely had drawn nearer to the curate, regarding him with projecting and slightly flushed face, and eyes that had even something of eagerness in them.

"I would have come earlier, only I thought it would be better not," said Mr. Fuller.

Mr. Kitely drew yet a step nearer, with the same expression on his face.

"You won't put any nonsense into her head, will you, sir?" he said, almost pleadingly.

"Not if I know it," answered Mr. Fuller, with a smile of kind humor. "I would rather take some out of it."

"For you see," Kitely went on, "that child never committed a sin in her life. It's all nonsense; and I won't have her talked to as if she was a little hell-cat."

"But you see we must go partly by what she thinks herself; and I suspect she won't say she never did anything wrong. I don't think I ever knew a child that would. But, after all, suppose you are right, and she never did anything, wrong—"

"I don't exactly say that, you know," interposed Mr. Kitely, in a tone of mingled candor and defense. "I only said she hadn't committed any sins."

"And where's the difference?" asked Mr. Fuller, quietly.

"Oh! you know quite well. Doing wrong, you know—why, we all do wrong sometimes. But to commit a sin, you know—I suppose that's something serious. That comes in the way of the Ten Commandments."

"I don't think your little girl would know the difference."

"But what's the use of referring to her always?"

"Just because I think she's very likely to know best. Children are wise in the affairs of their own kingdom."

"Well, I believe you're right; for she is the strangest child I ever saw. She knows more than any one would think for. Walk this way, sir. You'll find her in the back room."

"Won't you come, too, and see that I don't put any nonsense into her head?"

"I must mind the shop, sir," objected Kitely, seeming a little ashamed of what he had said.

Mr. Fuller nodded content, and was passing on, when he bethought himself, and stopped.

"Oh, Mr. Kitely," he said, "there was just one thing I was going to say, but omitted. It was only this: that suppose you were right about your little girl, or suppose even that she had never done anything wrong at all, she would want God all the same. And we must help each other to find Him."

If Mr. Kitely had any reply ready for this remark, which I doubt, Mr. Fuller did not give him time to make it, for he walked at once into the room, and found Mattie sitting alone in a half twilight, for the day was cloudy. Even the birds were oppressed, for not one of them was singing. A thrush hopped drearily about under his load of speckles, and a rose-ringed paroquet, with a very red nose, looked ashamed of the quantity of port-wine he had drunk. The child was reading the same little old book mentioned before. She laid it down, and rose from the window-sill to meet Mr. Fuller.

"Well, how do you do, sir?" she said. "I am glad you are come."

Any other child of her age Mr. Fuller would have kissed, but there was something about Mattie that made him feel it an unfit proceeding. He shook hands with her and offered her a white camellia.

"Thank you, sir," said Mattie, and laid the little transfiguration upon the table.

"Don't you like flowers?" asked Mr. Fuller, somewhat disappointed. "Isn't it beautiful now?"

"Well, where's the good?" answered and asked Mattie, as if she had been a Scotchwoman. "It will be ugly before to-morrow."

"Oh, no; not if you put it in water directly."

"Will it live forever, then?" asked Mattie.

"No, only a few days."

"Well, where's the odds, then? To-morrow or next week—where's the difference? It *looks* dead now when you know it's dying."

"Ah!" thought Mr. Fuller, "I've got something here worth looking into." What he said was, "You dear child!"

"You don't know me yet," returned Mattie. "I'm not dear at all. I'm cross and ill-natured. And I won't be petted."

"You like the birds, though, don't you?" said Mr. Fuller.

"Well, yes. Mr. Kitely likes them, and I always like what he likes. But they are not quite comfortable, you know. They won't last forever, you know. One of them is dead since I was taken ill. And father meant it for Miss Burton."

"Do you like Miss Burton, then?"

"Yes, I *do*. But she'll live forever, you know. I'll tell you something else I like."

"What is that, my child?"

"Oh, I'm no such a child! But I'll tell you what I like. There."

And she held out the aged little volume, open at the hymn about blind Bartimeus.

"Will this live forever, then?" he asked, turning the volume over in his hand, so that its withered condition suggested itself at once to Mattie.

"Now you puzzle me," answered Mattie. "But let me think. You know it's not the book I mean; it's the poem. Now I have it. If I know that poem by heart, and I live forever, then the poem will live forever. There!"

"Then the book's the body, and the poem the soul," said Mr. Fuller.

"One of the souls; for some things have many souls. I have two, at least."

Mr. Fuller felt instinctively, with the big forehead and the tiny body of the child before him, that they were getting on rather dangerous ground. But he must answer.

"Two souls! That must be something like what King David felt, when he asked God to join his heart into one. But do you like this poem?" he hastened to add. "May I read it to you?"

"Oh, yes; please do. I am never tired of hearing it. It will sound quite new if you read it."

So Mr. Fuller read slowly—"As Jesus went into Jericho town." And from the way Mattie listened, he knew what he must bring her next—not a camellia, but a poem. Still, how sad it was that a little child should not love flowers!

"When were you in the country last, Miss Kitely?"

"I never was in the country that I know of. My name is Mattie."

"Wouldn't you like to go, Mattie?"

"No I shouldn't—not at all."

"Why?"

"Well, because—because it's not in my way, you see."

"But surely you have some reason for not liking the country."

"Well, now, I will tell you. The country, by all I can hear, is full of things that die, and I don't like that. And I think people can't be nice that like the country."

Mr. Fuller resolved in his heart that he would make Mattie like the country before he had done with her. But he would say no more now, because he was not sure whether Mattie as yet regarded him with a friendly eye; and he must be a friend before he could speak about religion. He rose, therefore, and held out his hand.

Mattie looked at him with dismay.

"But I wanted you to tell me about the man that sat at Somebody's feet in his Sunday clothes."

Happily for his further influence with her, Mr. Fuller guessed at once whom she meant, and taking a New Testament from his pocket, read to her about the demoniac, who sat at the feet of Jesus, clothed, and in his right mind. He had not known her long before he discovered that all these stories of possession had an especial attraction for Mattie—she evidently associated them with her own visions of Syne and his men.

"Well, I was wrong. It wasn't his Sunday clothes," she said. "Or, perhaps, it was, and he had torn the rest all to pieces."

"Yes; I think that's very likely," responded Mr. Fuller.

"I know—it was Syne that told him, and he did it. But he wouldn't do it any more, would he, after he saw Somebody?"

"I don't think he would," answered Mr. Fuller, understanding her just enough to know the right answer to make. "But I will come and see you again to-morrow," he added, "and try whether I can't bring something with me that you will like."

"Thank you," answered the old-fashioned creature. "But don't be putting yourself to any expense about it, for I am not easy to please." And she lifted her hand to her head and gave a deep sigh, as if it was a very sad fact indeed. "I wish I was easier to please," she added, to herself; but Mr. Fuller heard her as he left the room.

"She's a very remarkable child that, Mr. Kitely—too much so, I fear," he said, reëntering the shop.

"I know that," returned the bookseller, curtly, almost angrily. "I wish she wasn't."

"I beg your pardon. I only wanted—"

"No occasion at all," interrupted Mr. Kitely.

"I only wanted," Mr. Fuller persisted, "to ask you whether you do not think she had better go out of town for a while."

"I dare say. But how am I to send her? The child has not a relation but me—and an aunt that she can't a-bear; and that wouldn't do—would it, sir? She would fret herself to death without someone she cared about."

"Certainly it wouldn't do. But mightn't Miss—I forget her name—"

"Miss Burton, I dare say you mean."

"I mean Miss Burton. Couldn't she help you? Is she any relation of yours?"

"None whatever. Nor she's not like it. I believe she's a stray, myself."

"What *do* you mean, Mr. Kitely?" asked Mr. Fuller, quite bewildered now.

"Well, sir, I mean that she's a stray angel," answered Mr. Kitely, smiling; "for she ain't like anyone else I know of but that child's mother, and she's gone back to where she came from—many's the long year."

"I don't wonder at your thinking that of her if she's as good as she looks," returned Mr. Fuller. And bidding the bookseller good-morning, he left the shop and walked home, cogitating how the child could be got into the country.

Next morning he called—earlier, and saw Lucy leaving the court just as he was going into the shop. He turned and spoke to her.

"Fancy a child, Miss Burton," he said, "that does not care about flowers—and her heart full of religion too! How is she to consider the lilies of the field? She knows only birds in cages; she has no idea of the birds of the air. The poor child has to lift everything out of that deep soul of hers, and the buckets of her brain can't stand such hard work." .

"I know, I know," answered Lucy. "But what can I do?"

"Besides," Mr. Fuller continued, "what notion of the simple grandeur of God can she have when she never had more than a peep of the sky from between these wretched houses? How can the heavens declare the glory of God to her? You don't suppose David understood astronomy, and that it was from a scientific point of view that he spoke, when he said that the firmament showed his handiwork? That was all he could say about it, for the Jewish nation was not yet able to produce a Ruskin. But it was, nevertheless, the spiritual power of the sky upon his soul—not the stars in their courses, but the stars up there in their reposeful depth of blue, their 'shining nest'— which, whatever theory of their construction he might have, yet impressed him with an awe, an infinitude, a shrinking and yet aspiring—made his heart swell within him, and sent him down on his knees. This little darling knows nothing of such an experience. We must get her into the open. She must love the wind that bloweth where it listeth, and the clouds that change and pass. She can't even like anything that does not last forever; and the mind needs a perishing bread sometimes as well as the body—though it never perishes when once made use of, as Mattie told me yesterday. But I beg your pardon; I am preaching a sermon, I think. What a thing it is to have the faults of a profession in addition to those of humanity! It all comes to this—you must get that child, with her big head and her big conscience, out of London, and give her heart a chance."

"Indeed, I wish I could," answered Lucy. "I will do what I can, and let you know. Are you going to see her now, Mr. Fuller?"

"Yes, I am. I took her a flower yesterday, but I have brought her a poem to-day. I am afraid, however, that it is not quite the thing for her. I thought I could easily find her one till I began to try, and then I found it very difficult indeed."

They parted—Lucy to Mrs. Morgenstern's, Mr. Fuller to Mattie.

I will give the hymn—for the sake, in part, of what Mattie said, and then I will close the chapter.

> "Come unto me," the Master says.
> But how? I am not good;
> No thankful song my heart will raise,
> Nor even wish it could.
>
> I am not sorry for the past,
> Nor able not to sin;
> The weary strife would ever last
> If once I should begin.

Hast thou no burden then to bear?
No action to repent?
Is all around so very fair?
Is thy heart quite content?

Hast thou no sickness in thy soul?
No labor to endure?
Then go in peace, for thou art whole,
Thou needest not His cure.

Ah! mock me not. Sometimes I sigh;
I have a nameless grief,
A faint, sad pain—but such that I
Can look for no relief.

Come then to Him who made thy heart;
Come in thyself distrest;
To come to Jesus is thy part,
His part to give thee rest.

New grief, new hope He will bestow,
Thy grief and pain to quell;
Into thy heart Himself will go,
And that will make thee well.

When Mr. Fuller had finished the hymn, he closed the book and looked toward Mattie. She responded—with a sigh—

"Well, I think I know what it means. You see I have such a big head, and so many things come and go just as they please, that if it weren't for Somebody I don't know what I should do with them all. But as soon as I think about Him, they grow quieter and behave better. But I don't know all that it means. Will you lend me the book, Mr. Fuller?"

All the child's thoughts took shapes, and so she talked like a lunatic. Still, as all the forms to which she gave an objective existence were the embodiments of spiritual realities, she could not be said to have yet passed the narrow line that divides the poet from the maniac. But it was high time that the subjects of her thoughts should be supplied from without, and that the generating power should lie dormant for a while. And the opportunity for this arrived sooner than her friends had expected.

CHAPTER XXVI
THE NINGPO IS LOST

Lucy was so full of Mattie and what Mr. Fuller had said that she told Mrs. Morgenstern all about it before Miriam had her lesson. After the lesson was over, Mrs. Morgenstern, who had, contrary to her custom, remained in the room all the time, said:

"Well, Lucy, I have been thinking about it, and I think I have arranged it all very nicely. It's clear to me that the child will go out of her mind if she goes on as she's doing. Now, I don't think Miriam has been quite so well as usual, and she has not been out of London since last August. Couldn't you take her down to St. Leonard's—or I dare say you would like Hastings better? You can go on with your lessons there all the same, and take little Mattie with you."

"But what will become of my grandmother?" said Lucy.

"She can go with you, can't she? I could ask her to go and take care of you. It would be much better for you to have her, and it makes very little difference to me, you know."

"Thank you very much," returned Lucy, "but I fear my grandmother will not consent to it. I will try her, however, and see what can be done. Thank you a thousand times, dear Mrs. Morgenstern. Wouldn't you like to go to Hastings, Miriam?"

Miriam was delighted at the thought of it, and Lucy was not without hopes that if her grandmother would not consent to go herself, she would at least wish her to go. Leaving Mattie out of view, she would be glad to be away from Thomas for a while, for, until he had done as he ought, she could not feel happy in his presence; and she made up her mind that she would write to him very plainly when she was away—perhaps tell him positively that if he would not end it, she must. I say *perhaps*, for ever as she approached the resolution, the idea of the poor lad's helpless desertion arose before her, and she recoiled from abandoning him. Nothing more could be determined, however, until she saw her grandmother.

But as she was going out she met Mr. Sargent in the hall. He had come to see her.

This very morning the last breath of the crew and passengers of the *Ningpo* had bubbled up in the newspapers; and all the world who cared to know it knew the fact, that the vessel had been dashed to pieces upon a rock of the Cape Verde Islands; all hands and passengers supposed to be lost. This the underwriters knew but a few hours before. Now it was known to Mr. Stopper and Mr. Worboise, both of whom it concerned even more than the underwriters. Mr. Stopper's first feeling was one of dismay, for the articles of partnership had not been completed before Mr. Boxall sailed. Still, as he was the only person who understood the business, he trusted in any case to make his position good, especially if he was right in imagining that old Mrs. Boxall must now be heir-at-law—a supposition which he scarcely allowed himself to doubt. Here, however, occurred the thought of Thomas. He had influence there, and that influence would be against him, for had he not insulted him? This he could not help yet. He would wait for what might turn up.

What Mr. Worboise's feelings were when first he read the paragraph in the paper I do not know, nor whether he had not an emotion of justice, and an inclination to share the property with Mrs. Boxall. But I doubt whether he very clearly recognized the existence of his friend's mother. In his mind, probably, her subjective being was thinned by age, little regard, and dependence, into a thing of no account—a shadow of the non-Elysian sort, living only in the waste places of human disregard. He certainly knew nothing of her right to any property in the possession of her son. Of one of his feelings only am I sure: he became more ambitious for his son, in whom he had a considerable amount of the pride of paternity.

Mrs. Boxall was the last to hear anything of the matter. She did not read the newspapers, and, accustomed to have sons at sea, had not even begun to look for news of the *Ningpo*.

"Ah, Miss Burton," said Mr. Sargent, "I am just in time. I thought perhaps you would not be gone yet. Will you come into the garden with me for a few minutes? I won't keep you long."

Lucy hesitated. Mr. Sargent had of late, on several occasions, been more confidential in his manner than was quite pleasant to her, because, with the keenest dislike to raise appearances, she yet could not take his attentions for granted, and tell him she was engaged to Thomas. He saw her hesitation, and hastened to remove it.

"I only want to ask you about a matter of business," he said. "I assure you I won't detain you."

Mr. Sargent knew something of Mr. Wither, who had very "good connections," and was indeed a favorite in several professional circles; and from him he had learned all about Lucy's relations, without even alluding to Lucy herself, and that her uncle and whole family had sailed in the *Ningpo.* Anxious to do what he could for her, and fearful lest, in their unprotected condition, some advantage should be taken of the two women, he had made haste to offer his services to Lucy, not without a vague feeling that he ran great risk of putting himself in the false position of a fortune-hunter by doing so, and heartily abusing himself for not having made more definite advances before there was any danger of her becoming an heiress; for although a fortune was a most desirable thing in Mr. Sargent's position, especially if he wished to marry, he was above marrying for money alone, and, in the case of Lucy, with whom he had fallen in love—just within his depth, it must be confessed—while she was as poor as himself, he was especially jealous of being unjustly supposed to be in pursuit of her prospects. Possibly the consciousness of what a help the fortune would be to him made him even more sensitive than he would otherwise have been. Still he would not omit the opportunity of being useful to the girl, trusting that his honesty would, despite of appearances, manifest itself sufficiently to be believed in by so honest a nature as Lucy Burton.

"Have you heard the sad news?" he said, as soon as they were in the garden.

"No," answered Lucy, without much concern; for she did not expect to hear anything about Thomas.

"I thought not. It is very sad. The *Ningpo* is lost."

Lucy was perplexed. She knew the name of her uncle's vessel; but for a moment she did not associate the thing. In a moment, however, something of the horror of the fact reached her. She did not cry, for her affections had no great part in anyone on board of the vessel, but she turned very pale. And not a thought of the possible interest she might have in the matter crossed her mind. She had never associated good to herself with her uncle or any of his family.

"How dreadful!" she murmured. "My poor cousins! What they must all have gone through! Are they come home?"

"They are gone home," said Mr. Sargent, significantly. "There can be but little doubt of that, I fear."

"You don't mean they're drowned?" she said, turning her white face on him, and opening her eyes wide.

"It is not absolutely certain; but there can be little doubt about it."

He did not show her the paragraph in the *Times*, though the paper was in his pocket: the particulars were too dreadful.

"Are there any other relations but your grandmother and yourself?" he asked, for Lucy remained silent.

"I don't know of any," she answered.

"Then you must come in for the property."

"Oh, no. He would never leave it to us. He didn't like me, for one thing. But that was my fault, perhaps. He was not over-kind to my mother, and so I never liked him."

And here at length she burst into tears. She wept very quietly, however, and Mr. Sargent went on.

"But you must be his heirs-at-law. Will you allow me to make inquiry — to do anything that may be necessary, for you? Don't misunderstand me," he added, pleadingly. "It is only as a friend—what I have been for a long time now, Lucy."

Lucy scarcely hesitated before she answered, with a restraint that appeared like coldness:

"Thank you, Mr. Sargent. The business cannot in any case be mine. It is my grandmother's, and I can, and will, take no hand in it."

"Will you say to your grandmother that I am at her service?"

"If it were a business matter, there is no one I would more willingly — ask to help us; but as you say it is a matter of friendship, I must refuse your kindness."

Mr. Sargent was vexed with himself, and disappointed with her. He supposed that she misinterpreted his motives. Between the two, he was driven to a sudden, unresolved action of appeal.

"Miss Burton," he said, "for God's sake, do not misunderstand me, and attribute to mercenary motives the offer I make only in the confidence that you will not do me such an injustice."

Lucy was greatly distressed. Her color went and came for a few moments, and then she spoke.

"Mr. Sargent, I am just as anxious that you should understand me; but I am in a great difficulty and have to throw myself on your generosity."

She paused again, astonished to find herself making a speech. But she did not pause long.

"I refuse your kindness," she said, "only because I am not free to lay myself under such obligation to you. Do not ask me to say more," she added, finding that he made no reply.

But if she had looked in his face, she would have seen that he understood her perfectly. Honest disappointment and manly suffering were visible enough on his countenance. But he did not grow ashy pale, as some lovers would at such an utterance. He would never have made, under any circumstances, a passionate lover, though an honest and true one; for he was one of those balanced natures which are never all in one thing at once. Hence the very moment he received a shock, was the moment in which he began to struggle for victory. Something called to him, as Una to the Red-Cross Knight when face to face with the serpent Error:

"Strangle her, else she sure will strangle thee."

Before Lucy's eyes and his met, he had mastered his countenance at last.

"I understand you, Miss Burton," he said, in a calm voice, which only trembled a little—and it was then that Lucy ventured to look at him—"and I thank you. Please to remember that if ever you need a friend, I am at your service."

Without another word, he lifted his hat and went away.

Lucy hastened home full of distress at the thought of her grandmother's grief, and thinking all the way how she could convey the news with least of a shock; but when she entered the room, she found her already in tears, and Mr. Stopper seated by her side comforting her with commonplaces.

CHAPTER XXVII
OF USEFUL ODDS AND ENDS

During all this time, when his visits to Lucy were so much interrupted by her attendance upon Mattie, Thomas had not been doing well. In fact, he had been doing gradually worse. His mother had, of course, been at home for a long time now, and Mr. Simon's visits had been resumed. But neither of these circumstances tended to draw him homeward.

Mrs. Worboise's health was so much improved by her sojourn at Folkestone, that she now meditated more energetic measures for the conversion of her son. What these measures should be, however, she could not for some time determine. At length she resolved that, as he had been a good scholar when at school—proved in her eyes by his having brought home prizes every year—she would ask him to bring his Greek Testament to her room, and help her to read through St. Paul's Epistle to the Romans with the fresh light which his scholarship would cast upon the page. It was not that she was in the least difficulty about the Apostle's meaning. She knew that as well at least as the Apostle himself; but she would invent an innocent trap to catch a soul with, and, if so it might be, put it in a safe cage, whose strong wires of exclusion should be wadded with the pleasant cotton of safety. Alas for St. Paul, his mighty soul, and his laboring speech, in the hands of two such! The very idea of such to read him, might have scared him from his epistle—if such readers there could have been in a time when the wild beasts of the amphitheatre kept the Christianity pure.

"Thomas," she said, one evening, "I want you to bring your Greek Testament, and help me out with something."

"O, mother, I can't. I have forgotten all about Greek. What is it you want to know?"

"I want you to read the Romans with me."

"Oh! really, mother, I can't. It's such bad Greek, you know."

"Thomas!" said his mother, sepulchrally, as if his hasty assertion with regard to St. Paul's scholarship had been a sin against the truth St. Paul spoke.

"Well, really, mother, you must excuse me. I can't. Why don't you ask Mr. Simon? He's an Oxford man."

To this Mrs. Worboise had no answer immediately at hand. From the way in which Thomas met her request my reader will see that he was breaking loose from her authority—whether for the better or the worse does not at this point seem doubtful, and yet perhaps it was doubtful. Still he was not prepared to brave her and his father with a confession, for such it appeared to him to be, of his attachment to Lucy.

Since he could see so little of her, he had spent almost all the time that used to be devoted to her with Molken. In consequence, he seldom reached home in anything like what he had been accustomed to consider decent time. When his mother spoke to him on the subject he shoved it aside with an "Ah! you were in bed, mother," prefacing some story, part true, part false, arranged for the occasion. So long as his father took no notice of the matter he did not much mind. He was afraid of him still; but so long as he was out of bed early enough in the morning, his father did not much care at what hour he went to it: he had had his own wild oats to sow in his time. The purity of his boy's mind and body did not trouble him much, provided that, when he came to take his position in the machine of things, he turned out a steady, respectable pinion, whose cogs did not miss, but held—the one till the other caught. He had, however, grown ambitious for him within the last few days—more of which by and by.

In the vacancy of mind occasioned by the loss of his visits to Lucy—for he had never entered heartily into any healthy pursuits in literature, art, or even amusement—Thomas had, as it were, gradually sauntered more and more into the power of Mr. Molken; and although he had vowed to himself, after his first experience, that he would, never play again, himself not being to himself a very awe-inspiring authority, he had easily broken that vow. It was not that he had any very strong inclination to play—the demon of play had not quite entered into him: it was only that whatever lord asserted dominion over Thomas, to him Thomas was ready to yield that which he claimed. Molken said, "Come along," and Thomas went along. Nor was it always to the gambling-house that he followed Molken; but although there was one most degrading species of vice from which his love to Lucy—for he loved Lucy with a real though not great love—did preserve him, there were several places to which his *friend* took him from which he could scarcely emerge as pure as he entered them. I suspect—thanks to what influence Lucy had with him, to what conscience he had left in him, to what good his mother and Mr. Simon had taught him, in a word, to the care of God over him—Mr. Molken found him rather harder to corrupt than, from his shilly-shally ways, he had expected. Above all, the love of woman, next to the love of God, is the power of God to a young man's salvation; for all is of God, everything, from first to last—nature, providence, and grace—it is all of our Father in Heaven; and what God hath joined let not man put asunder.

His gambling was a very trifle as far as money went: an affair of all but life and death as far as principle was concerned. There is nothing like the amount of in-door gambling that there used to be; but there is no great improvement in taking it to the downs and the open air, and making it librate on the muscles of horses instead of on the spinning power of a top or the turning up of cards. And whoever gambles, whether at *rouge-et-noir* or at Fly-away *versus* Staywell, will find that the laws of gambling are, like those of the universe, unalterable. The laws of gambling are discontent, confusion, and loss upon everyone who seeks to make money without giving moneys worth. It will matter little to the grumbler whether the retribution comes in this world, he thinking, like Macbeth, to "skip the life to come," or in the next. He will find that one day is with the Lord as a thousand years, and a thousand years as one day.

But for Thomas, the worst thing in the gambling, besides the bad company it led him into, was that the whole affair fell in so with his natural weakness. Gambling is the employment fitted for the man without principles and without will, for his whole being is but, as far as he is concerned, the roulette-ball of chance. The wise, on the contrary, do not believe in Fortune, yield nothing to her sway, go on their own fixed path regardless "of her that turneth as a ball," as Chaucer says. They at least will be steady, come to them what may. Thomas got gradually weaker and weaker, and, had it not been for Lucy, would soon have fallen utterly. But she, like the lady of an absent lord, still kept one fortress for him in a yielded and devastated country.

There was no newspaper taken in at Mr. Worboise's, for he always left home for his office as soon as possible. So, when Thomas reached the counting-house, he had heard nothing of the sad news about his late master and his family. But the moment he entered the place he felt that the atmosphere was clouded. Mr. Wither, whose face was pale as death, rose from the desk where he had been sitting, caught up his hat, and went out. Thomas could not help suspecting that his entrance was the cause of Mr. Wither's departure, and his thoughts went back to last night, and he wondered whether his fellow-clerks would cut him because of the company he had been in. His conscience could be more easily pricked by the apprehension of overt disapprobation than by any other goad. None of them took any particular notice of him; only a gloom as of a funeral hung about all their faces, and radiated from them so as to make the whole place look sepulchral. Mr. Stopper was sitting within the glass partition, whence he called for Mr. Worboise, who obeyed with a bad grace, as anticipating something disagreeable.

"There!" said Mr. Stopper, handing him the newspaper, and watching him as he read.

Thomas read, returned the paper, murmured something, and went back with scared face to the outer room. There a conversation arose in a low voice, as if it had been in the presence of the dead. Various questions were asked and conjectures hazarded, but nobody knew anything. Thomas's place was opposite the glass, and before he had been long seated he saw Mr. Stopper rake the key of the door of communication from a drawer, unlock the door, and with the *Times* in his hand walk into Mrs. Boxall's house, closing the door behind him. This movement was easy to understand, and set Thomas thinking. Then first the thought struck him that Lucy and her grandmother would come in for all the property. This sent a glow of pleasure through him, and he had enough ado to keep the funeral look which belonged to the occasion. Now he need not fear to tell his father the fact of his engagement— indeed, he might delay the news as long as he liked, sure that it would be welcome when it came. If his father were pleased, he did not care so much for his mother. But had he known how much she loved him, he could not have got so far away from her as he was now. If, on the other hand, he had fallen in with her way of things, she would have poured out upon him so much repressed affection that he would have known it. But till he saw as she saw, felt as she felt, and could talk as she talked, her motherhood saw an impervious barrier between her and him—a barrier she labored hard to remove, but with tools that could make no passage through an ever-closing mist.

I cannot help thinking that if he had told all now, the knowledge of his relation to Lucy would have been welcomed by his father, and would have set everything right. I cannot but believe that Mr. Worboise's mind was troubled about the property. With perfect law on his side, there was yet that against him which all his worldliness did not quite enable him to meet with coolness. But the longer the idea of the property rested upon his mind, the more, as if it had been the red-hot coin of the devil's gift, it burned and burrowed out a nest for itself, till it lay there stone-cold and immovably fixed, and not to be got rid of. Before many weeks had passed he not only knew that it was his by law, but felt that it was his by right—his own by right of possession, and the clinging of his heart-strings around it—his own because it was so good that he could not part with it. Still it was possible that something adverse might turn up, and there was no good in incurring odium until he was absolutely sure that the fortune as well as the odium would be his; therefore he was in no haste to propound the will.

But, as I have said, he began to be more ambitious for his son, and the more he thought about the property, the more he desired to increase it by the advantageous alliance which he had now no doubt he could command. This persuasion was increased by the satisfaction which his son's handsome person and pleasing manners afforded him; and a confidence of manner which had of late shown itself, chiefly, it must be confessed, from the experience of the world he had had in the company he of late frequented, had raised in his father's mind a certain regard for him which he had not felt before. Therefore he began to look about him and speculate. He had not the slightest suspicion of Thomas being in love; and, indeed, there was nothing in his conduct or appearance that could have aroused such a suspicion in his mind. Mr. Worboise believed, on the contrary, that his son was leading a rather wild life.

It may seem strange that Thomas should not by this time have sunk far deeper into the abyss of misery; but Molken had been careful in not trying to hook him while he was only nibbling; and, besides, until he happened to be able to lose something worth winning, he rather avoided running him into any scrape that might disgust him without bringing any considerable advantage to himself.

There was one adverse intelligence, of whom Mr. Worboise knew nothing, and who knew nothing of Mr. Worboise, ready to pounce upon him the moment he showed his game. This was Mr. Sargent. Smarting, not under Lucy's refusal so much as from the lingering suspicion that she had altogether misinterpreted his motives, he watched for an opportunity of proving his disinterestedness; this was his only hope; for he saw that Lucy was lost to him. He well knew that in the position of her and her grandmother, it would not be surprising if something with a forked tongue or a cloven foot should put its head out of a hole before very long, and begin to creep toward them; and therefore, as I say, he kept an indefinite but wide watch, in the hope which I have mentioned. He had no great difficulty in discovering that Mr. Worboise had been Mr. Boxall's man of business, but he had no right to communicate with him on the subject. This indeed Mr. Stopper, who had taken the place of adviser in general to Mrs. Boxall, had already done, asking him whether Mr. Boxall had left no will, to which he had received a reply only to the effect that it was early days, that there was no proof of his death, and that he was prepared to give what evidence he possessed at the proper time—an answer Mrs. Boxall naturally enough, with her fiery disposition, considered less than courteous. Of this

Mr. Sargent of course was not aware, but, as the only thing he could do at present, he entered a *caveat* in the Court of Probate.

Mr. Stopper did his best for the business in the hope of one day having not only the entire management as now, but an unquestionable as unquestioned right to the same. If he ever thought of anything further since he had now a free entrance to Mrs. Boxall's region, he could not think an inch in that direction without encountering the idea of Thomas.

It was very disagreeable to Thomas that Mr. Stopper, whom he detested, should have this free admission to what he had been accustomed to regard as his *peculium*. He felt as if the place were defiled by his presence, and to sit as he had sometimes to sit, knowing that Mr. Stopper was overhead, was absolutely hateful. But, as I shall have to set forth in the next chapter, Lucy was not at home; and that mitigated the matter very considerably. For the rest, Mr. Stopper was on the whole more civil to Thomas than he had hitherto been, and appeared even to put a little more confidence in him than formerly. The fact was, that the insecurity of his position made him conscious of vulnerability, and he wished to be friendly on all sides, with a vague general feeling of strengthening his outworks.

Mr. Wither never opened his mouth to Thomas upon any occasion or necessity, and from several symptoms it appeared that his grief, or rather perhaps the antidotes to it, were dragging him down hill.

Amy Worboise was not at home. The mother had seen symptoms; and much as she valued Mr. Simon's ghostly ministrations, the old Adam in her rebelled too strongly against having a curate for her son-in-law. So Amy disappeared for a season, upon a convenient invitation. But if she had been at home, she could have influenced events in nothing; for, as often happens in families, there was no real communication between mother and sister.

CHAPTER XXVIII
MATTIE IN THE COUNTRY

I now return to resume the regular thread of my story.

I do not know if my reader is half as much interested in Mattie as I am. I doubt it very much. He will, most probably, like Poppie better. But big-headed, strange, and conceited as Mattie was, she was altogether a higher being than Poppie. She thought; Poppie only received impressions. If she had more serious faults than Poppie, they were faults that belonged to a more advanced stage of growth; diseased, my reader may say, but diseased with a disease that fell in with, almost belonged to, the untimely development. All Poppie's thoughts, to speak roughly, came from without; all Mattie's from within. To complete Mattie, she had to go back a little, and learn to receive impressions too; to complete Poppie; she had to work upon the impressions she received, and, so to speak, generate thoughts of her own. Mattie led the life of a human being; Poppie of a human animal. Mattie lived; Poppie was there. Poppie was the type of most people; Mattie of the elect.

Lucy did not intend, in the sad circumstances in which she now was, to say a word to her grandmother about Mrs. Morgenstern's proposal. But it was brought about very naturally. As she entered the court she met Mattie. The child had been once more to visit Mr. Spelt, but had found the little nest so oppressive that she had begged to be put down again, that she might go to her own room. Mr. Spelt was leaning over his door and his crossed legs, for he could not stand up, looking anxiously after her; and the child's face was so pale and sad, and she held her little hand so pitifully to her big head, that Lucy could not help feeling that the first necessity among her duties was to get Mattie away.

After the fresh burst of her grandmother's grief at sight of her was over, after Mr. Stopper had gone back to the counting-house, and she had fallen into a silent rocking to and fro, Lucy ventured to speak.

"They're gone home, dear grannie," she said.

"And I shan't stay long behind them, my dear," grannie moaned.

"That's some comfort, isn't it, grannie?" said Lucy, for her own heart was heavy, not for the dead, but for the living; heavy for her own troubles, heavy for Thomas, about whom she felt very despondent, almost despairing.

"Ah! you young people would be glad enough to have the old ones out of the way," returned Mrs. Boxall, in the petulance of grief. "Have patience, Lucy, have patience, child; it won't be long, and then you can do as you like."

"Oh, grannie, grannie!" cried Lucy, bursting into tears. "I do everything I like now. I only wanted to comfort you," she sobbed. "I thought you would like to go too. *I* wish I was dead."

"*You*, child!" exclaimed Mrs. Boxall; "why should you wish you was dead? You don't know enough of life to wish for death." Then, as Lucy went on sobbing, her tone changed—for she began to be concerned at her distress. "What *is* the matter with my darling?" she said. "Are you ill, Lucy?"

Then Lucy went to her and kissed her, and knelt down, and laid her head in the old woman's lap. And her grannie stroked her hair, and spoke to her as if she had been one of her own babies, and, in seeking to comfort her, forgot her own troubles for the moment.

"You've been doing too much for other people, Lucy," she said. "We must think of you now. You must go to the sea-side for awhile. You shan't go about giving lessons any more, my lamb. There is no need for that any more, for they say all the money will be ours now."

And the old woman wept again at the thought of the source of their coming prosperity.

"I should like to go to the country very much, if you would go too, grannie."

"No, no, child, I don't want to go. I don't want any doing good to."

"But I don't like to leave you, grannie," objected Lucy.

"Never mind me, my dear. I shall be better alone for awhile. And I dare say there will be some business to attend to."

And so they went on talking, till Lucy told her all about Mrs. Morgenstern's plan, and how ill poor Mattie looked, and that she would be glad to go away for a little while herself. Mrs. Boxall would not consent to go, but she even urged Lucy to accept the proposed arrangement, and proceeded at once to inquire into her wardrobe, and talk about mourning.

Two days after, Lucy and Mattie met Mrs. Morgenstern and Miriam at the London Bridge railway station. Mattie looked quite dazed, almost stupid, with the noise and bustle; but when they were once in motion, she heaved a deep sigh, and looked comforted. She said nothing, however, for some time, and her countenance revealed no surprise. Whatever was out of the usual way always oppressed Mattie—not excited her; and, therefore, the more surprising anything was, the less did it occasion any outward shape of surprise. But as they flashed into the first tunnel, Lucy saw her start and shudder ere they vanished from each other in the darkness. She put out her hand and took hold of the child's. It was cold and trembling; but as she held it gently and warmly in her own, it grew quite still. By the time the light began to grow again, her face was peaceful, and when they emerged in the cutting beyond, she was calm enough to speak the thought that had come to her in the dark. With another sigh—

"I knew the country wasn't nice," she said.

"But you don't know what the country is yet," answered Lucy.

"I know quite enough of it," returned Mattie. "I like London best. I wish I could see some shops."

Lucy did not proceed to argue the matter with her. She did not tell her how unfair she was to judge the country by what lay between her and it. As well might she have argued with Thomas that the bitterness of the repentance from which he shrank was not the religion to which she wanted to lead him; that religion itself was to him inconceivable; and could but be known when he was in it. She had tried this plan with him in their last interview before she left. She had herself, under the earnest teaching of Mr. Fuller, and in the illumination of that Spirit for which she prayed, learned many a spiritual lesson, had sought eagerly, and therefore gained rapidly. For hers was one of the good soils, well prepared beforehand for the seed of the redeeming truth of God's love, and the Sonship of Christ, and his present power in the human soul. And she had tried, I say, to make Thomas believe in the blessedness of the man whoso iniquities are pardoned, whose sins are covered, to whom the Lord imputeth not his transgressions; but Thomas had replied only with some of the stock phrases of assent. A nature such as his could not think of law and obedience save as restraint. While he would be glad enough to have the weight of conscious wrong-doing lifted off him, he could not see that in yielding his own way and taking God's lay the only *freedom* of which the human being, made in the image of God, is capable.

Presently Mattie found another argument upon her side, that is, the town-side of the question. She had been sitting for half an hour watching the breath of the snorting engine, as it rushed out for a stormy flight over the meek fields, faltered, lingered, faded, melted, was gone.

"I told you so," said Mattie: "nothing lasts in the country."

"What are you looking at now?" asked Lucy, bending forward to see.

"Those white clouds," answered Mattie. "I've been expecting them to do something for ever so long. And they never do anything, though they begin in such a hurry. The green gets the better of them somehow. They melt away into it, and are all gone."

"But they do the grass some good, I dare say," returned Lucy—"in hot weather like this especially."

"Well, that's not what they set out for, anyhow," said Mattie. "They look always as if they were just going to take grand shapes, and make themselves up into an army, and go out and conquer the world."

"And then," suggested Lucy, yielding to the fancy of the child, "they think better of it, and give themselves up, and die into the world to do it good, instead of trampling it under their feet and hurting it."

"But how do they come to change their minds so soon?" asked Mattie, beginning to smile; for this was the sort of intellectual duel in which her little soul delighted.

"Oh, I don't think they do change their minds. I don't think they ever meant to trample down the world. That was your notion, you know, Mattie."

"Well, what do you think they set out for? Why do they rush out so fiercely all at once?"

"I will tell you what I think," answered Lucy, without perceiving more than the faintest glimmering of the human reality of what she said, "I think they rush out of the hot place in which they are got ready to do the fields good, in so much pain, that they toss themselves about in strange ways, and people think they are fierce and angry when they are only suffering—shot out into the air from a boiling kettle, you know, Mattie."

"Ah! yes; I see," answered Mattie. "That's it, is it? Yes, I dare say. Out of a kettle?"

Miriam had drawn near, and was listening, but she could make little of all this, for her hour was not yet come to ask, or to understand such questions.

"Yes, that great round thing in front of us is just a great kettle," said Lucy.

"Well, I will look at it when we get out. I thought there wasn't much in the country. I suppose we shall get out again, though. This isn't all the country, is it?"

Before they reached Hastings, Mattie was fast asleep. It was the evening. She scarcely woke when they stopped for the last time. Lucy carried her from the carriage to a cab, and when they arrived at the lodgings where they were expected, made all haste to get her to bed and asleep.

But she woke the earlier in the morning, and the first thing she was aware of was the crowing of a very clear-throated cock, such a cock as Henry Vaughan must have listened to in the morning of the day when he wrote

"Father of lights! what sunnie seed,
What glance of day hast thou confined
Into this bird? To all the breed
This busie Ray thou hast assigned;
Their magnetisme works all night,
And dreams of Paradise and light."

She could not collect her thoughts for some time. She was aware that a change had taken place, but what was it? Was she somebody else? What did they use to call her? Then she remembered Mr. Spelt's shop, and knew that she was Mattie Kitely. What then had happened to her? Something certainly had happened, else how could the cock crow like that? She was now aware that her eyes were open, but she did not know that Lucy was in another bed in the same room watching her—whence afterward, when she put Mattie's words and actions together, she was able to give this interpretation of her thoughts. The room was so different from anything she had been used to, that she could not understand it. She crept out of bed and went to the window. There was no blind to it, only curtains drawn close in front.

Now my reader must remember that when Mattie went to the window of her own room at home she saw into Guild Court. The house in which they now were was half way up one of the hills on the sides of which great part of Hastings is built. The sun was not shining upon the window at this hour of the morning, and therefore did not obstruct the view. Hence when Mattie went between the curtains she saw nothing but that loveliest of English seas—the Hastings sea—lying away out into the sky, or rather, as it appeared to her unaccustomed gaze, piled up like a hill against the sky, which domed it over, vast and blue, and triumphant in sunlight—just a few white sails below and a few white clouds above, to show how blue the sea and sky were in this glory of an autumn morning. She saw nothing of the earth on which she was upheld; only the sea and the sky. She started back with a feeling that she could never describe; there was terror, and loneliness, and helplessness in it. She turned and flew to her bed, but instead of getting into it, fell down on her knees by the side of it, clutched the bed-clothes, and sobbed and wept aloud. Lucy was by her side in a moment, took her in her arms, carried her into her own bed, and comforted her in her bosom.

Mattie had been all her life sitting in the camera-obscura of her own microcosm, watching the shadows that went and came, and now first she looked up and out upon the world beyond and above her. All her doings had gone on in the world of her own imaginings; and although that big brain of hers contained—no, I cannot say *contained*, but what else am I to say?—a being greater than all that is seen, heard, or handled, yet the outward show of divine imagination which now met her eyes might well overpower that world within her. I fancy that, like the blind to whom sight is given, she did not at first recognize the difference between herself and it, but felt as if it was all inside her and she did not know what to do with it. She would not have cried at the sight of a rose, as Poppie did. I doubt whether Mattie's was altogether such a refined nature as Poppie's—to begin with: she would have rather patronized the rose-tree, and looked down upon it as a presuming and rather unpleasant thing because it bore dying children; and she needed, some time or other, and that was now, just such a sight as this to take the conceit out of her. Less of a vision of the eternal would not have been sufficient. Was it worth while? Yes. The whole show of the universe was well spent to take an atom of the self out of a child. God is at much trouble with us, but he never weighs material expense against spiritual gain to one of his creatures. The whole universe existed for Mattie. There is more than that that the Father has not spared. And no human fault, the smallest, is overcome, save by the bringing in of true, grand things. A sense of the infinite and the near, the far yet impending, rebuked the conceit of Mattie to the very core, and without her knowing why or how. She clung to Lucy as a child would cling, and as, all through her illness, she had never clung before.

"What is the matter with you, Mattie, dear?" asked Lucy, but asked in vain. Mattie only clung to her the closer, and began a fresh utterance of sobs. Lucy therefore held her peace for some time and waited. And in the silence of that waiting she became aware that a lark was singing somewhere out in the great blue vault.

"Listen to the lark singing so sweetly," she said at length. And Mattie moved her head enough to show that she would listen, and lay still a long while listening. At length she said, with a sob:

"What is a lark? I never saw one, Miss Burton."

"A bird like a sparrow. You know what a sparrow is, don't you, dear?"

"Yes. I have seen sparrows often in the court. They pick up dirt."

"Well, a lark is like a sparrow; only it doesn't pick up dirt, and sings as you hear it. And it flies so far up into the sky that you can't see it—you can only hear the song it scatters down upon the earth."

"Oh, how dreadful!" said Mattie, burying her head again as if she would shut out hearing and sight and all.

"What is it that is dreadful? I don't understand you, Mattie."

"To fly up into that awful place up there. Shall we have to do that when we die?"

"It is not an awful place, dear. God is there, you know."

"But I am frightened. And if God is up there, I shall be frightened at him too. It is so dreadful! I used to think that God could see me when I was in London. But how he is to see me in this great place, with so many things about, cocks and larks, and all, I can't think. I'm so little! I'm hardly worth taking care of."

"But you remember, Mattie, what Somebody says—that God takes care of every sparrow."

"Yes, but that's the sparrows, and they're in the town, you know," said Mattie, with an access of her old fantastic perversity, flying for succor, as it always does, to false logic.

Lucy saw that it was time to stop. The child's fear was gone for the present, or she could not have talked such nonsense. It was just as good, however, as the logic of most of those who worship the letter and call it the word.

"Why don't you speak, Miss Burton?" asked Mattie at length, no doubt conscience-stricken by her silence.

"Because you are talking nonsense now, Mattie."

"I thought that was it. But why should that make you not speak? for I need the more to hear sense."

"No, Mattie. Mr. Fuller says that when people begin to talk falsely, it is better to be quite silent, and let them say what they please, till the sound of their own nonsense makes them ashamed."

"As it did me, Miss Burton, as soon as you wouldn't speak any more."

"He says it does no good to contradict them then, for they are not only unworthy to hear the truth—that's not it—if they would hear it—but they are not fit to hear it. They are not in a mood to get any good from it; for they are holding the door open for the devil to come in, and truth can't get in at the same door with the devil."

"Oh, how dreadful! To think of me talking like Syne!" said Mattie. "I won't do it again, Miss Burton. Do tell me what Somebody said about God and the sparrows. Didn't he say something about counting their feathers? I think I remember Mr. Spelt reading that to me one night."

"He said something about counting your hairs, Mattie."

"*Mine?*"

"Well, he said it to all the people that would listen to him. I dare say there were some that could not believe it because they did not care to be told it."

"That's me, Miss Burton. But I won't do it again. Well—what more?"

"Only this, Mattie: that if God knows how many hairs you have got on your head—"

"My big head," interrupted Mattie. "Well?"

"Yes, on your big head—if God knows that, you can't think you're too small for him to look after you."

"I will try not to be frightened at the big sky any more, dear Miss Burton; I will try."

In a few minutes she was fast asleep again.

Lucy's heart was none the less trustful that she had tried to increase Mattie's faith. He who cared for the sparrows would surely hear her cry for Thomas, nay, would surely look after Thomas himself. The father did not forget the prodigal son all the time that he was away; did not think of him only when he came back again, worn and sorrowful. In teaching Mattie she had taught herself. She had been awake long before her, turning over and over her troubled thoughts till they were all in a raveled sleeve of care. Now she too fell fast asleep in her hope, and when she awoke, her thoughts were all knit up again in an even resolve to go on and do her duty, casting her care upon Him that cared for her.

And now Mattie's childhood commenced. She had had none as yet. Her disputatiousness began to vanish. She could not indulge it in the presence of the great sky, which grew upon her till she felt, as many children and some conscience-stricken men have felt—that it was the great eye of God looking at her; and although this feeling was chiefly associated with awe at first, she soon began to love the sky, and to be sorry and oppressed upon cloudy days when she could no longer look up into it.

The next day they went down to the beach, in a quiet place, among great stones, under the east cliff. Lucy sat down on one of them, and began to read a book Mr. Fuller had lent her. Miriam was at a little distance, picking up shells, and Mattie on another stone nearer the sea. The tide was rising. Suddenly Mattie came scrambling in great haste over all that lay between her and Lucy. Her face was pale, scared, and eager.

"I'm so frightened again!" she said; "and I can't help it. The sea! What does it mean?"

"What do you mean, Mattie?" returned Lucy, smiling.

"Well, it's roaring at me, and coming nearer and nearer, as if it wanted to swallow me up. I don't like it."

"You must not be afraid of it. God made it, you know."

"Why does he let it roar at me, then?"

"I don't know. Perhaps to teach you not to be afraid."

Mattie said no more, stood a little while by Lucy, and then scrambled back to her former place.

The next day, they managed with some difficulty to get up on the East Hill; Mattie was very easily worn out, especially with climbing. She gazed at the sea below her, the sky over her head, the smooth grass under her feet, and gave one of her great sighs. Then she looked troubled.

"I feel as if I hadn't any clothes on," she said.

"How is that, Mattie?"

"Well, I don't know. I feel as if I couldn't stand steady—as if I hadn't anything to keep me up. In London, you know, the houses were always beside to hold a body up, and keep them steady. But here, if it weren't for Somebody, I should be so frightened for falling down—I don't know where!"

Lucy smiled. She did not see then how exactly the child symbolized those who think they have faith in God, and yet when one of the swaddling bands of system or dogma to which they have been accustomed is removed, or even only slackened, immediately feel as if there were no God, as if the earth under their feet were a cloud, and the sky over them a color, and nothing to trust in anywhere. They rest in their swaddling bands, not in God. The loosening of these is God's gift to them that they may grow. But first they are much afraid.

Still Mattie looked contemptuously on the flowers. Wandering along the cliff, they came to a patch that was full of daisies. Miriam's familiarity with the gorgeous productions of green-house and hot-house had not injured her capacity for enjoying these peasants of flowers. She rushed among them with a cry of pleasure, and began gathering them eagerly. Mattie stood by with a look of condescending contempt upon her pale face.

"Wouldn't you like to gather some daisies too, Mattie?" suggested Lucy.

"Where's the use?" said Mattie. "The poor things'll be withered in no time. It's almost a shame to gather them, I do think."

"Well, you needn't gather them if you don't want to have them," returned Lucy. "But I wonder you don't like them, they are so pretty."

"But they don't last. I don't like things that die. I had a little talk with Mr. Fuller about that."

Now Mr. Fuller had told Lucy what the child had said, and this had resulted in a good deal of talk. Mr. Fuller was a great lover of Wordsworth, and the book Lucy was now reading, the one he had lent her, was Wordsworth's Poems. She had not found what she now answered, either in Wordsworth's poems or in Mr. Fuller's conversation, but it came from them both, mingling with her love to God, and her knowledge of the Saviour's words, with the question of the child to set her mind working with them all at once. She thought for a moment, and then said:

"Listen, Mattie. You don't dislike to hear me talk, do you?"

"No, indeed," answered Mattie.

"You like the words I say to you, then?"

"Yes, indeed," said Mattie, wondering what would come next.

"But my words die as soon as they are out of my mouth."

Mattie began to see a glimmering of something coming, and held her peace and listened. Lucy went on.

"Well, the flowers are some of God's words, and they last longer than mine."

"But I understand your words. I know what you want to say to me. And I don't know the meaning of *them*."

"That's because you haven't looked at them long enough. You must suppose them words in God's book, and try to read them and understand them."

"I will try," said Mattie, and walked soberly toward Miriam.

But she did not begin to gather the daisies as Miriam was doing. She lay down in the grass just as Chaucer tells us he used to do in the mornings of May for the same purpose—to look at the daisy—"leaning on my elbow and my side"; and thus she continued for some time. Then she rose and came slowly back to Lucy.

"I can't tell what they mean," she said. "I have been trying very hard, too."

"I don't know whether I understand them or not, myself. But I fancy we get some good from what God shows us even when we don't understand it much."

"They are such little things!" said Mattie. "I can hardly fancy them worth making."

"God thinks them worth making, though, or he would not make them. He wouldn't do anything that he did not care about doing. There's the lark again. Listen to him, how glad he is. He is so happy that he can't bear it without singing. If he couldn't sing it would break his heart, I fancy. Do you think God would have made his heart so glad if he did not care for his gladness, or given him such a song to sing—for he must have made the song and taught it to the lark—the song is just the lark's heart coming out in sounds—would he have made all the lark if he did not care for it? And he would not have made the daisies so pretty if their prettiness was not worth something in his eyes. And if God cares for them, surely it is worth our while to care for them too."

Mattie listened very earnestly, went back to the daisies, and lay down again beside a group of them. Miriam kept running about from one spot to another, gathering them. What Mattie said, or what Miriam replied, I do not know, but in a little while Mattie came to Lucy with a red face—a rare show in her.

"I don't like Miss Miriam," she said. "She's not nice at all."

"Why, what's the matter?" asked Lucy, in some surprise, for the children had got on very well together as yet. "What has she been doing?"

"She doesn't care a bit for Somebody. I don't like her."

"But Somebody likes her."

To this Mattie returned no answer, but stood thoughtful. The blood withdrew from her face to its fountain, and she went back to the daisies once more.

The following day she began to gather flowers as other children do, even to search for them as for hidden treasures. And if she did not learn their meaning with her understanding, she must have learned it with her heart, for she would gaze at some of them in a way that showed plainly enough that she felt their beauty; and in the beauty, the individual loveliness of such things, lies the dim lesson with which they faintly tincture our being. No man can be quite the same he was after having *loved* a new flower.

Thus, by degrees, Mattie's thought and feeling were drawn outward. Her health improved. Body and mind reacted on each other. She grew younger and humbler. Every day her eyes were opened to some fresh beauty on the earth, some new shadowing of the sea, some passing loveliness in the heavens. She had hitherto refused the world as a thing she had not proved; now she began to find herself at home in it, that is, to find that it was not a strange world to which she had come, but a home; not, indeed, the innermost, sacredest room of the house where the Father sat, but still a home, full of his presence, his thoughts, his designs. Is it any wonder that a child should prosper better in such a world than in a catacomb filled with the coffined remains of thinking men? I mean her father's book-shop. Here, God was ever before her in the living forms of his thought, a power and a blessing. Every wind that blew was his breath, and the type of his inner breathing upon the human soul. Every morning was filled with his light, and the type of the growing of that light which lighteth every man that cometh into the world. And there are no natural types that do not dimly work their own spiritual reality upon the open heart of a human being.

Before she left Hastings, Mattie was almost a child.

CHAPTER XXIX
POPPIE IN TOWN

Between Mr. Spelt's roost and the house called No. 1 of Guild Court there stood a narrow house, as tall as the rest, which showed by the several bell-pulls, ranged along the side of the door, that it was occupied by different households. Mr. Spelt had for some time had his eye upon it, in the hope of a vacancy occurring in its top chambers, occupying which he would be nearer his work, and have a more convenient home in case he should some day succeed in taming and capturing Poppie. Things had been going well in every way with the little tailor. He had had a good many more private customers for the last few months, began in consequence to look down from a growing hight upon slop-work, though he was too prudent to drop it all at once, and had three or four pounds in the post-office savings-bank. Likewise his fishing had prospered. Poppie came for her sweets as regularly as a robin for his crumbs in winter. Spelt, however, did not now confine his bait to sweets; a fresh roll, a currant bun, sometimes—when his longing for his daughter had been especially strong the night before, even a Bath bun— would hang suspended by a string from the aerial threshold, so that Poppie could easily reach it, and yet it should be under the protection of the tailor from chance marauders. And every morning as she took it, she sent a sweet smile of thanks to the upper regions whence came her aid. Though not very capable of conversation, she would occasionally answer a few questions about facts—as, for instance, where she had slept the last night, to which the answer would commonly be, "Mother Flanaghan's;" but once, to the tailor's no small discomposure, was "The Jug." She did not seem to know exactly, however, how it was that she got incarcerated: there had been a crowd, and somebody had prigged something, and there was a scurry and a running, and she scudded as usual, and got took up. Mr. Spelt was more anxious than ever to take her home after this. But sometimes, the moment he began to talk to her she would run away, without the smallest appearance of rudeness, only of inexplicable oddity; and Mr. Spelt thought sometimes that he was not a single step nearer to the desired result than when he first baited his hook. He regarded it as a good omen, however, when, by the death of an old woman and the removal of her daughter, the topmost floor of the house, consisting of two small rooms, became vacant; and he secured them at a weekly rental quite within the reach of his improved means. He did not imagine how soon he would be able to put them to the use he most desired.

One evening, just as the light was fading and he proceeded to light a candle to enable him to go on with his work, he heard the patter of her bare feet on the slabs, for his ear was very keen for this most pleasant of sounds, and looking down, saw the child coming toward him, holding the bottom of her ragged frock up to her head. He had scarcely time to be alarmed before she stopped at the foot of his shop, looked up pale as death, with a dark streak of blood running through the paleness, and burst into a wail. The little man was down in a moment, but before his feet reached the ground Poppie had fallen upon it in a faint. He lifted the child in his arms with a strange mixture of pity and horror in his big heart, and sped up the three stairs to his own dwelling. There he laid her on his bed, struck a light, and proceeded to examine her. He found a large and deep cut in her head, from which the blood was still flowing. He rushed down again, and fortunately found Dolman on the point of leaving. Him he sent for the doctor, and returned like an arrow to his treasure. Having done all he could, with the aid of his best Sunday shirt, to stop the bleeding, he waited impatiently for the doctor's arrival, which seemed long delayed. Before he came the child began to revive; and, taught by the motion of her lips, he got some water and held to them. Poppie drank and opened her eyes. When she saw who was bending over her, the faintest ghost of a smile glimmered about her mouth, and she closed her eyes again, murmuring something about Mother Flanaghan.

As far as he could gather from piecing together what the child said afterward, Mr. Spelt came to the conclusion that Mrs. Flanaghan had come home a little the worse for "cream of the valley," and wanted more. Poppie happened to be alone in her room when she came, for we have seen that she sometimes forgot to lock the door, if, indeed, there was a lock on it. She had nothing to care for, however, but her gin-bottle; and that she thought she hid safely enough. Whether she had left it empty or not, I do not know, but she found it empty when she neither desired nor expected to find it so; and coming to the hasty and stupid conclusion that poor Poppie was the thief—just as an ill-trained child expends the rage of a hurt upon the first person within his reach—she broke the vile vessel upon Poppie's head with the result we have seen. But the child had forgotten everything between that and her waking upon Mr. Spelt's bed.

The doctor came and dressed her wound, and gave directions for her treatment.

And now Mr. Spelt was in the seventh heaven of delight—he had a little woman of his own to take care of. He was thirty-nine years of age; and now, for the first time in his life, saw a prospect of happiness opening before him. No—once before, when he led the splendid Mrs. Spelt home from church, he had looked into a rosy future; but the next morning the prospect closed, and had never opened again till now. He did not lie down all that night, but hovered about her bed, as if she had been a creature that might any moment spread out great wings and fly away from him forever. Sometimes he had to soothe her with kind words, for she wandered a good deal, and would occasionally start up with wild looks, as if to fly once more from Mother Flanaghan with the gin-bottle bludgeon uplifted in her hand; then the sound of Mr. Spelt's voice would instantly soothe her, and she would lie down again and sleep. But she scarcely spoke; for at no time was Poppie given to much speech.

When the light came, he hurried down-stairs to his shop, got his work and all his implements out, carried them up, and sat with them on the floor where he could see Poppie's face. There he worked away busily at a pair of cords for a groom, every now and then lifting his eyes from his seam to look down into the court, and finding them always met by the floor. Then his look would go up to the bed, seeking Poppie's pale face. He found he could not get on so fast as usual. Still he made progress; and it was a comfort to think that by working thus early he was saving time for nursing his little white Poppie.

When at length she woke, she seemed a little better; but she soon grew more feverish, and soon he found that he must constantly watch her, for she was ready to spring out of bed any moment. The father-heart grew dreadfully anxious before the doctor came; and all that day and the next he got very little work done, for the poor child was really in danger. Indeed it was more than a week before he began to feel a little easy about her; and ten days yet passed before she was at all able to leave her bed.

And herein lay the greatest blessing both for Spelt and Poppie. I doubt if anything else could have given him a reasonable chance, as we say, of taming the wild animal. Her illness compelled her into such a continuance of dependent association with him, that the idea of him had time to grow into her heart; while all her scudding propensities, which prevented her from making a quiet and thorough acquaintance with anybody, were not merely thwarted, but utterly gone, while she remained weak. The humanity of the child had therefore an opportunity of developing itself; obstructions removed, the well of love belonging to her nature began to pulse and to flow, and she was, as it were, compelled to love Mr. Spelt; so that, by the time old impulses returned with returning health, he had a chance against them.

CHAPTER XXX
MR. FULLER IN HIS CHURCH

Mr. Fuller's main bent of practical thought was how to make his position in the church as far as possible from a sinecure. If the church was a reality at all, if it represented a vital body, every portion of it ought to be instinct with life. Yet here was one of its cells, to speak physiologically, all but inactive—a huge building of no use all the week, and on Sundays filled with organ sounds, a few responses from a sprinkling of most indifferent worshipers, and his own voice reading prayers and crying "with sick assay" sometimes—to move those few to be better men and women than they were. Now, so far it was a center of life, and as such well worthy of any amount of outlay of mere money. But even money itself is a holy thing; and from the money point alone, low as that is, it might well be argued that this church was making no adequate return for the amount expended upon it. Not that one thought of honest comfort to a human soul is to be measured against millions of expense; but that what the money did might well be measured against what the money might do. To the commercial mind such a church suggests immense futility, a judgment correct in so far as it falls short of its possibilities. To tell the truth, and a good truth it is to tell, Mr. Fuller was ashamed of St. Amos's, and was thinking day and night how to retrieve the character of his church.

And he reasoned thus with himself, in the way mostly of question and answer:

"What is a Sunday?" he asked, answering himself—"A quiet hollow scooped out of the windy hill of the week." "Must a man then go for six days shelterless ere he comes to the repose of the seventh? Are there to be no great rocks to shadow him between?—no hiding-places from the wind to let him take breath and heart for the next struggle? And if there ought to be, where are they to be found if not in our churches?—scattered like little hollows of sacred silence scooped out of the roar and bustle of our cities, dumb to the questions—What shall we eat? what shall we drink? and wherewithal shall we be clothed?—but, alas! equally dumb to the question—Where shall I find rest, for I am weary and heavy-laden? These churches stand absolute caverns of silence amid the thunder of the busy city—with a silence which does not remind men of the eternal silence of truth, but of the carelessness of heart wherewith men regard that silence. Their work is nowhere till Sunday comes, and nowhere after that till the next Sunday or the next saint's day. How is this? Why should they not lift up the voice of silence against the tumult of care? against the dissonance of Comus and his crew? How is it that they do not—standing with their glittering, silent cocks and their golden, unopening keys high uplifted in sunny air? Why is it that their cocks do not crow, and their keys do not open? Because their cocks are busy about how the wind blows, and their keys do not fit their own doors. They may be caverns of peace, but they are caverns without entrance—sealed fountains—a mockery of the thirst and confusion of men." "But men do not want entrance. What is the use of opening the doors of our churches so long as men do not care to go in? Times are changed now." "But does not the very word Revelation imply a something coming from heaven—not certainly before men were ready for it, for God cannot be precipitate—but before they had begun to pray for it?" Mr. Fuller remembered how his own father used always to compel his children to eat one mouthful of any dish he heard them say at table that they did not like—whereupon they generally chose to go on with it. "But they won't come in." "How can you tell till you try, till you fulfill the part of the *minister* (good old beautiful Christian word), and be 'the life o' the building?'" "Presumption! Are not the prayers everything?" "At least not till you get people to pray them." "You make too much of the priest." "Leave him for God, and the true priest has all the seal of his priesthood that he wants." At least so thought Mr. Fuller. "What is the priest?" he asked, going on with the same catechism. "Just a man to be among men what the Sunday is among the work-days of the week—a man to remind you that there is a life within this life, or beyond and about it, if you like that mode better—for extremes meet in the truest figures—that care is not of God, that faith and confidence are truer, simpler, more of common sense than balances at bankers' or preference shares. He is a protest against the money-heaping tendencies of men, against the desire of rank or estimation or any kind of social distinction. With him all men are equal, as in the Church all have equal rights, and rank ceases on the threshold of the same, overpowered by the presence of the Son of Mary, who was married to a carpenter—overpowered by the presence of the God of the whole earth, who wrote the music for the great organ of the spheres, after he had created them to play the same." Such was the calling of the clergyman, as Mr. Fuller saw it. Rather a lofty one, and simply a true one. If the clergyman cannot rouse men to seek his God and their God, if he can only rest in his office, which becomes false the moment he rests in it, being itself for a higher end; if he has no message from the infinite to quicken the thoughts that cleave to the dust, the sooner he takes to grave-digging or any other honest labor, the sooner will he get into the kingdom of heaven, and the higher will he stand in it. But now came the question—from the confluence of all these considerations, "Why should the church be for Sundays only? And of all places in the world, what place wanted a week-day reminder of truth, of honesty, of the kingdom of heaven, more than London? Why should the churches be closed all the week, to the exclusion of the passers-by, and open on the Sunday to the weariness of those who entered? Might there not be too much of a good thing on the Sunday, and too little of it on a week-day?" Again Mr. Fuller said to himself, "What is a parson?" and once more he answered himself, that he was a man to keep the windows of heaven clean, that its light might shine through upon men below. What use, then, once more, could he make of the church of St. Amos?

And again, why should the use of any church be limited to the Sunday? Men needed religious help a great deal more on the week-day than on the Sunday. On the Sunday, surrounded by his family, his flowers, his tame animals, his friends, a man necessarily, to say the least of it, thinks less of making great gains, is more inclined to the family view of things generally; whereas, upon the week-day, he is in the midst of the struggle and fight; it is catch who can, then, through all the holes and corners, highways and lanes of the busy city: what would it not be then if he could strike a five minutes'—yea, even a one minute's—silence into the heart of the uproar? if he could entice one vessel to sail from the troubled sea of the streets, shops, counting-houses, into the quiet haven of the church, the doors of whose harbor stood ever open? There the wind of the world would be quiet behind them. His heart swelled within him as he thought of sitting there keeping open door of refuge for the storm-tossed, the noise-deafened, the crushed, the hopeless. He would not trouble them with many words. There should be no long prayers. "But," thought he, "as often as one came in, I would read the collect for the day; I would soothe him with comfort out of Handel or Mendelssohn, I would speak words of healing for the space of three minutes. I would sit at the receipt of such custom. I would fish for men—not to make churchmen of them—not to get them under my thumb"—(for Mr.

Fuller used such homely phrases sometimes that certain fledgling divines feared he was vulgar)—"not to get them under the Church's thumb, but to get them out of the hold of the devil, to lead them into the presence of Him who is the Truth, and so can make them free."

Therefore he said to himself that his church, instead of accumulating a weary length of service on one day, should be open every day, and that there he would be ready for any soul upon which a flask of silence had burst through the clouds that ever rise from the city life and envelop those that have their walk therein.

It was not long before his cogitations came to the point of action; for with men of Mr. Fuller's kind all their meditations have action for their result: he opened his church—set the door to the wall, and got a youth to whom he had been of service, and who was an enthusiast in music, to play about one o'clock, when those who dined in the city began to go in search of their food, such music as might possibly waken the desire to see what was going on in the church. For he said to himself that the bell was of no use now, for no one would heed it; but that the organ might fulfill the spirit of the direction that "the curate that ministereth in every parish church shall say the morning and evening prayer—where he ministereth, and shall cause a bell to be tolled thereunto a convenient time before he begins, that the people may come to hear God's word and to pray with him."

Over the crowded street, over the roar of omnibuses, carts, wagons, cabs, and all kinds of noises, rose the ordered sounds of consort. Day after day, day after day, arose the sounds of hope and prayer; and not a soul in the streets around took notice of the same. Why should they? The clergy had lost their hold of them. They believed that the clergy were given to gain and pleasure just as much as they were themselves. Those even of the passers-by who were ready to acknowledge worth where they saw it, were yet not ready to acknowledge the probability of finding it in the priesthood; for their experience, and possibly some of their prejudices, were against it. They were wrong; but who was to blame for it? The clergy of the eighteenth century, because so many of them were neither Christians nor gentlemen; and the clergy of the present century, because so many of them are nothing but gentlemen—men ignorant of life, ignorant of human needs, ignorant of human temptations, yea, ignorant of human aspirations; because in the city pulpits their voice is not uplifted against city vices—against speculation, against falsehood, against money-loving, against dishonesty, against selfishness; because elsewhere their voices are not uplifted against the worship of money and rank and equipage; against false shows in dress and economy; against buying and not paying; against envy and emulation; against effeminacy and mannishness; against a morality which consists in discretion. Oh! for the voice of a St. Paul or a St. John! But it would be of little use: such men would have small chance of being heard. They would find the one-half of Christendom so intent upon saving souls instead of doing its duty, that the other half thought it all humbug. The organ sounded on from day to day, and no one heeded.

But Mr. Fuller had the support of knowing that there were clergymen east and west who felt with him; men who, however much he might differ from them in the details of belief, yet worshiped the Lord Christ, and believed him to be the King of men, and the Saviour of men whose sins were of the same sort as their own, though they had learned them in the slums, and not at Oxford or Cambridge. He knew that there were greater men, and better workers than himself, among the London clergy; and he knew that he must work like them, after his own measure and fashion, and not follow the multitude. And the organ went on playing—I had written *praying*—for I was thinking of what our Lord said, that men ought always to pray, and not to faint.

At last one day, about a quarter past one o'clock, a man came into the church. Mr. Fuller, who sat in the reading-desk, listening to the music and praying to God, lifted up his eyes and saw Mr. Kitely.

The bookseller had been passing, and, having heard the organ, thought he would just look in and see what was doing in the church. For this church was a sort of link between him and his daughter now that she was away.

The moment he entered Mr. Fuller rose, and knelt, and began to read the collect for the day, in order that Mr. Kitely might pray with him. As soon as his voice arose the organ, which was then playing very softly, ceased; Mr. Kitely knelt, partly, it must be allowed, out of regard for Mr. Fuller; the organist came down and knelt beside him; and Mr. Fuller went on with the second and third collects. After this he read the Epistle and the Gospel for the foregoing Sunday, and then he opened his mouth and spoke—for not more than three minutes, and only to enforce the lesson. Then he kneeled and let his *congregation* depart with a blessing. Mr. Kitely rose and left the chapel, and the organist went back to his organ.

Now all this was out of order. But was it as much out of order as the omission of prayer altogether, which the Church enjoins shall be daily? Times had changed: with them the order of prayer might possibly be changed without offense. At least Mr. Fuller was not such a slave to the letter as to believe that not to pray at all was better than to alter the form by choice of parts. And although in the use of prayers the Church had made great changes upon what had been first instituted, he did not care to leave present custom for the sake merely of reverting to that which was older. He had no hope of getting business men to join in a full morning service—even such as it was at first—upon any week-day.

Mr. Kitely dropped in again before long, and again Mr. Fuller read the collect and went through the same form of worship. Thus he did every time any one appeared in the church, which was very seldom for the first month or so. But he had some friends scattered about the city, and when they knew of his custom they would think of it as they passed his church, until at length there were very few days indeed upon which two or three persons did not drop in and join in the collects, Epistle, and Gospel. To these he always spoke for a few minutes, and then dismissed them with the blessing.

CHAPTER XXXI
A DREARY ONE

"Couldn't you get a holiday on Saturday, Tom?" said Mr. Worboise. "I mean to have one, and I should like to take you with me."

"I don't know, father," answered Tom, who did not regard the proposal as involving any great probability of enjoyment; "my holiday is coming so soon that I should not like to ask for it, especially as Mr. Stopper—"

"What about Mr. Stopper? Not over friendly, eh? He is not a bad fellow, though, is Stopper. I'll ask for you, if you like that better."

"I would much rather you wouldn't, father."

"Pooh, pooh! nonsense, man! It's quite a different thing if I ask for it, you know."

Thomas made no further objection, for he had nothing at hand upon which to ground a fresh one; nor, indeed, could he well have persisted in opposing what seemed a kind wish of his father. It was not, however, merely because they had little to talk about, and that Thomas always felt a considerable restraint in his father's presence—a feeling not very uncommon to young men—but he lived in constant dread of something coming to light about Lucy. He feared his father much more than he loved him; not that he had ever been hardly treated by him; not that he had ever even seen him in a passion, for Mr. Worboise had a very fair command of his temper; it was the hardness and inflexibility read upon his face from earliest childhood, that caused fear thus to overlay love. If a father finds that from any cause such is the case, he ought at once to change his system, and to require very little of any sort from his child till a new crop has begun to appear on the ill-farmed ground of that child's heart.

Now the meaning of the holiday was this: Mr. Worboise had a city-client—a carpet-knight—by name Sir Jonathan Hubbard, a decent man, as the Scotch would say; jolly, companionable, with a husky laugh, and friendly unfinished countenance in which the color was of more weight than the drawing—for, to quote Chaucer of the Franklin, "a better envined man," either in regard of body or cellar, "was nowhere none;" upon Sir Jonathan's sociability Mr. Worboise had founded the scheme of the holiday. Not that he intended to risk any intrusion—Mr. Worboise was far too knowing a man for that. The fact was that he had appointed to wait upon his client at his house near Bickley on that day—at such an hour, however, as would afford cover to his pretense of having brought his son out with him for a holiday in the country. It was most probable that Sir Jonathan would invite them to stay to dinner, and so to spend their holiday with him. There was no Lady Hubbard alive, but there was a Miss Hubbard at the head of the house; and hence Mr. Worboise's strategy. Nor had he reckoned without his host, for if Sir Jonathan was anything he was hospitable; things fell out as the lawyer had forehoped, if not foreseen. Sir Jonathan was pleased with the young fellow, would not allow him to wait companionless in the drawing-room till business was over—sent, on the contrary, for his daughter, and insisted on the two staying to dinner. He was one of those eaters and drinkers who have the redeeming merit of enjoying good things a great deal more in good company. Sir Jonathan's best port would seem to him to have something the matter with it if he had no one to share it. If, however, it had come to the question of a half-bottle or no companion, I would not answer for Sir Jonathan. But his cellar would stand a heavy siege.

Thomas was seated in the drawing-room, which looked cold and rather cheerless; for no company was expected, and I presume Miss Hubbard did not care for color, save as reflected from her guests, seeing she had all her furniture in pinafores. How little some rich people know how to inherit the earth! The good things of it they only uncover when they can *make*, not *receive*, a show.

My dear reader—No, I will not take a liberty to which I have no right; for perhaps were he to see me he would not like me, and possibly were I to meet him I should not like him: I will rather say *My Reader*, without the impertinence or the pledge of an adjective—have a little patience while I paint Miss Hubbard just with the feather-end of my pen. I shall not be long about it.

Thomas sat in the drawing-room, I say, feeling vacant, for he was only waiting, not expecting, when the door opened, and in came a fashionable girl—rather tall, handsome, bright-eyed, well-dressed, and yet—What was it that Thomas did not like about her? Was it that she was dressed in the extreme of the fashion? I will not go on to say what the fashion was, for before I had finished writing it, it would have ceased to be the fashion; and I will not paint my picture *knowingly* with colors that must fade the moment they are laid on. To be sure she had ridden the fashion till it was only fit for the knacker's yard; but she soon made him forget that, for she was clever, pleasant, fast—which means affectedly unrefined, only her affectation did no violence to fact—and altogether amusing. I believe what Thomas did not like about her at first was just all wherein she differed from Lucy. Yet he could not help being taken with her; and when his father and Sir Jonathan came into the room, the two were talking like a sewing-machine.

"Laura, my dear," said the knight, "I have prevailed on Mr. Worboise to spend the day with us. You have no engagement, I believe?"

"Fortunately, I have not, papa."

"Well, I'll just give orders about dinner, and then I'll take our friends about the place. I want to show them my new stable. You had better come with us."

"SHE WAS CLEVER, PLEASANT, FAST—"

Sir Jonathan always ordered the dinner himself. He thought no woman was capable of that department of the household economy. Laura put on her hat—beautiful with a whole king-fisher—and they went out into the grounds to the stable—trim as her drawing-room—where her favorite horse ate apples out of her pocket; from the stable to the hothouses and kitchen-garden; then out at a back door into the lane—shadowy with trees—in which other colors than green were now very near carrying the vote of the leaves. Sweet scents of decay filled the air, waved about, swelling and sinking, on the flow of a west wind, gentle and soft, as if it had been fanned from the wings of spring when nearest to summer. Great white clouds in a brilliant sky tempered the heat of the sun. What with the pure air, the fine light, and the handsome girl by his side, Thomas was in a gayer mood than had been his for many a long day. Miss Hubbard talked plenteously—about balls and theatres and Mansion House dinners, about Rotten Row, and St. James's; and although of all these Thomas knew very little, yet being quick and sympathetic, he was able to satisfy the lady sufficiently to keep her going. He was fortunate enough, besides, to say one or two clever things with which she was pleased, and to make an excellent point once in a criticism upon a girl they both knew, which, slighting her, conveyed, by no very occult implication, a compliment to Miss Hubbard. By the time they had reached this stage of acquaintanceship, they had left stout Sir Jonathan and Mr. Worboise far behind; but Miss Hubbard was not in the least danger of being made uncomfortable by any squeamish notions of propriety; and, having nothing more amusing to do, and being out already, she proposed that they should go home by a rather longer road, which would lead them over a hill whence they would get a good view of the country.

"Do you like living in the country, Miss Hubbard?"

"Oh! dear no. London for me. I can't tell what made papa come to this dull place."

"The scenery is very lovely, though."

"People say so. I'm sure I don't know. Scenery wasn't taught where I went to school."

"Were you taught horses there?" asked Thomas, slyly.

"No. That comes by nature. Do you know I won this bracelet in a handicap last Derby?" she said, showing a very fine arm as well as bracelet, though it was only the morning, so-called.

Miss Hubbard had no design upon Thomas. How could she have? She knew nothing about him. She would have done the same with any gentleman she liked well enough to chatter to. And if Thomas felt it and thought that Laura Hubbard was more entertaining than sober Lucy Burton, he made up to Lucy for it in his own idea by asserting to himself that, after all, she was far handsomer than Miss Hubbard, handsome as she was. Yet I should never think of calling Lucy handsome. She was lovely—almost beautiful, too. *Handsome* always indicates more or less vulgarity—no, I mean commonness—in my ears. And certainly, whatever she might be capable of, had she been blessed with poverty, Miss Hubbard was as common as she was handsome. Thomas was fool enough to revert to Byron to try his luck with that. She soon made him ashamed of showing any liking for such a silly thing as poetry. That piqued him as well, however.

"You sing, I suppose?" he said.

"Oh, yes, when I can't help it—after dinner, sometimes."

"Well, you sing poetry, don't you?"

"I don't know. One must have some words or other just to make her open her mouth. I never know what they're about. Why should I? Nobody ever pays the least attention to them—or to the music either, except it be somebody that wants to marry you."

But why should I go further with the record of such talk? It is not interesting to me, and, therefore, can hardly be so to my reader. Even if I had the art to set it forth aright, I hope I should yet hold to my present belief, that nothing in which the art is uppermost is worth the art expended upon it.

Thomas was a little shocked at her coolness, certainly; but at the same time that very coolness seemed a challenge. Before they had reached the house again, he was vexed to find he had made no impression upon Miss Hubbard.

Farewell to such fencing. By the time he had heard her sing, and his father and he were on their way home again, I am glad to say that Thomas had had nearly enough of her. He thought her voice loud and harsh in speech, showy and distressing in song, and her whole being *bravura*. The contrasts in Lucy had come back upon him with a gush of memorial loveliness; for, as I have said, she still held the fortress of his heart, and held it for its lawful owner.

Scarcely were they seated in the railway carriage, of which they were the sole occupants, when the elder Worboise threw a shot across the bows of the younger.

"Well, Tom, my boy," he said, rubbing his lawyer palms, "how do you like Miss Hubbard?"

"Oh, very well, father," answered Thomas, indifferently. "She's a very jolly sort of girl."

"She's worth a hundred thousand," said his father, in a tone that would have been dry but for a touch of slight resentment at the indifference, possibly in the father's view irreverence, with which he spoke of her.

"Girls?" asked Thomas.

"Pounds," answered his father, clenchingly.

Tom was now convinced of his father's design in taking him out for a holiday. But even now he shrunk from confession. And how did he justify his sneaking now? By saying to himself, "Lucy can't have anything like that money; it won't do. I must wait a more fitting opportunity." But he thought he was very brave indeed, and actually seizing the bull of his father's will by the horns when he ventured to take his meaning for granted, and replied:

"Why, father, a fellow has no chance with a girl like that, except he could ride like Assheton Smith, and knew all the slang of the hunting-field as well as the race-course."

"A few children will cure her of that," said his father.

"What I say is," persisted Thomas, "that she would never look at a clerk."

"If I thought you had any chance, I would buy you a commission in the Blues."

"It wants blue blood for that," said Thomas, whose heart, notwithstanding, danced in his bosom at the sound of *commission*. Then, afraid lest he should lose the least feather of such a chance, he added hastily, "But any regiment would do."

"I dare say," returned his father, at right angles. "When you have made a little progress it will be time enough. She knows nothing about what you are now. Her father asked me, and I said I had not made up my mind yet what to do with you."

"But, as I said before," resumed Thomas, fighting somewhat feebly, "I haven't a chance with her. She likes better to talk about horses than anything else, and I never had my leg across a horse's back in my life—as you know, father," he added in a tone of reproach.

"You mean, Tom, that I have neglected your education. Well, it shall be so no longer. You shall go to the riding-school on Monday night. It won't be open to-morrow, I suppose."

I hope my reader is not so tired of this chapter as I am. It is bad enough to have to read such uninteresting things—but to have to write them! The history that is undertaken must be written, however, whether the writer weary sometimes of his task, or the interest of his labor carry him lightly through to the close.

Thomas, wretched creature, dallied with his father's proposal. He did not intend accepting it, but the very idea of marrying a rich, fashionable girl like that, with a knight for a father, flattered him. Still more was he excited at the notion, the very possibility of wearing a uniform. And what might he not do with so much money? Then, when the thought of Lucy came, he soothed his conscience by saying to himself, "See, how much I must love her when I am giving up all this for her sake!" Still his thoughts hovered about what he said he was giving up. He went to bed on Sunday night, after a very pathetic sermon from Mr. Simon, with one resolution, and one only, namely, to go to the riding-school in Finsbury on Monday night.

But something very different was waiting him.

CHAPTER XXXII
AN EXPLOSION

The whole ground under Thomas's feet was honey-combed and filled with combustible matter. A spark dropped from any, even a loving hand, might send everything in the air. It needed not an enemy to do it.

Lucy Burton had been enjoying a delightful season of repose by the seaside. She had just enough to do with and for the two children to gain healthy distraction to her thinking. But her thinking as well as her bodily condition grew healthier every day that she breathed the sea air. She saw more and more clearly than ever that things must not go on between her and Thomas as they were now going on. The very scent of the sea that came in at her bedroom window when she opened it in the morning, protested against it; the wind said it was no longer endurable; and the clear, blue autumn sky said it was a shame for his sake, if not for her own. She must not do evil that good might come; she must not allow Thomas to go on thus for the sake even of keeping a hold of him for his good. She would give him one chance more, an if he did not accept it, she would not see him again, let come of it what would. In better mood still, she would say, "Let God take care of that for him and me." She had not written to him since she came: that was one thing she could avoid. Now, she resolved that she would write to him just before her return, and tell him that the first thing she would say to him when she saw him would be—had he told his father? and upon his answer depended their future. But then the question arose, what address she was to put upon the letter; for she was not willing to write either to his home or to the counting-house for evident reasons. Nor had she come to any conclusion, and had indeed resolved to encounter him once more without having written, when from something rather incoherently expressed in her grandmother's last letter, which indeed referred to an expected absence of Mr. Stopper, who was now the old lady's main support, she concluded, hastily, I allow, that Mr. Worboise was from home, and that she might without danger direct a letter to Highbury.

Through some official at the Court of Probate, I fancy that Mr. Worboise had heard of a caveat having been entered with reference to the will of Mr. Richard Boxall, deceased. I do not know that this was the case, but I think something must have occurred to irritate him against those whom he, with the law on his side, was so sorely tempted to wrong. I know that the very contemplation of wrong is sufficient to irritate, and that very grievously, against one thus contemplated; but Lucy would have been a very good match, though not equal to Miss Hubbard, even in Mr. Worboise's eyes. On the other hand, however, if he could but make up, not his mind, but his conscience, to take Boxall's money, he would be so much the more likely to secure Miss Hubbard's; which, together with what he could leave him, would make a fortune over two hundred thousand—sufficient to make his son somebody. If Thomas had only spoken in time, that is, while his father's conscience still spoke, and before he had cast eyes of ambition toward Sir Jonathan's bankers! All that was wanted on the devil's side now was some personal quarrel with the rightful heirs; and if Mr. Worboise did not secure that by means of Mr. Sargent's caveat, he must have got it from what had happened on the Monday morning. Before Thomas came down to breakfast, the postman had delivered a letter addressed to him, with the Hastings postmark upon it.

When Thomas entered, and had taken his seat, on the heels of the usual cool *Good-morning*, his father tossed the letter to him across the table, saying, more carelessly than he felt:

"Who's your Hastings correspondent, Tom?"

The question, coming with the sight of Lucy's handwriting, made the eloquent blood surge into Tom's face. His father was not in the way of missing anything that there was to see, and he saw Tom's face.

"A friend of mine," stammered Tom. "Gone down for a holiday."

"One of your fellow-clerks?" asked his father, with a dry significance that indicated the possible neighborhood of annoyance, or worse. "I thought the writing of doubtful gender."

For Lucy's writing was not in the style of a field of corn in a hurricane: it had a few mistakable curves about it, though to the experienced eye it was nothing the less feminine that it did not affect feminity.

"No," faltered Tom, "he's not a clerk; he's a—well, he's a—teacher of music."

"Hm!" remarked Mr. Worboise. "How did you come to make his acquaintance, Tom?" And he looked at his son with awful eyes, lighted from behind with growing suspicion.

Tom felt his jaws growing paralyzed. His mouth was as dry as his hand, and it seemed as if his tongue would rattle in it like the clapper of a cracked bell if he tried to speak. But he had nothing to say. A strange tremor went through him from top to toe, making him conscious of every inch of his body at the very moment when his embarrassment might have been expected to make him forget it altogether. His father kept his eyes fixed on him, and Tom's perturbation increased every moment.

"I think, Tom, the best way out of your evident confusion will be to hand me over that letter," said his father, in a cool, determined tone, at the same time holding out his hand to receive it.

Tom had strength to obey only because he had not strength to resist. But he rose from his seat, and would have left the room.

"Sit down, sir," said Mr. Worboise, in a voice that revealed growing anger, though he could not yet have turned over the leaf to see the signature. In fact, he was more annoyed at his son's pusillanimity than at his attempted deception. "You make a soldier!" he added, in a tone of contempt that stung Tom—not to the heart, but to the backbone. When he had turned the leaf and saw the signature, he rose slowly from his chair and walked to the window, folding the letter as he went. After communing with the garden for awhile, he turned again to the table and sat down. It was not Mr. Worboise's way to go into a passion when he had anything like reasonable warning that his temper was in danger.

"Tom, you have been behaving like a fool. Thank heaven, it's not too late! How could you be such a fool? Believe me, it's not a safe amusement to go trifling with girls this way."

With a great effort, a little encouraged by the quietness of his father's manner, Tom managed to say, "I wasn't trifling."

"Do you mean to tell me," said his father, with more sternness than Tom had ever known him assume—"do you mean to tell me," he repeated, "that you have come under any obligation to this girl?"

"Yes, I have, father."

"You fool! A dress-maker is no fit match for you."

"She's not a dress-maker," said Tom, with some energy, for he was beginning to grow angry, and that alone could give a nature like his courage in such circumstances; "she's a lady, if ever there was one."

"Stuff and nonsense!" said his father. "Don't get on your high horse with me. She's a beggar, if ever there was one."

Tom smiled unbelievingly, or tried to smile; for now his tremor, under the influence of his wholesome anger, had abated, and his breath began to come and go more naturally. A little more, and he would feel himself a hero, stoutly defending his lady-love, fearless of consequences to himself. But he said nothing more just yet.

"You know better than I do, you think, you puppy! I tell you she's not worth a penny—no, nor her old witch of a grandmother, either. A pretty mess you've made of it! You just sit down and tell the poor girl—it's really too bad of you, Tom!—that you're sorry you've been such a confounded fool, but there's no help for it."

"Why should I say that?"

"Because it's true. By all that's sacred!" said Mr. Worboise, with solemn fierceness, "you give up that girl, or you give up me. Not that your father is anything to you: but I swear, if you carry on with that girl, you shall not cross my door as long as you do; and not a penny you shall have out of my pocket. You'll have to live on your salary, my fine fellow, and perhaps that'll bring down your proud stomach a bit. By Jove! You may starve for me. Come, my boy," he added with sudden gentleness, "don't be a fool."

Whether Mr. Worboise meant all he said, I cannot tell, but at least he meant Thomas to believe that he did. And Thomas did believe it. All the terrible contrast between a miserable clerkship, with lodging as well as food to be provided, and a commission in the army with unlimited pocket-money, and the very name of business forgotten, rose before him. A conflict began within him which sent all the blood to the surface of his body, and made him as hot now as he had been cold just before. He again rose from his seat, and this time his father, who saw that he had aimed well, did not prevent him from leaving the room. He only added as his son reached the door, "Mark what I say, Tom: *I mean it*; and when I mean a thing, it's not my fault if it's not done. You can go to the riding-school to-night, or you can look out for a lodging suitable to your means. I should recommend Wapping."

Thomas stood on the heel of one foot and the toes of the other, holding the handle of the door in his hand till his father had done speaking. He then left the room, without reply, closed the door behind him, took his hat and went out. He was half way to London before he remembered that he had left Lucy's letter in his father's hands and had not even read it. This crowned his misery. He dared not go back for it; but the thought of Lucy's words to him being at the mercy of his hard-hearted father moved him so, that he almost made up his mind never to enter the house again. And then how Lucy must love him when he had given up everything for her sake, knowing quite well, too, that she was not going to have any fortune after all? But he did not make up his mind; he never had made up his mind yet; or, if he had, he unmade it again upon meeting with the least difficulty. And now his whole "state of man" was in confusion. He went into the counting-house as if he had been walking in a dream, sat down to his desk mechanically, droned through the forenoon, had actually only a small appetite for his dinner, and when six o'clock arrived, and the place was closed, knew no more what he was going to do than when he started out in the morning.

But he neither went to the riding-school in Finsbury, nor to look for a lodging in Wapping.

CHAPTER XXXIII
DOWN AT LAST

In the very absence of purpose, he strolled up Guild Court to call upon Molken, who was always at home at that hour.

Molken welcomed him even more heartily than usual. After a few minutes' conversation they went out together: having no plan of his own, Thomas was in the hands of any one who had a plan of which he formed a part. They betook themselves to one of their usual haunts. It was too early yet for play, so they called for some refreshment, and Thomas drank more than he had ever drunk before, not with any definite idea of drowning the trouble in his mind, but sipping and sipping from mere restlessness and the fluttering motion of a will unable to act.

It was a cold evening. An autumn wind which had dropped in its way all the now mournful memories of nature, and was itself the more dreary therefore, tumbled a stray billow now and then through the eddies of its chimney-rocks and housetop-shoals upon the dirty window of the little dreary den in which they sat, drinking their gin and water at a degraded card-table whose inlaid borders were not yet quite obscured by the filth caked upon it from greasy fingers and dusters dirtier than the smoke they would remove. They talked—not about gaming—no: they talked about politics and poetry; about Goethe and Heine; and Molken exerted all his wit and sympathy to make himself agreeable to his dejected friend, urging him to rise above his dejection by an effort of the will; using, in fact, much the same arguments as Lady Macbeth when she tried to persuade her husband that the whole significance of things depended on how he chose to regard them: "These things must not be thought after these ways." Thomas, however, had not made a confidant of Molken. He had only dropped many words that a man like him would not fail to piece together into some theory regarding the condition and circumstances of one of whom he meant to make gain.

At length, what between Molken's talk and the gin, a flame of excitement began to appear in Thomas's weary existence; and almost at the same instant a sound of voices and footsteps was heard below; they came up the stair; the door of the room opened; and several fellows entered, all eager for the excitement of play as a drunkard for his drink, all talking, laughing, chaffing. A blast of wind laden with rain from a laboring cloud which had crept up from the west and darkened the place, smote on the windows, and soft yet keen the drops pattered on the glass. All outside was a chaos of windy mist and falling rain. They called for lights, and each man ordered his favorite drink; the face of Nature, who was doing her best to befriend them, was shut out by a blind of green and black stripes stained with yellow; two dirty packs of cards were produced—not from the pocket of any of the company, for none of the others would have trusted such a derivation, but from the archives of the house; and, drawing round the table, they began to offer their sacrifice to the dreary excitement for whose presence their souls had been thirsting all the day. Two of them besides Molken were foreigners, one of them apparently a German, a very quiet and rather a gentlemanly man, between whom and Molken, however, if Thomas had been on the outlook, he might, I fancy, have seen certain looks of no good omen interchanged.

They began playing very gently—and fairly no doubt; and Thomas for some time went on winning.

There was not even the pretense of much money among them. Probably a few gold pieces was the most any of them had. When one of them had made something at this sort of small private game, he would try his luck at one of the more public tables, I presume. As the game went on and they grew more excited, they increased their stakes a little. Still they seemed content to go on for a little. Thomas and Molken were partners, and still they won. Gradually the points were increased, and betting began. Thomas began to lose and lose, of course, more rapidly than he had won. He had had two or three pounds in his pocket when he began, but all went now—the last of it in a bet on the odd trick. He borrowed of Molken—lost; borrowed and lost, still sipping his gin and water, till Molken declared he had himself lost everything. Thomas laid his watch on the table, for himself and Molken— it was not of great value—a gift of his mother only. He lost it. What was to be done? He had one thing left—a ring of some value which Lucy had given him to wear for her. It had belonged to her mother. He pulled it off his finger, showed that it was a rose diamond, and laid it on the table. It followed the rest. He rose, caught up his hat, and, as so many thousands of gamblers have done before, rushed out into the rain and the darkness.

Through all the fumes of the gin which had begun to render "the receipt of reason a limbeck only," the thought gleamed upon his cloudy mind that he ought to have received his quarter's salary that very day. If he had had that, what might he not have done? It was his, and yet he could not have it. His mind was all in a confused despair, ready to grasp at anything that offered him a chance of winning back what he had lost. If he had gone home and told his father—but he was not capable of reasoning out anything. Lucy's ring was his chief misery: so much must be said for him. Something—he did not know what—drove him toward Guild Court. I believe, though in his after reflections he could not identify the impulse, that it was the same which he obeyed at last. Before he knew where he was going, he was at Mrs. Boxall's door. He found it ajar, and walked up the stair to the sitting-room. That door too was open, and there was no one there. But he saw at a glance, from the box on the floor and the shawl on the table, that Lucy had returned, and he supposed that her grandmother had gone up stairs with her. The same moment his eyes sought the wall, and there hung two keys. They were the keys of the door of communication and of the safe.

Mr. Stopper, wise in his generation, sought, as we have seen, to stand as well as possible with the next of kin and supposed heir to Mr. Boxall, namely, his mother. He had, therefore, by degrees, made himself necessary to her, in her fancy at least, by giving her good advice till she thought she could not do without his wisdom. Nor that alone; he had pleased her by a hundred little acknowledgments of her suzerainty, especially grateful to one who loved power as Mrs. Boxall did. Among the rest, one evening, after locking up the counting-house, he went to her with those two keys in his hand, and kept playing with them till he was taking his leave—then, as if a sudden thought had struck him, said:

"But I don't see the use of troubling myself with these keys. I may as well hang them up somewhere," he added, looking about for a place.

"I don't know that it's wise to leave them here," objected Mrs. Boxall.

"Oh! don't be uneasy, ma'am," returned Mr. Stopper. "You mustn't suppose we leave a mint of money in the house at night. If we did, *you* wouldn't be safe either. It's only what comes in after banking-hours—a matter of ten pounds, or thereabouts, sometimes more, sometimes less. The safe's more for the books—in case of fire, you know."

"I hope there's no danger of that, Mr. Stopper."

"Not as long as the neighbors don't take fire. I see every spark out when we have a fire before I turn my back on the premises. Indeed, I'm rather more careful over the fire than the cash-box."

In the meantime Mr. Stopper had discovered a brass-headed nail in the wall, and thereupon he had hung the keys, and there he had hung them every evening since, and there they hung at this moment when Thomas's eyes went in search of them.

When he considered the whole affair afterward, Thomas thought he must have been driven by a demon. He hardly knew whether he was thinking over or doing the thing that was present to him. No thought of resisting it as a temptation arose to meet it. He knew that there was eleven pounds odd shillings in the cash box, for he had seen one of the other clerks count it; he knew that the cash-box was in the safe; he knew that that was the key of it; he knew that the firm owed him twenty-five pounds; he could replace it again before the morning; and while thinking all this he was "doing the effect of his thinking," almost without knowing it: he found himself standing before the safe with the key already in the lock, and the cold handle of the door in his hand. But it was dark all around and within him. In there alone lay light and hope. In another moment the door was open, and the contents of the cash-box—gold, silver, copper—in his pocket. It is possible that even then he might have restored the money if he had not heard the step of the policeman at the street-door. He left the safe open as it was, with the key in it, and sped from the house.

Nothing more marked itself on his memory till he reached the room where he had left his *friends*. It was dark. There was no one there. They had gone to try their luck in a more venturous manner, where rogue met rogue, and fortune was umpire rather than cunning. He knew their haunts, followed and found them. But his watch and ring were gone. They told him, however, where they were. He would go and seek them to-morrow. Meantime he would play. He staked and lost—lost, won, won again; doubled his stakes, won still; and when he left the house it was with a hundred pounds in his pocket and a gray dawn of wretchedness in his heart.

CHAPTER XXXIV
MRS. BOXALL AND MR. STOPPER

Lucy was not up stairs with her grandmother when Thomas went into the room. She had arrived some time before, and had ran across to the bookseller's to put Mattie to bed, according to promise, leaving the door just ajar that she might not trouble her grandmother to come down and open it for her. She had come home hoping against hope that Thomas must by this time have complied, in some way or other, with her request—must have written to his father, or, at least, so positively made up his mind to tell him on his return, that he would be at the station to meet her with the assurance, or would appear in Guild Court some time during the evening with a response to her earnest appeal. When she had put the child to bed, she lingered a few moments with the bookseller in his back parlor, for the shop was shut up, telling him about Mattie, and listening to what little bits of news the worthy man had to impart in return. Their little chat ran something in this way:

"And how have you been, Mr. Kitely?"

"Oh, among the middlins, miss, thank you. How's yourself been?"

"Quite well, and no wonder."

"I don't know that, miss, with two young things a pullin' of you all ways at once. I hope Mattie wasn't over and above troublesome to you."

"She was no trouble at all. You must have missed her, though."

"I couldn't ha' believed how I'd miss her. Do you know the want of her to talk to made me do what I ain't done for twenty year?"

"What's that, Mr. Kitely? Go to church of a Sunday?"

"More than that, miss," answered the bookseller, laughing—a little sheepishly. "Would you believe it of me? I've been to church of a week-day more than once. Ha! ha! But then it wasn't a long rigmarole, like—"

"You mustn't talk about it like that—to me, you know, Mr. Kitely."

"I beg your pardon, miss. I only meant he didn't give us a Sundayful of it, you know. I never could ha' stood that. We had just a little prayer, and a little chapter, and a little sermon—good sense, too, upon my word. I know I altered a price or two in my catalogue when I come home again. I don't know as I was right, but I did it, just to relieve my mind and make believe I was doin' as the minister told me. If they was all like Mr. Fuller, I don't know as I should ha' the heart to say much agen them."

"So it's Mr. Fuller's church you've been going to? I'm so glad! How often has he service, then?"

"Every day, miss. Think o' that. It don't take long, though, as I tell you. But why should it? If there is any good in talking at all, it comes more of being the right thing than the muchness of it, as my old father used to say—for he was in the business afore me, miss, though I saw a great deal more o' the world than ever he did afore I took to it myself—says he, 'It strikes me, Jacob, there's more for your money in some o' those eighteen mos, if you could only read 'em, than in some o' them elephants. I ha' been a watchin',' says he, 'the sort o' man that buys the one and that buys the tother. When a little man with a shabby coat brings in off the stall one o' them sixpenny books in Latin, that looks so barbarious to me, and pops it pleased like into the tail of his coat—as if he meant to have it out again the minute he was out of the shop—then I thinks there's something in that little book—and something in that little man,' says father, miss. And so I stick up for the sermons and the little prayers, miss. I've been thinking about it since; and I think Mr. Fuller's right about the short prayers. They're much more after the manner of the Lord's Prayer anyhow. I never heard of anybody getting tired before *that* was over. As you are fond of church, miss, you'd better drop into Mr. Fuller's to-morrow mornin'. If you go once, you'll go again."

Long after, Lucy told Mr. Fuller what the bookseller had said, and it made him think yet again whether our long prayers—*services*, as we call them, forsooth—are not all a mistake, and closely allied to the worship of the Pagans, who think they shall be heard for their much speaking.

She went out by the side-door into the archway. As she opened it, a figure sped past her, fleet and silent. She started back. Why should it remind her of Thomas? She had scarcely seen more in the darkness than a deeper darkness in motion, for she came straight from the light.

She found the door not as she left it.

"Has Thomas been here, grannie?" she asked, with an alarm she could not account for.

"No, indeed. He has favored us with little of his company this many a day," answered grannie, speaking out of the feelings which had gradually grown from the seeds sown by Stopper. "The sooner you're off with him, my dear, the better, for you!" she continued. "He's no good, I doubt." With a terrible sinking at the heart, Lucy heard her grandmother's words. But she would fight Thomas's battles to the last.

"If ever that man dares to say a word against Thomas in my hearing," she said, "I'll—I'll—I'll leave the room."

O most lame and impotent conclusion! But Lucy carried it farther than her words; for when Mr. Stopper entered the next morning, with a face scared into the ludicrous, she, without even waiting to hear what he had to say, though she foreboded evil, rose at once and left the room. Mr. Stopper stood and looked after her in dismayed admiration; for Lucy was one of those few whose anger even is of such an unselfish and unspiteful nature, that it gives a sort of piquancy to their beauty.

"I hope I haven't offended the young lady," said Mr. Stopper, with some concern.

"Never you mind, Mr. Stopper. I've been giving her a hint about Thomas, and she's not got over it yet. Never you mind her. It's me you've got to do with, and I ain't got no fancies."

"It's just as well, perhaps, that she did walk herself away," said Mr. Stopper.

"You've got some news, Mr. Stopper. Sit ye down. Will you have a cup o' tea?"

"No, thank you. Where's the keys, Mrs. Boxall?"

The old lady looked up at the wall, then back at Mr. Stopper.

"Why, go along! There they are in your own hand."

"Yes; but where do you think I found them?—Hanging in the door of the safe, and all the money gone from the cash-box. I haven't got over the shock of it yet."

"Why, good heavens! Mr. Stopper," said the old lady, who was rather out of temper with both herself and Lucy, "you don't think *I've* been a-robbing of your cash-box, do you?"

Mr. Stopper laughed aloud.

"Well, ma'am, that would be a roundabout way of coming by your own. I don't think we could make out a case against you if you had. Not quite. But, seriously, who came into the house after I left? I hung the keys on that wall with my own hands."

"And I saw them there when I went to bed," said Mrs. Boxall, making a general impression ground for an individual assertion.

"Then somebody must have come in after you had gone to bed—some one that knew the place. Did you find the street door had been tampered with?"

"Lucy opened it this morning."

Mrs. Boxall went to the door and called her grand-daughter. Lucy came, thinking Mr. Stopper must be gone. When she saw him there, she would have left the room again, but her grandmother interfered.

"Come here, child," she said, peremptorily. "Was the house-door open when you went down this morning?"

Lucy felt her face grow pale with the vaguest foreboding—associated with the figure which had run through the archway and her finding the door open. But she kept her self-command.

"No, grannie. The door was shut as usual."

"Did nobody call last night?" asked Mr. Stopper, who had his suspicions, and longed to have them confirmed in order to pay off old scores at once.

"Nobody; that I'll give my word for," answered Mrs. Boxall.

"A most unaccountable thing, ladies," said Stopper, rubbing his forehead as if he would fain rouse an idea in his baffled brain.

"Have you lost much money?" asked the old lady.

"Oh, it's not the money; that's a flea-bite. But justice, you know—that's the point," said Mr. Stopper, with his face full of meaning.

"Do you suspect any one, Mr. Stopper?"

"I do. I found something on the floor. If Mr. Worboise were come," he continued, looking hard at Lucy, "he might be able to help us out with it. Sharp fellow that. But it's an hour past his time, and he's not made his appearance yet. I fear he's been taking to fast ways lately. I'll just go across the court to Mr. Molken, and see if he knows anything about him."

"You'll oblige *me*," said Lucy, who was cold to the very heart, but determined to keep up, "by doing nothing of the sort. I will not have his name mentioned in the matter. Does any one but yourself know of the—the robbery, Mr. Stopper?"

"Not a soul, miss. I wouldn't do anything till I had been to you. I was here first, as I generally am."

"Then, if I am to have anything to say at all," she returned with dignity, "let the matter rest in the mean time—at least till you have some certainty. If you don't you will make suspicion fall on the innocent. It might have been grannie or myself, for anything you can tell yet."

"Highty-tighty, lass!" said her grandmother. "We're on our high horse, I believe."

Before she could say more, however, Lucy had left the room. She just managed to reach her bed, and fell fainting upon it.

Money had evidently, even in the shadow it cast before it, wrought no good effect upon old Mrs. Boxall. The bond between her and her granddaughter was already weakened. She had never spoken thus to her till now.

"Never you mind what the wench says," she went on to Stopper. "The money's none of hers, and shan't be except I please. You just do as you think proper, Mr. Stopper. If that young vagabond has taken the money, why you take him, and see what the law will say to it. The sooner our Lucy is shut of him the better for her—and may be for you too, Mr. Stopper," added the old lady, looking insinuatingly at him.

But whether the head clerk had any design upon Lucy or not, he seemed to think that her favor was of as much consequence as that of her grandmother. He might have reasoned in this way—that he could not expose Thomas without making Lucy his enemy, both from her regard to him and because of the disgrace that would come upon her by having her name associated with his; and Mrs. Boxall was old, and Lucy might take her place any day in the course of nature. Whereas, so long as he kept the secret and strengthened the conclusions against Thomas without divulging them, he had a hold over Lucy, even a claim upon her gratitude, he would say, which he might employ as he saw occasion, and as prudence should direct, holding his revenge still ready in his hands in case there should be nothing to be gained by foregoing it. Therefore, when the clerk in whose charge the money-box was, opened it, he found in it only a ticket with Mr. Stopper's initials, and the sum abstracted in figures, by which it was implied that Mr. Stopper had taken the contents for his own use. So, although it seemed queer that he should have emptied it of the whole sum, even to the few coppers, there was nothing to be said, and hardly anything to be conjectured even.

As Thomas did not make his appearance all day, not a doubt remained upon Mr. Stopper's mind that he had committed the robbery. But he was so well acquainted with the minutest details of the business that he knew very well that the firm was the gainer by Thomas's absconding as nearly as possible to the same amount that he had taken. This small alleviation of Thomas's crime, however, Mr. Stopper took no pains to communicate to Lucy, chuckling only over his own good fortune in getting rid of him so opportunely; for he would no longer stand in his way, even if he were to venture on making advances to Lucy; she could never have anything more to do with a fellow who could be tried for burglary if he chose to apply for a warrant for his apprehension.

Intending that his forbearance should have the full weight of obedience to her wishes, Mr. Stopper went up in the evening after the counting-house was closed. Lucy was not there. She had not left her room since the morning, and the old woman's tenderness had revived a little.

"Perhaps you'd better not hang them keys up there, Mr. Stopper. I don't care about the blame of them. I've had enough of it. There's Lucy, poor dear, lying on her bed like a dead thing; and neither bit nor sup passed her lips all day. Take your keys away with you, Mr. Stopper. I'll have nothing more to do wi' them, I can tell you. And don't you go and take away that young man's character, Mr. Stopper."

"Indeed I should be very sorry, Mrs. Boxall. He hasn't been here all day, but I haven't even made a remark on his absence to any one about the place."

"That's very right, Mr. Stopper. The young gentleman may be at home with a headache."

"Very likely," answered Mr. Stopper, dryly. "Good-night, Mrs. Boxall. And as the keys must have an unpleasant look after what has happened, I'll just put them in my pocket and take them home with me."

"Do ye that, Mr. Stopper. And good-night to you. And if the young man comes back to-morrow, don't 'ee take no notice of what's come and gone. If you're sure he took it, you can keep it off his salary, with a wink for a warning, you know."

"All right, ma'am," said Mr. Stopper, taking his departure in less good humor than he showed.

I will not say much about Lucy's feelings. For some time she was so stunned by the blow as to be past conscious suffering. Then commenced a slow oscillation of feeling: for one half hour, unknown to her as time, she would be declaring him unworthy of occasioning her trouble; for the next she would be accusing his attachment to her, and her own want of decision in not absolutely refusing to occupy the questionable position in which she found herself, as the combined causes of his ruin: for as ruin she could not but regard such a fall as his. She had no answer to her letter—heard nothing of him all day, and in the evening her grandmother brought her the statement of Mr. Stopper that Thomas had not been there. She turned her face away toward the wall, and her grandmother left her, grumbling at girls generally, and girls in love especially. Meantime a cherub was on its way toward her, bearing a little bottle of comfort under its wing.

CHAPTER XXXV
MATTIE FALLS AND RISES AGAIN

Mattie had expected Lucy to call for her in the forenoon and take her out to Wyvil Place to see Miriam. Spending the morning with her father in the shop, amidst much talk, conducted with the most respectful docility on the part of the father, and a good deal of condescending assertion on the part of the child, she had run out twenty times to look at the clock at St. Jacob's; and at length, finding that Lucy did not come, had run up and knocked at her door, giving Mr. Spelt a promissory nod as she passed. Hearing from Mrs. Boxall, however, that Miss Burton was too tired to go out with her, she turned in some disappointment, and sought Mr. Spelt.

"Well, mother, how do *you* do?" she asked, perking up her little gray face, over which there was now a slight wash of rose-color, toward the watch-tower of the tailor.

"Quite well, Mattie. And you look well," answered Mr. Spelt.

"And I am well, I assure you; better than I ever expected to be in this world, mother. I mean to come up beside you a bit. I want to tell you something."

"I don't know, Mattie," answered Mr. Spelt, with some embarrassment. "Is it anything in particular?"

"In particular! Well, I should think so," returned Mattie, with a triumph just dashed with displeasure, for she had not been accustomed to any hesitation in accepting her advances on the part of Mr. Spelt. "I should think so." Then, lowering her voice to a keen whisper, she added, "I've been to see God in his own house."

"Been to church, have you?" said Mr. Spelt.

Now I am sorry to say that Spelt was behaving dishonestly—not from choice, but from embarrassment and fear springing from a false conscientiousness. And Mattie felt at once that Mr. Spelt was not behaving like himself.

"No, Mr. Spelt," she answered with dignity—bridling indeed; "I've not been to church. You don't call that God's house, do you? *Them!* They're nothing but little shops like your own, Mr. Spelt. But God's house!—Take me up, I say. Don't make me shout such things in the open street."

Thus adjured, Mr. Spelt could stand out no longer. He stooped over his threshold and lifted Mattie toward him. But the moment her head reached the level of his floor, she understood it all. In *her* old place in the corner sat the little demoniac Poppie, clothed and in her right mind. A true observer, however, would have seen from her pale, thin face that possibly her quietude was owing more to weakness than to any revolution in her nature.

"Well!" said Mattie, with hauteur. "Will you set me down again, if you please, Mr. Spelt."

"I think, perhaps," said the tailor, meekly, holding the child still suspended in the air, "I could find room for you both. The corner opposite the door there, Mattie," he added, looking round suggestively in the direction of the spot signified.

"Put me down," insisted Mattie, in such a tone that Mr. Spelt dared not keep her in suspense any longer, but lowered her gently to the ground. All the time Poppie had been staring with great black eyes, which seemed to have grown much larger during her illness, and, of course, saying nothing.

As soon as the soles of Mattie's feet touched the ground, she seemed to gather strength like Antæus; for instead of turning and walking away, with her head as high, morally considered, as that of any giant, she began to parley with the offending Mr. Spelt.

"I have heard, mother—Mr. Spelt—that you should be off with the old love before you're on with the new. You never told me what you were about."

"But you was away from home, Mattie."

"You could have written. It would only have cost a penny. I shouldn't have minded paying it."

"Well, Mattie, shall I turn Poppie out?"

"Oh! *I* don't want you to turn her out. You would say I drove her to the streets again."

"Do you remember, Mattie, that you wouldn't go to that good lady's house because she didn't ask Poppie, too. Do you?"

A moment's delay in the child's answer revealed shame. But she was ready in a moment.

"Hers is a big house. That's my own very corner."

"Don't you see how ill Poppie is?"

"Well!" said the hard little thing, with a side nod of her head over the speaking corner of her mouth.

Mr. Spelt began to be a little vexed. He took the upper hand now and came home to her. She was turning to go away, when he spoke in a tone that stopped her. But she stood with her back half turned toward him.

"Mattie, do you remember the story Somebody told us about the ragged boy that came home again, and how his brother, with the good clothes on, was offended, and wouldn't go in because he thought he was taking his place? You're behaving just the same as the brother with the good clothes."

"I don't know that. There's some difference, I'm sure. I don't think you're telling the story right. I don't think there's anything about taking his place. I'll just go and look. I can read it for myself, Mr. Spelt."

So saying, Mattie walked away to the house, with various backward tosses of the head. Mr. Spelt drew his head into his shell, troubled at Mattie's naughtiness. Poppie stared at him, but said nothing, for she had nothing to say.

When Mattie entered the shop, her father saw that something was amiss with her.

"What's the matter with my princess?" he asked.

"Oh, nothing much," answered Mattie, with tears in her eyes. "I shall get over it, I dare say. Mr. Spelt has been very naughty," she added; in a somewhat defiant tone; and before her father could say anything more she had reached the stairs, and went to her own room.

My reader must imagine her now taking down a huge family Bible her father him given her for the sake of the large print. She lugs it along and heaves it upon her bed; then, by a process known only to herself, finds the place, and begins to spell out the story once more, to discover whether the tailor has not garbled it to her condemnation. But, as she reads, the story itself lays hold upon her little heart, and she finds a far greater condemnation there than she had found in her friend's reproof. About half an hour after, she ran—Mattie seldom ran—past Mr. Spelt and Poppie, not venturing to look up, though, ere she came too near, the tailor could see the red eyes in the white face, and knocked at Mrs. Boxall's door.

Lucy was still lying on her bed when she heard little knuckles at her door, and having answered without looking round, felt, a moment after, a tiny hand steal into hers. She opened her eyes, and saw Mattie by her bedside. Nor was she too much absorbed in her own griefs to note that the child had hers, too.

"What is the matter with you, Mattie, my dear?" she asked, in a faint voice.

Mattie burst into tears—a rare proceeding with the princess. It was some moments before she could sob out:

"I've been *so* naughty, Miss Burton—so *very* naughty!"

Lucy raised herself, sat on the side of the bed, and took the child's hand. Mattie could not look up.

"I'm sorry to hear that, Mattie. What have you done?"

"Such a shame. Poppie! Far country. Elder brother."

These were almost the only words Lucy could hear for the sobs of the poor child. Hence she could only guess at the cause of her grief, and her advice must be general.

"If you have done wrong to Poppie, or any one, you must go and tell her so, and try to make up for it."

"Yes, I will, for I can't bear it," answered Mattie, beginning to recover herself. "Think of doing the very same as the one I was so angry with when mother read the story! I couldn't bear to see Poppie in my place in mother's shop, and I was angry, and wouldn't go in. But I'll go now, as soon as I get my poor eyes dried."

Lucy was not able to say much to her, and Mattie was so taken up with her own repentance that she did not see that Lucy was in trouble, too. In a few minutes the child announced her intention of going to Mr. Spelt at once, and left Lucy to her own thoughts. I will first tell how Mattie finished her repentance, and then return to Lucy.

She walked right under Mr. Spelt's door, and called aloud, but with a wavering voice:

"Mother, take me up directly. I'm very sorry."

Over the threshold came a pair of arms, and Mattie was hoisted into the heaven of her repentant desire. As soon as she was in it she crawled on her hands and knees—even she could scarcely have stood in the place—toward Poppie.

"How do you do, prodigal?" she said, putting her arms round the bewildered Poppie, who had no more idea of what she meant than a child born in heaven would have had. "I'm very glad to see you home again. Put on this ring, and we'll both be good children to mother there."

So saying, she took a penny ring, with a bit of red and two bits of green glass in it, from her finger, and put it upon Poppie's, who submitted speechless, but was pleased with the glitter of the toy. She did not kiss in return, though: Poppie liked to be kissed, but she had not learned to kiss yet.

"Mother," Mattie went on, "I was behaving like—like—like—a wicked Pharisee and Sadducee. I beg your pardon, mother. I will be good. May I sit in the corner by the door?" "I think," answered the little tailor, greatly moved, and believing in the wind that bloweth where it listeth more than ever he had believed before—"I think if I were to move a little, you could sit in the corner by the window, and then you would see into the court better. Only," he said, as he drew his work about his new position, "you must not lean much against the sash, for it is not very sound, and you might tumble in the court, you know."

So Mattie and Poppie sat side by side, and the heart of the tailor had a foretaste of heaven.

Presently Mattie began to talk to Poppie. She could scarcely, however, draw a single response from her, for she had nothing to say. Interchange of thought was unknown to the elder child, and Mattie's words were considerably less intelligible to Poppie than the autumn wind that blew round their nest. Mattie was annoyed. The romance of the reconciliation was dimmed. Instinctively she felt that the only way to restore it was to teach Poppie, and she took her in hand at once.

There was more hope for Poppie, and Spelt, too, now that Mattie was in the work, for there is no teacher of a child like a child. All the tutors of Oxford and Cambridge will not bring on a baby as a baby a year older will. The child-like is as essential an element in the teacher as in the scholar. And the train of my story is not going so fast but that I may pull up at this siding for a moment to say that those who believe they have found a higher truth, with its higher mode of conveyance, are very apt to err in undervaluing, even to the degree of wishing to remove the lower forms in which truth, if not embodied exactly, is at least wrapt up. Truth may be presented in the grandeur of a marble statue, or in a brown-paper parcel. I choose the sculpture; my last son prefers the parcel. The only question is whether there is truth—not in the abstract, but as assimilable by the recipient—present in the form. I cannot, however, resume without a word on the other side. To the man who sees and feels the higher and nobler form, it is given to teach *that*. Let those to whom the lower represents the sum of things, teach it with their whole hearts. *He* has nothing to do with it, for he cannot teach it without being false. The snare of the devil holds men who, capable of teaching the higher, talk of the people not being ready to receive it, and therefore teach them in forms which are to their own souls an obstruction. There is cowardice and desertion in it. They leave their own harder and higher work to do the easier and clumsier work of their neighbor. It is wasteful of time, truth, and energy. The man who is most careful over the truth that lies in forms not his own, will be the man most careful to let no time-serving drag him down—not to the level of the lower teachers, for they are honest—but to the level of Job's friends, who lied for God; nay, lower still; for this will soon cease to be lying even for God, and become lying for himself.

When Mattie left her, Lucy again threw herself down, and turned her face to the wall, and the story of which Mattie had been talking straightway began to mingle with all that filled her troubled mind. For who was a prodigal son but her lost Thomas? Lost indeed! But there was another word in the parable to balance that—there was *found* as well. Thomas might be found again. And if the angels in heaven rejoiced over the finding of such a lost wanderer, why should she cut the cable of Love, and let him go adrift from her heart? Might she not love him still? Ought she not to love him still? Was he not more likely to come back some day if she went on loving him? The recent awaking of Lucy's spiritual nature—what would be called by some, her conversion—had been so interpenetrated with the image, the feeling, the subjective presence of Thomas—she had thought so much of him while stooping her own shoulders to the easy yoke, that she could not leave him out now, and it seemed as if, were she to give him up, she would lose half the incentive to press forward herself. The fibres of her growth had so twined around him, that if the idea of his regeneration departed from her, the hope of her own would sicken, at least, if not die. True, Pride hinted at the disgrace of being allied to such a man—a man who had stolen; but Faith replied, that if there were joy in heaven over him, she too might rejoice over him when he came back; and if the Father received the prodigal with all his heart, she too might receive him with all hers. But she would have no right to receive him thus if she did nothing to restore Him; nor would she have any right to put forth in full her reclaiming influence except she meant thus to receive him. Her conscience began to reproach her that she had not before done all that she could to reclaim him, and, if she only knew the way, she was now at least prepared to spend and be spent for him. But she had already done all that she was, at this juncture of his history, to be allowed to do for the wretched trifler. God had taken the affair out of her hands, and had put it into those of somewhat harder teachers.

CHAPTER XXXVI
BUSINESS

When Mr. Worboise found that Thomas did not return that night, he concluded at once that he had made up his mind to thwart him in his now cherished plan, to refuse the daughter of Sir Jonathan Hubbard, and marry the girl whom his father disliked. He determined at once, even supposing he might be premature as regarded the property, to have the satisfaction of causing the Boxalls sharp uneasiness at least. His son would not have dared to go against his wishes but for the enticements of "that minx," in the confidence that her uncle's property was about to be hers. He would teach her, and him too, a lesson. Either her uncle or some one or more of his family were not drowned, or they were all drowned: in neither case was the property hers. If one of the family was alive, the property remained where it was; if they were all gone, the property was his. He thought himself into a rage over her interference with his plans, judged himself an injured person, and thereby freed of any trifling obligation that a fastidious conscience might have fancied to exist to the prejudice of his claims upon the property of his friend, supposed to be deceased. He was now ready to push his rights to the uttermost—to exact the pound of flesh that the law awarded him. He went the next morning but one after Thomas's disappearance and propounded the will.

In due time this came to the knowledge of Mr. Sargent. He wrote to Mrs. Boxall a stiff business letter acquainting her with the fact, and then called upon Mr. Worboise to see whether some arrangement could not be come to; for, having learned the nature of the will, he saw that almost any decent division of the property, for which he could only appeal to the justice of the man, would be better than a contest. Mr. Worboise received him with a graciousness reaching almost to kindness, talked lightly of the whole as a mere matter of business about which there was no room for disputing, smiled aside at every attempt made by Mr. Sargent to approach the subject from another quarter, and made him understand, without saying a word to that effect, that he was prepared to push matters to the extreme of extremity. He even allowed him to see that he had reasons beyond the value of the money for setting about the matter in the coolest, most legal fashion in the world. Mr. Sargent went away baffled—to devise upon what ground he could oppose the grant of probate.

While Mr. Sargent was having his interview, Mr. Stopper was awaiting his departure in the clerk's room. It must be remembered that Mr. Stopper was now between two stools; and while he came to plead the cause of the widow and fatherless, he must be especially careful for his own sake not to give offense. Him, too, Mr. Worboise received with the greatest good humor; assured him that there was no mistake in the matter, and he believed no flaw in the will; informed him that he had drawn it up himself, and had, at his friend's request, entered his own name as contingent reversioner. His friend might have done it in joke; he did not know; but he had not any intention of foregoing his rights, or turning out of Luck's way when she met him in the teeth. On the contrary, he meant to have the money and to use it; for, at all events, it could not have been in joke that his friend had omitted his mother and his niece. He must have had some good reason for so doing; and he was not one to treat a dead friend's feeling with disrespect—and so on, all in pleasant words, and with smiling delivery, ended by a hearty, easy "good-morning." For, ere he had finished, Mr. Stopper, coming to the conclusion that nothing was to be done, rose to take his leave. At the door he turned, and said:

"I hope nothing is amiss with your son, Mr. Worboise. I hope he is not ill."

"Why do you ask?" returned Mr. Worboise, just a little staggered; for he was not prepared to hear that Thomas was missing from Bagot Street as well as from home. When he heard the fact, however, he merely nodded his head, saying:

"Well, Mr. Stopper, he's too old for me to horsewhip him. I don't know what the young rascal is after. I leave him in your hands. That kind of thing won't do, of course. I don't know that it wouldn't be the best thing to discharge him. It's of no consequence to me, you know, and it would be a lesson to him, the young scapegrace! That's really going too far, though you and I can make allowances, eh, Stopper?"

Mr. Stopper was wise enough not to incur the odium of a Job's messenger, by telling what even Mr. Worboise would have considered bad news; for he had a reverence for locks and money, and regarded any actionable tampering with either as disgraceful. "Besides," thought Stopper, "if it was only to spite the young jackanapes, I could almost marry that girl without a farthing. But I shouldn't have a chance if I were to leak about Tom."

Mr. Worboise was uneasy, though. He told his wife the sum of what had passed between Tom and himself, but I fear enjoyed her discomfiture at the relation; for he said spitefully, as he left her room:

"Shall I call on Mr. Simon as I go to town, and send him up, Mrs. Worboise?"

His wife buried her face in her pillow, and made no reply. Perhaps the husband's heart smote him; but I doubt it, though he did call on Mr. Simon and send him to her.

All the result of Mr. Simon's inquiries was the discovery that Thomas had vanished from the counting-house, too. Thereupon a more real grief than she had ever known seized the mother's heart; her conscience reproached her as often as Mr. Simon hinted that it was a judgment upon her for having been worldly in her views concerning her son's marriage; and she sent for Amy home, and allowed things to take their way.

All the comfort Mr. Worboise took was to say to himself over and over, "The young rascal's old enough to take care of himself. He knows what he's about, too. He thinks to force me to a surrender by starving me of his precious self. We'll see. I've no doubt he's harbored in that old woman's house. Stay a bit, and if I don't fire him out—by Jove! She'll find I'm not one to take liberties with, the old hag!"

The best that Mr. Sargent could do at present was to resist probate on the ground of the uncertainty of the testator's death, delaying thus the execution of the will. He had little hope, however, of any ultimate success—except such as he might achieve by shaming Mr. Worboise into an arrangement.

Mrs. Boxall sent for him, and with many acknowledgments begged him to do his best for them, saying that, if he were successful, she would gladly pay him whatever he demanded. He repudiated all idea of payment, however, and indeed considered himself only too fortunate to be permitted to call as often as he pleased, for then he generally saw Lucy. But he never made the smallest attempt to renew even the slight intimacy which had formerly existed between them.

CHAPTER XXXVII
MR. SARGENT LABORS

That large room in Guild Court, once so full of aged cheerfulness and youthful hope, was now filled with an atmosphere of both moral and spiritual perturbation. The first effect of her son's will upon Mrs. Boxall was rage and indignation against Mr. Worboise, who, she declared, must have falsified it. She would not believe that Richard could have omitted her name, and put in that of his attorney. The moment she heard the evil tidings, she rose and went for her bonnet, with the full intention of giving "the rascal a bit of her mind." It was all that her grand-daughter and Mr. Stopper could do to prevent her. For some time she would yield no ear to their representations of the bad consequences of such a proceeding. She did not care. If there was justice to be had on the earth she would have it, if she went to the Queen herself to get it. I half suspect that, though she gave in at last, she did carry out her intention afterward without giving any one the chance of preventing her. However that may be, the paroxysm of her present rage passed off in tears, followed by gloomy fits, which were diversified by outbreaks of temper against Lucy, although she spoke of her as a poor dear orphan reduced to beggary by the wickedness and greed of lawyers in general, who lived like cannibals upon the flesh and blood of innocents. In vain would Lucy try to persuade her that they were no worse now than they had been, reminding her that they were even happier together before the expectation of more than plenty came in to trouble them; beside her late imagination of wealth, her present feeling was that of poverty, and to feel poor is surely the larger half of being poor.

On Lucy my reader will easily believe that this change of prospect had little effect. Her heart was too much occupied with a far more serious affair to be moved about money. Had everything been right with Thomas, I have no doubt she would have built many a castle of the things she would do; but till Thomas was restored to her, by being brought to his right mind, no one thing seemed more worth doing than another. Sadness settled upon her face, her walk, her speech, her whole expression. But she went about her work as before, and did what she could to keep her sorrow from hurting others. The reality of the late growth of religious feeling in her was severely tested; but it stood the test; for she sought comfort in holding up her care to God; and what surer answer to such prayer could there be, than that she had strength to do her work? We are saved by hope, and Lucy's hope never died; or if it did wither away under the dry blasts of her human judgment, the prayers that went up for submission to His will soon returned in such dews as caused the little flower once more to lift its head in the sun and wind. And often as she could—not every day, because of her engagements with Miriam Morgenstern—she went to Mr. Fuller's church, and I think I may say that she never returned without what was worth going for. I do not say that she could always tell what she had learned, but she came away with fresh strength, and fresh resolution to do what might show itself to be right. And the strength came chiefly from this, that she believed more and more what the apostle Peter came to be so sure of before he died, that "He careth for us." She believed that the power that made her a living soul was not, could not be, indifferent to her sorrows, however much she might have deserved them, still less indifferent because they were for her good—a ready excuse for indifference with men—and if only he cared that she suffered, if he knew that it was sad and hard to bear, she could bear it without a word, almost without a thought of restlessness. And then, why should she not hope for Thomas as well as for herself? If we are to love our neighbor as ourself, surely we must hope and pray for him as for ourself; and if Lucy found that she could love Thomas at least as herself, for him she was in that very love bound to pray and to hope as for herself.

Mr. Sargent was soon thoroughly acquainted with all Mrs. Boxall's affairs. And he had so little hope of success in regard to the will, that, when he found that she had no vouchers to produce for her own little property placed in her son's hands, he resolved, before going any further in a course which must irritate Mr. Worboise, to see whether he could not secure that first. Indeed he was prepared, seeing how ill matters looked for his clients, to offer to withdraw from the contest, provided the old lady's rights were acknowledged. With this view he called once more upon Mr. Worboise, who received him just as graciously as before. A conversation something like this followed:

"Mrs. Boxall informs me, Mr. Worboise, that her son, at the time of his death, was, and had been for many years, in possession of some property of hers, amounting to somewhere between two and three thousand pounds. The old lady is a very simple woman—"

"Is she?" interjected, rather than interrupted, Mr. Worboise, in a cold parenthesis. Mr. Sargent went on.

"Indeed she does not know the amount exactly, but that could be easily calculated from the interest he was in the habit of paying her."

"But whatever acknowledgment she holds for the money will render the trouble unnecessary," said Mr. Worboise, who saw well enough to what Mr. Sargent was coming.

"Unfortunately—it was very wrong of a man of business, or anybody, indeed—her son never gave her any acknowledgment in writing."

"Oh!" said Mr. Worboise, with a smile, "then I don't exactly see what can be done. It is very awkward."

"You can be easily satisfied of the truth of the statement."

"I am afraid not, Mr. Sargent."

"She is a straightforward old lady, and—"

"I have reason to doubt it. At all events, seeing that she considers the whole of the property hers by right, an opinion in which you sympathize with her—as her legal adviser, I mean—it will not be very surprising if, from my point of view, I should be jealous of her making a statement for the sake of securing a part of those *rights*. With such temptation, and such an excuse, it is just possible—I've heard of such a thing as evil that good might come, eh, Mr. Sargent?—even if she were as straightforward as you think her. Let her produce her vouchers, I say."

"I have no fear—at least I hope Mr. Stopper will be able to prove it. There will be evidence enough of the interest paid."

"As interest, Mr. Sargent? I suspect it will turn out to be only an annuity that the good fellow allowed her, notwithstanding the reasons he must have had for omitting her name from his will."

"I confess this much to you, Mr. Worboise—that our cause is so far from promising that I should advise Mrs. Boxall to be content with her own, and push the case no further."

"Quite right, Mr. Sargent. The most prudent advice you can give her."

"You will then admit the debt, and let the good woman have her own?"

"Admit the debt by no means; but certainly let her have her own as soon as she proves what is her own," answered Mr. Worboise, smiling.

"But I give you my word, Mr. Worboise," said Mr. Sargent, doing his best to keep his temper, "that I believe the woman's statement to be perfectly true."

"I believe you, Mr. Sargent, but I do not believe the woman," returned Mr. Worboise, again smiling.

"But you know it will not matter much, because, coming into this property as you do, you can hardly avoid making some provision for those so nearly related to the testator, and who were dependent upon him during his lifetime. You cannot leave the old lady to starve."

"It will be time enough to talk about that when my rights are acknowledged. Till then I decline to entertain the question."

There was a something in Mr. Worboise's manner, and an irrepressible flash of his eye, that all but convinced Mr. Sargent that there was nothing not in the bond to be got from him. He therefore left him, and started a new objection in opposing the probate of the will. He argued the probability of all or one or other of the daughters surviving the father—that is, not of their being yet alive, but of their having outlived him. Now this question, though plain as the alphabet to those who are acquainted with law, requires some explanation to those who are not, numbering possibly the greater part of my readers.

The property would come to Mr. Worboise only in the case of all those mentioned in the will dying before Mr. Boxall. A man can only will that which is his own at the time of his death. If he died before any of his family, Mr. Worboise had nothing to do with it. It went after the survivor's death to *her* heirs. Hence if either of the daughters survived father and mother, if only for one provable moment, the property would be hers, and would go to her heir, namely, her grandmother. So it would in any case, had not Mr. Worboise been mentioned, except Mrs. Richard Boxall had survived her husband and family, in which case the money would have gone to her nearest of kin. This alternative, however, was not started, for both sides had an equal interest in opposing it—and indeed the probable decision upon probabilities would have been that the wife would die first. The whole affair then turned upon the question: whether it was more likely that Richard Boxall or every one of his daughters died first; in which question it must be remembered that there was nothing cumulative in the three daughters. He was as likely to die before or to survive all three as any one of them, except individual reasons could be shown in regard to one daughter which did not exist in regard to another.

One more word is necessary. Mr. Sargent was not in good practice and would scarcely have been able—I do not use the word *afforded* because I do not know what it means—to meet the various expenses of the plea. But the very day he had become acquainted with the contents of the will, he told Mr. Morgenstern of the peculiar position in which his governess and her grandmother found themselves. Now Mr. Morgenstern was not only rich—that is common; nor was he only aware that he was rich; if that is not so common, it is not yet very uncommon; but he felt that he had something to spare. Lucy was a great favorite with him; so was Sargent. He could not but see that Sargent was fond of Lucy, and that he was suffering from some measure of repulse. He therefore hoped, if not to be of any material assistance to Lucy—for from Sargent's own representation he could not see that the matter was a promising one—at least to give the son of his old friend a chance of commending himself to the lady by putting it in his power to plead her cause. And conducted as Mr. Sargent conducted the affair, it did not put Mr. Morgenstern to an amount of expense that cost him two thoughts; while even if it had been serious, the pleasure with which his wife regarded his generosity would have been to him reward enough.

CHAPTER XXXVIII
HOW THOMAS DID AND FARED

I flatter myself that my reader is not very much interested in Thomas; I never meant he should be yet. I confess, however, that I am now girding up my loins with the express intention of beginning to interest him if I can. For I have now almost reached the point of his history which I myself feel to verge on the interesting. When a worthless fellow begins to meet with his deserts, then we begin to be aware that after all he is our own flesh and blood. Our human heart begins to feel just the least possible yearning toward him. We hope he will be well trounced, but we become capable of hoping that it may not be lost upon him. At least we are content to hear something more about him.

When Thomas left the gambling-house that dreary morning, he must have felt very much as the devil must feel. For he had plenty of money and no home. He had actually on this raw morning, when nature seemed to be nothing but a drizzle diluted with gray fog, nowhere to go to. More, indeed; he had a good many places, including the principal thoroughfares of London, where he must not go. There was one other place which he did all he could to keep out of, and that was the place where the little thinking that was considered necessary in his establishment was carried on. He could not help peeping in at the window, however, and now and then putting his ear to the keyhole. And what did he hear? That he, Thomas Worboise, gentlemen, was a thief, a coward, a sneak. Now, when Thomas heard this, for the first time in his life, his satisfaction with himself gave way utterly; nor could all his admiration for Lara or the Corsair—I really forget whether they are not one and the same phantom—reconcile him to become one of the fraternity. The Corsair at least would not have sold Medora's ring to save his life. Up to this point, he had never seen himself contemptible. Nor even now could he feel it much, for, weary and sick, all he wanted was some place to lay down his head and go to sleep in. After he had slept, he would begin to see things as they were, and, once admitted possible that he could do an ungentlemanly action, fresh accusations from quarters altogether unsuspected of unfriendliness would be lodged in that court of which I have already spoken. But for a time mere animal self-preservation would keep the upper hand. He was conscious of an inclination to dive into every court that he came near—of a proclivity toward the darkness. This was the same Thomas Worboise that used to face the sunshine in gay attire, but never let the sun farther in than his brain; so the darkness within him had come at last to the outside, and swathed all in its funereal folds. Till a man's indwelling darkness is destroyed by the deep-going light of truth, he walks in darkness, and the sooner this darkness comes out in action and shows itself to be darkness, the better for the man. The presence of this darkness, however, is sooner recognized by one man than by another. To one the darkness within him is made manifest by a false compliment he has just paid to a pretty girl; to Thomas it could only be revealed by theft and the actual parting for money with the jewel given him by a girl whom he loved as much as he could love, which was not much—yet; to a third—not murder, perjury, hypocrisy, hanging, will reveal it; he will go into the other world from the end of a rope, not mistaking darkness for light, but knowing that it is what it is, and that it is his, and yet denying the possession of the one, and asserting the possession of the other.

Thomas forgot all about where he was, till suddenly he found himself far west in the Strand. The light of the world was coming nearer; no policeman was in sight: and the archway leading down under the Adelphi yawned like the mouth of hell at his side. He darted into it. But no sooner was he under the arches than he wished himself out again. Strange forms of misery and vice were coming to life here and there in the darkness where they had slept away the night. He was of their sort, yet he did not like his own kin. Nay, some of them might be worthy compared to him, yet he shrunk from them. He rushed out. Heaven was full of lights and hell was full of horrors; where was his own place? He hurried back toward the city.

But as the light grew his terror increased. There was no ground for immediate alarm, for no one yet knew what he had done; but with the light discovery drew nearer. When he reached Farringdon Street he turned down toward Blackfriars Bridge, then eastward again by Earl Street into Thames Street. He felt safer where the streets were narrow, and the houses rose high to shut out the dayspring, which the Lord says to Job he had "caused to know its place, that it might take hold of the ends of the earth," like a napkin, "that the wicked might be shaken out of it." He hurried on, not yet knowing what he was, only seeing revelation at hand clothed in terror. And the end of it was, that he buried his head in the public-house where the mischief of the preceding night had begun, and was glad to lie down in a filthy bed. The ways of transgressors are always hard in the end. Happy they who find them hard in the beginning.

Ill at ease as he was, both in body and mind, he was yet so worn out that he fell fast asleep; and still on the stream of sleep went drifting toward the vengeance that awaited him—the vengeance of seeing himself as he was.

When he woke, it was afternoon. He had to make several efforts before his recollection combined with his observation to tell him where he was. He felt, however, that a horror was coming, and when it came his whole being was crushed before it. It must be confessed, however, that it was the disgrace, and not the sin, that troubled him. But honor, although a poor substitute for honesty or religion, is yet something; and the fear of disgrace is a good sword to hang over the heads of those who need such attendance. Thomas's heart burned like a hot coal with shame. In vain he tried to persuade himself, in vain he partially succeeded in persuading himself, that he was not himself when he took the money. Allowing whatever excuse might lie in the state to which he had first brought himself, he knew that no defense of that sort would have any influence in restoring to him the place he had lost. He was an outcast. He lay in moveless torture. He knew himself, and he knew his crime; and he knew that himself had committed that crime. Wide awake, he did not think of rising; for the whole world of activity lay beyond the impassable barrier of his shame. There was nothing for him to do, nowhere for him to go. At length he heard voices in the room below him: they were voices he knew; and he was lying over the scene of last night's temptation. He sprung from the bed, hurried on his clothes, crept down the stairs, paid for his lodging at the bar, and went out into the street. He felt sick at the thought of joining them; he had had a surfeit of wickedness.

But he was too near his former haunts; and the officers of justice must be after him. He turned from one narrow street into another, and wandered on till he came where the bow-sprit of a vessel projected over a wall across a narrow lane, and he knew by this that he must be near the Thames. The sun was going down, and the friendly darkness was at hand. But he could not rest. He knew nothing of the other side, and it seemed to him therefore that he would be safer there. He would take a boat and be put across. A passage between two houses led toward the river. Probably there were stairs at the end. He turned into the passage. Half a dozen bills were up on the walls. He stopped to look. They all described bodies found in the river. He turned away, and started at the sight of a policeman regarding him from a door three or four yards off. It was a police station. He had all but put his head into the lion's mouth. He had just presence of mind enough to prevent him from running, but not enough to keep his legs steady under him. His very calves seemed to feel the eyes of the policeman burning upon them, and shrank away with a sense of unprotected misery. He passed several stairs before he ventured to look round. Then finding no reason to suppose he was watched, he turned down the next opening, found a boat, and telling the waterman to put him across to Rotherhithe, of which district he just knew the name, sat down in the stern. The man rowed up the river. The sun was going down behind the dome of St. Paul's, which looked like the round shoulder of a little hill; and all the brown masts and spars of the vessels shone like a forest of gold-barked trees in winter. The dark river caught the light, and threw it shimmering up on the great black hulls, which shone again in the water below; and the Thames, with all its dirt and all its dead, looked radiant. But Thomas felt nothing of its beauty. If Nature had ever had a right of way in his heart, she was now shut out. What was it to him, despised in his own eyes, that the sun shone? He looked up at the sky only to wish for the night. What was it to him that the world was for a moment gay, even into the heart of London? Its smile could not reach his heart: it needs an atmosphere as well as a sun to make light. The sun was in the heavens, yea, the central sun of truth shone upon the universe; but there was no atmosphere of truth in Thomas's world to be lighted up by it; or if there was, it was so filled with smoke and vapor that for the time the sun could not make it smile. As they passed under a towering hull, he envied a monkey that went scrambling out of one of the port-holes and in at another. And yet the scene around was as strange as it was beautiful. The wide river, the many vessels, the multitudinous wilderness of gray houses on every side, all disorder to the eye, yet blended by the air and the light and the thin fog into a marvelous whole; the occasional vista of bridge-arches; the line of London Bridge lying parallel with the lines of green and gray and gold in the sky—its people, its horses, its carriages creeping like insects athwart the sunset—one of the arches cut across near the top by the line of a new railway-bridge, and the segment filled with a moving train; all this light and life to the eye, while, save for the splash of the oars, and the general hum like an aroma of sound that filled the air, all was still to the ear—none of it reached the heart of outcast Thomas.

Soon, as if by magic, the scene changed. The boatman had been rowing up the river, keeping in the quiet water as the tide hurried out. Now he was crossing toward Cherry Garden Stairs. As they drew near the Surrey-side, all at once Thomas found himself in the midst of a multitude of boats, flitting about like water-flies on the surface of a quiet pool. What they were about he could not see. Now they would gather in dense masses, in every imaginable position to each other, the air filled with shouting, objurgation, expostulation, and good-humored chaff, varied with abuse. Again they would part asunder and vanish over the wide space. Guns were firing, flags were flying, Thames liveries gleaming here and there. The boats were full of men, women, and children; some in holiday garments, most of them dark with the darkness of an English mob. It was an aquatic crowd—a people exclusively living on and by the river—assembled to see a rowing-match between two of their own class for a boat, probably given by the publicans of the neighborhood—who would reap ten times the advantage. But although there were thousands assembled, the uproar troubled such a small proportion of the river's surface, that one might have rowed up and down in the middle space between Rotherhithe and Wapping for hours and know nothing about it.

But Thomas did not see the race, not because he was in haste to get ashore, but because something happened. His waterman, anxious to see the sport, lingered in the crowd lining the whole of that side of the river. In a boat a little way farther up was a large family party, and in it a woman who was more taken up with the baby in her arms than with all that was going on around her. In consequence of her absorption in the merry child, which was springing with all the newly-discovered delight of feet and legs, she was so dreadfully startled when the bows of another boat struck the gunwale just at her back, that she sprung half up from her seat, and the baby, jerking itself forward, dropped from her arms into the river. Thomas was gazing listlessly at the water when he saw the child sweep past him a foot or so below the surface. His next remembered consciousness was in the water. He was a fair swimmer, though no rider. He caught the child, and let himself drift with the tide, till he came upon the cable of a vessel that lay a hundred yards below. Boats came rushing about him; in a moment the child was taken from him and handed across half a dozen of them to his mother; and in another moment he, too, was in a boat. When he came to himself a gin-faced, elderly woman, in a small threadbare tartan shawl, was wiping his face with a pocket-handkerchief, and murmuring some feminine words over him, while a coarse-looking, dough-faced man was holding a broken cup with some spirit in it to his mouth.

"Go ashore with the gentleman, Jim," said the woman. "There's the India Arms. That's a respectable place. You must go to bed, my dear, till you gets your clo'es dried."

"I haven't paid my man," said Tom, feebly. He was now shivering with cold; for, after the night and day he had spent, he was in no condition to resist the effects of the water.

"Oh, we'll pay him. Here, Fluke," cried two or three—they seemed all to know each other.

"Come along, sir," cried twenty shrill voices over his head. He looked up and saw that they were alongside of a great barge which was crowded with little dirty creatures, row above row. "Come this way—solid barges, sir, all the way. Ketch hold of the gen'lm'n's hand, Sammy. There. Now, Bill."

They hauled and lifted Thomas on to the barge, then led him along the side and across to the next yawning wooden gulf, and so over about seven barges to a plank, which led from the last on to a ladder ascending to the first floor of a public-house, the second floor of which, supported upon piles, projected over high water. There his conductors, two ragged little mudlarks, left him.

Through an empty kind of bar-room, he went into the bar, which communicated with the street. Here first he found that he had been followed by the same man who had given him the gin. He now passed before him to the counter, and said to the woman who was pumping a pot of beer:

"This gen'leman, Mrs. Cook, 's been and just took a child out o' the water ma'am. He 'ain't got a change in his wescut-pocket, so if you'll do what ye can for 'im, there's many on us'll be obliged to ye, ma'am."

"Lor', whose child was it, Jim?"

"I don't know as you know her, ma'am. The man's name's Potts. He keeps a public down about Limehouse, someveres."

Thomas stood shivering—glad, however, that the man should represent his case for him.

"The gentleman had better go to bed till we get his clo'es dried for him," said the landlady. "I think that's the best we can do for him."

"Take a drop o' summat, sir," said the man, turning to Thomas. "They keeps good licker here. Put a name upon it, sir."

"Well, I'll have a small glass of pale brandy," said Thomas—"neat, if you please. And what'll you have yourself? I'm much obliged to you for introducing me here, for I must look rather a queer customer."

"It's what *you'll* have, not what I'll have, sir, if you'll excuse *me*," returned the man.

"I beg your pardon," said Thomas, who had just received his brandy. He drank it, and proceeded to put his hand in his pocket—no easy matter in the state of his garments.

"*I'm*, a goin' to pay for this," interposed the man, in a determined tone, and Thomas was hardly in a condition to dispute it.

At the same moment the landlady, who had left the bar after she had helped Thomas, returned, saying, "Will you walk this way, sir?" Thomas followed, and found himself in a neat enough little room, where he was only too glad to undress and go to bed. As he pulled off his coat, it occurred to him to see that his money was safe. He had put it, mostly in sovereigns, into a pocket-book of elaborate construction, which he generally carried in the breast-pocket of what the tailors call a lounging-coat. It was gone. His first conclusion was, that the man had taken it. He rushed back into the bar, but he was not there. It must be confessed that, in the midst of his despair, a fresh pang at the loss of his money shot through Thomas's soul. But he soon came to the conclusion that the man had not taken it. It was far more likely that, as he went overboard, the book slipped from his pocket into the water, and in this loss an immediate reward of almost his first act of self-forgetfulness had followed. The best thing that can happen to a man, sometimes, is to lose his money; and, while people are compassionate over the loss, God may regard it as the first step of the stair by which the man shall rise above it and many things besides with which not only his feet, but his hands and his head, are defiled. Then first he began to feel that he had no ground under his feet—the one necessity before such a man could find a true foundation. Until he lost it, he did not know how much, even in his misery, the paltry hundred pounds had been to him. Now it was gone, things looked black indeed. He emptied his pockets of two or three sovereigns and some silver, put his clothes out at the door, and got into bed. There he fell a thinking. Instead of telling what he thought, however, I will now turn to what my reader may be, and I have been, thinking about his act of rescue.

What made him, who has been shown all but incapable of originating a single action, thus at the one right moment do the one right thing? Here arises another question: Does a man *always* originate his own actions? Is it not possible, to say the least of it, that, just to give him a taste of what well-doing means, some moment, when selfishness is sick and faint, may be chosen by the power in whom we live and move and have our being to inspire the man with a true impulse? We must think what an unspeakable comfort it must have been to Thomas, in these moments of hopeless degradation of which he felt all the bitterness, suddenly to find around him, as the result of a noble deed into which he had been unaccountably driven, a sympathetic, yes, admiring public. No matter that they were not of his class, nor yet that Thomas was not the man to do the human brotherhood justice; he could not help feeling the present power of humanity, the healing medicine of approbation, in the faces of the *common* people who had witnessed and applauded his deed. I say *medicine* of approbation; for what would have been to him in ordinary, a poison, was now a medicine. There was no fear of his thinking himself too much of a hero at present.

It may be objected that the deed originated only in a carelessness of life resulting from self-contempt. I answer, that no doubt that had its share in making the deed possible, because it removed for the time all that was adverse to such a deed; but self-despite, however true and well-grounded, cannot inspirit to true and noble action. I think it was the divine, the real self, aroused at the moment by the breath of that wind which bloweth where it listeth, that sprung thus into life and deed, shadowing, I say *shadowing* only, that wonderful saying of our Lord that he that loseth his life shall find it. It had come—been given to him—that a touch of light might streak the dark cloud of his fate, that he might not despise himself utterly, and act as unredeemable—kill himself or plunge into wickedness to drown his conscience. It was absolutely necessary that he should be brought to want; but here was just one little opening—not out of want, but into the light of a higher region altogether, the region of well-being—by which a glimmer of the strength of light could enter the chaos of his being. Any good deed partakes of the life whence it comes, and is a good to him who has done it. And this act might be a beginning.

Poor weak Thomas, when he got his head down on the pillow, began to cry. He pitied himself for the helplessness to which he was now reduced, and a new phase of despair filled his soul. He even said in his thoughts that his ill-gotten gain had, like all the devil's money, turned to rubbish in his hands. What he was to do he could not tell. He was tolerably safe, however, for the night, and, worn and weary, soon fell into a sleep which not even a dream disturbed.

When he woke all was dark, and he welcomed the darkness as a friend. It soothed and comforted him a little. If it were only always dark! If he could find some cave to creep into where he might revel in—feed upon the friendly gloom! If he could get among the snowy people of the north, blessed with half a year of gentle sunlessness! Thomas had plenty of fancy. He leaned on his elbow and looked out. His clothes had been placed by him while he slept. He rose and put them on, opened the door of his room, saw light somewhere, approached it softly, and found himself in a small room, like a large oriel window. The day had changed from gold to silver; the wide expanse of the great river lay before him, and up, and down, and across, it gleamed in the thoughtful radiance of the moon. Never was a picture of lovelier peace. It was like the reflex of the great city in the mind of a saint—all its vice, its crime, its oppression, money-loving, and ambition, all its fearfulness, grief, revenge, and remorse, gently covered with the silver mantle of faith and hope. But Thomas could not feel this. Its very repose was a reproach to him. There was no repose for him henceforth forever. He was degraded to all eternity. And herewith the thought of Lucy, which had been hovering about his mind all day, like a bird looking for an open window that it might enter, but which he had not dared to admit, darted into its own place, and he groaned aloud. For in her eyes, as well as in his own, he was utterly degraded. Not a thousand good actions, not the applause of a thousand crowds, could destroy the fact that he had done as he had done. The dingy, applauding multitude, with its many voices, its kind faces, its outstretched hands, had vanished, as if the moon had melted it away from off the water. Never to all eternity would that praising people, his little consoling populace, exist again, again be gathered from the four corners whither they had vanished, to take his part, to speak for him that he was not all lost in badness, that they at least considered him fit company for them and their children.

Thoughts like these went to and fro in his mind as he looked out upon the scene before him. Then it struck him that all was strangely still. Not only was there no motion on the river, but there was no sound—only an occasional outcry in the streets behind. The houses across in Wapping showed rare lights, and looked sepulchral in the killing stare of the moon, which, high above, had not only the whole heavens but the earth as well to herself, and seemed to be taking her own way with it in the consciousness of irresistible power. What that way was, who can tell? The troubled brain of the maniac and the troubled conscience of the malefactor know something about it; but neither can tell the way of the moon with the earth. Fear laid hold upon Thomas. He found himself all alone with that white thing in the sky; and he turned from the glorious window to go down to the bar. But all the house was dark, the household in bed, and he alone awake and wandering "in the dead waste and middle of the night." A horror seized him when he found that he was alone. Why should he fear? The night covered him. But there was God. I do not mean for a moment that he had a conscious fear of the Being he had been taught to call God. Never had that representation produced in him yet any sense of the reality, any the least consciousness of presence—anything like the feeling of the child who placed two chairs behind the window-curtain, told God that that one was for him, and sat down to have a talk with him. It was fear of the unknown God, manifested in the face of a nature which was strange and unfriendly to the evil-doer. It is to God alone that a man can flee from such terror of the unknown in the fierceness of the sea, in the ghastly eye of the moon, in the abysses of the glaciers, in the misty slopes of the awful mountain-side; but to God Thomas dared not or could not flee. Full of the horror of wakefulness in the midst of sleeping London, he felt his way back into the room he had just left, threw himself on a bench, and closed his eyes to shut out everything. His own room at Highbury, even that of his mother with Mr. Simon talking in it, rose before him like a haven of refuge. But between him and that haven lay an impassable gulf. No more returning thither. He must leave the country. And Lucy? He must vanish from her eyes, that she might forget him and marry some one else. Was not that the only justice left him to do her? But would Lucy forget him? Why should she not? Women could forget honorable men whom they had loved, let them only be out of their sight long enough; and why should not Lucy forget a —? He dared not even think the word that belonged to him now. A fresh billow of shame rushed over him. In the person of Lucy he condemned himself afresh to utter and ineffaceable shame, confusion, and hissing. Involuntarily he opened his eyes. A ghostly whiteness, the sails of a vessel hanging loose from their yards, gleamed upon him. The whole of the pale region of the moon, the spectral masts, the dead houses on the opposite shore, the glitter of the river as from eyes that would close no more, gleamed in upon him, and a fresh terror of loneliness in the presence of the incomprehensible and the unsympathetic overcame him. He fell on his knees, and sought to pray; and doubtless in the ear that is keen with mercy it sounded as prayer, though to him that prayed it seemed that no winged thought arose to the infinite from a "heart as dry as dust." Mechanically, at length, all feeling gone, both of fear and of hope, he went back to his room and his bed.

When he woke in the morning his landlady's voice was in his ears.

"Well, how do we find ourselves to-day, sir? None the worse, I hope?"

He opened his eyes. She stood by his bedside, with her short arms set like the handles of an urn. It was a common face that rose from between them, red, and with eyes that stood out with fatness. Yet Thomas was glad to see them looking at him, for there was kindness in them.

"I am all right, thank you," he said.

"Where will you have your breakfast?" she asked.

"Where you please," answered Thomas.

"Will you come down to the bar-parlor, then?"

"I shall be down in a few minutes."

"Jim Salter's inquirin' after ye."

"Who?" said Thomas, starting.

"Only Jim Salter, the man that brought you in last night, sir. I told him to wait till I came up."

"I shall be down in one minute," said Thomas, a hope of his money darting into his mind.

He had to pass through the bar to the little room at the back. Against the counter leaned Jim, smoking a short pipe, with his hand upon a pot of beer. When Thomas entered, he touched his cap to him, saying:

"Glad to see you lookin' middlin', guvnor. Is there anything I can do for you to-day?"

"Come into the room here," said Thomas, "and have something. I'm rather late, you see. I haven't had my breakfast yet."

Salter followed him with his pewter in his hand. Thomas disliked his appearance less than on the preceding evening. What was unpleasant in his face was chiefly owing to the small-pox. He was dirty and looked *beery*, but there seemed to be no harm in him. He sat down near the door which led to the ladder already mentioned, and put his pot on the window-sill. Thomas asked him if he would have a cup of coffee, but he preferred his beer and his pipe.

"You wanted to see me?" said Thomas, opening a conversation.

"Oh! nothin' perticlar, guvnor. I only wanted to see if I could do anything for you," said Jim.

"I was in hopes you had heard of something I lost, but I suppose it's at the bottom of the river," said Thomas.

"Not your watch?" asked Salter, with some appearance of anxious interest.

"A great deal worse," answered Thomas; "a pocket-book."

"Much in it?" asked Jim, with a genuine look of sympathetic discomfiture.

"More than I like to think of. Look," said Thomas, turning out the contents of his pocket, "that is all I have in the world."

"More than ever I had," returned Salter; "keep me a month."

Thomas relapsed into thought. This man was the only resemblance of a friend he had left. He did not like to let him go loose in the wilds of London, without the possibility of finding him again. If this man vanished, the only link Thomas felt between him and the world of men would be broken. I do not say Thomas *thought* this. He only felt that he would be absolutely alone when this man left him. Why should he not go away somewhere with him?

"Where do you live?" he asked.

"Stepney way," answered Jim.

"I want to see that part of London. What do you do now? I mean, what do you work at?"

"Oh! nothin' perticlar, guvnor. Take a day at the docks now and then. Any job that turns up. I'm not perticlar. Only I never could stick to one thing. I like to be moving. I had a month in Bermondsey last—in a tan-yard, you know. I knows a bit of everthing."

"Well, where are you going now?"

"Nowheres—anywhere you like, guvnor. If you want to see them parts, as you say, there's nobody knows 'em better than I do—Tiger-bay and all."

"Come, then," said Thomas. But here a thought struck him. "Wouldn't it be better, though," he added—"they're queer places, some of those, ain't they?—to put on a workman's clothes?"

Jim looked at him. Thomas felt himself wince under his gaze. But he was relieved when he said, with a laugh:

"You won't look much like a workman, guvnor, put on what you like."

"I can't wear these clothes, anyhow," said Thomas; "they look so wretchedly shabby after their ducking. Couldn't you take me somewhere where they'd change them for a suit of fustian? I should like to try how they feel for a few days. We're about the same size—I could give them to you when I had done with them."

Jim had been observing him, and had associated this wish of Thomas's with the pocket-book, and his furtive, troubled looks. But Jim was as little particular about his company as about anything else, and it was of no consequence to him whether Thomas had or had not deeper reasons than curiosity for seeking to disguise himself.

"I tell you what," he said, "if you want to keep quiet for a day or two, I'm your man. But if you put on a new suit of fustian you'll be more looked at than in your own clo'es."

Thomas had by this time finished his breakfast; it was not much he could eat.

"Well," he said, rising, "if you've nothing particular to do, I'll give you a day's wages to go with me. Only let's go into Stepney, or away somewhere in that direction, as soon as possible."

He called the landlady, settled his very moderate bill, and then found that his hat must be somewhere about the Nore by this time. Jim ran to a neighboring shop, and returned with a cloth cap. They then went out into a long, narrow street, Rotherhithe Street, I think, very different in aspect from any he had seen in London before. Indeed it is more like a street in Cologne. Here we must leave him with his misery and Jim Salter, both better companions than Molken.

CHAPTER XXXIX
POPPIE CHOOSES A PROFESSION

When their native red began to bloom again upon the cheeks of Poppie, she began to grow restless, and the heart of the tailor to grow anxious. It was very hard for a wild thing to be kept in a cage against her will, he thought. He did not mind sitting in a cage, but then he was used to it, and frequented it of his own free will; whereas his child Poppie took after her grandfather— her mother's father, who was a sailor, and never set his foot on shore but he wanted to be off again within the week.

He therefore began to reason with himself as to what ought to be done with her. So soon as she was quite strong again all her wandering habits would return, and he must make some provision for them. It would not only be cruel to try to break her of them all at once, but assuredly fruitless. Poppie would give him the slip some day, return to her Arab life, and render all sealing of the bond between father and daughter impossible. The streets were her home. She was used to them. They made life pleasant to her. And yet it would not do to let her run idle about the streets. He thought and thought what would be best.

Meantime the influence of Mattie had grown upon Poppie. Although there was as yet very little sign of anything like thought in her, the way she deferred to the superior intelligence in their common pursuits proved that she belonged to the body of humanity, and not to unassociated animality. Her love of bright colors now afforded the first hold by which to commence her education. Remembering her own childhood, Mattie sought to interest her pupil in dolls, proceeding to dress one, which she called Poppie, in a gorgeous scarlet cloth which the tailor procured for the purpose. And Poppie was interested. The color drew her to the process. By degrees, she took a part; first only in waiting on Mattie, then in sewing on a button or string, at which she was awkward enough, as Mattie took more than necessary pains to convince her, learning, however, by slow degrees, to use her needle a little. But what was most interesting to find was, that a certain amount of self-consciousness began to dawn during and apparently from the doll-dressing. Her causative association with the outer being of the doll, led to her turning an eye upon her own outer being; and Poppie's redemption—I do not say regeneration—first showed itself in a desire to be dressed. Consciousness begins with regard to the body first. A baby's first lesson of consciousness lies in his blue shoes. But one may object, "You do not call it a sign of redemption in a baby that, when you ask where baby's shoes are, he holds up his little feet with a smile of triumph." I answer, it must be remembered that Poppie had long passed the age when such interest indicates natural development, and therefore she was out of the natural track of the human being, and a return to that track, indicating an awakening of the nature that was in her, may well be called a sign of redemption. And with a delicate instinct of his own, nourished to this particular manifestation by his trade, the tailor detected the interest shown in the doll by Poppie, as a most hopeful sign, and set himself in the midst of his work to get a dress ready for her, such as she would like. Accustomed, however, only to work in cloth, and upon male subjects, the result was, to say the least of it, remarkable—altogether admirable in Poppie's eyes, though somewhat strange in those of others. She appeared one day in a scarlet jacket, of fine cloth, trimmed with black, which fitted her like her skin, and, to complete the dress, in a black skirt, likewise of cloth, which, however picturesque and accordant with the style of Poppie's odd beauty, was at least somewhat peculiar and undesirable in a city like London, which persecutes men's tastes if it leaves their convictions free.

This dress Mr. Spelt had got ready in view of a contemplated walk with Poppie. He was going to take her to Highgate on a Sunday morning, with his Bible in his pocket. I have already said that he was an apparent anomaly, this Mr. Spelt, loving his New Testament, and having no fancy for going to church. How this should come about I hardly understand. Not that I do not know several instances of it in most excellent men, but not in his stratum. Yet what was his stratum? The Spirit of God teaches men in a thousand ways, and Mr. Spelt knew some of the highest truths better than nine out of ten clergymen, I venture to say. Yet Mr. Spelt was inwardly reproached that he did not go to church, and made the attempt several times, with the result that he doubted the truth of the whole thing for half the week after. Some church-going reader must not condemn him at least for preferring Highgate to the church-yard gate.

It was a bright frosty morning, full of life and spirit, when the father and daughter—for thus we accept the willful conviction of the tailor, and say no more about it—set out for Highgate. Poppie was full of spirits, too full for her father's comfort, for, every time she drew her hand from his, and danced away sideways or in front, he feared lest he had seen the last of her, and she would never more return to lay her hand in his. On one of these occasions, it was to dart a hundred yards in advance upon another little girl, who was listlessly standing at a crossing, take the broom from her hand, and begin to sweep vigorously. Nor did she cease sweeping till she had made the crossing clean, by which time her father had come up. She held out her hand to him, received in it a ready penny, and tossed it to the girl. Then she put her hand in his again, and trotted along with him, excited and sedate both at once.

"Would you like to sweep a crossing, Poppie?" asked he.

"Wouldn't I just, daddie? I should get no end o' ha'pence."

"What would you do with them when you got them?"

"Give them to poor girls. I don't want them, you see, now I'm a lady."

"What makes a lady of you, then?"

"I've got a father of my own, all to myself—that makes a lady of me, I suppose. Anyhow I know I am a lady now. Look at my jacket."

I do not know that Mr. Spelt thought that her contempt of money, or rather want of faith in it, went a good way to make her a very peculiar lady indeed; but he did think that he would buy her a broom the first day he saw the attraction of the streets grow too strong for Guild Court.

This day, things did not go quite to the tailor's mind. He took Poppie to a little public-house which he had known for many years, for it was kept by a cousin of his. There he ordered his half-pint of beer, carried it with him to a little arbor in the garden, now getting very bare of its sheltering leaves, sat down with Poppie, pulled out big Bible, and began to read to her. But he could not get her to mind him. Every other moment she was up and out of the arbor, now after one thing, now after another; now it was a spider busily rolling up a fly in his gluey weft; now it was a chicken escaped from the hen-house, and scratching about as if it preferred finding its own living even in an irregular fashion; and now a bird of the air that sowed not nor reaped, and yet was taken care of.

"Come along, Poppie," said her father; "I want you to listen."

"Yes, daddie," Poppie would answer, returning instantly; but in a moment, ere a sentence was finished, she would be half across the garden. He gave it up in despair.

"Why ain't you reading, daddie?" she said, after one of these excursions.

"Because you won't listen to a word of it, Poppie."

"Oh! yes; here I am," she said.

"Come, then; I will teach you to read."

"Yes," said Poppie, and was off after another sparrow.

"Do you know that God sees you, Poppie?" asked Mr. Spelt.

"I don't mind," answered Poppie.

He sighed and closed his book, drank the last of his half-pint of beer, and rose to go. Poppie seemed to feel that she had displeased him, for she followed without a word. They went across the fields to Hampstead, and then across more fields to the Finchley Road. In passing the old church, the deeper notes of the organ reached their ears.

"There," said Poppie; "I suppose that's God making his thunder. Ain't it, daddie?"

"No. It's not that," answered Spelt.

"It's there he keeps it, anyhow," said Poppie. "I've heard it coming out many a time."

"Was you never in one o' them churches?" asked her father.

"No," answered Poppie.

"Would you like to go?" he asked again, with the hope that something might take hold of her.

"If you went with me," she said.

Now Mr. Spelt had heard of Mr. Fuller from Mr. Kitely, and had been once to hear him preach. He resolved to take Poppie to his church that evening.

My reader will see that the child had already made some progress. She talked at least. How this began I cannot explain. No fresh sign of thought or of conscience in a child comes into my notice but I feel it like a miracle—a something that cannot be accounted for save in attributing it to a great Thought that can account for it.

They got upon an omnibus, to Poppie's great delight, and rode back into the city. After they had had some tea they went to the evening service, where they saw Lucy, and Mattie with her father. Mattie was very devout, and listened even when she could not understand; Poppie only stared, and showed by her restlessness that she wanted to be out again. When they were again in the street she asked just one question: "Why did Jesus Christ put on that ugly black thing?"

"That wasn't Jesus Christ," said Mattie, with a little pharisaical horror.

"Oh! wasn't it?" said Poppie, in a tone of disappointment. "I thought it was."

"Oh, Poppie, Poppie!" said poor Mr. Spelt; "haven't I told you twenty times that Jesus Christ was the Son of God?"

But he might have told her a thousand times. Poppie could not recall what she had no apprehension of when she heard it. What was Mr. Spelt to do? He had tried and tried, but he had got no idea into her yet. But Poppie had no objection either to religion in general, or to any dogma whatever in particular. It was simply that she stood in no relation of consciousness toward it or any part or phrase of it. Even Mattie's attempts resulted in the most grotesque conceptions and fancies. But that she was willing to be taught, an instance which soon followed will show.

Her restlessness increasing, and her father dreading lest she should be carried away by some sudden impulse of lawlessness, he bought her a broom one day—the best he could find, of course—and told her she might, if she pleased, go and sweep a crossing. Poppie caught at the broom, and vanished without a word. Not till she was gone beyond recall did her father bethink himself that the style of her dress was scarcely accordant with the profession she was about to assume. She was more like a child belonging to a traveling theater than any other. He remembered, too, that crossing-sweepers are exceedingly tenacious of their rights, and she might get into trouble. He could not keep quiet; his work made no progress; and at last he yielded to his anxiety and went out to look for her. But he wandered without success, lost half his day, and returned disconsolate.

At their dinner-hour Poppie came home; but, alas! with her brilliant jacket nearly as dirty as her broom, the appearance of which certainly indicated work. Spelt stooped, as usual, but hesitated to lift her to his nest.

"Oh, Poppie," he expostulated, "what a mess you've made of yourself!"

"'Tain't me, daddie," she answered. "It's them nasty boys would throw dirt at me. 'Twasn't their crossing I took—they hadn't no call to chivy me. But I give it them."

"What did you do, Poppie?" asked her father, a little anxiously.

"I looks up at St. Pauls's, and I says, 'Please, Jesus Christ, help me to give it 'em.' And then I flies at 'em with my broom, and I knocks one o' them down, and a cart went over his leg, and he's took to the 'ospittle. I believe his leg's broke."

"Oh, Poppie! And didn't they say anything to you? I wonder they didn't take you up."

"They couldn't find me. I thought Jesus Christ would help me. He did."

What was Mr. Spelt to say? He did not know; and, therefore, unlike some, who would teach others even when they have nothing to impart, he held his peace. But he took good care not to let her go out in that dress any more.

"Didn't you get any ha'pence?" he asked.

"Yes. I gave 'em all to the boy. I wouldn't if the cart hadn't gone over him, though. Catch me!"

"Why did you give them to him?"

"Oh, I don't know. I wanted to."

"Did he take them?"

"Course he did. Why shouldn't he? I'd ha' tookt 'em."

Mr. Spelt resolved at last to consult Mr. Fuller about the child. He went to see him, and told him all he knew concerning her. To his surprise, however, when he came to her onset with the broom, Mr. Fuller burst into a fit of the heartiest laughter. Spelt stood with his mouth open, staring at the sacred man. Mr. Fuller saw his amazement.

"You don't think it was very wicked of your poor child to pray to God and shoulder her broom, do you?" he said, still laughing.

"We're told to forgive our enemies, sir. And Poppie prayed against hers."

"Yes, yes. You and I have heard that, and, I hope, learned it. But Poppie, if she has heard it, certainly does not understand it yet. Do you ever read the Psalms?"

"Yes, sometimes. Some of them pretty often, sir."

"You will remember, then, how David prays against his enemies?"

"Yes, sir. It's rather awful, sometimes."

"What do you make of it? Was it wicked in David to do so?"

"I daren't say that, sir."

"Then why should you think it was in Poppie?"

"I think perhaps David didn't know better."

"And you think Poppie ought to know better than David?"

"Why, you see, sir, if I'm right, as I fancy, David lived before our Saviour came into the world to teach us better."

"And so you think Poppie more responsible than a man like David, who loved God as not one Christian in a million, notwithstanding that the Saviour is come, has learned to love him yet? A man may love God, and pray against his enemies. Mind you, I'm not sure that David hated them. I know he did not love them, but I am not sure that he hated them. And I am sure Poppie did not hate hers, for she gave the little rascal her coppers, you know."

"Thank you, sir," said Spelt, grateful to the heart's core that Mr. Fuller stood up for Poppie.

"Do you think God heard David's prayers, against his enemies?" resumed Mr. Fuller.

"He gave him victory over them, anyhow."

"And God gave Poppie the victory, too. I think God heard Poppie's prayer. And Poppie will be the better for it. She'll pray for a different sort of thing before she's done praying. It is a good thing to pray to God for anything. It is a grand thing to begin to pray."

"I wish you would try and teach her something, sir. I have tried and tried, and I don't know what to do more. I don't seem to get anything into her."

"You're quite wrong, Mr. Spelt. You have taught her. She prayed to God before she fell upon her enemies with her broom."

"But I do want her to believe. I confess to you, sir, I've never been much of a church-goer, but I do believe in Christ."

"It doesn't much matter whether you go to church or not if you believe in him. Tell me how you came to hear or know about him without going to church."

"My wife was a splendid woman, sir—Poppie's mother, but—you see, sir—she wasn't—she didn't—she was a bit of a disappointment to me."

"Yes. And what then?"

"I took to reading the Bible, sir."

"Why did you do that?"

"I don't know, sir. But somehow, bein' unhappy, and knowin' no way out of it, I took to the Bible, sir. I don't know why or wherefore, but that's the fact. And when I began to read, I began to think about it. And from then I began to think about everything that came in my way—a tryin' to get things all square in my own head, you know, sir."

Mr. Fuller was delighted with the man, and having promised to think what he could do for Poppie, they parted. And here I may mention that Spelt rarely missed a Sunday morning at Mr. Fuller's church after this. For he had found a fellow-man who could teach him, and that the Bible was not the sole means used by God to make his children grow: their brothers and sisters must have a share in it too.

Mr. Fuller set about making Poppie's acquaintance. And first he applied to Mattie, in order to find out what kind of thing Poppie liked. Mattie told him *lollipops*. But Mr. Fuller preferred attacking the town of Mansoul at the gate of one of the nobler senses, if possible.—He tried Lucy, who told him about the bit of red glass and the buttons. So Mr. Fuller presented his friendship's offering to Poppie in the shape of the finest kaleidoscope he could purchase. It was some time before she could be taught to shut one eye and look with the other; but when at length she succeeded in getting a true vision of the wonders in the inside of the thing, she danced and shouted for joy. This confirmed Mr. Fuller's opinion that it was through her eyes, and not through her ears, that he must approach Poppie's heart. She had never been accustomed to receive secondary impressions: all her impressions, hitherto, had come immediately through the senses. Mr. Fuller therefore concluded that he could reach her mind more readily through the seeing of her eyes than such hearing of the ears as had to be converted by the imagination into visual forms before it could make any impression. He must get her to ask questions by showing her eyes what might suggest them. And Protestantism having deprived the Church of almost all means of thus appealing to the eye as an inlet of truth, he was compelled to supply the deficiency as he best could. I do not say that Mr. Fuller would have filled his church with gorgeous paintings as things in general, and artists in especial, are. He shrunk in particular from the more modern representations of our Lord given upon canvas, simply because he felt them to be so unlike him, showing him either as effeminately soft, or as pompously condescending; but if he could have filled his church with pictures in which the strength exalted the tenderness, and the majesty was glorified by the homeliness, he would have said that he did not see why painted windows should be more consistent with Protestantism than painted walls. Lacking such aids, he must yet provide as he could that kind of instruction which the early Church judged needful for those of its members who were in a somewhat similar condition to that of Poppie. He therefore began searching the print-shops, till he got together about a dozen of such engravings, mostly from the old masters, as he thought would represent our Lord in a lovable aspect, and make the child want to have them explained. For Poppie had had no big family Bible with pictures, to pore over in her homeless childhood; and now she had to go back to such a beginning.   .

By this time he had so far ingratiated himself with her that she was pleased to accompany Mattie to tea with him, and then the pictures made their appearance. This took place again and again, till the pictures came to be looked for as part of the entertainment—Mr. Fuller adding one now and then, as he was fortunate in his search, for he never passed a fresh print-shop without making inquiry after such engravings.

Meantime Poppie went out crossing-sweeping by fits and starts. Her father neither encouraged nor prevented her.

One afternoon of a cold day, when the wind from the east was blowing the darkness over the city, and driving all who had homes and could go to them home for comfort, they were walking hand in hand in Farringdon Street—a very bleak, open place. Poppie did not feel the cold nearly so much as her father, but she did blow upon the fingers of her disengaged hand now and then notwithstanding.

"Have a potato to warm you, Poppie," said her father, as they came up to one of those little steam-engines for cooking potatoes, which stand here and there on the edges of the pavements about London, blowing a fierce cloud of steam from their little funnels, so consoling to the half-frozen imagination.

"Jolly!" cried Poppie, running up to the man, and laying her hand on the greasy sleeve of his velveteen coat.

"I say, Jim, give us a ha'porth," she said.

"Why, 'tain't never you, Poppie?" returned the man.

"Why ain't it?" said Poppie. "Here's my father. I've found one, and a good 'un, Jim."

The man looked at Poppie's dress, then at Mr. Spelt, touched the front of his cloth cap, and said:

"Good evenin', guvnor." Then in an undertone he added,

"I say, guvnor, you never did better in your life than takin' that 'ere pretty creetur off the streets. You look well arter her. She's a right good un, I know. Bless you, she ain't no knowledge what wickedness means."

In the warmth of his heart, Mr. Spelt seized the man's hand, and gave it a squeeze of gratitude.

"Come, Jim, ain't your taters done yet?" said Poppie.

"Bustin' o' mealiness," answered Jim, throwing back the lid, and taking out a potato, which he laid in the hollow of his left hand. Then he caught up an old and I fear dirty knife, and split the potato lengthways. Then, with the same knife, he took a piece of butter from somewhere about the apparatus—though how it was not oil instead of butter I cannot think—laid it into the cleft as if it had been a trowelful of mortar, gave it a top-dressing of salt and a shake of the pepper-box, and handed it to Poppie.

"Same for you, sir?" he asked.

"Well, I don't mind if I do have one," answered Spelt. "Are they good?"

"The best *and* the biggest at the price in all London," said Jim. "Taste one," he went on, as he prepared another, "and if you like to part with it then, I'll take it back and eat it myself."

Spelt paid for the potatoes—the sum of three ha'pence—and Poppie, bidding Jim good-night, trotted away by his side, requiring both her hands now for the management of her potato, at which she was more expert than her father, for he, being nice in his ways, found the butter and the peel together troublesome.

"I say, ain't it jolly?" remarked Poppie. "I call that a good trade now."

"Would you like to have one o' them things and sell hot potatoes?" asked her father.

"Just wouldn't I?"

"As well as sweeping a crossing?"

"A deal better," answered Poppie. "You see, daddie, it's more respectable—a deal. It takes money to buy a thing like that. And I could wear my red jacket then. Nobody could say anything then, for the thing would be my own, and a crossing belongs to everybody."

Mr. Spelt turned the matter over and over in his mind, and thought it might be a good plan for giving Poppie some liberty, and yet keeping her from roving about everywhere without object or end. So he began at once to work for a potato-steamer for Poppie, and, in the course of a fortnight, managed to buy her one. Great was Poppie's delight.

She went out regularly in the dusk to the corner of Bagot Street. Her father carried the machine for her, and leaving her there with it, returned to his work. In following her new occupation, the child met with little annoyance, for this was a respectable part of the city, and the police knew her, and were inclined to protect her. One of her chief customers was Mr. Spelt himself, who would always once, sometimes twice, of an evening, lay down his work, scramble from his perch, and, running to the corner of the street, order a potato, ask her how she was getting on, pay his ha'penny or penny, and hurry back with the hot handful to console him for the absence of his darling. Having eaten it, chuckling and rejoicing, he would attack his work with vigor so renewed as soon to make up for the loss of time involved in procuring it. But keeping out of view the paternal consumption, Poppie was in a fair way of paying all the expense of the cooking apparatus. Mr. and Miss Kitely were good customers, too, and everything looked well for father and daughter.

Every night, at half-past nine, her father was by her side to carry the "murphy-buster"—that was Jim's name for it—home. There was no room for it in the shop, of course. He took it up the three flights of stairs to Poppie's own room; and there, with three-quarters of a pint of beer to wash them down, they finished the remaining potatoes, "*with* butter, *with* pepper, and *with* salt," as Poppie would exclaim, in the undisguised delight of her sumptuous fare. Sometimes there were none left, but that gave only a variety to their pleasures; for as soon as the engine, as Mr. Spelt called it, was deposited in safety, they set out to buy their supper. And great were the consultations to which, in Mr. Spelt's desire to draw out the choice and judgment of his daughter, this proceeding gave rise. At one time it was a slice of beef or ham that was resolved upon, at another a bit of pudding, sometimes a couple of mutton-pies or sausages, with bread *ad libitum*. There was a cook-shop in the neighborhood, whose window was all beclouded with jets of steam, issuing as from a volcanic soil, and where all kinds of hot dainties were ready for the fortunate purchaser: thither the two would generally repair, and hold their consultation outside the window. Then, the desirable thing once agreed upon, came the delight of buying it, always left to Poppie; of carrying it home, still left to Poppie; of eating it, not left to Poppie, but heightened by the sympathetic participation of her father. Followed upon all, the chapter in the Bible, the Lord's Prayer, bed, and dreams of Mrs. Flanaghan and her gin-bottle, or, perhaps, of Lucy and her first kiss.

CHAPTER XL
THOMAS'S MOTHER

Meantime Mrs. Worboise had taken to her bed, and not even Mr. Simon could comfort her. The mother's heart now spoke louder than her theology.

She and her priest belonged to a class more numerous than many of my readers would easily believe, a great part of whose religion consists in arrogating to themselves exclusive privileges, and another great part in defending their supposed rights from the intrusion of others. The thing does not look such to them, of course, but the repulsiveness of their behavior to those who cannot use the same religious phrases, indicating the non-adoption of their particular creed, compels others so to conclude concerning their religion. Doubtless they would say for themselves, "We do but as God has taught us; we believe but as he has told us; we exclude whom he has excluded, and admit whom he has admitted." But, alas for that people! the god of whose worship is altogether such a one as themselves, or worse; whose god is paltry, shallow-minded and full of party spirit; who sticks to a thing *because* he has said it, accepts a man because of his assent, and condemns him because of his opinions; who looks no deeper than a man's words to find his thoughts, and no deeper than his thoughts to find his will! True, they are in the hands of another God than that of their making, and such offenses must come; yet, alas for them! for they are of the hardest to redeem into the childhood of the kingdom.

I do not say that Mrs. Worboise began to see her sin as such, when the desolation of Thomas's disappearance fell upon her, but the atmosphere of her mind began to change, and a spring-season of mother's feelings to set in. How it came about I cannot explain. I as well as any of my readers might have felt as if Mrs. Worboise were almost beyond redemption; but it was not so. *Her* redemption came in the revival of a long suppressed motherhood. Her husband's hardness and want of sympathy with her sufferings had driven her into the arms of a party of exclusive *Christians*, whose brotherhood consisted chiefly, as I have already described it, in denying the great brotherhood, and refusing the hand of those who followed not with them. They were led by one or two persons of some social position, whose condescending assumption of superiority over those that were without was as offensive as absurd, and whose weak brains were their only excuse. The worst thing of this company was that it was a company. In many holding precisely the same opinions with them, those opinions are comparatively harmless, because they are more directly counteracted by the sacred influences of God's world and the necessities of things, which are very needful to prevent, if possible, self-righteous Christians from sending themselves to a deeper hell than any they denounce against their neighbors. But when such combine themselves into an esoteric school, they foster, as in an oven or a forcing-pit, all the worst distinctions for the sake of which they separate themselves from others. All that was worst in poor Mrs. Worboise was cherished by the companionship of those whose chief anxiety was to save their souls, and who thus ran the great risk set forth by the Saviour of losing them. They treated the words of the Bible like talismans or spells, the virtue of which lay in the words, and in the assent given to them, or at most, the feelings that could be conjured up by them, not in the doing of the things they presupposed or commanded. But there was one thing that did something to keep her fresh and prevent her from withering into a dry tree of supposed orthodoxy, the worst dryness of all, because it is the least likely to yield to any fresh burst of living sap from the forgotten root—that was her anxiety to get her son within the "garden walled around," and the continual disappointment of her efforts to that end.

But now that the shock of his flight had aggravated all the symptoms of her complaint, which was a serious one though slow in the movement of its progressive cycles, now that she was confined to her bed and deprived of the small affairs that constituted the dull excitements of her joyless life, her imagination, roused by a reaction from the first grief, continually presented to her the form of her darling in the guise of the prodigal, his handsome face worn with hunger and wretchedness, or still worse, with dissipation and disease; and she began to accuse herself bitterly for having alienated his affections from herself by too assiduously forcing upon his attention that which was distasteful to him. She said to herself that it was easy for an old woman like her, who had been disappointed in everything, and whose life and health were a wreck, to turn from the vanities of the world; but how could her young Thomas, in the glory of youth, be expected to see things as she saw them? How could he flee from the wrath to come when he had as yet felt no breath of that wrath on his cheek? She ought to have loved him, and borne with him, and smiled upon him, and never let him fancy that his presence was a pain to her because he could not take her ways for his. Add to this certain suspicions that arose in her mind from what she considered unfriendly neglect on the part of the chief man of their chosen brotherhood, and from the fact that her daughter Amy had already wrought a questionable change on Mr. Simon, having persuaded him to accompany her—not to the theatre at all—only to the Gallery of Illustration, and it will be seen that everything tended to turn the waters of her heart back into the old channel with the flow of a spring-tide toward her son. She wept and prayed—better tears and better prayers because her love was stronger. She humbled her heart, proud of its acceptance with God, before a higher idea of that God. She began to doubt whether she was more acceptable in his sight than other people. There must be some who were, but she could not be one of them. Instead of striving after assurance, as they called it, she began to shrink from every feeling that lessened her humility; for she found that when she was most humble then she could best pray for her son. Not that had her assurance rested in the love of God it would ever have quenched her prayer; but her assurance had been taught to rest upon her consciousness of faith, which, unrealized, tended to madness—realized, to spiritual pride. She lay thus praying for him, and dreaming about him, and hoping that he would return before she died, when she would receive him as son had never before been welcomed to his mother's bosom.

But Mr. Worboise's dry, sand-locked bay was open to the irruption of no such waters from the great deep of the eternal love. Narrow and poor as it was, Mrs. Worboise's religion had yet been as a little wedge to keep her door open to better things, when they should arrive and claim an entrance, as they had now done. But her husband's heart was full of money and the love of it. How to get money, how not to spend it, how to make it grow—these were the chief cares that filled his heart. His was not the natural anxiety the objects of which, though not the anxiety, were justified by the Lord when he said, "Your Father knoweth that ye have need of these things." It was not what he needed that filled his mind with care, but what he did not need, and never would need; nay, what other people needed, and what was not his to take—not his in God's sight, whatever the law might say. And to God's decision everything must come at last, for that is the only human verdict of things, the only verdict which at last will satisfy the whole jury of humanity. But I am wrong; this was not all that filled his heart. One demon generally opens the door to another—they are not jealous of exclusive possession of the human thrall. The heart occupied by the love of money will be only too ready to fall a prey to other evils; for selfishness soon branches out in hatred and injustice. The continued absence of his son, which he attributed still to the Boxalls, irritated more than alarmed him; but if sometimes a natural feeling of dismay broke in upon him, it only roused yet more the worst feelings of his heart against Lucy and her grandmother. Every day to which Thomas's absence extended itself, his indignation sank deeper rather than rose higher. Every day he vowed that, if favored by fortune, he would make them feel in bitterness how deeply they had injured him. To the same account he entered all the annoyance given him by the well-meaning Mr. Sargent, who had only as yet succeeded in irritating him without gaining the least advantage over him. His every effort in resistance of probate failed. The decision of the court was that Mr. Boxall, a strong, healthy, well-seasoned, middle-aged man, was far more likely to have outlived all his daughters, than any one of them have outlived him; therefore Mr. Worboise obtained probate and entered into possession.

Although Mr. Sargent could not but have at least more than doubted the result, he felt greatly discomfited at it. He went straight to Mr. Morgenstern's office to communicate his failure and the foiling of the liberality which had made the attempt possible. Mr. Morgenstern only smiled, and wrote him a check for the costs. Of course, being a Jew, he did not enjoy parting with his money for nothing—no Christian would have minded it in the least. Seriously, Mr. Morgenstern did throw half his cigar into the fire from annoyance. But his first words were:

"What's to be done for those good people, then, Sargent?"

"We must wait till we see. I think I told you that the old lady has a claim upon the estate, which, most unfortunately, she cannot establish. Now, however, that this cormorant has had his own way, he will perhaps be inclined to be *generous*; for justice must be allowed in this case to put on the garb of generosity, else she will not appear in public, I can tell you. I mean to make this one attempt more. I confess to considerable misgiving, however. To-morrow, before his satisfaction has evaporated, I will make it, and let you know the result."

By this time Mr. Morgenstern had lighted another cigar.

CHAPTER XLI
LUCY'S NEW TROUBLE

Mr. Sargent's next application to Mr. Worboise, made on the morning after the decision of the court in his favor, shared the fate of all his preceding attempts. Mr. Worboise smiled it off. There was more inexorableness expressed in his smile than in another's sullen imprecation. The very next morning Mrs. Boxall was served with notice to quit at the approaching quarter-day; for she had no agreement, and paid no rent, consequently she was tenant only on sufferance. And now Mr. Stopper's behavior toward them underwent a considerable change; not that he was in the smallest degree rude to them; but, of course, there was now no room for that assumption of the confidential by which he had sought to establish the most friendly relations between himself and the probable proprietors of the business in which he hoped to secure his position, not merely as head-clerk, but as partner. The door between the house and the office was once more carefully locked, and the key put in his drawer, and having found how hostile his new master was to the inhabitants of the house, he took care to avoid every suspicion of intimacy with them.

Mrs. Boxall's paroxysm of indignant rage when she received the notice to quit was of course as impotent as the bursting of a shell in a mountain of mud. From the first, however, her anger had had this effect, that everybody in the court, down to lowly and lonely Mr. Dolman, the cobbler, knew all the phases of her oppression and injury. Lucy never said a word about it, save to Mr. and Mrs. Morgenstern, whose offer of shelter for herself and her grandmother till they could see what was to be done, she gratefully declined, knowing that her grandmother would die rather than accept such a position.

"There's nothing left for me in my old age but the work-house," said Mrs. Boxall, exhausted by one of her outbursts of fierce vindictive passion against the author of her misfortunes, which, as usual, ended in the few bitter tears that are left to the aged to shed.

"Grannie, grannie," said Lucy, "don't talk like that. You have been a mother to me. See if I cannot be a daughter to you. I am quite able to keep you and myself too as comfortable as ever. See if I can't."

"Nonsense, child. It will be all that you can do to keep yourself; and I'm not a-going to sit on the neck of a young thing like you, just like a nightmare, and have you wishing me gone from morning to night."

"I don't deserve that you should say that of me, grannie. But I'm sure you don't think as you say. And as to being able, with Mrs. Morgenstern's recommendation I can get as much teaching as I can undertake. I am pretty sure of that, and you know it will only be paying you back a very little of your own, grannie."

Before Mrs. Boxall could reply, for she felt reproached for having spoken so to her grand-daughter, there was a tap at the door, and Mr. Kitely entered.

"Begging your pardon, ladies, and taking the liberty of a neighbor, I made bold not to trouble you by ringing the bell I've got something to speak about in the way of business."

So saying, the worthy bookseller, who had no way of doing anything but going at it like a bull, drew a chair near the fire.

"With your leave, ma'am, it's as easy to speak sitting as standing. So, if you don't object, I'll sit down."

"Do sit down, Mr. Kitely," said Lucy. "We're glad to see you—though you know we're in a little trouble just at present."

"I know all about that, and I don't believe there's a creature in the court, down to Mrs. Cook's cat, that isn't ready to fly at that devil's limb of a lawyer. But you see, ma'am, if we was to murder him it wouldn't be no better for you. And what I come to say to you is this: I've got a deal more room on my premises than I want, and it would be a wonderful accommodation to me, not to speak of the honor of it, if you would take charge of my little woman for me. I can't interfere with her, you know, so as to say she's not to take care of me, you know, for that would go nigh to break her little heart; but if you would come and live there as long as convenient to you, you could get things for yourselves all the same as you does here, only you wouldn't have nothing to be out of pocket for house-room, you know. It would be the making of my poor motherless Mattie."

"Oh! we're not going to be so very poor as grannie thinks, Mr. Kitely," said Lucy, trying to laugh, while the old lady sat rocking herself to and fro and wiping her eyes. "But I should like to move into your house, for there's nowhere I should be so much at home."

"Lucy!" said her grandmother, warningly.

"Stop a bit, grannie. Mr. Kitely's a real friend in need; and if I had not such a regard for him as I have, I would take it as it's meant. I'll tell you what, Mr. Kitely; it only comes to this, that I have got to work a little harder, and not lead such an idle life with my grannie here."

"You idle, miss!" interrupted the bookseller. "I never see any one more like the busy bee than yourself, only that you was always a-wastin' of your honey on other people; and that they say ain't the way of the bees."

"But you won't hear me out, Mr. Kitely. It would be a shame of me to go and live in anybody's house for nothing, seeing I am quite able to pay for it. Now, if you have room in your house—"

"Miles of it," cried the bookseller.

"I don't know where it can be, then; for it's as full of books from the ground to the garret as—as—as my darling old grannie here is of independence."

"Don't you purtend to know more about my house, miss, than I does myself. Just you say the word, and before quarter-day you'll find two rooms fit for your use and at your service. What I owe to you, miss, in regard of my little one, nothing I can do can ever repay. They're a bad lot them Worboises—son *and* father! and that I saw—leastways in the young one."

This went with a sting to poor Lucy's heart. She kept hoping and hoping, and praying to God: but her little patch of blue sky was so easily overclouded! But she kept to the matter before her.

"Very well, Mr. Kitely; you ought to know best. Now for my side of the bargain. I told you already that I would rather be in your house than anywhere else, if I must leave this dear old place. And if you will let me pay a reasonable sum, as lodgings go in this court, we'll regard the matter as settled. And then I can teach Mattie a little, you know."

Mrs. Boxall did not put in a word. The poor old lady was beginning to weary of everything, and for the first time in her life began to allow her affairs to be meddled with—as she would no doubt even now consider it. And the sound of paying for it was very satisfactory. I suspect part of Lucy's desire to move no farther than the entrance of the court, came from the hope that Thomas would some day or other turn up in that neighborhood, and perhaps this emboldened her to make the experiment of taking the matter so much into her own hands. Mr. Kitely scratched his head, and looked a little annoyed.

"Well, miss," he said, pausing between every few words, a most unusual thing with him, "that's not a bit of what I meant when I came up the court here. But that's better than nothing—for Mattie and me, I mean. So if you'll be reasonable about the rent, we'll easily manage all the rest. Mind you, miss, it'll be all clear profit to me."

"It'll cost you a good deal to get the rooms put in order as you say, you know, Mr. Kitely."

"Not much, miss. I know how to set about things better than most people. Bless you, I can buy wall-papers for half what you'd pay for them now. I know the trade. I've been a-most everything in my day. Why, miss, I lived at one time such a close shave with dying of hunger, that, after I was married, I used to make picture frames and then pawn my tools to get glass to put into them, and then carry them about to sell, and when I had sold 'em I bought more gold-beading and redeemed my tools, and did it all over again. Bless you! I know what it is to be hard up, if anybody ever did. I once walked from Bristol to Newcastle upon fourpence. It won't cost me much to make them rooms decent. And then there's the back parlor at your service. I shan't plague you much, only to take a look at my princess now and then."

After another interview or two between Lucy and Mr. Kitely, the matter was arranged, and the bookseller proceeded to get his rooms ready, which involved chiefly a little closer packing, and the getting rid of a good deal of almost unsalable rubbish, which had accumulated from the purchase of lots.

Meantime another trial was gathering for poor Lucy. Mr. Sargent had met Mr. Wither, and had learned from him all he knew about Thomas. Mr. Wither was certain that everything was broken off between Lucy and him. It was not only known to all at the office that Thomas had disappeared, but it was perfectly known as well that for some time he had been getting into bad ways, and his disappearance was necessarily connected with this fact, though no one but Mr. Stopper knew the precise occasion of his evanishment, and this he was, if possible, more careful than ever to conceal. Not even to the lad's father did he communicate what he knew: he kept this as a power over his new principal. From what he heard, Mr. Sargent resolved to see if he could get anything out of Molken, and called upon him for that purpose. But the German soon convinced him that, although he had been intimate with Thomas, he knew nothing about him now. The last information he could give him was that he had staked and lost his watch and a lady's ring that he wore; that he had gone away and returned with money; and, having gained considerably, had disappeared and never been heard of again. It was easy for Mr. Sargent to persuade himself that a noble-minded creature like Lucy, having come to know the worthlessness of her lover, had dismissed him forever; and to believe that she would very soon become indifferent to a person so altogether unworthy of her affection. Probably he was urged yet the more to a fresh essay from the desire of convincing her that his motives in the first case had not been so selfish as accident had made them appear; nor that his feelings toward her remained unaltered notwithstanding the change in her prospects. He therefore kept up his visits, and paid them even more frequently now that there was no possible excuse on the score of business. For some time, however, so absorbed were Lucy's thoughts that his attentions gave her no uneasiness. She considered the matter so entirely settled, that no suspicion of the revival of any farther hope in the mind of Mr. Sargent arose to add a fresh trouble to the distress which she was doing all she could to bear patiently. But one day she was suddenly undeceived. Mrs. Boxall had just left the room.

"Miss Burton," said Mr. Sargent, "I venture to think circumstances may be sufficiently altered to justify me in once more expressing a hope that I may be permitted to regard a nearer friendship as possible between us."

Lucy started as if she had been hurt. The occurrence was so strange and foreign to all that was in her thoughts, that she had to look all around her, as it were, like a person suddenly awaking in a strange place. Before she could speak, her grandmother reëntered. Mr. Sargent went away without any conviction that Lucy's behavior indicated repugnance to his proposal.

Often it happens that things work together without any concerted scheme. Mrs. Morgenstern had easily divined Mr. Sargent's feelings, and the very next day began to talk about him to Lucy. But she listened without interest, until Mrs. Morgenstern touched a chord which awoke a very painful one. For at last her friend had got rather piqued at Lucy's coldness and indifference.

"I think at least, Lucy, you might take a little interest in the poor fellow, if only from gratitude. A girl may acknowledge that feeling without compromising herself. There has Mr. Sargent been wearing himself out for you, lying awake at night, and running about all day, without hope of reward; and, you are so taken up with your own troubles that you haven't a thought for the man who has done all that lay in human being's power to turn them aside."

Could Lucy help comparing this conduct with that of Thomas? And while she compared it, she could as little help the sudden inroad of the suspicion that Thomas had forsaken her that he might keep well with his father—the man who was driving them, as far as lay in his power, into the abysses of poverty; and that this disappearance was the only plan he dared to adopt for freeing himself—for doubtless his cowardice would be at least as great in doing her wrong as it had been in refusing to do her right. And she did feel that there was some justice in Mrs. Morgenstern's reproach. For if poor Mr. Sargent was really in love with her, she ought to pity him and feel for him some peculiar tenderness, for the very reason that she could not grant him what he desired. Her strength having been much undermined of late, she could not hear Mrs. Morgenstern's reproaches without bursting into tears. And then her friend began to comfort her; but all the time supposing that her troubles were only those connected with her reverse of fortune. As Lucy went home, however, a very different and terrible thought darted into her mind: "What if it was her duty to listen to Mr. Sargent!" There seemed no hope for her any more. Thomas had forsaken her utterly. If she could never be happy, ought she not to be the more anxious to make another happy? Was there any limit to the sacrifice that ought to be made for another—that is of one's self? for, alas! it would be to sacrifice no one besides. The thought was indeed a terrible one.

All the rest of the day her soul was like a drowning creature—now getting one breath of hope, now with all the billows and waves of despair going over it. The evening passed in constant terror, lest Mr. Sargent should appear, and a poor paltry little hope grew as the hands of the clock went round, and every moment rendered it less likely that he would come. At length she might go to bed without annoying her grandmother, who, by various little hints she dropped, gave her clearly to understand that she expected her to make a good match before long, and so relieve her mind about her at least.

She went to bed, and fell asleep from very weariness of emotion. But presently she started awake again; and, strange to say, it seemed to be a resolution she had formed in her sleep that brought her awake. It was that she would go to Mr. Fuller, and consult him on the subject that distressed her. After that she slept till the morning.

She had no lesson to give that day, so as soon as Mr. Fuller's church-bell began to ring, she put on her bonnet. Her grandmother asked where she was going. She told her she was going to church.

"I don't like this papist way of going to church of a week-day—at least in the middle of the day, when people ought to be at their work."

Lucy made no reply; for, without being one of those half of whose religion consists in abusing the papists, Mrs. Boxall was one of those who would turn from any good thing of which she heard first as done by those whose opinions differed from her own. Nor would it have mitigated her dislike to know that Lucy was going for the purpose of asking advice from Mr. Fuller. She would have denounced that as *confession*, and asked whether it was not more becoming in a young girl to consult her grandmother than go to a priest. Therefore, I say, Lucy kept her own counsel.

There were twenty or thirty people present when she entered St. Amos's; a grand assembly, if we consider how time and place were haunted—swarming with the dirty little demons of money-making and all its attendant beggarly cares and chicaneries—one o'clock in the City of London! It was a curious psalm they were singing, so quaint and old-fashioned, and so altogether unlike London in the nineteenth century!—the last in the common version of Tate and Brady. They were beginning the fifth verse when she entered:

> "Let them who joyful hymns compose
> To cymbals set their songs of praise;
> Cymbals of common use, and those
> That loudly sound on solemn days."

Lucy did not feel at all in sympathy with cymbals. But she knew that Mr. Fuller did, else he could not have chosen that psalm to sing. And an unconscious operation of divine logic took place in her heart, with result such as might be represented in the following process: "Mr. Fuller is glad in God—not because he thinks himself a favorite with God, but because God is what he is, a faithful God. He is not one thing to Mr. Fuller and another to me. He is the same though I am sorrowful, I will praise him too. He will help me to be and do right, and that can never be anything unworthy of me." So, with a trembling voice, Lucy joined in the end of the song of praise. And when Mr. Fuller's voice arose in the prayer—"O God, whose nature and property is ever to have mercy and to forgive, receive our humble petitions, and though we be tied and bound with the chain of our sins, yet let the pitifulness of thy great mercy loose us: for the honor of Jesus Christ, our Mediator and Advocate. Amen"—she joined in it with all her heart, both for herself and Thomas. Then, without the formality of a text, Mr. Fuller addressed his little congregation something as follows:

"My friends, is it not strange that with all the old church-yards lying about in London, unbusinesslike spots in the midst of shops and warehouses, 'and all the numberless goings on of life,' we should yet feel so constantly as if the business of the city were an end in itself? How seldom we see that it is only a means to an end! I will tell you in a few words one cause of this feeling as if it were an end; and then to what end it really is a means. With all the reminders of death that we have about us, not one of us feels as if he were going to die. We think of other people—even those much younger than ourselves—dying, and it always seems as if we were going to be alive when they die: and why? Just because we are not going to die. This thinking part in us feels no symptom of ceasing to be. We think on and on, and death seems far from us, for it belongs only to our bodies—not to us. So the soul forgets it. It is no part of religion to think about death. It is the part of religion, when the fact and thought of death come in, to remind us that we live forever, and that God, who sent his Son to die, will help us safe through that somewhat fearful strait that lies before us, and which often grows so terrible to those who fix their gaze upon it that they see nothing beyond it, and talk with poor Byron of the day of death as 'the first dark day of nothingness.' But this fact that *we* do not die, that only our bodies die, adds immeasurably to the folly of making what is commonly called the business of life an end instead of a means. It is not the business of life. The business of life is that which has to do with the life—with the living *us*, not with the dying part of us. How can the business of life have to do with the part that is always dying? Yet, certainly, as you will say, it must be done—only, mark this, not as an end, but as a means. As an end it has to do only with the perishing body; as a means it has infinite relations with the never-ceasing life. Then comes the question, To what end is it a means? It is a means, a great, I might say the great, means to the end for which God sends us individually into a world of sin; for that he does so, whatever the perplexities the admission may involve, who can deny, without denying that God makes us? If we were sent without any sinful tendencies into a sinless world, we should be good, I dare say; but with a very poor kind of goodness, knowing nothing of evil, consequently never choosing good, but being good in a stupid way because we could not help it. But how is it with us? We live in a world of constant strife—a strife, as the old writers call it, following St. Paul, between the flesh and the spirit; the things belonging to the outer life, the life of the senses, the things which our Saviour sums up in the words, 'what we shall eat, and what we shall drink, and wherewithal we shall be clothed,' forcing themselves constantly on our attention, and crowding away the thought and the care that belong to the real life—the life that consists in purity of heart, in love, in goodness of all kinds—that embraces all life, using our own life only as the standpoint from which to stretch out arms of embracing toward God and toward all men. For the feeding and growth of this life, London city affords endless opportunity. Business is too often regarded as the hindrance to the spiritual life. I regard it as among the finest means the world affords for strengthening and causing to grow this inner real life. For every deed may be done according to the fashion of the outward perishing life, as an end; or it may be done after the fashion of the inward endless life—done righteously, done nobly, done, upon occasion, magnificently—

ever regarded as a something to be put under the feet of the spiritual man to lift him to the height of his high calling. Making business a mean to such end, it will help us to remember that this world and the fashion of it passeth away, but that every deed done, as Jesus would have done it if he had been born to begin his life as a merchant instead of a carpenter, lifts the man who so does it up toward the bosom of Him who created business and all its complications, as well as our brains and hands that have to deal with them. If you were to come and ask me, 'How shall I do in this or that particular case?' very possibly I might be unable to answer you. Very often no man can decide but the man himself. And it is part of every man's training that he should thus decide. Even if he should go wrong, by going wrong he may be taught the higher principle that would have kept him right, and which he has not yet learned. One thing is certain, that the man who wants to go right will be guided right; that not only in regard to the mission of the Saviour, but in regard to everything, he that is willing to do the will of the Father shall know of the doctrine.—Now to God the Father," etc.

The worship over, and the congregation having retired, Lucy bent her trembling steps toward the vestry, and there being none of those generally repellent ministers, pew-openers, about, she knocked at the door. By the way, I wish clergymen were more acquainted with the nature and habits of those who in this *lowly*—alas, how far from humble—office represent the gospel of welcome. They ought to have at least one sermon a year preached to them upon their duties before the whole congregation. The reception the servants of any house afford has no little share in the odor of hospitality which that house enjoys, and hospitality is no small Christian virtue. Lucy's troubled heart beat very fast as she opened the door in answer to Mr. Fuller's cheerful "Come in." But the moment she saw Mr. Fuller she felt as if she had been guilty of an act of impropriety, and ought to have waited in the church till he came out. She drew back with a murmured "I beg your pardon," but Mr. Fuller at once reassured her. He came forward; holding out his hand.

"How do you do, Miss Burton? I am delighted to see you. By your coming to the vestry, like a brave woman, I suppose there is something I can do for you. Let me hear all about it. Sit down."

So saying, he gave her a chair, and seated himself on the only remaining one. And as soon as she saw that Mr. Fuller was not shocked at her forwardness, such was Lucy's faith in him, that her courage returned, and with due regard to his time and her own dignity, she proceeded at once to explain to him the difficulty in which she found herself. It was a lovely boldness in the maiden, springing from faith and earnestness and need, that enabled her to set forth in a few plain words the main points of her case—that she had been engaged for many months to a youth who seemed to have forsaken her, but whom she did not know to have done so, though his conduct had been worse than doubtful, seeing he had fallen into bad company. She would never have troubled Mr. Fuller about it for that, for it was not sympathy she wanted; but there was a gentleman—and here she faltered more—to whom she was under very great obligation, and who said he loved her; and she wanted much to know whether it was her duty to yield to his entreaties.

My reader must remember that Lucy was not one of those clear-brained as well as large-hearted women who see the *rights* of a thing at once. Many of the best women may be terribly puzzled, especially when an opportunity of self-sacrifice occurs. They are always ready to think that the most painful way is the right one. This indicates a noble disposition. And the most painful way *may* be the right one; but it is not the right one *because* it is the most painful. It is the right way because it is the right way, whether it be painful or delightful; and the notion of self-sacrifice may be rooted in spiritual pride. Whether it be so or not, the fact that the wrong way is the least self-indulgent, is the most painful, will not prevent it from bringing with it all the consequences that belong to it: wrong-doing cannot set things right, however noble the motive may be. Of course the personal condemnation and the individual degradation are infinitely less than if the easiest and pleasantest way is chosen only because it is the easiest and pleasantest. But God will not make of law a child's toy, to indulge the vagaries of his best children.

When Lucy had finished setting forth her case, which the trembling of her voice, and the swelling of her tears, hardly interrupted, Mr. Fuller said:

"Now you must allow me, Miss Burton, to ask you one or two plain questions."

"Certainly, sir. Ask me whatever you please. I will answer honestly."

"That I have no doubt about. Do you love this man to whom you say you are obliged?"

"Indeed I do not. I hope I am grateful to him, and I would do anything in return, except—"

"I understand you. It seems to me, though this kind of thing involves many questions too delicate to be easily talked about, that, whatever he may desire at the time, it is doing any man a grievous wrong to marry him without loving him. Blinded by his love, he may desire it none the less even if you tell him that you do not love him; but the kindest thing, even to him, is to refuse. This is what seems to me the truth."

While Mr. Fuller spoke, Lucy heaved such a deep sigh of relief, that if any corroboration of what she represented as the state of her feelings had been necessary, Mr. Fuller had it. After a little pause, he went on:

"Now, one question more: Do you love the other still?"

"I do," said Lucy, bursting at last into a passion of tears. "But, perhaps," she sobbed, "I ought to give him up altogether. I am afraid he has not behaved well at all."

"To you?"

"I didn't mean that. I wasn't thinking about myself just then."

"Has he let you understand that he has forsaken you?"

"No, no. He hasn't said a word. Only I haven't seen him for so long."

"There is, then, some room for hope. If you were to resolve upon anything now, you would be doing so without knowing what you were doing, because you do not know what he is doing. It is just possible it may be a healthy shame that is keeping him away from you. It may become your duty to give him up, but I think when it is so, it will be clearly so. God gives us all time: we should give each other time, too. I wish I could see him."

"I wish, indeed, you could, sir. It seems to me that he has not been well brought up. His father is a dreadfully hard and worldly man, as my poor grandmother knows too well; and his mother is very religious, but her religion seems to me to have done my poor Thomas more harm than his father's worldliness."

"That is quite possible. When you do see him again, try to get him to come and see me. Or I will go and see him. I shall not overwhelm him with a torrent of religion which he cannot understand, and which would only harden him."

"There is nothing I should wish more. But tell me one thing, Mr. Fuller: would it be right to marry him? I want to understand. Nothing looks farther off; but I want to know what is right."

"I think," returned Mr. Fuller, "that every willing heart will be taught what is right by the time that action is necessary. One thing seems clear, that while you love him—"

"I shall always love him," interrupted Lucy.

"LUCY NEVER LIFTED HER EYES."

"I must speak generally," said Mr. Fuller; "and there have been a few instances," he added, with the glimmer of a smile through the seriousness of his countenance, "of young maidens, and young men no less, changing their minds about such matters. I do not say you will. But while you love him it is clear to me, that you must not accept the attentions of any one else. I could put a very hard and dreadful name upon that. There is another thing equally clear to me—that while he is unrepentant, that is, so long as he does not change his ways—turn from evil toward good—think better of it, that is—you would be doing very wrong to marry him. I do not say when, or that ever you are bound to stop loving him; but that is a very different thing from consenting to marry him. Any influence for good that a woman has over such a man, she may exercise as much before marriage as after it. Indeed, if the man is of a poor and selfish nature, she is almost certain, as far as my observation goes, to lose her influence after her marriage. Many a woman, I fear, has married a man with the hope of reforming him, and has found that she only afforded him opportunity for growth in wickedness. I do not say that no good at all comes of it, so long as she is good, but it is the wrong way, and evil comes of it."

"I am sure you are right, Mr. Fuller. It would be dreadful to marry a bad man—or a man who had not strength, even for love of a wife, to turn from bad ways. But you won't think the hardest of my poor Thomas yet? He has been led astray, and has too much good in him to be easily made all bad."

"I too will hope so, for your sake as well as his own."

Lucy rose.

"Good-morning, Mr. Fuller. I do not know how to thank you. I only wanted leave to go on loving him. Thank you a thousand times."

"Do not thank me as if I could give you leave to do this or that. I only tell you what seems to me the truth of the matter."

"But is not that the best thing to give or to receive?"

"Yes, it is," answered Mr. Fuller, as Lucy left the vestry.

It was with a heart wonderfully lightened that she went home to her grandmother. This new cloud of terror had almost passed away; it only lightened a little on the horizon when she thought of having again to hear what Mr. Sargent wanted to say.

That same evening he came. Lucy never lifted her eyes to his face, even when she held out her hand to him. He misinterpreted her embarrassment; and he found argument to strengthen his first impression; for a moment after, summoning all her courage, and remembering very conveniently a message she had had for him, Lacy said to her grandmother:

"Mr. Kitely said he would like to see you, grannie, about the papers for our rooms. He has got some patterns."

"I have done with this world, child, and all its vanities," said Mrs. Boxall, with a touch of asperity.

"It would only be polite, though, grannie, as he is taking so much trouble about it, to go and see them. He is so kind!"

"We're going to pay him for his kindness," said the old dame, soured out of her better judgment, and jealous of Mr. Sargent supposing that they were accepting charity.

"No, grannie. That nobody ever could do. Kindness is just what can't be paid for, do what you will."

"I see you want to get rid of me," she said, rising; "so I suppose I had better go. Things are changed. Old people must learn to do as they're bid. You'll be teaching me my catechism next, I suppose."

Mrs. Boxall walked out of the room with as stiff a back as she had ever assumed in the days of her prosperity. The moment the door closed, Mr. Sargent approached Lucy, who had remained standing, and would have taken her hand, but she drew it away, and took the lead.

"I am very sorry if I have led you into any mistake, Mr. Sargent. I was so distressed at what you said the other evening, that I made this opportunity for the sake of removing at once any misapprehension. I wish to remind you, that I considered the subject you resumed then as quite settled."

"But excuse me, Miss Burton. I too considered it settled; but circumstances having altered so entirely—"

"Could you suppose for a moment, that because I had lost the phantom of a fortune which I never possessed, I would accept the man—whose kindness I was always grateful for, but whose love I had refused before because I could not give him any in return?"

"No. I did not suppose so. You gave me a reason for refusing my attentions then, which I have the best ground for believing no longer exists."

"What was the reason I gave you then?"

"That you loved another."

"And what ground have I given you for supposing that such has ceased to be the case?"

"You have not given me any. He has."

Lucy started. The blood rushed to her forehead, and then back to her heart.

"Where is he?" she cried, clasping her hands. "For God's sake, tell me."

"That at least is answer enough to my presumptuous hope," returned Mr. Sargent, with some bitterness.

"Mr. Sargent," said Lucy, who, though trembling greatly, had now recovered her self-command, "I beg your pardon for any pain I may have occasioned you. But, by surprising the truth, you have saved me the repetition of what I told you before. Tell me what you know of Mr. Worboise."

But Mr. Sargent's feelings—those especially occupied with himself—got the better of him now, bitterly as he regretted it afterward. He felt it a wrong that such a woman should pass him by for the sake of such a man; and he answered in the heat of injury:

"All I care to know about him is, that for the sake of his game among a low set of gamblers, he staked and lost a diamond ring—a rose-diamond, which one of his companions seemed to know as the gift of a lady. That is the man for whom Lucy Burton is proud to express her devotion!"

Lucy had grown very pale; but she would hold out till Mr. Sargent was gone. She had an answer on her lips; but if she spoke he would stay. Still she *would* say one word for Thomas.

"Your evidence is hardly of the most trustworthy kind, Mr. Sargent. Good-evening."

"It is of *his* kind, anyhow, whatever that may be," he retorted, and left the room. Before he reached the bottom of the stairs, he despised himself most heartily, and rushed up again to attempt an apology. Opening the room door, he saw Lucy lying on the floor. He thought she had fainted. But the same moment, Mrs. Boxall, who had only gone up stairs, came down behind him, and he thought it best to leave and write a letter. But Lucy had not fainted. She had only thrown herself on the floor in that agony which would gladly creep into the grave to forget itself. In all grief unmingled with anger there is the impulse to lie down. Lucy had not heard Mr. Sargent return or her grandmother reënter, for she had been pressing her ears with her hands, as if the last sounds that had entered had wounded them grievously.

"Well, I'm sure! what next?" remarked Mrs. Boxall. "I dare say fashions *have* come to that at last!"

What she meant was not very clear; but the moment she spoke, Lucy started from the floor and left the room. She had not been long in her chamber, however, before, with the ingenuity of a lover, she had contrived to draw a little weak comfort even out of what Mr. Sargent had told her. She believed that he had done worse than part with her ring; but when the thought struck her that it must have been for the sake of redeeming that ring that he had robbed his employer, which was indeed the case, somehow or other, strange as it may seem, the offenses appeared mutually to mitigate each other. And when she thought the whole matter over in the relief of knowing that she was free of Mr. Sargent, she quite believed that she had discovered fresh grounds for taking courage.

CHAPTER XLII
MRS. BOXALL FINDS A COMPANION
IN MISFORTUNE

At last the day arrived that Lucy and her grandmother had fixed for removing into the bookseller's house. The furniture was all Mrs. Boxall's own, though, if Mr. Worboise had thought proper to dispute the fact, there was nobody left who could have home witness against it. Mr. Kitely shut shop a little earlier; Mr. Spelt descended from his perch: and Mr. Dolman crept out of his hole—all to bear a hand in the moving of it. It was dusk when they began, but the darkness did not hinder their diligence, and, in the course of a couple of hours, all the heavier articles were in their new places. When everything was got into something like order, it did not appear that, save for the diminution of space, they had had such a terrible downcome. Lucy was heartily satisfied with their quarters, and the feeling that she had now to protect and work for her grandmother gave a little cheerfulness to her behavior, notwithstanding the weight on her heart. Mattie was important, with an importance which not even the delight of having Miss Burton to live with them could assuage; for she had to preside at a little supper which Mr. Kitely had procured, in honor of the occasion, from the cook-shop which supplied the feasts of Spelt and Poppie. But when things were partially arranged for the night, Mrs. Boxall, who was in a very despondent condition, declared her intention of going to bed. Lucy would gladly have done the same, but she could not think of doing dishonor to the hospitality of their kind friend.

"Well, I am sorry the old lady can't be prevailed upon," said Mr. Kitely. "Them sassages I know to be genuine—none of your cats or cats' meat either. I know the very tree they grew upon—eh, princess? And now we shan't be able to eat 'em up."

"Why don't you ask Mr. Spelt to come in and help us?" said Mattie.

"Bless you! he's gone to fetch his kid; and before they'll come home they'll have bought their supper. They always do. I know their ways. But I do believe that's them gone up the court this minute. I'll run and see."

Mr. Kitely hurried out, and returned with Mr. Spelt, Poppie, and the steam-engine, which was set down in the middle of the room.

"Ain't I been fort'nate?" said the bookseller. "Poppie ain't sold all her potatoes. They was a-going to eat 'em up by the way of savin'. So we've agreed to club, and go share and share. Ain't that it, Poppie?"

Poppie grinned and gave no other answer. But her father took up the word.

"It's very kind of you to put it so, Mr. Kitely. But it seems to me we're hardly fit company for a lady like Miss Burton."

"Surely, Mr. Spelt, we haven't been neighbors so long without being fit to have our supper together?" said Lucy.

"That's very neighborly of you, miss. Let me assist you to a potato," said Spelt, going toward the steamer. "It's my belief there ain't no better taters in London, though I says it as buys 'em," he added, throwing back the lid.

"But we ain't going to begin on the taters, Spelt. You come and sit down here, and we'll have the taters put on a plate. That's the right way, ain't it, princess?"

"Well, I should say so, Mr. Kitely," answered Mattie, who had hitherto been too full of her own importance even to talk. But Mr. Spelt interfered.

"Them taters," said he, with decision, "ought to be eaten fresh out of the steamer. If you turn 'em out on to a plate, I don't answer for the consequences. We'll put 'em nearer the table, and I'll sit by 'em, with your leave, Miss Burton, and help everybody as wants one."

It was remarkable with how much more decision than had belonged to him formerly, Mr. Spelt now spoke. Mr. Kitely, after a half hour's meditation, next day, as to whether the cause of it was Poppie or the potatoes, came to the wise conclusion that between them they had made a man of him.

By this time they were all seated round the table.

"Mr. Spelt, you be parson, and say grace," said Kitely, in his usual peremptory tone.

"Why should you ask me, Mr. Kitely?" said the tailor, humbly.

"Because you know more about that sort o' thing than I do—and you know it."

Mr. Spelt said grace so devoutly that nobody could hear him.

"Why do you say grace as if you was ashamed of it, Spelt? If I was to say grace, now, I would let you hear me."

"I didn't know you cared about such things," returned Spelt, evasively.

"Well," said Mr. Kitely, "no more I do—or did, rather; for I'm afraid that Mr. Fuller will get me into bad habits before he has done with me. He's a good man, Mr. Fuller, and that's more than I'd say for every one of the cloth. They're nothing but cloth—meaning no offense, Mr. Spelt, to a honest trade."

"Perhaps there are more good ones among 'em than you think, Mr. Kitely," said Lucy.

"There ud need to be, miss. But I declare that man has almost made me hold my tongue against the whole sect of them. It seems a shame, with him in St. Amos's, to say a word against Mr. Potter in St. Jacob's. I never thought I should take to the church in my old age."

"Old age, Mr. Kitely!" Mattie broke in. "If you talk in that way, think what you make of me!"

A general laugh greeted this remark. But Mattie was serious, and did not even smile.

Poppie never opened her lips, except to smile. But she behaved with perfect propriety. Mr. Spelt had civilized her so far, and that without much trouble. He never told any one, however, that it was with anxiety that he set out every night at half-past nine to bring her home; for more than once he had found her potato-steamer standing alone on the pavement, while she was off somewhere, looking at something, or following a crowd. He had stood nearly half an hour before she came back upon one of those occasions. All she said when she returned was, "I thought I should find you here, daddy."

But I must not linger with the company assembled in the bookseller's back-parlor; for their conversation will not help my reader on with my story.

A very little man, with very short, bandy legs, was trudging along a wide and rather crowded thoroughfare, with a pair of workman's boots in his hand. It was Mr. Spelt's *sub*, Mr. Dolman, the cobbler.

"Well, Dolly, how do?" said a man in a long velveteen coat, with a short pipe in his mouth and a greasy cloth cap on his head. "You're late to-night, ain't you, Dolly?"

"Them lawyers; them lawyers, Jim!" returned Dolman, enigmatically.

"What the blazes have you got to do with lawyers?" exclaimed Jim Salter, staring at the cobbler, who for the sake of balance had now got one boot in each hand, and stood weighing the one against the other.

"Not much for my own part," returned Dolman, who was feeling very important from having assisted at his neighbors' *flitting*. "But there's good people in our court could tell you another story."

I have said that Mrs. Boxall did anything but hold her tongue about her affairs, and Dolman had heard Mr. Worboise's behavior so thoroughly canvassed between Mr. Kitely and Mr. Spelt, that he was familiar with the main points of the case.

"Come and have a drop of beer," said Jim, "and tell us all about it."

No greater temptation could have been held out to Dolman. But he had a certain sense of duty that must first be satisfied.

"No, Jim. I never touch a drop till I've taken my work home."

"Where's that?" asked Jim.

"Down by the Minories," answered the cobbler.

"Come along, then. I'll help you carry it."

"'Taint heavy. I'll carry it myself," answered Dolman, who, having once been robbed on a similar occasion, seemed, in regard to boots, to have lost his faith in humanity.

"I can't think, Dolly, why you roost so far from your work. Now it's different with me. My work's here and there and everywhere; but yours is allus in the same place."

"It gives me a walk, Jim. Besides it's respectable. It's having two places of one's own. My landlady, Mrs. Dobbs, knows that my shop's in a fashionable part, and she's rather proud of me for a lodger in consekence. And my landlord, that's Mr. Spelt, a tailor, and well-to-do—how's he to know that I ain't got a house in the suburbs?" answered Dolman, laughing.

The moment he had got his money, and delivered the boots—for that was the order of business between Dolman and his customers—they betook themselves to a public-house in the neighborhood, where Dolman conveyed to Jim, with very tolerable correctness, the whole story of Mrs. Boxall's misfortunes. Before he reached the end of it, however, Jim, who had already "put a name upon something" with two of his acquaintances that night, got rather misty, and took his leave of Dolman with the idea that Lucy and her grandmother had been turned out, furniture and all, into the street, without a place to go to.

Much as she had dreaded leaving her own house, as she had always considered it, Mrs. Boxall had a better night in her new abode than she had

had for months, and rose in the morning with a surprising sense of freshness. Wonderful things come to us in sleep—none perhaps more wonderful than this reviving of the colors of the faded soul from being laid for a few hours in the dark—in *God's ebony box*, as George Herbert calls the night. It is as if the wakeful angels had been busy all the night preening the draggled and ruffled wings of their sleeping brothers and sisters. Finding that Lucy was not yet dressed, she went down alone to the back parlor, and, having nothing else to do, began to look at the birds, of which, I have already informed my reader, Mr. Kitely kept a great many, feeding and cleaning them himself, and teaching the more gifted, starlings and parrots, and such like birds of genius, to speak. If he did anything in the way of selling as well as buying them, it was quite in a private way—as a gentleman may do with his horses.

"Good-morning, sir," screamed a huge gray parrot the moment she entered, regardless of the sex of his visitor. It was one the bookseller had bought of a sailor somewhere about the docks, a day or two before, and its fame had not yet spread through the neighborhood, consequently Mrs. Boxall was considerably startled by the salutation. "Have you spliced the main-brace this morning, sir?" continued the parrot, and, without waiting for a reply, like the great ladies who inquire after an inferior's family and then look out of the window, burst into the song, "There's a sweet little cherub," and, stopping as suddenly at the word, followed it with the inquiry, "How's your mother?" upon which point Mrs. Boxall may, without any irreverence, be presumed to have been a little in the dark. The next moment the unprincipled animal poured forth his innocent soul in a torrent of imprecations which, growing as furious as fast, reached the ears of Mr. Kitely. He entered in a moment and silenced the animal with prompt rebuke, and the descent of an artificial night in the shape of a green cloth over his cage—the vengeance of the lower Jove. The creature exploded worse than ever for a while, and then subsided. Meantime the bookseller turned to Mrs. Boxall to apologize.

"I haven't had him long, ma'am—only a day or two. He's been ill brought up, as you see, poor bird! I shall have a world of trouble to cure him of his bad language. If I can't cure him I'll wring his neck."

"The poor creature doesn't know better," said Mrs. Boxall. "Wouldn't it be rather hard to kill him for it?"

"Well, but what am I to do? I can't have such words running out and in of my princess's ears all day." .

"But you could sell him, or give him away, you know, Mr. Kitely."

"A pretty present he would be, the rascal! And for selling him, it would be wickedness to put the money in my pocket. There was a time, ma'am, when I would have taught him such words myself, and thought no harm of it; but now, if I were to sell that bird, ma'am—how should I look Mr. Fuller in the face next Sunday? No; if I can't cure him, I must twist his neck. We'll eat him, ma'am; I dare say he's nice."

He added, in a whisper: "I wanted him to hear me. There's no telling how much them creatures understand."

But before Mr. Kitely had done talking, Mrs. Boxall's attention was entirely taken up with another bird, of the paroquet species. It was the most awfully grotesque, the most pitiably comic animal in creation. It had a green head, with a band of red round the back of it; while white feathers came down on each side of its huge beak, like the gray whiskers of a retired military man. This head looked enormous for the rest of the body, for from the nape of the neck to the tail, except a few long feathers on the shoulders of its wings, blue like those of a jay, there was not another feather on its body: it was as bare as if it had been plucked for roasting. A more desolate, poverty-stricken, wretched object, can hardly be conceived. The immense importance of his head and beak and gray whiskers, with the abject nakedness—more than nakedness, *pluckedness*—of his body was quite beyond laughing at. It was far fitter to make one cry. But the creature was so absolutely, perfectly self-satisfied, without a notion of shame, or even discomfort, that it appeared impossible he could ever have seen himself behind. He must sorely have fancied himself as glorious as in his palmiest days. And his body was so thin, and his skin so old and wrinkled—I wish I could set him in the margin for my younger readers to see him. He hopped from place to place, and turned himself round before the spectators with such an absence of discomposure, that one could not help admiring his utter *sang-froid*, almost envying his perfect self-possession. Observing that his guest was absorbed in the contemplation of the phenomenon, Mr. Kitely said:

"You're a-wondering at poor Widdles. Widdles was an old friend of mine I named the bird after before he lost his greatcoat all but the collar. Widdles! Widdles!"

The bird came close up to the end of his perch, and, setting his head on one side, looked at his master with one round yellow eye.

"He's the strangest bird I ever saw," said Mrs. Boxall. "If you talked of wringing *his* neck, now, I shouldn't wonder, knowing you for a kind-hearted man, Mr. Kitely."

"Wring Widdles' neck!" exclaimed the bookseller. "His is the last neck I would think of wringing. See how bravely he bears misfortune. Nobody could well lose more than Widdles, and nobody could well take it lighter. He's a sermon, is that bird. His whole worldly wealth consists in his wig. They was a fine pair once, only he was always henpecked. His mate used to peck him because he wasn't able to peck her, for he was the smaller of the two. They always reminded me of Spelt and his wife. But when they were took ill, both of them, she gave in, and he wouldn't. Death took his feathers, and left him jolly without them. Bless him, old Widdles."

"Well, it's a curious taste of yours, I must say, Mr. Kitely. But some people, no more than some birds, ain't to be accounted for."

Mr. Kitely chose to consider this a good sally of wit, and laughed loud and long. Mrs. Boxall laughed a little too, and was pleased with herself. And from that moment she began to take to the bird.

"Try him with a bit of sugar," said Mr. Kitely, going to the carved cabinet to get a piece, which he then handed to Mrs. Boxall.

The bird was friendly and accepted it. Mrs. Boxall was pleased with him now as well as with herself, and before long a firm friendship was established between the two, which went so far that Widdles would, when she put her hand into his cage, perch upon her bony old finger, and allow himself to be lifted out. There was no fear of his even attempting to fly away, for he was perfectly aware of his utter incapacity in that direction of bird-like use and custom. Before many days had passed she had become so much attached to the bird that his company did not a little to shield her from the inroads of recurrent regret, mortification, and resentment.

One evening when she came home from her now rather numerous engagements, Lucy found her grandmother seated at the table, with the bird in her hand, rubbing him all over very gently for fear of hurting him, with something she took with her finger from a little pot on the table.

"What *are* you doing with Widdles, grannie?" she said.

"Trying a little bear's grease, child. Why shouldn't I?" she added, angrily, when Lucy laughed.

"No reason in the world why you shouldn't, grannie. You mustn't mind my laughing."

"I don't see why anybody should laugh at misfortune," returned Mrs. Boxall, severely. "How would you like to be in the condition of this bird yourself?" — without a feather, she was going to say, but just pulled up in time. She could not help laughing herself now, but she went on, nevertheless, with her work of charity. "Who knows," she said, "but they may grow again?"

"Grow again!" shrieked the gray parrot, in the tone of a violin in unskillful hands.

"Yes, grow again, you witch!" said Mrs. Boxall. "I don't see why the devil shouldn't be in you as well as in your betters. Why shouldn't they grow again?"

"Grow again!" reiterated the gray parrot. "Grow again! Widdles! Widdles! Widdles! Ha! ha! ha!"

"It shall grow again," retorted the old lady. "If bear's grease won't do, I'll spend my last penny on a bottle of Macassar; and if it doesn't grow then I'll pluck your back and stick them into his."

Mrs. Boxall had got into a habit of talking thus with the bird, which the bookseller had already nearly cured of his wicked words by instant punishment following each offense.

"Stick them into his!" cried the bird like an echo, and refused to speak again.

Sometimes, however, he would say a naughty word evidently for the sake of testing his master, or as if he wondered what punishment he would have this time — for the punishments were various. On such occasions he would shriek out the word, "Duck his head," and dart to the opposite side of the cage, keeping one eye full on his master, with such an expression that his profile looked like a whole face with a Cyclopean one eye in it.

Whether Mrs. Boxall was at last successful in her benevolent exertions I am unable to say, for her experiments were still going on when the period arrived with which my story must close. She often asserted that she saw them beginning to sprout; and to see her with spectacles on nose, examining the poor withered bluish back of Widdles, was ludicrous or touching, according to the humor of the beholder. Widdles seemed to like the pains she took with him, however; and there is no doubt of one thing, that she was rewarded for her trouble tenfold in being thus withdrawn from the contemplation of her own wrongs and misfortunes. Widdles thus gave her many a peaceful hour she would not in all-probability have otherwise enjoyed. Nor were her attentions confined to him; through him, she was introduced to the whole regiment of birds, which she soon began assisting Mr. Kitely to wait upon. Mattie had never taken to them. While grannie, as she, too, called her, was busy with them, Mattie would sit beside at her needlework, scarcely looking up even when she addressed an occasional remark to grannie. It was a curious household, and fell into many singular groups.

But here I must leave Mrs. Boxall with her bird-companions, which, save for the comfort they afforded her in taking her mind off herself, have no active part in the story. Through Mrs. Morgenstern's influence and exertions, Lucy soon had as much to do in the way of teaching as she could compass, and her grandmother knew no difference in her way of living from what she had been accustomed to.

CHAPTER XLIII
WHAT THOMAS WAS ABOUT

When Thomas left Rotherhithe with Jim Salter, he had no idea in his head but to get away somewhere. Like the ostrich, he wanted some sand to stick his head into. But wherever he went there were people, even policemen, about, and not one of the places they went through looked more likely to afford him shelter than another. Had he given Jim any clearer information concerning the necessity he was in of *keeping dark*, perhaps he would have done differently with him. As it was, he contented himself with piloting him about the lower docks and all that maritime part of London. They walked about the whole day till Thomas was quite weary. Nor did refuge seem nearer than before. All this time the police might be on his track, coming nearer and nearer like the bloodhounds that they were. They had some dinner at an eating-house, where Thomas's fastidiousness made yet a farther acquaintance with dirt and disorder, and he felt that he had fallen from his own sphere into a lower order of things, and could never more climb into the heaven from whence he had fallen. But the fear of yet a lower fall into a prison and the criminal's dock kept him from dwelling yet upon what he had lost. At night Jim led him into Ratcliff Highway, the Paradise of sailors at sea—the hell of sailors on shore. Thomas shrunk from the light that filled the street from end to end, blazing from innumerable public-houses, through the open doors of which he looked across into back parlors, where sailors and women sat drinking and gambling, or down long passages to great rooms with curtained doorways, whence came the sounds of music and dancing, and through which passed and re-passed seafaring figures and gaily bedizened vulgar girls, many of whom, had the weather been warmer, would have been hanging about the street-doors, laughing and *chaffing* the passers-by, or getting up a dance on the pavement to the sound of the music within. It was a whole streetful of low revelry. Poor Jack! Such is his coveted reward on shore for braving Death, and defying him to his face. He escapes from the embrace of the bony phantom to hasten to the arms of his far more fearful companion—the nightmare Life-in-Death— "who thicks man's blood with cold." Well may that pair casting their dice on the skeleton ship symbolize the fate of the sailor, for to the one or the other he falls a victim.

Opposite an open door Jim stopped to speak to an acquaintance. The door opened directly upon a room ascending a few steps from the street. Round a table sat several men—sailors, of course—apparently masters of coasting vessels. A lithe lascar was standing with one hand on the table, leaning over it, and talking swiftly, with snaky gestures of the other hand. He was in a rage. The others burst out laughing. Thomas saw something glitter in the hand of the Hindoo. One of the sailors gave a cry, and started up, but staggered and fell.

Before he fell the lascar was at the door, down the steps with a bound, and out into the street. Two men were after him at full speed, but they had no chance with the light-built Indian.

"The villain has murdered a man, Jim," said Thomas—"in there—look!"

"Oh, I dare say he ain't much the worse," returned Jim. "They're always a outing with their knives here."

For all his indifference, however, Jim started after the Hindoo, but he was out of sight in another moment.

Jim returned.

"He's crowding all sail for Tiger Bay," said he. "I shouldn't care to follow him there. Here's a Peeler."

"Come along, Jim," said Thomas. "Don't stand here all the night."

"Why *you* ain't afraid o' the place, are you, guv'nor?"

Thomas tried to laugh, but he did not enjoy the allusion—in the presence of a third person especially.

"Well, good-night," said Jim to his acquaintance.

"By the way," he resumed, "do you know the figure of Potts's ken?"

"What Potts? I don't know any Potts."

"Yes you do. Down somewhere about Lime 'us, you know. We saw him that night—"

Here Jim whispered his companion, who answered aloud:

"Oh, yes, I know. Let me see. It's the Marmaid, I think. You ain't a-going there, are you?"

"Don't know. Mayhap. I'm only taking this gen'leman a sight-seeing. He's from the country."

"Good-night, then." And so they parted.

It was a sudden idea of Jim's to turn in the direction of the man whose child Thomas had saved. But Thomas did not know where he was taking him.

"Where will you sleep to-night, guv'nor?" asked Jim, as they walked along.

"I don't know," answered Thomas. "I must leave you to find me a place. But I say, Jim, can you think of anything I could turn to? for my money won't last me long."

"Turn to!" echoed Jim. "Why a man had need be able to turn to everything by turns to make a livin' nowadays. You ain't been used to hard work, by your hands. Do you know yer Bible well?"

"Pretty well," answered Thomas; "but I don't know what that can have to do with making a living."

"Oh, don't you, guv'nor? Perhaps you don't know what yer Bible means. It means pips and pictures."

"You mean the cards. No, no, I've had enough of that. I don't mean ever to touch them again."

"Hum! Bitten," said Jim to himself, but so that Thomas heard him.

"Not very badly, Jim. In the pocket-book I told you I lost I had a hundred pounds, won at cards the night before last."

"My eye!" exclaimed Jim. "What a devil of a pity! But why don't you try your luck again?" he asked, after a few moments of melancholy devoted to the memory of the money.

"Look here, Jim. I don't know where to go to sleep. I have a comfortable room that I dare not go near; a father—a rich man, I believe—who would turn me out; and, in short, I've ruined myself forever with card-playing. The sight of a pack would turn me sick, I do believe."

"Sorry for you, guv'nor. I know a fellow, though, that makes a good thing of the thimble."

"I've no turn for tailoring, I'm afraid."

"Beggin' your pardon, guv'nor, but you are a muff! You never thought I meant a gen'leman like you to take to a beastly trade like that. I meant the thimble and peas, you know, at fairs, and such like. It's all fair, you know. You tell 'em they don't know where the pea is and they don't. I know a friend o' mine'll put you up to it for five or six bob. Bless you! there's room for free trade and money made." ·

Thomas could hardly be indignant with Jim for speaking according to his kind. But when he looked into it, it stung him to the heart to think that every magistrate would regard him as capable of taking to the profession of thimble-rigging after what he had been already guilty of. Yet in all his dealings with cards Thomas had been scrupulously honorable. He said no more to Jim about finding something to do.

They had gone a good way, and Thomas's strength was beginning to fail him quite. Several times Jim had inquired after the *Marmaid*, always in public-houses, where he paid for the information or none, as the case might be, by putting a name upon something at Thomas's expense; so that he began to be rather uplifted.

At length he called out joyfully:

"Here's a fishy one, guv'nor, *at last!* Come along."

So saying, he pushed the swing door, to which was attached a leather strap to keep it from swinging outward, and entered. It admitted them to a bar served by a big fat man with an apron whose substratum was white at the depth of several strata of dirt, and a nose much more remarkable for color than drawing, being in both more like a half-ripe mulberry than anything else in nature. He had little round, watery eyes, and a face indicative of nothing in particular, for it had left its original conformation years behind. As soon as they entered, Jim went straight up to the landlord, and stared at him for a few moments across the counter. "You don't appear to know me, guv'nor?" he said, for the many things he had drank to find the way had made him *barky*. His vocabulary of address, it will be remarked, was decidedly defective.

"Well, I can't take upon me to say as I do," answered the man, putting his thumbs in the strings of his apron, and looking at Jim with a mixture of effort and suspicion on his puffy face. "And I'll be bound to say," remarked Jim, turning toward Thomas, "that you don't know this gen'leman either. Do 'ee now guv'nor? On yer honor, right as a trivet? No, ye don't."

"Can't say I do."

"Look at him, then. Ain't he fit to remember? Don't he look respectable?"

"Come, none o' your chaff! Say what you've got to say. What do you want?"

"Cut it short, Jim," said Thomas.

"How's your young marmaid as took to the water so nat'ral at the Horsleydown tother day, Mr. Potts?" asked Jim, leaning on his elbows on the counter.

"Jolly," answered the landlord. "Was you by?"

"Wasn't I, then! And there's a guv'nor was nearer than I was. Mr. Potts, that's the very gen'leman as went a header into the water and saved her, Mr. Potts. Hold up yer head, guv'nor."

"You're a chaffin of me, I know," said Potts.

"Come, come, Jim, don't make a fool of me," said Thomas.

"I wish I had known you were bringing me here. Come along. I won't stand it."

But Jim was leaning over the counter, speaking in a whisper to the down-bent landlord.

"You don't mean it?" said the latter.

"Ask the mis'ess, then," said Jim.

"You don't mean it!" repeated the landlord, in a husky voice, and with increase of energy. Then looking toward Thomas, "What will he take?" and with the words turned his back upon Jim, and his face toward a shelf on which stood his choicest bottles between two cask-like protuberances. He got down one of brandy, but Thomas, who was vexed at being brought there as if he wanted some acknowledgment of the good deed he had been fortunate enough to perform, refused to take anything.

"What *will* you take then?" said the man, whose whole stock of ideas seemed to turn upon *taking*.

But at the moment a woman entered from behind the shop.

"There, mis'ess," said her husband, "can *you* tell who that gentleman is?"

She looked at him for a moment, and exclaimed:

"Bless my soul! It's the gentleman that took our Bessie out of the water. How do you do, sir?" she continued, with mingled pleasure and respect, as she advanced from behind the counter, and curtsied to Thomas.

"None the worse for my ducking, thank you," said Thomas, holding out his hand in the delight a word of real friendship always gives.

She shook it warmly, and would hardly let it go.

"Oh! isn't he, then?" muttered Jim, mysteriously, but loud enough for Potts to hear.

"Won't you come in, sir?" said the woman, turning to lead the way.

"Thank you," answered Thomas. "I have been walking about all day, and am very tired. If you would let me sit down awhile—and—perhaps it wouldn't be giving you too much trouble to ask for a cup of tea, for my head aches rather."

"Come in, sir," she said, in a tone of truest hospitality. "That I will, with pleasure, I'm sure."

Thomas followed her into a dingy back room, where she made him lie down on a sofa from which he would have recoiled three days ago, but for which he was very grateful now. She then bustled about to get him some tea, and various little delicacies besides, in the shape of ham, and shrimps, etc., etc. It was pretty clear from her look, and the way she pressed her offerings of gratitude, that she had a true regard for inward comforts, if not for those outward luxuries of neatness and cleanliness.

The moment Thomas was out of the shop, Jim Salter began to be more communicative with Mr. Potts.

"None the worse!" said he, reflectively. "Oh, no. That's the way your quality talk about a few bank-notes. Nothing but a hundred pounds the worst. Oh, no."

"You don't mean it?" said Mr. Potts, making his eyes as round as two sixpences.

"Well, to be sure," said Salter, "I can't take my davy on it; 'cause as how I've only his word for it. But he don't look like a cony-catcher, do he? He's a deal too green for that, I can tell you. Well, he is green!" repeated Jim, bursting into a quiet chuckle.

"I don't mean he's a fool, neither. There's a vasty heap o' difference betwixt a leek in yer eye and a turnip in yer brain-box. Ain't there now, guv'nor?"

"You don't mean it?" said Mr. Potts, staring more than ever.

"What don't I mean, Mr. Potts?"

"You don't mean that that 'ere chap? What *do* you mean about them hundred pounds?"

"Now I'll tell 'ee, guv'nor. It's a great pleasure to me to find I can tell a story so well."

"There you are—off again, no mortal man can tell to where. You ain't told me no story yet."

"Ain't I? How came it then, guv'nor, that I ha' made you forget your usual 'ospitable manners? If I hadn't ha' been telling you a story, you'd ha'—I know you'd ha' asked me to put a name upon something long ago."

Mr. Potts laughed, and saying, "I beg yer pardon, Mr. Salter, though I'm sure I don't remember ever meetin' of you afore, only that's no consequence; the best o' friends must meet some time for the first time," turned his face to the shelf as he had done before, and, after a little hesitation, seemed to conclude that it would be politic to take down the same bottle. Jim tossed off the half of his glassful, and, setting the rest on the counter, began his story. Whether he wished to represent himself as Thomas's confidant, or, having come to his conclusions to the best of his ability, believed himself justified in representing them as the facts of the case, it is not necessary to inquire; the account he gave of Thomas's position was this: That when Thomas went overboard after little Bessie, he had in the breast of his coat a pocket-book, with a hundred pounds of his master's in it; that he dared not go home without it; that the police were after him; and, in short, that he was in a terrible fix. Mr. Potts listened with a general stare, and made no reply.

"You'll give him a bed to-night, won't you, guv'nor? I'll come back in the morning and see what can be done."

Jim finished his glass of brandy as if it had been only the last drops, and set it on the counter with a world of suggestion in the motion, to which Mr. Potts mechanically replied by filling it again, saying as he did so, in a voice a little huskier than usual, "All right." Jim tossed off the brandy, smacked his lips, said "Thank you, and good-night," and went out of the beer-shop. Mr. Potts stood for five minutes motionless, then went slowly to the door of the back parlor, and called his wife. Leaving Thomas to finish his meal by himself, Mrs. Potts joined her husband and they had a talk together. He told her what Jim had just communicated to him, and they held a consultation, the first result of which was that Mrs. Potts proceeded to get a room—the best she could offer—ready for Thomas. He accepted her hospitality with gratitude, and was glad to go to bed.

Meantime, leaving his wife to attend to the thirst of the public, Mr. Potts set out to find his brother-in-law, the captain of a collier trading between Newcastle and London, who was at the moment in the neighborhood, but whose vessel was taking in ballast somewhere down the river. He came upon him where he had expected to find him, and told him the whole story.

The next morning, when Thomas, more miserable than ever, after rather a sleepless night, came down stairs early, he found his breakfast waiting for him, but not his breakfast only: a huge seafaring man, with short neck and square shoulders, dressed in a blue pilot-coat, was seated in the room. He rose when Thomas entered, and greeted him with a bow made up of kindness and patronage. Mrs. Potts came in the same moment.

"This is my brother, Captain Smith, of the *Raven*," she said, "come to thank you, sir, for what you did for his little pet, Bessie."

"Well, I donnow," said the captain, with a gruff breeziness of manner. "I came to ask the gentleman if, bein' on the loose, he wouldn't like a trip to Newcastle, and share my little cabin with me."

It was the first glimmer of gladness that had lightened Thomas's horizon for what seemed to him an age.

"Thank you, thank you!" he said; "it is the very thing for me."

And, as he spoke, the awful London wilderness vanished, and open sea and sky filled the world of his imaginings.

"When do you sail?" he asked.

"To-night, I hope, with the ebb," said the captain; "but you had better come with me as soon as you've had your breakfast, and we'll go on board at once. You needn't mind about your chest. You can rough it a little, I dare say. I can lend you a jersey that'll do better than your 'longshore togs."

Thomas applied himself to his breakfast with vigor. Hope even made him hungry. How true it is that we live by hope! Before he had swallowed his last mouthful, he started from his seat.

"You needn't be in such a hurry," said the captain. "There's plenty of time. Stow your prog."

"I have quite done. But I must see Mr. Potts for a minute."

He went to the bar, and, finding that Jim had not yet made his appearance, asked the landlord to change him a sovereign, and give half to Jim.

"It's too much," said Mr. Potts.

"I promised him a day's wages."

"Five shillings is over enough, besides the brandy I gave him last night. He don't make five shillings every day."

Thomas, however, to the list of whose faults stinginess could not be added, insisted on Jim having the half sovereign, for he felt that he owed him far more than that.

In pulling out the small remains of his money, wondering if he could manage to buy a jersey for himself before starting, he brought out with it two bits of pasteboard, the sight of which shot a pang to his heart: they were the pawn-tickets for his watch and Lucy's ring, which he had bought back from the holder on that same terrible night on which he had lost almost everything worth having. It was well he had only thrust them into the pocket of his trousers, instead of putting them into his pocket-book. They had stuck to the pocket, and been dried with it, had got loose during the next day, and now came to light, reminding him of his utter meanness, not to say dishonesty, in parting with the girl's ring that he might follow his cursed play. The gleam of gladness which the hope of escaping from London gave him had awaked his conscience more fully; and he felt the despicableness of his conduct as he had never felt it before. How could he have done it? The ring, to wear which he had been proud because it was not his own, but Lucy's, he had actually exposed to the contamination of vile hands—had actually sent from her pure, lovely person into the pocket of a foul talker, and thence to a pawnbroker's shop. He could have torn himself to pieces at the thought. And now that she was lost to him forever, was he to rob her of her mother's jewel as well? He *must* get it again. But if he went after it now, even if he had the money to redeem it, he might run into the arms of the searching Law, and he and it too would be gone. But he had not the money. The cold dew broke out on his face, as he stood beside the pump-handles of the beer-shop. But Mr. Potts had been watching him for some time. He knew the look of those tickets, and dull as his brain was, with a dullness that was cousin to his red nose, he divined at once that Thomas's painful contemplation had to do with some effects of which those tickets were the representatives. He laid his hand on Thomas's shoulder from behind. Thomas gave a great start.

"I beg your pardon for frightening of you, sir," said Mr. Potts; "but I believe a long experience in them things makes me able to give you good advice."

"What things?" asked Thomas.

"Them things," repeated Potts, putting a fat forefinger first on the one and then on the other pawn-ticket. "'Twasn't me, nor yet Bessie. 'Tis long since I was in my uncle's. All I had to do there was a-getting of 'em down the spout. I never sent much up it; my first wife, Joan—not Bessie, bless her! Now I ain't no witch, but I can see with 'alf a heye that you've got summat at your uncle's you don't like to leave there, when you're a-goin' a voyagin' to the ends o' the earth. Have you got the money as well as the tickets?"

"Oh dear, no!" answered Thomas, almost crying.

"Come now," said Potts, kindly, "sweep out the chimley. It's no use missing the crooks and corners, and having to send a boy up after all. Sweep it out. Tell me all about it, and I'll see what I can do—or can't do, it may be."

Thomas told him that the tickets were for a watch—a gold watch, with a compensation balance—and a diamond ring. He didn't care about the watch; but he would give his life to get the ring again.

"Let me look at the tickets. How much did you get on 'em separate?"

Thomas said he did not know, but gave him the tickets to examine.

Potts looked at them. "You don't care so much for the watch?" he said.

"No, I don't," answered Thomas; "though my mother did give it to me," he added, ruefully.

"Why don't you offer 'em both of the tickets for the ring, then?" said Potts.

"What?" said Thomas. "I don't see—"

"You give 'em to me," returned Potts. "Here, Bess! you go in and have a chat with the captain—I'm going out, Bessie, for an hour. Tell the captain not to go till I come back."

So saying, Potts removed his white apron, put on a black frock coat and hat, and went out, taking the tickets with him.

Mrs. Potts brought a tumbler of grog for her brother, and he sat sipping it. Thomas refused to join him; for he reaped this good from his sensitive organization, that since the night on which it had helped to ruin him, he could scarcely endure even the smell of strong drink. It was rather more than an hour before Mr. Potts returned, during which time Thomas had been very restless and anxious. But at last his host walked into the back room, laid a small screw of paper before him, and said:

"There's your ring, sir. You won't want your watch this voyage. I've got it, though; but I'm forced to keep it, in case I should be behind with my rent. Any time you look in, I shall have it, or know where it is."

Thomas did what he could to express his gratitude, and took the ring with a wonderful feeling of relief. It seemed like a pledge of farther deliverance. He begged Mr. Potts to do what he pleased with the watch; he didn't care if he never saw it again; and hoped it would be worth more to him than what it had cost him to redeem them both. Then, after many kind farewells, he took his leave with the captain of the *Raven*. As they walked along, he could not help looking round every few yards; but after his new friend had taken him to a shop where he bought a blue jersey and a glazed hat, and tied his coat up in a handkerchief—his sole bundle of luggage—he felt more comfortable. In a couple of hours he was on board of the *Raven*, a collier brig of a couple of hundred tons. They set sail the same evening, but not till they reached the Nore did Thomas begin to feel safe from pursuit.

The captain seemed a good deal occupied with his own thoughts, and there were few things they understood in common, so that Thomas was left mostly to his own company; which, though far from agreeable, was no doubt the very best for him under the circumstances. For it was his real self that he looked in the face—the self that told him what he was, showed him whence he had fallen, what he had lost, how he had hitherto been wasting his life, and how his carelessness had at length thrown him over a precipice up which he could not climb—there was no foothold upon it. But this was not all: he began to see not only his faults, but the weakness of his character, the refusal to combat which had brought him to this pass. His behavior to Lucy was the bitterest thought of all. She looked ten times more lovely to him now that he had lost her. That she should despise him was terrible—even more terrible the likelihood that she would turn the rich love of her strong heart upon some one else. How she had entreated him to do her justice! and he saw now that she had done so even more for his sake than for her own. He had not yet any true idea of what Lucy was worth. He did not know how she had grown since the time when, with all a girl's inexperience, she had first listened to his protestations. While he had been going down the hill, she had been going up. Long before they had been thus parted, he would not have had a chance of winning her affections had he had then to make the attempt. But he did see that she was infinitely beyond him, infinitely better than—to use a common phrase—he could have deserved if he had been as worthy as he fancied himself. I say *a common phrase*, because no man can ever *deserve* a woman. Gradually—by what gradations he could not have told—the truth, working along with his self-despising, showed him something of all this; and it was the first necessity of a nature like his to be taught to look down on himself. As long as he thought himself more than somebody, no good was to be expected of him. Therefore, it was well for him that the worthlessness of his character should break out and show itself in some plainly worthless deed, that he might no longer be able to hide himself from the conviction and condemnation of his own conscience. Hell had come at last; and he burned in its fire.

He was very weary, and went to bed in a berth in the cabin. But he was awaked while it was yet quite dark by the violent rolling and pitching of the vessel, and the running to and fro overhead. He got up at once, dressed in haste, and clambered up the companion-ladder. It was a wild scene. It had come on to blow hard. The brig was under reefed topsails and jib: but Thomas knew nothing of sea affairs. She was a good boat, and rode the seas well. There was just light enough for him to see the water by the white rents in its darkness. Fortunately, he was one of those few favored individuals in whose nerves the motion of a vessel finds no response—I mean he did not know what sea-sickness was. And that storm came to him a wonderful gift from the Father who had not forgotten his erring child—so strangely did it harmonize with his troubled mind. New strength, even hope, invaded his weary heart from the hiss of the wind through the cordage as it bellied out from the masts; his soul rejoiced in the heave of the wave under the bows and its swift rush astern; and though he had to hold hard by the weather shrouds, not a shadow of fear crossed his mind. This may have partly come from life being to him now a worthless thing, save as he had some chance of—he did not know what; for although he saw no way of recovering his lost honor, and therefore considered that eternal disgrace was his, even if God and man forgave him, there was yet a genuine ray of an unknown hope borne into him, as I say, from the crests of those broken waves. But I think it was natural to Thomas to fear nothing that merely involved danger to himself. In this respect he possessed a fine physical courage. It was in moral courage—the power of looking human anger and contempt in the face, and holding on his own way—that he was deficient. I believe that this came in a great measure from a delicate, sensitive organization. He could look a storm in the face; but a storm in a face he could not endure; he quailed before it. He would sail over a smooth human sea, if he might; when a wind rose there, he would be under bare poles in a moment. Of course this sensitiveness was not in itself an evil, being closely associated with his poetic tendencies, which ought to have been the center from which all the manlier qualities were influenced for culture and development; but he had been spoiled in every way, not least by the utterly conflicting discords of nature, objects, and character in his father and mother. But although a man may be physically brave and morally a coward—a fact too well known to be insisted upon—a facing of physical danger will help the better courage in the man whose will is at all awake to cherish it; for the highest moral courage is born of the will, and not of the organization. The storm wrought thus along with all that was best in him. In the fiercest of it that night, he found himself often kissing Lucy's ring, which, as soon as he began to know that they were in some danger, and not till then, he had, though with a strong feeling of the sacrilege of the act, ventured to draw once more upon his unworthy hand.

The wind increased as the sun rose. If he could only have helped the men staggering to and fro, as they did on the great sea in the days of old! But he did not know one rope from another. Two men were at the tiller. One was called away on some emergency aloft. Thomas sprang to his place.

"I will do whatever you tell me," he said to the steersman; "only let me set a man free."

Then he saw it was the captain himself. He gave a nod, and a squirt of tobacco-juice, as cool as if he had been steering with a light gale over a rippling sea. Thomas did his best, and in five minutes had learned to obey the word the captain gave him as he watched the binnacle. About an hour after the sun rose the wind began to moderate; and before long the captain gave up the helm to the mate, saying to Thomas:

"We'll go and have some breakfast. You've earned your rations, anyhow. Your father ought to have sent you to sea. It would have made a man of you."

This was not very complimentary. But Thomas had only a suppressed sigh to return for answer. He did not feel himself worth defending any more.

CHAPTER XLIV
THOMAS RETURNS TO LONDON

After this Thomas made rapid progress in the favor of Captain Smith. He had looked upon him as a landlubber before, with the contempt of his profession; but when he saw that, clerk as he was, he was yet capable at sea, he began to respect him. And as Thomas wakened up more and more to an interest in what was going on around him, he did not indulge in giving him fool's answers to the questions he asked, as so many sea-farers would have been ready to do; and he soon found that Thomas's education, though it was by no means a first-rate one, enabled him to ask more questions with regard to the laws of wind and water and the combination of forces than he was quite able to solve. Before they reached the end of the voyage, Thomas knew the rigging pretty well, and could make himself useful on board. Anxious to ingratiate himself with the captain—longing almost unconsciously for the support of some human approbation, the more that he had none to give himself—he laid himself out to please him. Having a tolerably steady head, he soon found himself able to bear a hand in taking in a reef in the foretop-sail, and he could steer by the course with tolerable steadiness. The sailors were a not unsociable set of men, and as he presumed upon nothing, they too gave him what help they could, not without letting off a few jokes at his expense, in the laughter following on which he did his best to join. The captain soon began to order him about like the rest, which was the best kindness he could have shown him; and Thomas's obedience was more than prompt—it was as pleasant as possible. He had on his part some information to give the captain; and their meals in the cabin together were often merry enough.

"Do you think you could ever make a sailor of me?" asked Tom, one day.

"Not a doubt of it, my boy," the captain answered. "A few voyages more, and you'll go aloft like a monkey."

"Where do you think of making your next voyage, sir?" asked Tom.

"Well, I'm part owner of the brig, and can do pretty much as I like. I did think of Dundee."

"I should have thought they have coal enough of their own thereabouts."

"A cargo of English coal never comes amiss. It's better than theirs by a long way."

"Would you take me with you?"

"To be sure, if you can't do better."

"I can't. I don't want anything but my rations, you know."

"You'll soon be worth your wages. I can't say you are yet, you know."

"Of course not. You must have your full crew besides."

"We're one hand short this voyage; and you've done something to fill the gap."

"I'm very glad, I'm sure. But what would you advise me to do when we reach Newcastle? It will be some time before you get off again."

"Not long. If you like to take your share in getting the cargo on board, you can make wages by that."

"With all my heart," said Thomas, whom this announcement greatly relieved.

"It's dirty work," said the captain.

"There's plenty of water about," answered Thomas.

When they came to Newcastle, Thomas worked as hard as any of them, getting the ballast out and the new cargo in. He had never known what it was to work before; and though it tired him dreadfully at first, it did him good.

"THOMAS WORKED AS HARD AS ANY OF THEM."

Among the men was one whom he liked more than the rest. He had been in the merchant service, and had sailed to India and other places. He knew more than his shipmates, and had only taken to the coasting for a time for family reasons. With him Thomas chiefly consorted when their day's work was over. With a growing hope that by some means he might rise at last into another kind of company, he made the best he could of what he had, knowing well that it was far better than he deserved, and far better than what of late he had been voluntarily choosing. His hope, however, alternated with such fits of misery and despair, that if it had not been for the bodily work he had to do, he thought he would have lost his reason. I believe not a few keep hold of their senses in virtue of doing hard work. I knew an earl's son, an heir, who did so. And I think that not a few, especially women, lose their senses just from having nothing to do. Many more, who are not in danger of this, lose their health, and more still lose their purity and rectitude. In other words, health—physical, mental, moral, and spiritual—requires, for its existence and continuance, work, often hard and bodily labor.

This man lived in Newcastle, and got Thomas a decent room near his own dwelling, where he slept. One evening they had been walking together about the place till they were tired. It was growing late, and as they were some distance from home, they went into a little public house which Robins knew, to get a bit of bread and cheese and some ale. Robins was a very sober man, and Thomas felt no scruple in accompanying him thus, although one of the best things to be said for Thomas was, that ever since he went on board the *Raven* he had steadily refused to touch spirits. Perhaps, as I have hinted before, there was less merit in this than may appear, for the very smell was associated with such painful memories of misery that it made him shudder. Sometimes a man's physical nature comes in to help him to be good. For such a dislike may grow into a principle which will last after the dislike has vanished.

They sat down in a little room with colored prints of ships in full sail upon the walls, a sanded floor, in the once new fashion which superseded rushes, and an ostrich egg hanging from the ceiling. The landlady was a friend of Robins, and showed them this attention. On the other side of a thin partition was the ordinary room, where the ordinary run of customers sat and drank their grog. There were only two or three in there when our party entered. Presently, while Thomas and Robins were sitting at their supper, they heard two or three more come in. A hearty recognition took place, and fresh orders were given. Thomas started and listened. He thought he heard the name *Ningpo*.

Now, from Thomas's having so suddenly broken off all connection with his friends, he knew nothing of what had been going on with regard to the property Mr. Boxall had left behind him. He thought, of course, that Mrs. Boxall would inherit it. It would not be fair to suppose, however, that this added to his regret at having lost Lucy, for he was humbled enough to be past that. The man who is turned out of Paradise does not grieve over the loss of its tulips, or, if he does, how came he ever to be within its gates? But the very fact that the name of Boxall was painful to him, made the name of that vessel attract and startle him at once.

"What's the matter?" said Robins.

"Didn't you hear some one in the next room mention the *Ningpo*?" returned Thomas.

"Yes. She was a bark in the China trade."

"Lost last summer on the Cape Verdes. I knew the captain—at least, I didn't know him, but I knew his brother and his family. They were all on board and all lost."

"Ah!" said Robins, "that's the way of it, you see. People oughtn't to go to sea but them as has business there. Did you say the crew was lost as well?"

"So the papers said."

Robins rose, and went into the next room. He had a suspicion that he knew the voice. Almost the same moment a rough burst of greeting came to Thomas's ears: and a few minutes after, Robins entered, bringing with him a sailor so rough, so hairy, so brown, that he looked as if he must be proof against any attack of the elements—case-hardened against wind and water.

"Here's the gentleman," said Robins, "as knew your captain, Jack."

"Do, sir?" said Jack, touching an imaginary sou'wester.

"What'll you have?" asked Tom.

This important point settled, they had a talk together, in which Jack opened up more freely in the presence of Robins than he would have felt interest enough to do with a stranger alone who was only a would-be sailor at best—a fact which could not be kept a secret from an eye used to read all sorts of signals. I will not attempt to give the story in Jack's lingo. But the certainty was that he had been on board the *Ningpo* when she went to pieces—that he had got ashore on a spar, after sitting through the night on the stern, and seeing every soul lost, as far as he believed, but himself. He had no great power of description, and did not volunteer much; but he returned very direct answers to all the questions Thomas put to him. Had

Thomas only read some of the proceedings in the Court of Probate during the last few months, he would have known better what sort of questions to put to him. Almost the only remark Jack volunteered was:

"Poor little July! how she did stick to me, to be sure! But she was as dead as a marlin-spike long afore the starn broke up."

"Were you long on the island?" asked Tom.

"No, not long," answered the sailor. "I always was one of the lucky ones. I was picked up the same day by a brigantine bound from Portingale to the Sambusy."

Little did Tom think how much might be involved in what Jack said. They parted, and the friends went home together. They made a good voyage, notwithstanding some rough weather, to Dundee, failed in getting a return cargo, and went back to Newcastle in ballast. From Newcastle their next voyage was to London again.

"If you would rather not go to London," said the master to Tom, "there's a friend of mine here who is just ready to start for Aberdeen. I dare say if I were to speak to him he would take you on board."

But Tom's heart was burning to see Lucy once more—if only to see her and restore her ring. If, he thought, he might but once humble himself to the dust before her—if he might but let her see that, worthless as he was, he worshiped her, his heart would be easier. He thought, likewise, that what with razoring and tanning, and the change of his clothes, he was not likely to be recognized. And besides, by this time the power must be out of Mr. Stopper's hands; at least Lucy must have come to exert her influence over the affairs of the business, and she would not allow them to drive things to extremity with him, worthless as he was. He would venture, come of it what might. So he told the captain that he would much prefer to work his passage to London again. It was a long passage this time, and very rough weather.

It was with strange feelings that Thomas saw once more the turrets of the Tower of London. Danger—exposure, it might be—lay before him, but he thought only of Lucy, not of the shame now. It was yet early morning when Captain Smith and he went on shore at Shadwell. The captain was going to see an old friend in the neighborhood, and after that to Limehouse, to the Mermaid, to see his sister. Thomas wanted to be alone, for he had not yet succeeded in making up his mind what he was going to do. So he sent a grateful message by the captain, with the addition that he would look in upon them in the evening.

Left alone, without immediate end or aim, he wandered on, not caring whither he went, but, notwithstanding his heavy thoughts, with something of the enjoyment the sailor feels in getting on shore even after only a fortnight at sea. It was a bright, cold, frosty morning, in the month of March. Without knowing his course, Thomas was wandering northward; and after he had gone into a coffee-shop and had some breakfast, he carelessly resumed his course in the same direction. He found that he was in the Cambridge Road, but whither that led he had no idea. Nor did he know, so absorbed was he in his own thoughts, even after he came into a region he knew, till, lifting up his head, he saw the gray, time-worn tower, that looks so strong and is so shaky, of the old church of Hackney, now solitary, its ancient nave and chancel and all having vanished, leaving it to follow at its leisure, wearied out with disgust at the church which has taken its place, and is probably the ugliest building in Christendom, except the parish-church of a certain little town in the north of Aberdeenshire. This sent a strange pang to his heart, for close by, that family used to live whose bones were now whitening among those rocky islands of the Atlantic. He went into the church-yard, sat down on a grave-stone, and thought. Now that the fiction of his own worth had vanished like an image in the clouds of yesterday, he was able to see clearly into his past life and conduct; and he could not conceal from himself that his behavior to Mary Boxall might have had something to do with the loss of the whole family. He saw more and more the mischief that had come of his own weakness, lack of courage, and principle. If he could but have defended his own conduct where it was blameless, or at least allowed it to be open to the daylight and the anger of those whom it might not please, he would thus have furnished his own steps with a strong barrier against sliding down that slope down which he had first slidden before falling headlong from the precipice at its foot. In self-abasement he rose from the grave-stone, and walked slowly past the house. Merry faces of children looked from upper windows, who knew nothing of those who had been there before them. Then he went away westward toward Highbury. He would just pass his father's door. There was no fear of his father seeing him at this time of the day, for he would be at his office, and his mother could not leave her room. Ah, his mother! How had he behaved to her? A new torrent of self-reproach rushed over his soul as he walked along the downs toward Islington. Some day, if he could only do something first to distinguish himself in any way, he would go and beg her forgiveness. But what chance was there of his ever doing any thing now? He had cut all the ground of action from under his own feet. Not yet did Thomas see that his duty was to confess his sin, waiting for no means of covering its enormity. He walked on. He passed the door, casting but a cursory glance across the windows. There was no one to be seen. He went down the long walk with the lime-trees on one side, which he knew so well, and just as he reached the gates there were his sister Amy and Mr. Simon coming from the other side. They were talking and laughing merrily, and looking in each others face. He had never seen Mr. Simon look so pleasant before. He almost felt as if he could speak to him. But no sooner did Mr. Simon see that this sailor-looking fellow was regarding them, than the clerical mask was on his face, and Thomas turned away with involuntary dislike.

"It is clear," he said to himself, "that they don't care much what is become of me." He turned then, westward again, toward Highgate, and then went over to Hampstead, paused at the pines, and looked along the valley beneath; then descended into it, and went across the heath till he came out on the road by Wildwood. This was nearly the way he had wandered on that stormy Christmas Day with Mary Boxall. He had this day, almost without conscious choice, traversed the scenes of his former folly. Had he not been brooding repentantly over his faults, I doubt if he could have done so, even unconsciously. He turned into the Bull and Bush, and had some dinner; then, as night was falling, started for London, having made up his mind at last what he would do. At the Bull and Bush he wrote a note to Lucy, to the following effect. He did not dare to call her by her name, still less to use any term of endearment.

"I am not worthy to speak or write your name," he said; "but my heart is dying to see you once more. I have likewise to return you your mother's ring, which, though it has comforted me often in my despair, I have no longer any right to retain. But I should just like to tell you that I am working honestly for my bread. I am a sailor now. I am quite clear of all my bad companions, and hope to remain so. Dare I ask you to meet me once—to-morrow night, say, or any night soon, for I am not safe in London? I will tell you all when I see you. Send me one line by the bearer of this to say where you will meet me. Do not, for the sake of your love to me once, refuse me this. I want to beg your forgiveness, that I may go away less miserable than I am. Then I will go to Australia, or somewhere out of the country, and you will never hear of me more. God bless you."

He cried a good deal over this note. Then came the question how he was to send it. He could, no doubt, find a messenger at the Mermaid, but he was very unwilling to make any line of communication between that part of London and Guild Court, or, more properly, to connect himself, whose story was there known, with Lucy's name. He would go to the neighborhood of Guild Court and there look out for a messenger, whom he could then watch.

CHAPTER XLV
THOMAS IS CAPTURED

As soon as he had resolved upon this he set out. There was plenty of time. He would walk. Tired as he was beginning to be, motion was his only solace. He walked through Hampstead, and by Haverstock Hill, Tottenham Court Road, and Holborn to the City. By this time the moon was up. Going by Ludgate Hill, he saw her shining over St. Paul's right through the spire of St. Martin's, where the little circle of pillars lays it open to the sky and the wind; she seemed to have melted the spire in two. Then he turned off to the left, now looking out for a messenger. In his mind he chose and rejected several, dallying with his own eagerness, and yielding to one doubt after another about each in succession. At last he reached the farther end of Bagot Street. There stood Poppie with her "murphy-buster." Had it been daylight, when her dress and growth would have had due effect upon her appearance, probably Thomas would not have known her; but seeing her face only by the street-lamp, he just recollected that he had seen the girl about Guild Court. He had no suspicion that she would know him. But Poppie was as sharp as a needle; she did know him.

"Do you know Guild Court, my girl?" he asked.

"I believe you," answered Poppie.

"Would you take this letter for me, and give it to Miss Burton, who lives there, and wait for an answer? If she's not at home, bring it back to me. I will take care of your potatoes, and give you a shilling when you come back."

Whether Poppie would have accepted the office if she had not recognized Thomas, I do not know. She might, for she had so often forsaken her machine and found it all right when she returned that I think the promise of the shilling would have enabled her to run the risk. As it was, she scudded. While she was gone he sold three or four of her potatoes. He knew how to deliver them; but he didn't know the price, and just took what they gave him. He stood trembling with hope.

Suddenly he was seized by the arm from behind, and a gruff voice he thought he knew, said:

"Here he is. Come along, Mr. Worboise. You're wanted."

Thomas had turned in great alarm. There were four men, he saw, but they were not policemen. That was a comfort. Two of them were little men. None of them spoke but the one who seized him. He twisted his arm from the man's grasp, and was just throwing his fist at his head, when he was pinioned by two arms thrown round him from behind.

"Don't strike," said the first man, "or it'll be the worse for you. I'll call the police. Come along, and I swear nothing but good will come of it—to you as well as to other people. I'm not the man to get you into trouble, I can tell you. Don't you know me?—Kitely, the bookseller. Come along. I've been in a fix myself before now."

Thomas yielded, and they led him away.

"But there's that child's potatoes!" he said. "The whole affair will be stolen. Just wait till she comes back."

"Oh! she's all right," said Kitely. "There she is, buttering a ha'p'orth. Come along."

They led him through streets and lanes, every one of which Thomas knew better than his catechism a good deal. All at once they hustled him in at a church door. In the vestibule Thomas saw that there were but two with him—Mr. Kitely, whom he now recognized, and a little man with his hair standing erect over his pale face, like corn on the top of a chalk-cliff. Him too he recognized, for Mr. Spelt had done many repairs for him. The other two had disappeared. Neither Mr. Salter nor Mr. Dolman cared to tempt Providence by coming farther. It was Jim who had secured his arms, and saved Kitely's head. Mr. Kitely made way for Thomas to enter first. Fearful of any commotion, he yielded still, and went into a pew near the door. The two men followed him. It is time I should account for the whole of this strange proceeding.

Jim Salter did not fail to revisit the Mermaid on the day of Tom's departure, but he was rather late, and Tom was gone. As to what had become of him, Mr. Potts thought it more prudent to profess ignorance. He likewise took another procedure upon him, which, although well-meant, was not honest. Regardless of Thomas's desire that Jim should have a half-sovereign for the trouble of the preceding day, Mr. Potts, weighing the value of Jim's time, and the obligation he was himself under to Tom, resolved to take Tom's interests in his own hands, and therefore very solemnly handed a half-crown and a florin, as what Thomas had left for him, across the counter to Jim. Jim took the amount in severe dudgeon. The odd sixpence was especially obnoxious. It was grievous to his soul.

"Four and sixpence! Four bob and one tanner," said Jim, in a tone of injury, in which there certainly was no pretense—"after a-riskin' of my life, not to mention a-wastin' of my precious time for the ungrateful young snob. Four and sixpence!"

Mr. Potts told him with equal solemnity, a righteous indignation looking over the top of his red nose, to hold his jaw, or go out of his tavern. Whereupon Jim gave a final snuff, and was silent, for where there was so much liquor on the premises it was prudent not to anger the Mermaid's master. Thereupon the said master, probably to ease his own conscience Jim-ward, handed him a glass of old Tom, which Jim, not without suspicion of false play, emptied and deposited. From that day, although he continued to call occasionally at the Mermaid, he lost all interest in his late client, never referred to him, and always talked of Bessy Potts as if he himself had taken her out of the water.

The acquaintance between Dolman and him began about this time to grow a little more intimate; and after the meeting which I have described above, they met pretty frequently, when Mr. Dolman communicated to him such little facts as transpired about "them lawyers," namely, Mr. Worboise's proceedings. Among the rest was the suspicious disappearance of the son, whom Mr. Dolman knew, not to speak to, but by sight, as well as his own lap-stone. Mr. Salter, already suspicious of his man, requested a description of the missing youth, and concluded that it was the same in whom he had been so grievously disappointed, for the odd sixpence represented any conceivable amount of meanness, not to say wickedness. This increased intimacy with Jim did Dolman no good, and although he would not yet forsake his work during work-hours, he would occasionally permit Jim to fetch a jug of beer from a neighboring tavern, and consume it with him in his shop. On these occasions they had to use great circumspection with regard to Dolly's landlord, who sat over his head. But in the winter nights, Mr. Spelt would put up the outside shutter over his window to keep the cold out, only occasionally opening his door to let a little air in. This made it possible to get the beer introduced below without discovery, when Dolman, snail-like, closed the mouth of his shell also, in which there was barely room for two, and stitched away while Jim did the chief part of the drinking and talking—in an undertone—for him—not so low, however, but that Spelt could hear not a little that set him thinking. It was pretty clear that young Worboise was afraid to show himself, and this and other points he communicated to his friend Kitely. This same evening they were together thus when they heard a hurried step come up and stop before the window, and the voice of Mr. Kitely, well known to Dolman, call to the tailor overhead.

"Spelt, I say. Spelt!"

Mr. Spelt looked out at his door.

"Yes, Mr. Kitely. What's the matter?"

"Here's that young devil's lamb, Worboise, been and sent a letter to Miss Burton by your Poppie, and he's a-waitin' an answer. Come along, and we'll take him alive."

"But what do you want to do with him?" asked Spelt.

"Take him to Mr. Fuller."

"But what if he won't come?"

"We can threaten him with the police, as if we knew all about it. Come along, there's no time to be lost."

"But what would you take him to Mr. Fuller for?"

My reader may well be inclined to ask the same question. I will explain. Mr. Kitely was an original man in thinking, and a rarely practical man in following it up, for he had confidence in his own conclusions. Ever since he had made the acquaintance of Mr. Fuller, through Mattie's illness, he had been feeling his influence more and more, and was gradually reforming his ways in many little things that no one knew of but himself. No one in London knew him as any thing but an honest man, but I presume there are few men so honest that if they were to set about it seriously, they could not be honester still. I suspect that the most honest man of my acquaintance will be the readiest to acknowledge this; for honesty has wonderful offshoots from its great tap-root. Having this experience in himself, he had faith in the moral power of Mr. Fuller. Again, since Lucy had come to live in the house, he had grown to admire her yet more, and the attention and kindness she continued to show to his princess, caused an equal growth in his gratitude. Hence it became more and more monstrous in his eyes that she should be deprived of her rights in such a villainous manner by the wickedness of "them Worboises." For the elder, he was afraid that he was beyond redemption; but if he could get hold of the younger, and put him under Mr. Fuller's pump, for that was how he represented the possible process of cleansing to himself, something might come of it. He did not know that Thomas was entirely ignorant of his father's relation to the property of the late Richard Boxall, and that no man in London would have less influence with Worboise, senior, than Worboise, junior. He had had several communications with Mr. Fuller on the subject, and had told him all he knew. Mr. Fuller likewise had made out that this must be the same young man of whom Lucy had spoken in such trouble. But as he had disappeared, nothing could be done—even if he had had the same hope of good results from the interview as Mr. Kitely, whose simplicity and eagerness amused as well as pleased him. When Mr. Kitely, therefore, received from Poppie Thomas's letter to give to Lucy, who happened to be out, he sped at once, with his natural promptitude, to secure Mr. Spelt's assistance in carrying out his conspiracy against Thomas.

As soon as the two below heard Mr. Spelt scramble down and depart with Mr. Kitely, they issued from their station; Mr. Dolman anxious to assist in the capture, Mr. Salter wishing to enjoy his disgrace, for the odd sixpence rankled. As soon as they saw him within the inner door of the church they turned and departed. They knew nothing about churches, and were unwilling to enter. They did not know what they might be in for, if they went in. Neither had they any idea for what object Thomas was taken there. Dolman went away with some vague notion about the Ecclesiastical Court; for he tried to read the papers sometimes. This notion he imparted with equal vagueness to the brain of Jim Salter, already muddled with the beer he had drunk. Dolman went back to his work, hoping to hear about it when Spelt came home. Jim wandered eastward to convey a somewhat incorrect idea of what had happened to the inhabitants of the Mermaid. Having his usual design on the Mermaid's resources, his story lost nothing in the telling, and, in great perplexity, and greater uneasiness, Captain Smith and Mr. Potts started to find out the truth of the matter. Jim conducted them to the church door, which was still open, and retired round the corner.

Meantime the captors and the culprit waited till the service was over. As soon as Mr. Fuller had retired to the vestry, and the congregation had dispersed, Mr. Kitely intimated to Thomas that he must follow him, and led the way up the church. With the fear of the police still before his eyes, Thomas did follow, and the little tailor brought up the rear. Hardly waiting, in his impatience, to knock at the door, Mr. Kitely popped his head in as Mr. Fuller was standing in his shirt-sleeves, and said with ill-suppressed triumph:

"Here he is, sir! I've got him!"

"Whom do you mean?" said Mr. Fuller, arrested by surprise with one arm in his coat and the other hand searching for the other sleeve.

"Young Worboise. The lawyer-chap, you know sir," he added, seeing that the name conveyed no idea.

"Oh!" said Mr. Fuller, prolongedly. "Show him in, then." And on went his coat.

Thomas entered, staring in bewilderment. Nor was Mr. Fuller quite at his ease at first, when the handsome, brown sailor-lad stepped into the vestry. But he shook hands with him, and asked him to take a chair. Thomas obeyed. Seeing his conductors lingered, Mr. Fuller then said:

"You must leave us alone now, Mr. Kitely. How do you do, Mr. Spelt?"

They retired, and, after a short consultation together in the church, agreed that they had done their part and could do no more, and went home.

CHAPTER XLVI
THE CONFESSION

As soon as the door closed behind them, Mr. Fuller turned to Tom, saying, as he took a chair near him, "I'm very glad to see you, Mr. Worboise. I have long wanted to have a little talk with you."

"Will you tell me," said Tom, with considerable uneasiness, notwithstanding the pacific appearance of everything about him, "why those people have made me come to you? I was afraid of making a row in the street, and so I thought it better to give in. But I have not an idea why I am here."

Mr. Fuller thought there must be some farther reason, else a young man of Thomas's appearance would not have so quietly yielded to the will of two men like Kitely and Spelt. But he kept this conclusion to himself.

"It certainly was a most unwarrantable proceeding if they used any compulsion. But I have no intention of using any—nor should I have much chance," he added, laughing, "if it came to a tussle with a young fellow like you, Mr. Worboise."

This answer restored Tom to his equanimity a little.

"Perhaps you know my father," he said, finding that Mr. Fuller was silent. In fact, Mr. Fuller was quite puzzled how to proceed. He cared little for the business part, and for the other, he must not compromise Lucy. Clearly the lawyer-business was the only beginning. Ana this question of Tom's helped him to it.

"I have not the pleasure of knowing your father. I wish I had. But, after all, it is better I should have a chat with you first."

"Most willingly," said Tom, with courtesy.

"It is a very unconventional thing I am about to do. But very likely you will give me such information as will enable me to set the minds of some of my friends at rest. I am perfectly aware what a lame introduction this is, and I must make a foolish figure indeed, except you will kindly understand that sometimes a clergyman is compelled to meddle with matters which he would gladly leave alone."

"I have too much need of forbearance myself not to grant it, sir—although I do not believe any will be necessary in your case. Pray make me understand you."

Mr. Fuller was greatly pleased with this answer, and proceeded to business at once.

"I am told by a man who is greatly interested in one of the parties concerned, that a certain near relative of yours is in possession of a large property which ought by right, if not by law, to belong to an old lady who is otherwise destitute. I wish to employ your mediation to procure a settlement upon her of such small portion of the property at least as will make her independent. I am certainly explicit enough, now," concluded Mr. Fuller, with a considerable feeling of relief in having discharged himself, if not of his duty, yet of so creditable a beginning of it.

"I am as much in the dark as ever, sir," returned Thomas. "I know nothing of what you refer to. If you mean my father, I am the last one to know anything of his affairs. I have not seen him or heard of him for months."

"But you cannot surely be ignorant of the case. It has been reported in the public prints from time to time. It seems that your father has come in for the contingent reversion—I think that is the phrase, I'm not sure—of all the property of the late Richard Boxall—"

"By Jove!" cried Thomas, starting to his feet in a rage, then sinking back on his chair in conscious helplessness. "He did make his will," he muttered.

"Leaving," Mr. Fuller went on, "the testator's mother and his niece utterly unprovided for."

"But she had money of her own in the business. I have heard her say so a thousand times."

"She has nothing now."

"My father is a villain!" cried Thomas, starting once more to his feet, and pacing up and down in the little vestry like a wild beast in a cage. "And what am I?" he added, after a pause. "I have brought all this upon her." He could say no more. He sat down, hid his face in his hands, and sobbed.

Thomas was so far mistaken in this, that his father, after things had gone so far as they had, would have done as he had done, whatever had been Thomas's relations to the lady. But certainly, if he had behaved as he ought, things could not have gone thus far. He was the cause of all the trouble.

Nothing could have been more to Mr. Fuller's mind.

"As to Miss Burton," he said, "I happen to know that she has another grief, much too great to allow her to think about money. A clergyman, you know, comes to hear of many things. She never told me who he was," said Mr. Fuller, with hesitation; "but she confessed to me that she was in great trouble."

"Oh, sir, what *shall* I do?" cried Thomas; "I love her with all my heart, but I can never, never dare to think of her more. I came up to London at the risk of—of—I came up to London only to see her and give her back this ring, and beg her to forgive me, and go away forever. And now I have not only given her pain—"

"Pain!" said Mr. Puller. "If she weren't so good, her heart would have broken before now."

Thomas burst out sobbing again. He turned his face away from Mr. Puller and stood by the wall, shaken with misery. Mr. Puller left him alone for a minute or two. Then, going up to him, he put his hand on his shoulder, kindly, and said:

"My dear boy, I suspect you have got into some terrible scrape, or you would not have disappeared as they tell me. And your behavior seems to confirm the suspicion. Tell me all about it, and I have very little doubt that I can help you out of it. But you must tell me *everything*."

"I will, sir; I will," Tom sobbed.

"Mind, no half-confessions. I have no right to ask you to confess but on the ground of helping you. But if I am to help you, I must know all. Can I trust you that you will be quite straightforward and make a clean breast of it?"

Tom turned round, and looked Mr. Fuller calmly in the face. The light of hope shone in his eyes: the very offer of hearing all his sin and misery gave him hope. To tell it, would be to get rid of some of the wretchedness.

"I hate myself so, sir," he said, "that I do not feel it worth while to hide anything. I will speak the truth. When you wish to know more than I tell, ask me any questions you please, and I will answer them."

At this moment a tap was heard at the vestry door, and it opened, revealing two strange figures with scared, interrogating faces on the top— the burly form of Captain Smith, and the almost as bulky, though differently arranged, form of Mr. Potts.

"Don't'ee be too hard on the young gentleman, sir," said Mr. Potts, in the soothing tone of one who would patch up a family quarrel. "He won't do it again, I'll go bail. You don't know, sir, what a good sort he is. Don't'ee get him into no trouble. He lost his life—all but—a reskewing of my Bessie. He did now. True as the Bible, sir," added Mr. Potts, with conciliatory flattery to the clergyman's profession, whom they both took for the father or uncle of Thomas.

"You just let me take him off again, sir," put in Captain Smith, while the face of Mr. Potts, having recovered its usual complexion, looked on approvingly like a comic but benevolent moon.

Mr. Fuller had a wise way of never interrupting till he saw in what direction the sense lay. So he let them talk, and the seaman went on:

"Everybody knows the sea's the place for curing the likes o' them fine fellows that carries too much sail ashore. They soon learns their reef-points there. Why, parson, sir, he's been but three or four voyages, and I'll take him for an able-bodied seaman to-morrow. He's a right good sort, though he may ha' been a little frolicsome on shore. We was all young once, sir."

"Are these men friends of yours, Mr. Worboise?" asked Mr. Fuller.

"Indeed they are," answered Thomas. "I think I must have killed myself before now, if it hadn't been for those two."

So saying, he shook hands with Mr. Potts, and, turning to the captain, said:

"Thank you, thank you, captain, but I am quite safe with this gentleman. I will come and see you to-morrow."

"He shall sleep at my house to-night," said Mr. Fuller; "and no harm shall happen to him, I promise you."

"Thank you, sir;" and "Good-night, gentlemen," said both, and went through the silent, wide church with a kind of awe that rarely visited either of them.

Without further preface than just the words, "Now, I will tell you all about it, sir," Thomas began his story. When he had finished it, having answered the few questions he put to him in its course, Mr. Fuller was satisfied that he did know all about it, and that if ever there was a case in which he ought to give all the help he could, here was one. He did not utter a word of reproof. Thomas's condition of mind was such that it was not only unnecessary, but might have done harm. He had now only to be met with the same simplicity which he had himself shown. The help must match the confession.

"Well, we must get you out of this scrape, somehow," he said, heartily.

"I don't see how you can, sir."

"It rests with yourself chiefly. Another can only help. The feet that walked into the mire must turn and walk out of it again. I don't mean to reproach you—only to encourage you to effort."

"What effort?" said Tom. "I have scarcely heart for anything. I have disgraced myself forever. Suppose all the consequences of my—doing as I did"—he could not yet call the deed by its name—"were to disappear, I have a blot upon me to all eternity, that nothing can wash out. For there is the fact. I almost think it is not worth while to do anything."

"You are altogether wrong about that," returned Mr. Fuller. "It is true that the deed is done, and that that cannot be obliterated. But a living soul may outgrow all stain and all reproach—I do not mean in the judgment of men merely, but in the judgment of God, which is always founded on the actual fact, and always calls things by their right names, and covers no man's sin, although he forgives it and takes it away. A man may abjure his sin so, cast it away from him so utterly, with pure heart and full intent, that, although he did it, it is his no longer. But, Thomas Worboise, if the stain of it were to cleave to you to all eternity, that would be infinitely better than that you should have continued capable of doing the thing. You are more honorable now than you were before. Then you were capable of the crime; now, I trust, you are not. It was far better that, seeing your character was such that you could do it, you should thus be humbled by disgracing yourself, than that you should have gone on holding up a proud head in the world, with such a deceitful hollow of weakness in your heart. It is the kindest thing God can do for his children, sometimes, to let them fall in the mire. You would not hold by your Father's hand; you struggled to pull it away; he let it go, and there you lay. Now that you stretch forth the hand to him again, he will take you, and clean, not your garments only, but your heart, and soul, and consciousness. Pray to your Father, my boy. He will change your humiliation into humility, your shame into purity."

"Oh, if he were called anything else than *Father*! I am afraid I hate my father."

"I don't wonder. But that is your own fault, too."

"How is that, sir? Surely you are making even me out worse than I am."

"No. You are afraid of him. As soon as you have ceased to be afraid of him, you will no longer be in danger of hating him."

"I can't help being afraid of him."

"You must break the bonds of that slavery. No slave can be God's servant. His servants are all free men. But we will come to that presently. You must not try to call God your Father, till *father* means something very different to you from what it seems to mean now. Think of the grandest human being you can imagine—the tenderest, the most gracious whose severity is boundless, but hurts himself most—all against, evil, all for the evil-doer. God is all that and infinitely more. You need not call him by any name till the name bursts from your heart. God our Saviour means all the names in the world, and infinitely more! One thing I can assure you of, that even I, if you will but do your duty in regard to this thing, will not only love—yes, I will say that word—will not only love, but honor you far more than if I had known you only as a respectable youth. It is harder to turn back than to keep at home. I doubt if there could be such joy in heaven over the repenting sinner if he was never to be free of his disgrace. But I like you the better for having the feeling of eternal disgrace now."

"I will think God is like you, sir. Tell me what I am to do."

"I am going to set you the hardest of tasks, one after the other. They will be like the pinch of death. But they *must* be done. And after that—peace. Who is at the head of the late Mr. Boxall's business now?"

"I suppose Mr. Stopper. He was head-clerk."

"You must go to him and take him the money you stole."

Thomas turned ashy pale.

"I haven't got it, sir."

"How much was it, did you say?"

"Eleven pounds—nearly twelve."

"I will find you the money. I will lend it to you."

"Thank you, thank you, sir. I will not spend a penny I can help till I repay you. But—"

"Yes, now come the *buts*," said Mr. Fuller, with a smile of kindness. "What is the first *but*?"

"Stopper is a hard man, and never liked me. He will give me up to the law."

"I can't help it. It must be done. But I do not believe he will do that. I will help you so far as to promise you to do all that lies in my power in every way to prevent it. And there is your father; his word will be law with him now."

"So much the worse, sir. He is ten times as hard as Stopper."

"He will not be willing to disgrace his own family, though."

"I know what he will do. He will make it a condition that I shall give up Lucy. But I will go to prison before I will do that. Not that it will make any difference in the end, for Lucy won't have a word to say to me now. She bore all that woman could bear. But she shall give me up—she has given me up, of course; but I will never give her up that way."

"That's right, my boy. Well, what do you say to it?"

Tom was struggling with himself. With a sudden resolve, the source of which he could not tell, he said, "I will, sir." With a new light in his face he added, "What next?"

"Then you must go to your father."

"That is far worse. I am afraid I can't."

"You must—if you should not find a word to say when you go—if you should fall in a faint on the floor when you try."

"I will, sir. Am I to tell him everything?"

"I am not prepared to say that. If he had been a true father to you, I should have said 'Of course.' But there is no denying the fact that such he has not been, or rather, that such he is not. The point lies there. I think that alters the affair. It is one thing to confess to God and another to the devil. Excuse me, I only put the extremes."

"What ought I to tell him, then?"

"I think you will know that best when you see him. We cannot tell how much he knows."

"Yes," said Thomas, thoughtfully; "I will tell him that I am sorry I went away as I did, and ask him to forgive me. Will that do?"

"I must leave all that to your own conscience, heart, and honesty. Of course, if he receives you at all, you must try what you can do for Mrs. Boxall."

"Alas! I know too well how useless that will be. It will only enrage him the more at them. He may offer to put it all right, though, if I promise to give Lucy up. *Must* I do that, sir?"

Knowing more about Lucy's feelings than Thomas, Mr. Fuller answered at once—though if he had hesitated, he might have discovered ground for hesitating—

"On no account whatever."

"And what must I do next?" he asked, more cheerfully.

"There's your mother."

"Ah! you needn't remind me of her."

"Then you must not forget Miss Burton. You have some apology to make to her too, I suppose."

"I had just sent her a note, asking her to meet me once more, and was waiting for her answer, when the bookseller laid hold of me. I was so afraid of making a row, lest the police should come, that I gave in to him. I owe him more than ever I can repay."

"You will when you have done all you have undertaken."

"But how am I to see Lucy now? She will not know where I am. But perhaps she will not want to see me."

Here Tom looked very miserable again. Anxious to give him courage, Mr. Fuller said:

"Come home with me now. In the morning, after you have seen Mr. Stopper, and your father and mother, come back to my house. I am sure she will see you."

With more thanks in his heart than on his tongue, Tom followed Mr. Fuller from the church. When they stepped into the street, they found the bookseller, the seaman, and the publican, talking together on the pavement.

"It's all right," said Mr. Fuller, as he passed them. "Good-night." Then, turning again to Mr. Kitely, he added, in a low voice, "He knows nothing of his father's behavior, Kitely. You'll be glad to hear that."

"I ought to be glad to hear it for his own sake, I suppose," returned the bookseller. "But I don't know as I am, for all that."

"Have patience, have patience," said the parson, and walked on, taking Thomas by the arm.

For the rest of the evening Mr. Fuller avoided much talk with the penitent, and sent him to bed early.

CHAPTER XLVII
THOMAS AND MR. STOPPER

Thomas did not sleep much that night, and was up betimes in the morning. Mr. Fuller had risen before him, however, and when Thomas went down stairs, after an invigorating cold bath which his host had taken special care should be provided for him, along with clean linen, he found him in his study reading. He received him very heartily, looking him, with some anxiety, in the face, as if to see whether he could read action there. Apparently he was encouraged, for his own face brightened up, and they were soon talking together earnestly. But knowing Mr. Stopper's habit of being first at the counting-house, Thomas was anxious about the time, and Mr. Fuller hastened breakfast. That and prayers over, he put twelve pounds into Thomas's hand, which he had been out that morning already to borrow from a friend. Then, with a quaking heart, but determined will, Thomas set out and walked straight to Bagot Street. Finding no one there but the man sweeping out the place, he went a little farther, and there was the bookseller arranging his stall outside the window. Mr. Kitely regarded him with doubtful eyes, vouchsafing him a "good-morning" of the gruffest.

"Mr. Kitely," said Thomas, "I am more obliged to you than I can tell, for what you did last night."

"Perhaps you ought to be; but it wasn't for your sake, Mr. Worboise, that I did it."

"I am quite aware of that. Still, if you will allow me to say so, I am as much obliged to you as if it had been."

Mr. Kitely grumbled something, for he was not prepared to be friendly.

"Will you let me wait in your shop till Mr. Stopper comes?"

"There he is."

Thomas's heart beat fast; but he delayed only to give Mr. Stopper time to enter the more retired part of the counting-house. Then he hurried to the door and went in.

Mr. Stopper was standing with his back to the glass partition, and took the entrance for that of one of his clerks. Thomas tapped at the glass door, but not till he had opened it and said "Mr. Stopper," did he take any notice. He started then, and turned; but, having regarded him for a moment, gave a rather constrained smile, and, to his surprise, held out his hand.

"It is very good of you to speak to me at all, Mr. Stopper," said Thomas, touched with gratitude already. "I don't deserve it."

"Well, I must say you behaved rather strangely, to say the least, of it. It might have been a serious thing for you, Mr. Thomas, if I hadn't been more friendly than you would have given me credit for. Look here."

And he showed him the sum of eleven pounds thirteen shillings and eightpence halfpenny put down to Mr. Stopper's debit in the petty cash-book.

"You understand that, I presume, Mr. Thomas. You ran the risk of transportation there."

"I know I did, Mr. Stopper. But just listen to me a moment, and you will be able to forgive me, I think. I had been drinking, and gambling, and losing all night; and I believe I was really drunk when I did that. Not that I didn't know I was doing wrong. I can't say that. And I know it doesn't clear me at all, but I want to tell you the truth of it. I've been wretched ever since, and daren't show myself. I have been bitterly punished. I haven't touched cards or dice since. Here's the money," he concluded, offering the notes and gold.

Mr. Stopper did not heed the action at first. He was regarding Thomas rather curiously. Thomas perceived it.

"Yes," Thomas said, "I am a sailor. It's an honest way of living, and I like it."

"But you'll come back now, won't you?"

"That depends," answered Thomas. "Would you take me, now, Mr. Stopper?" he added, with a feeble experimental smile. "But there's the money. Do take it out of my hands."

"It lies with your father now, Mr. Thomas. Have you been to Highbury? Of course, I took care not to let him know."

"Thank you heartily. I'm just going there. Do take the horrid money, and let me feel as if I weren't a thief after all."

"As for the money, eleven pound, odd," said Mr. Stopper, without looking at it, "that's neither here nor there. It was a burglary, there can be no doubt, under the circumstances. But I owe you a quarter's salary, though I should not be bound to pay it, seeing you left as you did. Still, I want to be friendly, and you worked very fairly for it. I will hand you over the difference."

"No, never mind that, I don't care about the money. It was all that damned play," said Thomas.

"Don't swear, Mr. Thomas," returned Stopper, taking out the checkbook, and proceeding to write a check for thirteen pounds six shillings and fourpence.

"If you had suffered as much from it as I have, Mr. Stopper, you would see no harm in damning it."

Mr. Stopper made no reply, but handed him the check, with the words:

"Now we're clear, Mr. Thomas. But don't do it again. It won't pass twice. I've saved you this time."

"Do it again!" cried Thomas, seizing Mr. Stopper's hand; "I would sooner cut my own throat. Thank you, thank you a thousand times, Mr. Stopper," he added, his heart brimful at this beginning of his day of horror.

Mr. Stopper very coolly withdrew his hand, turned round on his stool, replaced his check-book in the drawer, and proceeded to arrange his writing materials, as if nobody were there but himself. He knew well enough that it was not for Thomas's sake that he had done it; but he had no particular objection to take the credit of it. There was something rudely imposing in the way in which he behaved to Thomas, and Thomas felt it and did not resent it: for he had no right to be indignant: he was glad of any terms he could make. Let us hope that Mr. Stopper had a glimmering of how it might feel to have been kind, and that he was a little more ready in consequence to do a friendly deed in time to come, even when he could reap no benefit from it. Though Mr. Stopper's assumption of faithful friendship could only do him harm, yet perhaps Thomas's ready acknowledgment of it might do him good; for not unfrequently to behave to a man as good rouses his conscience and makes him wish that he were as good as he is taken for. It gives him almost a taste of what goodness is like—certainly a very faint and far-off taste—yet a something.

Thomas left the counting-house a free man. He bounded back to Mr. Fuller, returned the money, showed him the check, and told him all.

"There's a beginning for you, my boy!" said Mr. Fuller, as delighted almost as Thomas himself. "Now for the next."

There came the rub. Thomas's countenance fell. He was afraid, and Mr. Fuller saw it.

"You daren't go near Lucy till you have been to your father. It would be to insult her, Thomas."

Tom caught up his cap from the table and left the house, once more resolved. It would be useless to go to Highbury at this hour; he would find his father at his office in the city. And he had not far to go to find him— unfortunately, thought Tom.

CHAPTER XLVIII
THOMAS AND HIS FATHER

When he was shown into his father's room he was writing a letter. Looking up and seeing Tom he gave a grin—that is, a laugh without the smile in it—handed him a few of his fingers, pointed to a chair, and went on with his letter. This reception irritated Tom, and perhaps so far did him good that it took off the edge of his sheepishness—or rather, I should have said, put an edge upon it. Before his father he did not feel that he appeared exactly as a culprit. He had told him either to give up Lucy, or not to show his face at home again. He had lost Lucy, it might be—though hope had revived greatly since his interview with Mr. Stopper; but, in any case, even if she refused to see him, he would not give her up. So he sat, more composed than he had expected to be, waiting for what should follow. In a few minutes his father looked up again, as he methodically folded his letter, and casting a sneering glance at his son's garb, said:

"What's the meaning of this masquerading, Tom?"

"It means that I am dressed like my work," answered Tom, surprised at his own coolness, now that the ice was broken.

"What's your work, then, pray?"

"I'm a sailor."

"You a sailor! A horse-marine, I suppose! Ha, ha!"

"I've made five coasting voyages since you turned me out," said Tom.

"I turned you out! You turned yourself out. Why the devil did you come back, then? Why don't you stick to your new trade?"

"You told me either to give up Lucy Burton, or take lodgings in Wapping. I won't give up Lucy Burton."

"Take her to hell, if you like. What do you come back here for with your cursed impudence? There's nobody I want less."

This was far from true. He had been very uneasy about his son. Yet now that he saw him—a prey to the vile demon that ever stirred up his avarice till the disease, which was as the rust spoken of by the prophet St. James, was eating his flesh as it were fire—his tyrannical disposition, maddened by the resistance of his son, and the consequent frustration of his money-making plans, broke out in this fierce, cold, blasting wrath.

"I come here," said Thomas—and he said it merely to discharge himself of a duty, for he had not the thinnest shadow of a hope that it would be of service—"I come here to protest against the extreme to which you are driving your legal *rights*—which I have only just learned—against Mrs. Boxall."

"And her daughter. But I am not aware that I am driving my *rights*, as you emphasize the word," said Mr. Worboise, relapsing into his former manner, so cold that it stung; "for I believe I *have* driven them already almost as far as my knowledge of affairs allows me to consider prudent. I have turned those people out of the house."

"You have!" cried Thomas, starting to his feet. "Father! father! you are worse than even I thought you. It is cruel; it is wicked."

"Don't discompose yourself about it. It is all your own fault, my son."

"I am no son of yours. From this moment I renounce you, and call you *father* no more," cried Thomas, in mingled wrath and horror and consternation at the atrocity of his father's conduct.

"By what name, then, will you be pleased to be known in future, that I may say when I hear it that you are none of mine?"

"Oh, the devil!" burst out Tom, beside himself with his father's behavior and treatment.

"Very well. Then I beg again to inform you, Mr. Devil, that it is your own fault. Give up that girl, and I will provide for the lovely siren and her harridan of a grandam for life; and take you home to wealth and a career which you shall choose for yourself."

"No, father. I will not."

"Then take yourself off, and be—" It is needless to print the close of the sentence.

Thomas rose and left the room. As he went down the stairs, his father shouted after him, in a tone of fury:

"You're not to go near your mother, mind."

"I'm going straight to her," answered Tom, as quietly as he could.

"If you do, I'll murder her."

Tom came up the stairs again to the door next his father's where the clerks sat. He opened this and said aloud:

"Gentlemen, you hear what my father has just said. There may be occasion to refer to it again." Then returning to his father's door, he said, in a low tone which only he could hear: "My mother may die any moment, as you very well know, sir. It may be awkward after what has just passed."

Having said this, he left his father a little abashed. As his wrath ebbed, he began to admire his son's presence of mind, and even to take some credit for it: "A chip of the old block!" he muttered to himself. "Who would have thought there was so much in the rascal? Seafaring must agree with the young beggar!"

Thomas hailed the first hansom, jumped in, and drove straight to Highbury. Was it strange that notwithstanding the dreadful interview he had just had—notwithstanding, too, that he feared he had not behaved properly to his father, for his conscience had already begun to speak about comparatively little things, having been at last hearkened to in regard to great things—that notwithstanding this, he should feel such a gladness in his being as he had never known before? The second and more awful load of duty was now lifted from his mind. True, if he had loved his father much, as it was simply impossible that he should, that load would have been replaced by another—misery about his father's wretched condition and the loss of his love. But although something of this would come later, the thought of it did not intrude now to destroy any of the enjoyment of the glad reaction from months—he would have said years—yea, a whole past life of misery—for the whole of his past life had been such a poor thing, that it seemed now as if the misery of the last few months had been only the misery of all his life coming to a head. And this indeed was truer than his judgment would yet have allowed: it was absolute fact, although he attributed it to an overwrought fancy.

CHAPTER XLIX
THOMAS AND HIS MOTHER

When the maid opened the door to him she stared like an idiot, yet she was in truth a woman of sense; for, before Thomas had reached the foot of the stairs, she ran after him, saying:

"Mr. Thomas! Mr. Thomas! you mustn't go up to mis'ess all of a sudden. You'll kill her if you do."

Thomas paused at once.

"Run up and tell her, then. Make haste."

She sped up the stairs, and Thomas followed, waiting outside his mother's door. He had to wait a little while, for the maid was imparting the news with circumspection. He heard the low tone of his mother's voice, but could not hear what she said. At last came a little cry, and then he could hear her sob. A minute or two more passed, which seemed endless to Thomas, and then the maid came to the door, and asked him to go in. He obeyed.

His mother lay in bed, propped up as she used to be on the sofa. She looked much worse than before. She stretched out her arms to him, kissed him, and held his head to her bosom. He had never before had such an embrace from her.

"My boy! my boy!" she cried, weeping. "Thank God! I have you again. You'll tell me all about it, won't you?"

She went on weeping and murmuring words of endearment and gratitude for some time. Then she released him, holding one of his hands only.

"There's a chair there. Sit down and tell me about it. I am afraid your poor father has been hard upon you."

"We won't talk about my father," said Thomas. "I have faults enough of my own to confess, mother. But I won't tell you all about them now. I have been very wicked—gambling and worse; but I will never do so any more. I am ashamed and sorry; and I think God will forgive me. Will you forgive me, mother?"

"With all my heart, my boy. And you know that God forgives every one that believes in Jesus. I hope you have given your heart to him, at last. Then I shall die happy."

"I don't know, mother, whether I have or not; but I want to do what's right."

"That won't save you, my poor child. You'll have a talk with Mr. Simon about it, won't you? I'm not able to argue anything now."

It would have been easiest for Thomas to say nothing, and leave his mother to hope, at least; but he had begun to be honest, therefore he would not deceive her. But in his new anxiety to be honest, he was in great danger of speaking roughly, if not rudely. Those who find it difficult to oppose are in more danger than others of falling into that error when they make opposition a point of conscience. The unpleasantness of the duty irritates them.

"Mother, I will listen to anything you choose to say; but I won't see that—" *fool* he was going to say, but he changed the epithet—"I won't talk about such things to a man for whom I have no respect."

Mrs. Worboise gave a sigh; but, perhaps partly because her own respect for Mr. Simon had been a little shaken of late, she said nothing more. Thomas resumed.

"If I hadn't been taken by the hand by a very different man from him, mother, I shouldn't have been here to-day. Thank God! Mr. Fuller is something like a clergyman!"

"Who is he, Thomas? I think I have heard the name."

"He is the clergyman of St. Amos's in the city."

"Ah! I thought so. A Ritualist, I am afraid, Thomas. They lay snares for young people."

"Nonsense, mother!" said Thomas, irreverently. "I don't know what you mean. Mr. Fuller, I think, would not feel flattered to be told that he belonged to any party whatever but that of Jesus Christ himself. But I should say, if he belonged to any, it would be the Broad Church."

"I don't know which is worse. The one believes all the lying idolatry of the Papists; the other believes nothing at all. I'm sadly afraid, Thomas, you've been reading Bishop Colenso."

Mrs. Worboise believed, of course, in no distinctions but those she saw; and if she had heard the best men of the Broad Church party repudiate Bishop Colenso, she would only have set it down to Jesuitism.

"A sailor hasn't much time for reading, mother."

"A sailor, Thomas! What do you mean? Where have you been all this time?" she asked, examining his appearance anxiously.

"At sea, mother."

"My boy! my boy! that is a godless calling. However—"

Thomas interrupted her.

"They that go down to the sea in ships were supposed once to see the wonders of the Lord, mother."

"Yes. But when will you be reasonable? That was in David's time."

"The sea is much the same, and man's heart is much the same. Anyhow, I'm a sailor, and a sailor I must be. I have nothing else to do."

"Mr. Boxall's business is all your father's now, I hear; though I'm sure I cannot understand it. Whatever you've done, you can go back to the counting-house, you know."

"I can't, mother. My father and I have parted forever."

"Tom!"

"It's true, mother."

"Why is that? What have you been doing?"

"Refusing to give up Lucy Burton."

"Oh, Tom, Tom! Why do you set yourself against your father?"

"Well, mother, I don't want to be impertinent; but it seems to me it's no more than you have been doing all your life."

"For conscience' sake, Tom. But in matters indifferent we ought to yield, you know."

"Is it an indifferent matter to keep one's engagements, mother? To be true to one's word?"

"But you had no right to make them."

"They are made, anyhow, and I must bear the consequences of keeping them."

Mrs. Worboise, poor woman, was nearly worn out. Tom saw it, and rose to go.

"Am I never to see you again, Tom?" she asked, despairingly.

"Every time I come to London—so long as my father doesn't make you shut the door against me, mother."

"That shall never be, my boy. And you really are going on that sea again?"

"Yes, mother. It's an honest calling. And believe me, mother, it's often easier to pray to God on shipboard than it is sitting at a desk."

"Well, well, my boy!" said his mother, with a great sigh of weariness. "If I only knew that you were possessed of saving faith, I could bear even to hear that you had been drowned. It may happen any day, you know, Thomas."

"Not till God please. I shan't be drowned before that."

"God has given no pledge to protect any but those that put faith in the merits of his Son."

"Mother, mother, I can't tell a bit what you mean."

"The way of salvation is so plain that he that runneth may read."

"So you say, mother; but I don't see it so. Now I'll tell you what: I want to be good."

"My dear boy!"

"And I pray, and will pray to God to teach me whatever he wants me to learn. So if your way is the right one, God will teach me that. Will that satisfy you, mother?"

"My dear, it is of no use mincing matters. God has told us plainly in his holy Word that he that puts his trust in the merits of Christ shall be saved; and he that does not shall be sent to the place of misery for ever and ever."

The good woman believed that she was giving a true representation of the words of Scripture when she said so, and that they were an end of all controversy.

"But, mother, what if a man can't believe?"

"Then he must take the consequences. There's no provision made for that in the Word."

"But if he wants to believe, mother?" said. Tom, in a small agony at his mother's hardness.

"There's no man that can't believe, if he's only willing. I used to think otherwise. But Mr. Simon thinks so, and he has brought me to see that he is right."

"Well, mother, I'm glad Mr. Simon is not at the head of the universe, for then it would be a paltry affair. But it ill becomes me to make remarks upon anybody. Mr. Simon hasn't disgraced himself like me after all, though I'm pretty sure if I had had such teaching as Mr. Fuller's, instead of his, I should never have fallen as I have done."

Thomas said this with some bitterness as he rose to take his leave. He had no right to say so. Men as good as he, with teaching as good as Mr. Fuller's, have yet fallen. He forgot that he had had the schooling of sin and misery to prepare the soil of his heart before Mr. Fuller's words were sown in it. Even Mr. Simon could have done a little for him in that condition, if he had only been capable of showing him a little pure human sympathy.

His mother gave him another tearful embrace. Thomas's heart was miserable at leaving her thus fearful, almost hopeless about him. How terrible it would be for her in the windy nights, when she could not sleep, to think that if he went to the bottom, it must be to go deeper still! He searched his mind eagerly for something that might comfort her. It flashed upon him at last.

"Mother dear," he said, "Jesus said, 'Come unto me, all ye that are weary and heavy-laden, and I will give you rest.' I will go to him. I will promise you that if you like. That is all I can say, and I think that ought to be enough. If he gives me rest, shall I not be safe? And whoever says that he will not if I go to him—"

"In the appointed way, my dear."

"He says nothing more than *go to him*. I say I will go to him, the only way that a man can when he is in heaven and I am on the earth. And if Mr. Simon or anybody says that he will not give me rest, he is a liar. If that doesn't satisfy you, mother, I don't believe you have any faith in him yourself."

With this outburst, Thomas again kissed his mother, and then left the room. Nor did his last words displease her. I do not by any means set him up as a pattern of filial respect even toward his mother; nor can I approve altogether of the form his confession of faith took, for there was in it a mixture of that graceless material—the wrath of man; but it was good, notwithstanding; and such a blunt utterance was far more calculated to carry some hope into his mother's mind than any amount of arguing upon the points of difference between them.

As he reached the landing, his sister Amy came rushing up the stairs from the dining-room, with her hair in disorder, and a blushing face.

"Why Tom!" she said, starting back.

Tom took her in his arms.

"How handsome you have grown, Tom!" said Amy; and breaking from him, ran up to her mother's room.

Passing the dining-room door, Tom saw Mr. Simon looking into the fire. The fact was he had just made Amy an offer of marriage. Tom let him stand, and hurried back on foot to his friend, his heart full, and his thoughts in confusion.

He found him in his study, where he had made a point of staying all day that Tom might find him at any moment when he might want him. He rose eagerly to meet him.

"'Now I see by thine eyes that this is done,'" he said, quoting King Arthur.

They sat down, and Tom told him all.

"I wish you had managed a little better with your father," he said.

"I wish I had, sir. But it's done, and there's no help for it."

"No; I suppose not—at present, at least."

"As far as Lucy is concerned, it would have made no difference, if you had been in my place—I am confident of that."

"I dare say you are right. But you have earned your dinner anyhow; and here comes my housekeeper to say it is ready. Come along."

Thomas's face fell.

"I thought I should have gone to see Lucy, now, sir."

"I believe she will not be at home."

"She was always home from Mrs. Morgenstern's before now."

"Yes. But she has to work much harder now. You see her grandmother is dependent on her now."

"And where are they? My father told me himself he had turned them out of the house in Guild Court."

"Yes. But they are no farther off for that; they have lodgings at Mr. Kitely's. I think you had better go and see your friends the sailor and publican after dinner, and by the time you come back, I shall have arranged for your seeing her. You would hardly like to take your chance, and find her with her grandmother and Mattie."

"Who is Mattie? Oh! I know—that dreadful little imp of Kitely's."

"I dare say she can make herself unpleasant enough," said Mr. Fuller, laughing; "but she is a most remarkable and very interesting child. I could hardly have believed in such a child if I had not known her. She was in great danger, I allow, of turning out a little prig, if that word can be used of the feminine gender, but your friend Lucy has saved her from that."

"God bless her!" said Thomas, fervently. "She has saved me too, even if she refuses to have anything more to do with me. How *shall* I tell her everything? Since I have had it over with my father and Stopper, I feel as if I were whitewashed, and to have to tell her what a sepulchre I am is dreadful—and she so white outside and in!"

"Yes, it's hard to do, my boy, but it must be done."

"I would do it—I would insist upon it, even if she begged me not, Mr. Fuller. If she were to say that she would love me all the same, and I needn't say a word about the past, for it was all over now, I would yet beg her to endure the ugly story for my sake, that I might hear my final absolution from her lips."

"That's right," said Mr. Fuller.

They were now seated at dinner, and nothing more of importance to our history was said until that was over. Then they returned to the study, and, as soon as he had closed the door, Mr. Fuller said:

"But now, Worboise, it is time that I should talk to you a little more about yourself. There is only One that can absolve you in the grand sense of the word. If God himself were to say to you, 'Let by-gones be by-gones, nothing more shall be said about them'—if he only said that, it would be a poor thing to meet our human need. But he is infinitely kinder than that. He says, 'I, even I am he that taketh away thine iniquities.' He alone can make us clean—put our heart so right that nothing of this kind will happen again—make us simple God-loving, man-loving creatures, as much afraid of harboring an unjust thought of our neighbors as of stealing that which is his; as much afraid of pride and self-confidence as of saying with the fool, 'There is no God;' as far from distrusting God for the morrow, as from committing suicide. We cannot serve God and Mammon. Hence the constant struggle and discomfort in the minds of even good men. They would, without knowing what they are doing, combine a little Mammon-worship with the service of the God they love. But that cannot be. The Spirit of God will ever and always be at strife with Mammon, and in proportion as that spirit is victorious, is peace growing in the man. You must give yourself up to the obedience of his Son entirely and utterly, leaving your salvation to him, troubling yourself nothing about that, but ever seeking to see things as he sees them, and to do things as he would have them done. And for this purpose you must study your New Testament in particular, that you see the glory of God in the face of Christ Jesus; that receiving him as your master, your teacher, your saviour, you may open your heart to the entrance of his spirit, the mind that was in him, that so he may save you. Every word of his, if you will but try to obey it, you will find precious beyond words to say. And he has promised without reserve the Holy Spirit of God to them that ask it. The only salvation is in being filled with the Spirit of God, the mind of Christ."

"I believe you, sir, though I cannot quite see into all you say. All I can say is, that I want to be good henceforth. Pray for me, sir, if you think there is any good in one man praying for another."

"I do, indeed—just in proportion to the love that is in it. I cannot exactly tell how this should be; but if we believe that the figure St. Paul uses about our all being members of one body has any true, deep meaning in it, we shall have just a glimmering of how it can be so. Come, then, we will kneel together, and I will pray with you."

Thomas felt more solemn by far than he had ever felt in his life when he rose from that prayer.

"Now," said Mr. Fuller, "go and see your friends. When you think of it, my boy," he added, after a pause, during which he held Tom's hand in a warm grasp, "you will see how God has been looking after you, giving you friend after friend of such different sorts to make up for the want of a father, and so driving you home at last, home to himself. He had to drive you; but he will lead you now. You will be home by half-past six or seven?"

Thomas assented. He could not speak. He could only return the grasp of Mr. Fuller's hand. Then he took his cap and went.

It is needless to give any detailed account of Thomas's meeting with the Pottses. He did not see the captain, who had gone down to his brig. Mrs. Potts (and Bessie too, after a fashion) welcomed him heartily; but Mr. Potts was a little aggrieved that he would drink nothing but a glass of bitter ale. He had the watch safe, and brought it out gladly when Thomas produced his check.

Jim Salter dropped in at the last moment. He had heard the night before that Thomas was restored to society and was expected to call at the Mermaid some time that day. So he had been in or looking in a dozen times since the morning. When he saw Tom, who was just taking his leave, he came up to him, holding out his hand, but speaking as with a sense of wrong.

"How de do, guv'nor? Who'd ha' thought to see you here! Ain't you got ne'er another sixpence to put a name upon it? You're fond o' sixpences, *you* are, guv'nor."

"What do you mean, Jim?" asked Thomas, in much bewilderment.

"To think o' treatin' a man and a brother as you've treated me, after I'd been and devoted my life, leastways a good part of it, to save you from the police! Four *and* sixpence!"

Still bewildered, Thomas appealed to Mr. Potts, whose face looked as like a caricature of the moon as ever, although he had just worked out a very neat little problem in diplomacy.

"It's my fault, Mr. Worboise," he responded in his usual voice, which seemed to come from a throat lined with the insides of dates. "I forgot to tell you, sir, that, that—Don't you see, Jim, you fool!" he said, changing the object of his address abruptly—"you wouldn't have liked to rob a gentleman like that by takin' of half a suvering for loafin' about for a day with him when he was hard up. But as he's come by his own again, why there's no use in keeping it from you any longer. So there's your five and sixpence. But it's a devil of a shame. Go out of my house."

"Whew!" whistled; Jim Salter. "Two words to that, guv'nor o' the Marmaid. You've been and kep' me all this many a day out of my inheritance, as they say at the Britanuary. What do you say to that, sir? What do you think o' yerself, sir? I wait a reply, as the butcher said to the pig."

While he spoke, Jim pocketed the money. Receiving no reply except a sniff of Mr. Potts's red nose, he broke out again, more briefly:

"I tell 'ee what, guv'nor *of* the Marmaid, I *don't* go out o' your house till I've put a name upon it."

Quite defeated and rather dejected, Mr. Potts took down his best brandy, and poured out a bumper.

Jim tossed it off, and set down the glass. Then, and not till then, he turned to Thomas, who had been looking on, half vexed with Mr. Potts, and half amused with Jim.

"Well, I *am* glad, Mr. Wurbus, as you've turned out a honest man arter all. I assure you, sir, at one time, and that not much farther off than that 'ere glass o' rum—"

"Brandy, you loafing rascal! the more's the pity," said Mr. Potts.

"Than that 'ere glass o' rum," repeated Jim, "I had my doubts. I wasn't so sure of it, as the fox was o' the goose when he had his neck atwixt his teeth."

So saying, and without another word, Jim Salter turned and left the Mermaid. Jim was one of those who seem to have an especial organ for the sense of wrong, from which organ no amount or kind of explanation can ever remove an impression. They prefer to cherish it. Their very acknowledgments of error are uttered in a tone that proves they consider the necessity of making them only in the light of accumulated injury.

CHAPTER L
THOMAS AND LUCY

When Lucy came home the night before, she found her grandmother sitting by the fire, gazing reproachfully at the coals. The poor woman had not yet reconciled herself to her altered position. Widdles was in vain attempting to attract her attention; but, not being gifted with speech like his gray brother in the next cage to his—whose morals, by the way, were considerably reformed, thanks to his master's judicious treatment of him—he had but few modes of bringing his wishes to bear at a distance. He could only rattle his beak on the bars of his cage, and give a rending shriek.

The immediate occasion of her present mood was Thomas's note, which was over her head on the mantel-piece. Notes had occasionally passed between him and Lucy, and she knew the handwriting. She regarded him with the same feelings with which she regarded his father, but she knew that Lucy did not share in these feelings. And forgetting that she was now under Lucy's protection, she was actually vowing with herself at the moment Lucy entered that if she had one word of other than repudiation to say to Thomas, she would turn her out of the house. *She* was not going to encourage such lack of principle. She gave her no greeting, therefore, when she entered; but Lucy, whose quick eye caught sight of the note at once, did not miss it. She took the note with a trembling hand, and hurried from the room. Then Mrs. Boxall burst into a blaze.

"Where are you off to now, you minx?" she said.

"I am going to put my bonnet off, grannie," answered Lucy, understanding well enough, and waiting no farther parley.

She could hardly open the note, which was fastened with a wafer, her hands trembled so much. Before she had read it through she fell on her knees, and thus, like Hezekiah, "spread it before the Lord," and finished it so.

And now, indeed, was her captivity turned. She had nothing to say but. "Thank God!" she had nothing to do but weep. True, she was a little troubled that she could not reply: but when she made inquiry about the messenger, to see if she could learn anything of where Tom was to be found,

Mr. Kitely, who, I have said, returned home immediately after Mr. Fuller dismissed him (though in his anxiety he went back and loitered about the church door), told her that young Worboise was at that moment with Mr. Fuller in his vestry. He did not tell her how he came to be there. Nothing, therefore, remained for her but to be patient, and wait for what would come next. And the next thing was a note from Mr. Fuller, telling her that Thomas was at his house, bidding her be of good cheer, and saying that she should hear from him again to-morrow. She did not sleep much that night.

But she had a good deal to bear from her grandmother before she reached the haven of bed. First of all, she insisted on knowing what the young villain had written to *her* about. How *dared* he?—and so on. Lucy tried to pacify her, and said she would tell her about it afterward. Then she broke out upon herself, saying she knew it was nothing to Lucy what became of her. No doubt she would be glad enough to make her own terms, marry her grandmother's money, and turn her out of doors. But if she dared to say one word to the rascal after the way he had behaved to her, one house should not hold them both, and that she told her. But it is ungracious work recording the spiteful utterances of an ill-used woman. They did not go very deep into Lucy, for she knew her grandmother by this time. Also her hope for herself was large enough to include her grandmother.

And soon as Thomas left him in the morning, Mr. Fuller wrote again— only to say that he would call upon her in the evening. He did not think it necessary to ask her to be at home; nor did he tell her anything of Tom's story. He thought it best to leave that to himself. Lucy was strongly tempted to send excuses to her pupils that morning and remain at home, in case Thomas might come. But she concluded that she ought to do her work, and leave possibilities where alone they were determined. So she went and gave her lessons with as much care as usual, and more energy.

When she got home she found that Mr. Fuller had been there, but had left a message that he would call again. He was so delighted with the result of his efforts with Tom, that he could not wait till the evening. Still, he had no intention of taking the office of a mediator between them. That, he felt, would be to intrude for the sake of making himself of importance; and he had learned that one of the virtues of holy and true service is to get out of the way as soon as possible.

About six o'clock he went again, and was shown into the bookseller's back parlor, where he found both Lucy and her grandmother.

"Will you come out with me, Miss Burton, for an hour or so?" he said.

"I wonder at you, Mr. Fuller," interposed Mrs. Boxall—"a clergyman, too!"

It is a great pity that people should so little restrain themselves when they are most capable of doing so, that when they are old, excitement should make them act like the fools that they are not.

Mr. Fuller was considerably astonished, but did not lose his self-possession.

"Surely you are not afraid to trust her with me, Mrs. Boxall?" he said, half merrily.

"I don't know that, sir. I hear of very strange goings-on at your church. Service every day, the church always open, and all that! As if folks had nothing to do but say their prayers."

"I don't think you would talk like that, Mrs. Boxall," said Mr. Fuller, with no less point that he said it pleasantly, "if you had been saying your prayers lately."

"You have nothing to do with my prayers, sir."

"Nor you with my church, Mrs. Boxall. But come—don't let us quarrel, I don't wonder at your being put out sometimes, I'm sure; you've had so much to vex you. But it hasn't been Lucy's fault; and I'm sure I would gladly give you your rights if I could."

"I don't doubt it, sir," said the old lady, mollified. "Don't be long, Lucy. And don't let that young limb of Satan talk you over. Mind what I say to you."

Not knowing how to answer, without offending her grandmother, Lucy only made haste to get her bonnet and cloak. Mr. Fuller took her straight to his own house. The grimy, unlovely streets were, to Lucy's enlightened eyes, full of a strange, beautiful mystery, as she walked along leaning on her friend's arm. She asked him no questions, content to be led toward what was awaiting her. It was a dark and cloudy night, but a cool west wind, that to her feelings was full of spring, came down Bagot Street, blowing away the winter and all its miseries. A new time of hope was at hand. Away with it went all thought of Thomas's past behavior. He was repentant. The prodigal had turned to go home, and she would walk with him and help his homeward steps. She loved him, and would love him more than ever. If there was more joy in heaven over one such than over ninety-and-nine who were not such, why not more joy in her soul? Her heart beat so violently as she crossed Mr. Fuller's threshold, that she could hardly breathe. He took her into the sitting-room, where a most friendly fire was blazing, and left her.

Still she had asked no questions. She knew that she was going to see Thomas. Whether he was in the house or not, she did not know. She hardly cared. She could sit there, she thought, for years waiting for him; but every ring of the door-bell made her start and tremble. There were so many rings that her heart had hardly time to quiet itself a little from one before another set it beating again worse than ever. At length there came a longer pause, and she fell into a dreamy study of the fire. The door opened at length, and she thought it was Mr. Fuller, and, not wishing to show any disquietude, sat still. A moment more, and Thomas was kneeling at her feet. He had good cause to kneel. He did not offer to touch her. He only said, in a choked voice, "Lucy," and bowed his head before her. She put her hands on the bowed head before her, drew it softly on her knees, gave one long, gentle, but irrepressible wail like a child, and burst into a quiet passion of tears. Thomas drew his head from her hands, sank on the floor, and lay sobbing, and kissing her feet. She could not move to make him cease. But when she recovered herself a little, after a measureless time to both of them, she stopped, put her hands round upon his face, and drew him upward. He rose, but only to his knees.

"Lucy, Lucy," he sobbed, "will you forgive me?"

He could not say more yet. She bent forward and kissed his forehead.

"I have been very wicked. I will tell you all about it—everything."

"No, no, Thomas. Only love me."

"I love you—oh! I love you with all my heart and soul. I don't deserve to be allowed to love one of your hands; but if you will only let me love you I will be your slave forever. I don't even ask you to love me one little bit. If you will only let me love you!"

"Thomas," said Lucy, slowly, and struggling with her sobs, "my heart is so full of love and gladness that it is like to break. I can't speak."

By degrees they grew calmer, but Thomas could not rest till she knew all.

"Lucy," he said, "I can't be sure that all you give me is really mine till I've told you everything. Perhaps you won't love me—not so much—when you know all. So I must tell you."

"I don't care what it is, Thomas, for I am sure you won't again."

"*I will not*," said Thomas, solemnly. "But please, Lucy darling, listen to me—for my sake, not for your own, for it will hurt you so."

"If it will make you easier, Thomas, tell me everything." ·

"I will—I will. I will hide nothing."

And Thomas did tell her everything. But Lucy cried so much, that when he came to the part describing his adventures in London after he took the money, he felt greatly tempted, and yielded to the temptation, to try to give her the comical side as well. And at the very first hint of fun in the description he gave of Jim Salter, Lucy burst into such a fit of laughter, that Thomas was quite frightened, for it seemed as if she would never stop. So that between the laughing and crying Thomas felt like Christian between the quagmire and the pitfalls, and was afraid to say anything. But at length the story was told; and how Lucy did, besides laughing and crying, at every new turn of the story—to show my reader my confidence in him I leave all that to his imagination, assuring him only that it was all right between them. My women readers will not require even this amount of information, for they have the gift of understanding without being told.

When he came to the point of his father offering to provide for them if he would give up Lucy, he hesitated, and said:

"Ought I to have done it, Lucy, for your sake?"

"For my sake, Tom! If you had said for granny's—But I know her well enough to be absolutely certain that she would starve rather than accept a penny from him, except as her right. Besides, I can make more money in a year than he would give her, I am pretty sure. So if you will keep me, Tom, I will keep her."

Here Lucy discovered that she had said something very improper, and hid her face in her hands. But a knock came at the door, and then both felt so shy that neither dared to say, *Come in.* Therefore Mr. Fuller put his head in without being told, and said:

"Have you two young people made it up yet?"

"Have we, Tom?" said Lucy.

"I don't know," said Tom. "What was it, sir?"

Mr. Fuller laughed heartily, came near, put a hand on the head of each, and said:

"God bless you. I too am glad at my very heart. Now you must come to supper."

But at supper, which the good man had actually cleared his table to have in the study that he might not disturb them so soon, Thomas had a good many questions to ask. And he kept on asking, for he wanted to understand the state of the case between Mrs. Boxall and his father. All at once, at one reply, he jumped from his seat, looking very strange.

"I must be off, Lucy. You won't hear from me for a day or two. Good-bye, Mr. Fuller. I haven't time for a word," he said, pulling out his watch. "Something may be done yet. It may all come to nothing. Don't ask me any questions, I may save months."

He rushed from the room, and left Mr. Fuller and Lucy staring at each other. Mr. Fuller started up a moment after and ran to the door, but only to hear the outer door bang, and Thomas shout—"Cab ahoy!" in the street. So there was nothing for it but to take Lucy home again. He left her at Mr Kitely's door.

"Well, miss, what have you been about?" said her grandmother.

"Having a long talk with Thomas, grannie," answered Lucy.

"You have!" exclaimed Mrs. Boxall, who had expected nothing else, rising slowly from her seat with the air of one about to pronounce a solemn malediction.

"Yes, grannie; but he knew nothing till this very night of the way his father has behaved to us."

"He made you believe that, did he?"

"Yes, grannie."

"Then you're a fool. He didn't know, did he? Then you'll never see him again. He comes of a breed bad enough to believe anything of. You give him up or I give you up."

"No, I won't, grannie," said Lucy, smiling in her face.

"You or I leave this house, then."

"*I* won't, grannie."

"Then *I will.*"

"Very well, grannie," answered Lucy, putting her arms round her, and kissing her. "Shall I fetch your bonnet?"

Grannie vouchsafed no reply, but took her candle and went—up to bed.

CHAPTER LI
JACK OF THE NINGPO

My reader will know better than Lucy or Mr. Fuller what Thomas was after. Having only a hope, he did not like to say much, and therefore, as well as that he might not lose the chance of a night train, he hurried away. The first thing he did was to drive to a certain watchmaker's, to raise money if he could, once more on his watch and on Lucy's ring, which I need not say remained in his possession. But the shop was shut. Then he drove to the Mermaid, and came upon Captain Smith as he was emptying his tumbler of grog preparatory to going to bed.

"I say, captain, you must let Robins off this voyage. I want him to go to Newcastle with me."

"What's up now? Ain't he going to Newcastle? And you can go with him if you like."

"I want him at once. It's of the greatest importance."

"You won't find him to-night, I can tell you. You'd better sit down and have something, and tell us all about it."

When Thomas thought, he saw that nothing could be done till next day. Without money, without Robins, without a train in all probability, he was helpless. Therefore he sat down and told the captain what he was after, namely, to find Robins's friend Jack, whose surname he did not know, and see what evidence he could give upon the question of the order of decease in the family of Richard Boxall. He explained the point to the captain, who saw at once that Robins's services must be dispensed with for this voyage— except, indeed, he returned before they weighed anchor again, which was possible enough. When Tom told him what he had heard Jack say about little Julia, the captain, pondering it over, gave it as his judgment that Jack, being the only one saved, and the child being with him till she died, there was a probability almost of his being able to prove that she outlived the rest. At all events, he said, no time must be lost in finding this Jack.

Mr. Potts having joined them, they sat talking it over a long time. At last Tom said:

"There's one thing, I shall be more easy when I've told you: that lawyer is my father."

"God bless my soul!" said Mr. Potts, while Captain Smith said something decidedly different. "So you'll oblige me," Tom went on, "if you'll say nothing very hard of him, for I hope he will live to be horribly ashamed of himself."

"Here's long life to him!" said Captain Smith.

"And no success this bout!" added Mr. Potts.

"Amen to both, and thank you," said Tom.

Mrs. Potts would have got the same bed ready for him that he had had before, but as the captain was staying all night, Tom insisted on sleeping on the sofa. He wanted to be off to find Robins the first thing in the morning. It was, however, agreed that the captain should go and send Robins, while Thomas went to get his money. In a few hours Robins and he were off for Newcastle.

CHAPTER LII
LUCY, AND MATTIE, AND POPPIE

The Saturday following Tom's departure Lucy had a whole holiday, and she resolved to enjoy it. Not much resolution was necessary for that; for everything now was beautiful, and not even her grannie's fits of ill-humor could destroy her serenity. The old woman had, however, her better moments, in which she would blame her other self for her unkindness to her darling; only that repentance was forgotten the moment the fit came again. The saddest thing in the whole affair was to see how the prospect of wealth, and the loss of that prospect, worked for the temperamental ruin of the otherwise worthy old woman. Her goodness had had little foundation in principle; therefore, when the floods came and the winds blew, it could not stand against them. Of course prosperity must be better for some people, so far as we can see, for they have it; and adversity for others, for they have it; but I suspect that each must have a fitting share of both; and no disposition, however good, can be regarded as tempered, and tried, and weather-proof, till it has had a trial of some proportion of both. I am not sure that both are absolutely necessary to all; I only say that we cannot be certain of the character till we have seen it outstand both. The last thing Mrs. Boxall said to Lucy as she went out that morning, rousing herself from a dark-hued reverie over the fire, was:

"Lucy, if you marry that man I'll go to the work-house."

"But they won't take you in, grannie, when you've got a grand-daughter to work for you."

"I won't take a farthing of my own properly but as my own right."

"Thomas won't have a farthing of it to offer you, grannie, I'm afraid. He quarreled with his father just about that, and he's turned him out."

"Then I *must* go to the work-house."

"And I'll bring you packets of tea and snuff, as they do for the old goodies in the dusters, grannie," said Lucy, merrily.

"Go along with you. You never had any heart but for your beaux."

"There's a little left for you yet, dear grannie. And for beaux, you know as well as I do that I never had but one."

So saying, she ran away, and up the court to Mr. Spelt's shop.

"Where's Poppie, Mr. Spelt?" she asked.

"In the house, I believe, miss."

"Will you let her come with me to the Zoölogical Gardens to-day?"

"With all my heart, miss. Shall I get down, and run up and tell her?"

"No, thank you; on no account. I'll go up myself."

She found Poppie actually washing cups and saucers, with her sleeves tucked up, and looking not merely a very lovely, but a very orderly maiden. No doubt she was very odd still, and would be to the end of her days. What she would do when she was too old (which would not be till she was too frail) to scud, was inconceivable. But with all such good influences around her—her father, Mattie, Mr. Fuller, Lucy Burton—it was no wonder that the real woman in her should have begun to grow, and, having begun, should promise well for what was yet to be. There is scarcely anything more marvelous in the appearance of simple womanliness under such circumstances in the child of the streets, than there is in its existence in the lady who has outgrown the ordinarily evil influences of the nursery, the school-room, and the boarding-schools. Still, I must confess that anything like other people might well be a little startling to one who had known Poppie a year before and had not seen her since. Lucy had had a great deal to do with the change; for she had been giving her regular lessons with Mattie for the last few months. The difficulty was, to get Poppie to open her mental eyes to any information that did not come by the sight of her bodily eyes. The conveyance of facts to her, not to say of thoughts or feelings, by words, except in regard to things she was quite used to, was almost an impossibility. For a long time she only stared and looked around her now and then, as if she would be so glad to scud, if she dared. But she loved Lucy, who watched long and anxiously for some sign of dawning interest. It came at last. Nor let my reader suspect the smallest atom of satire in her most innocent remark: "Was Jesus a man? I s'posed he wor a clergyman!" But having once got a glimpse of light, her eyes, if they opened slowly, strengthened rapidly. Her acquisition was not great, that is, but she learned to think with an amount of reality which showed that, while she retained many of the defects of childhood, she retained also some of its most valuable characteristics.

The contrast with Mattie was very remarkable. Poppie was older than Mattie, I have said; but while Mattie talked like an old woman, Poppie talked like a baby. The remarks of each formed a strange opposition, both in manner and form, to her appearance, as far as bodily growth was concerned. But the faces were consistent with the words. There was, however, a very perceptible process of what may be called a double endosmose and exosmose going on between them. Poppie was getting wiser, and Mattie was getting merrier. Sometimes, to the delight of Mr. Kitely, they would be heard frolicking about his house like kittens. Such a burst, however, would seldom last long; for Mrs. Boxall resented it as unfeeling toward her misfortunes, and generally put a stop to it. This did not please Mr. Kitely at all. It was, in fact, the only thing that he found annoying in the presence of Mrs. Boxall in his house. But he felt such a kindly pity for the old woman that he took no notice of it, and intimated to Mattie that it was better to give up to her.

"The old lady is cranky to-day. She don't feel comfortable in her inside," he would say; and Mattie would repeat the remark to Poppie, as if it were her own. There was one word in it, however, which, among others of her vocabulary, making the antique formality of her speech so much the more ludicrous, she could not pronounce.

"The old lady don't feel over comfibittle in her inside to-day. We must drop it, or she'll be worse," Mattie would gravely remark to Poppie, and the tumult would be heard no more that day, or at least for an hour, when, if they were so long together, it might break out again.

Every now and then some strange explosion of Arab habits or ways of thinking would shock Mattie: but from seeing that it did not shock Miss Burton so much, she became, by degrees, considerably less of a little prig. Childhood revived in her more and more.

"Will you come with me to-day, Poppie, to see the wild beasts?" said Lucy.

"But they'll eat us, won't they?"

"Oh, no, child. What put that into your head?"

"I thought they always did."

"They always would if they could. But they can't."

"Do they pull their teeth out, then?"

"You come and see. I'll take care of you."

"Is Mattie going?"

"Yes."

"Then I'll come."

She threw down the saucer she was washing, dried her hands in her apron, and stood ready to follow.

"No, no, Poppie; that won't do. You must finish washing up and drying your breakfast things. Then you must put on your cloak and hat, and make yourself look nice and tidy, before I can take you."

"If it's only the beasts, miss! They ain't very particular, I guess."

Was this the old word of Chaucer indigenous, or a slip from the American slip?

"It's not for the beasts, but because you ought always to be tidy. There will be people there, of course, and it's disrespectful to other people to be untidy."

"I didn't know, miss. Would they give I to the bears?"

"Poppie, you're a goose. Come along. Make haste."

The children had never seen any but domestic animals before, and their wonder and pleasure in these strange new forms of life were boundless. Mattie caught the explosive affection from Poppie, and Lucy had her reward in the outbursts of interest, as varied in kind as the animals themselves, that rose on each side of her. The differences, too, between the children were very notable. Poppie shrieked with laughter at the monkeys; Mattie turned away, pale with dislike. Lucy overcame her own feelings in the matter for Poppie's sake, but found that Mattie had disappeared. She was standing outside the door, waiting for them.

"I can't make it out," she said, putting her hand into Lucy's.

"What can't you make out, Mattie?"

"I can't make out why God made monkeys." Now, this was a question that might well puzzle Mattie. Indeed, Lucy had no answer to give her. I dare say Mr. Fuller might have had something to say on the subject, but Lucy could only reply, "I don't know, my dear;" for she did not fancy it a part of a teacher's duty to tell lies, pretending acquaintance with what she did not know anything about. Poppie had no difficulty about the monkeys; but the lions and tigers, and all the tearing creatures were a horror to her; and if she did not put the same question as Mattie had put about the monkeys, it was only because she had not yet felt any need for understanding the creation of God in relation to him. In other words, she had not yet begun to construct her little individual scheme of the universe, which, sooner or later, must, I presume, be felt by every one as an indispensable necessity. Mr. Fuller would have acknowledged the monkeys as to him a far more important difficulty than the ferocious animals, and would probably have accepted the swine as a greater perplexity than either. Perhaps the readiest answer—I say *readiest* only, but I would not use the word answer at all, except it involved the elements of solution—for Lucy to give would have been:

"They disgust you, you say, Mattie? Then that is what God made them for."

A most incomplete, but most true and important reply—and the *readiest*.

Poppie shouted with delight to see the seals tumble into the water, dive deep, then turn on their backs and look up at her. But their large, round, yet pathetic, dog-like eyes, fixed upon her, made the tears come in Mattie's eyes, as they dreamed up and down and athwart the water-deeps with such a gentle power as destroyed all notion of force to be met or force to overcome.

Another instance or two, to show the difference between the children, and we shall return to the business of my story. There are, or were then, two or three little animals in a cage—I forget the name of them: they believe in somersaults—that the main object of life is to run round and round, doing the same thing with decency and order—that is, turning heels over head every time they arrive at a certain spot.

With these pretty enough, and more than comical enough creatures, Poppie was exquisitely delighted. She laughed and clapped her hands and shouted:

"Now, now! Do it again. There you are! Heels over head. All right, little one! Round you go. Now, now! There you are!" and so on.

Mattie turned away, saying only to Lucy:

"They don't make anything of it. They're no farther on at night than they were in the morning. I hate roundabouts. Poor little things!"

They came to the camel's house, and, with other children, they got upon his back. After a short and not over comfortable ride, they got down again. Poppie took hold of Lucy's sleeve, and, with solemn face, asked:

"Is it alive, miss?"

"How can you ask such a question, Poppie?"

"I only wanted to know if it was alive."

She was not sure that he did not go by machinery. Mattie gazed at her with compassionate superiority, and said:

"Poppie, I should like to hear what you tell Mr. Spelt when you get home. You *are* ignorant."

At this Poppie only grinned. She was not in the least offended. She even, I dare say, felt some of the same admiration for herself that one feels for an odd plaything.

Lucy's private share of the day's enjoyment lay outside the gardens. There the buds were bursting everywhere. Out of the black bark, all begrimed with London smoke and London dirt, flowed the purest green. Verily there is One that can bring a clean thing out of an unclean. Reviving nature was all in harmony with Lucy's feelings this day. It was the most simply happy day she had ever had. The gentle wind with its cold and its soft streaks fading and reviving, the blue sky with its few flying undefined masses of whiteness, the shadow of green all around—for when she looked through the trees, it was like looking through a thin green cloud or shadow—the gay songs of the birds, each of which, unlike the mocking-bird within, was content to sing his own song—a poor thing, it might be, but his own—his notion of the secret of things, of the well-being of the universe—all combined in one harmony with her own world inside, and made her more happy than she had ever been before, even in a dream.

She was walking southward through the Park, for she wanted to take the two children to see Mrs. Morgenstern. They were frolicking about her, running hither and thither, returning at frequent intervals to claim each one of her hands, when she saw Mr. Sargent coming toward her. She would not have avoided him if she could, for her heart was so gay that it was strong as well. He lifted his hat. She offered her hand. He took it, saying:

"This is more than I deserve, Miss Burton, after the abominable way I behaved to you last time I saw you. I see you have forgiven me. But I dare hardly accept your forgiveness. It is so much more than I deserve."

"I know what it is to suffer, Mr. Sargent, and there is no excuse I could not make for you. Perhaps the best proof I can give that I wish to forget all that passed on that dreadful evening is to be quite open with you still. I have seen Mr. Worboise since then," she went on, regardless of her own blushes. "He had been led astray, but not so much as you thought. He brought me back the ring you mentioned."

If Mr. Sargent did not place much confidence in the reformation Lucy hinted at, it is not very surprising. No doubt the fact would destroy any possibly lingering hope he yet cherished, but this was not all; he was quite justified in regarding with great distrust any such change as her words implied. He had known, even in his own comparatively limited experience, so many cases of a man's having, to all appearance, entirely abjured his wicked ways for the sake of a woman, only to return, after marriage, like the sow that was washed, to his wallowing in the mire, that his whole soul shrunk from the idea of such an innocent creature falling a prey to her confidence in such a man as Worboise most probably was. There was nothing to be said at present on the subject, however, and after a few more words they parted—Lucy, to pursue her dream of delight—Mr. Sargent, lawyer-like, to make further inquiry.

CHAPTER LIII
MOLKEN ON THE SCENT

Now it had so happened that Mr. Molken had caught sight of Tom as he returned from his visit to his mother, and had seen him go into Mr. Fuller's house. His sailor's dress piqued the curiosity which he naturally felt with regard to him; and as, besides, the rascal fed upon secrets, gave him hope of still making something out of him if he could but get him again in his power. Therefore he watched the house with much patience, saw Mr. Fuller go out and return again with Lucy, whom he knew by sight, and gave to the phenomenon what interpretation his vile nature was capable of, concluding that Tom was in want of money—as he himself generally was—and would get something out of Lucy before they parted: he had stored the fact of the ring in his usual receptacle for such facts. Besides, he had been in communication with a lawyer, for he could see well enough that Mr. Sargent belonged to that profession, concerning this very Thomas Worboise: perhaps he *was wanted*, and if so, why should not he reap what benefit might be reaped from aiding in his capture? With all these grounds for hope, he was able to persevere in watching the house till Thomas came out alone evidently in great haste and excitement. He accosted him then as he hurried past, but Tom, to whom the sight of him recalled no cherished memories, and who did not feel that he owed him any gratitude for favors received, felt that it would be the readiest and surest mode of procedure to cut him at once, and did so, although he could not prevent Molken from seeing that he knew him, and did not choose to know him. This added immeasurably to Molken's determination, for now his feelings as a *gentleman* were enlisted on the same side. He was too prudent, if not too cowardly, to ask him what he meant; nor would that mode have served his turn; it fitted his nature and character better to lurk and watch. When Tom got into a cab, Molten therefore got into another, and gave the driver directions to keep Tom's in sight, but not to follow so closely as to occasion suspicion. He ran him to earth at the Mermaid. There he peeped in at the door, and finding that he must have gone into the house, became more and more satisfied that he was after something or other which he wanted to keep dark—something fitted, in fact, for Molken to do himself, or to turn to his advantage if done by another. He entered the bar, called for a glass of hot gin and water, and got into conversation with Mr. Potts. The landlord of the Mermaid, however, although a man of slow mental processes, had instinct enough, and experience more than enough, to dislike the look of Molken. He gave him, therefore, such short answers as especially suited his own style, refused to be drawn into conversation, and persisted in regarding him merely as the purchaser of a glass of gin and water, hot with. On such an occasion Mr. Potts's surly grandeur could be surpassed by no other bar-keeper in England. But this caution completed Molken's conviction that Thomas was about something dark, and that the landlord of the Mermaid was in it, too; the more conclusively when, having, by way of experiment, mentioned Thomas's name as known to Mr. Potts, the latter cunningly repudiated all knowledge of "the party." Molken therefore left the house, and after doubling a little, betook himself to a coffee-shop opposite, whence he could see the door of the Mermaid from the window, and by a proper use of shillings, obtained leave to pass as much of the night there as he pleased. He thought he saw Thomas, with a light in his hand, draw down the dingy blind of an upper window; and concluding that he had gone to bed, Molken threw himself on one of the seats, and slept till daylight, when he resumed his watch. At length he saw him come out with another man in the dress of a sailor like himself, but part with him at the door, and walk off in the direction of the city. He then followed him, saw him go into the watchmaker's, and come out putting something in his trousers' pocket, followed him again, and observed that the ring, which he knew, and which he had seen on his hand as he came behind him from Limehouse, was gone, as well as his watch, which he had seen him use the night before, while now he looked up at every clock he passed. Nor did he leave his track till he saw him get into a train at King's Cross, accompanied by another sailor, not the one he had seen in the morning, whom he met evidently by appointment at the station. Here the condition of his own funds brought Molten to a pause, or he would very likely have followed his wild-goose chase to Newcastle at least. As it was, he could only find out where they were going, and remain behind with the hope of being one day called upon to give evidence that would help to hang him. Nor had he long to wait before something seemed likely to come of all his painstaking. For after a few days he had a second visit from Mr. Sargent, to whom, however, he was chary of his information till bribed by a couple of sovereigns. Then he told him all. The only point Mr. Sargent could at once lay hold of was the ring. He concluded that he had recovered the ring merely to show it to her, and again make away with it, which must even in her eyes look bad enough to justify any amount of jealousy as to the truth of his reformation. Acting on this fresh discovery, he went to the watchmaker's—a respectable man who did business in a quiet way and had accommodated Tom only for old acquaintance' sake, not, however, knowing much about him. Mr. Sargent told him who he was, gave him his card, and easily prevailed on him to show the watch and the ring. The latter especially Mr. Sargent examined, and finding quite peculiarity enough about it to enable him to identify it by description, took his leave.

Now, had it not been for Thomas's foolish, half-romantic way of doing things, no evil could have come of this. If, when he found that he had still a little time, he had returned and fully explained to his friends what his object was when he left them so suddenly, all would have been accounted for. He liked importance, and surprises, and secrecy. But this was self-indulgence, when it involved the possibility of so much anxiety as a lengthened absence must occasion Lucy, and Mr. Fuller too. They had a right, besides, to know everything that he was about, after all that they had done for him, and still more from the fact that they were both so unselfishly devoted to his best good, and must keep thinking about him. Regarding his behavior in its true light, however, and coming to the obvious conclusion between themselves that Tom had a clew to some evidence, they remained at ease on the matter—which ease was a little troubled when Lucy received the following note from Mr. Sargent. Without the least intention of being unjust, he gave, as people almost always do, that coloring to his representation which belonged only to the colored medium of prejudication through which he viewed the object:

> "Dear Madam,—Perfectly aware that I am building an insurmountable barrier between myself and my own peace, I am yet sufficiently disinterested to have some regard for yours. If you will only regard the fact as I have now stated it—that I have no hope for myself, that, on the contrary, I take the position, with all its obloquy, of the bringer of unwelcome tidings—you will, however you may regard me, be a little more ready to listen to what I have to communicate. From one of a certain gentleman's companions, of such unquestionable character that he refused information until I bribed him with the paltry sum of two pounds—(I at least am open, you see)—I learned that he had again parted with the ring, the possession of which he had apparently recovered only for the sake of producing it upon occasion of his late interview with you. You will say such testimony is no proof; but I will describe the ring which I found in the possession of the man to whom I was directed, leaving you to judge

whether it is yours or not: A good-sized rose-diamond, of a pale straw color, with the figures of two serpents carved on the ring, the head of each meeting the body of the other round opposite sides of the diamond. Do not take the trouble to answer this letter, except I can be of service to you. All that it remains possible for me to request of you now is, that you will believe it is for your sake, and not for my own, that I write this letter. In God's name I beg that you will not give yourself into the power of a man whose behavior after marriage has not the benefit of even a doubt when regarded in the light of his behavior before it. If you will not grant me the justice of believing in my true reasons for acting as I do, I yet prefer to bear the consequences of so doing to the worse suffering of knowing that there was one effort I might have made and did not make for your rescue from the worst fate that can befall the innocent."

"Your obedient servant,
"J. Sargent."

Lucy gave a little laugh to herself when she read the letter. There was no doubt about the ring being hers; but if Thomas had set out on the supposed errand it was easy to see that the poor fellow, having no money, must have parted with the ring for the sake of procuring the means of doing her justice. But if this was so plain, why was it that Lucy sat still and pale for an hour after, with the letter in her hand, and that when she rose it was to go to Mr. Fuller with it? It was the source alone of Mr. Sargent's information that occasioned her the anxiety. If he had been as explicit about that as he was about the ring, telling how Molken had watched and followed Thomas, she would not have been thus troubled. And had Mr. Sargent been as desirous of being just to Thomas as of protecting Lucy, perhaps he would have told her more. But there are a thousand ways in which a just man may do injustice.

My reader must not suppose, however, that Lucy really distrusted Thomas. The worst that she feared was that he had not quite broken with his bad companions; and the very thought of Molken, returning upon her as she had seen him that night in the thunder-storm, and coming along with the thought of Thomas, was a distress to her. To be made thus unhappy it is not in the least necessary that one should really doubt, but that forms, ideas of doubt, should present themselves to the mind. They cannot always be answered in a quiet, triumphant fashion, for women have been false and men have been hypocrites in all ages; and the mind keeps seeking the triumphant answer and cannot find it.

In something of this mood, and yet more vexed that such disquietude should have any place in her mind, regarding it as vile unfaithfulness on her part, she rose, and for the sake of hearing Mr. Fuller's answer justify her own confidence, took him the letter.

Having read it, the first words Mr. Fuller spoke, were:

"The writer of this is honest."

"Then you think it is all true!" said Lucy, in some dismay.

"What he tells as fact, no doubt is fact," answered. Mr. Fuller. "It does not follow, however, that his conclusions are in the least correct. The most honest man is, if not as liable, yet as certainly liable to mistake as the most dishonest. It is indubitable out of regard for your welfare that he has written the letter; but you know all the other side of which he knows nothing. You don't believe it yourself, Lucy—the inference of Thomas's hypocrisy, I mean?"

"No, no," cried Lucy. "I do not."

"Facts are certainly stubborn things, as people say. But it is equally certain that they are the most slippery things to get a hold of. And even when you have got a hold of them, they can be used with such different designs—after such varying fashions, that no more unlike buildings can be constructed of the same bricks or hewn stones, than conclusions arrived at from precisely the same facts. And this because all the facts round about the known facts, and which keep those facts in their places, compelling them to combine after a certain fashion, are not known, or perhaps are all unknown. For instance, your correspondent does not know—at least he does not give you to understand that he knows—how his informant arrived at the knowledge of the facts upon which he lays such stress. When I recall Thomas's whole bearing and conduct I cannot for a moment accept the conclusions arrived at by him, whatever may be the present appearance of the facts he goes upon. Facts are like faces—capable of a thousand expressions and meanings. Were you satisfied entirely with Thomas's behavior in the talk you had with him?"

"Entirely. It left nothing to wish more, or different."

"Then you have far deeper ground to build upon than any of those facts. They can no more overturn your foundation than the thickest fog can remove the sun from the heavens. You cannot *prove* that the sun is there. But neither can you have the smallest real doubt that he is there. You must wait with patience, believing all things, hoping all things."

"That is just what I have been saying to myself. Only I wanted to hear you say it too. I wanted it to come in at my ears as well as out of my heart."

When a month had passed away, however, bringing no news of Thomas; when another month had passed, and still he neither came nor wrote, hope deferred began to work its own work and make Lucy's heart sick. But she kept up bravely, through the help of her daily labor. Those that think it hard to have to work hard as well as endure other sore trials, little know how much those other trials are rendered endurable by the work that accompanies them. They regard the work as an additional burden, instead of as the prop which keeps their burdens from crushing them to the earth. The same is true of pain—sometimes of grief, sometimes of fear. And all of these are of the supports that keep the weight of evil within us, of selfishness, and the worship of false gods, from sinking us into Tophet. They keep us in some measure from putting our trust in that which is weak and bad, even when they do but little to make us trust in God.

Nor did this season of trial to Lucy pass by without bringing some little measure of good to the poor, disappointed, fretful soul of her grandmother. How much Widdles had to do with it—and my reader must not despise Widdles; many a poor captive has been comforted by a mouse, a spider, a rat even; and I know a lady who, leading a hard life while yet a child, but possessing one little garret-room as her own, with a window that opened on the leads, cultivated green things there enough to feed a few pet snails, to each of which she gave the name of one of her best friends, great names, too, and living names, so that I will not, as she most innocently and lovingly did, associate them with snails, though even thus they were comforters to her brave heart;—how much Widdles had to do with it, I say, and how much the divine help of time, and a sacred deprivation of that hope in chance which keeps man sometimes from hoping in God, I cannot tell; it was the work of the all-working Spirit, operating in and on her mind mediately or immediately. She grew calmer, and began to turn her thoughts a little away from what she fancied might have been if things had not gone wrong so perversely, and to reflect on the fact, which she had often expressed in words, but never really thought about before—that it would be all the same a hundred years after—a saying which, however far from true—although, in fact, taken logically as it stands, absolutely false—yet has, wrapt up in it, after a clumsy fashion, a very great and important truth. By slow degrees her former cheerfulness began to show a little light over her hitherto gloomy horizon; her eyes became less turbid; she would smile occasionally, and her communications with Widdles grew more airy. I do most potently believe that Widdles was, not only in the *similarity*, but in the *infinitesimality* (I am sorry to have to coin a word) of his influence, homeopathically operative in working a degree of cure in the troubled nature of the old woman.

"Ah, Widdles, Widdles!" she would say, as she rubbed the unavailing Balm of Columbia on his blue back, "you and I know what trouble is! Don't we, old bird?"

She began to have a respect for her own misfortunes, which indicated that they had begun to recede a little from the point of her vision. To have had misfortunes is the only distinction some can claim. How much that can distinguish one man from another, judge, oh Humanity. But the heart that knows its own bitterness, too often forgets that there is more bitterness in the world than that.

Widdles would cock his magnificent head and whiskers on one side, and wink with one eye, as much as to say, "I believe you, old girl." Then he would turn his denuded, featherless back upon her, as much as to add, with more solemnity: "Contemplate my condition, madam. Behold me. Imagine what I once was, that you may understand the spite of fortune which has reduced me to my present bareness. Am I not a spectacle to men and angels? And am I not therefore distinguished above my fellows?" Perhaps, however, I am all wrong in giving this interpretation to the actions of the bird. Perhaps the influence that flowed from him into the heart of Mrs. Boxall was really such as, put in words, would amount to this: "Here I am without a feather to hide my somewhat skinny proportions; but what the worse am I? Who cares? So long as you don't, I don't. Let's turn about once more. My dancing days are over; but life is life, even without feathers."

If Mrs. Boxall had had her way with Widdles, he would have turned out a resplendent bird in spite of fate. But if you had told her not to be distressed at his nakedness, for God cared for Widdles, not as much, but as well as for her, she would have judged you guilty of something like blasphemy. Was it because the bird was comical, as even she admitted, that you must not speak of God's care in relation to him? Certainly, however, he sowed not neither did he reap; and as for a barn to store his winter-grain in—poor Widdles! Yet, was he forgotten? Mrs. Boxall was the last person who could say so, with her sugar, her nuts, her unguents of price—though the latter, clearly a striving against Providence, were not of so much account in the eyes of the bird. I dare say he found them soothing, though.

However all these things may have been, one thing is certain, that Mrs. Boxall began to recover her equanimity, and at length even her benevolence toward men in general—with one class exception, that of lawyers, and two individual exceptions, those of old Worboise and young Worboise. I believe she had a vague conviction that it was one of the malignant class above mentioned that had plucked Widdles. "Ah, my poor Widdles! Them lawyers!" she would say. "You would have been a very different person indeed, Widdles, if it hadn't been for them. But it'll be all the same in a hundred years, Widdles. Keep up heart, old bird. It'll all be over soon. If you die before me, I'll put you on a winding-sheet that'll be a deal more comfortable than dead feathers, and I'll bury you with my own hands. But what'll you do for me, if I die first, you little scarecrow? You'll look about for me, won't you? That's about all you can do. And you'll miss the bits of sugar. Mattie, my dear, mind that Widdles has his sugar, and everything regular after I'm dead and gone."

She began to take to Mattie again, and even to make her read to her of a Sunday. But this, as of old, gave rise to much difference of opinion between them, which, however, resulted in the old woman's learning something from the child, if not in the immediate case, yet in the next similar case. For it often happens that a man who has opposed another's opinion bitterly in regard to the individual case that occasioned the difference, will act entirely according to that others judgment in the next precisely similar case that occurs; although if you were to return to the former, he would take up his former position with an access of obstinacy in the reaction from having yielded to argument. Something like this took place between Grannie and Mattie. It was amusing to hear now the former would attribute all the oddities of the latter to the fact that she belonged to the rising generation, never seeming to suspect that Mattie was an exception to children in general, as peculiar as Widdles in relation to birds.

CHAPTER LIV
GRANNIE APPEALS TO WIDDLES

One sultry evening in summer, Lucy was seated at her piano, which had its place in Mr. Kitely's back parlor, near the black oak cabinet, but she was not playing. She had just been singing a little song from some unknown pen, which she had found with music of her father's in the manuscripts he had left her. This was the song:

1.

Sunshine fair,
In the air,
On the earth!
Everywhere
Waking mirth!
Stay not there.
I sit apart
By the hearth
Of my heart
In the dark.
Dost thou mark
How I sit
In the dark,
With my grief,
Nursing it?
Bring relief,
Sunny gold!
Look, I set
Open door
Thee before,
And the fold
Of my curtain draw aside.
Enter, enter, golden tide.

2.

Summer Wind,
Nature's laughter!

Of sweet smiling
Waker, wafter!
Care beguiling,
Toying, wiling,
Never glance
Throw behind.
In the dance
Still advance,
To the past
Deaf and blind,
Follow after,
Fleet and fast,
Newer gladness,
Careless wind!
See the sadness
Of my mind.
Over river.
Hill and hollow,
Resting never,
Thou dost follow
Other graces,
Lovelier places,
Newer flowers,
Leafier bowers:
I still sit
Nursing it—
My old sorrow—
Night and morrow.
All my mind
Looks behind,
And I fret.
Look, I set
A wide door
Thee before,
And my casement open lay:
Come, and blow my cares away.

3.

Sunshine fair!
Of the saint
Gild the hair;
Wake the child,

With his mirth
Send him wild.
To the faint
Give new breath;
From the earth
Take the death,
Take the dearth.
'Tis in vain
To complain,
And implore
Thee to glide,
Thee to glow,
In my mind;
For my care
Will nevermore
Rise and go.
Open door,
Windows wide,
I do find
Yield no way
To the mind.
Glow and play,
Come and go,
Glance and glow,
To and fro,
Through the air!
Thou would'st say,
As ye use,
Thou and Wind,
Forget;
But not yet
I would choose
That way:
Shine and glitter, come and go;
Pass me by, and leave me so.

4.

And I whisper
To the wind,
Evening lisper
In the curl
Of the girl,

Who, all kind,
Waits her lover—
Waft and hover,
Linger over
Her bright color,
Waft her dolor
O'er the ocean,
With a faint,
Reviving motion.
Blow her plaint
From the maiden
Sorrow-laden;
Take all grief,
Which to lose
Were relief.
Leave me, leave me, for I choose
Still to clasp my grief.

5.

Sunshine fair!
Windy air!
Come and go,
Glance and glow,
Shine and show,
Waft and blow!
Neither choosing
Nor refusing,
Neither fretting
Nor forgetting
I will set
Open yet
Door and pane.
You may come,
Or the rain:
I will set,
Indifferent,
Open yet
Door and pane.
Sun and wind,
Rain-cloud blind,
Parted, blent,
There is room,

Go and come.
Loving only
To be lonely,
To be sad.
I repent,
Sun and wind,
That I went
You to find:
I was rent
In my mind.
Sun and wind, do what ye will;
I sit looking backward still.

Lucy, I say, had finished this song, and was sitting silent before the instrument, with her hands laid on the keys, which had just ceased the long-drawn sound, and again sunk into stillness. Two arms came round her from behind. She did not start. She was taken by but not with surprise. She was always with him in mood, if not in thought, and his bodily presence therefore overcame her only as a summer cloud. She leaned back into his embrace, and burst into tears. Then she would rise to look at him, and he let her go. She saw him rather ragged, rather dirty, quite of a doubtful exterior to the eye of the man who lives to be respectable, but her eye saw deeper. She looked into his face—the window of his being—and was satisfied. Truth shone there from the true light and fire within. He did not fall at her feet as once before. The redeemed soul stood and looked her in the face. He put out his arms once more, and she did not draw back. She knew that he was a man, that he was true, and she was his. And he knew, in the testimony thus given him, that the last low-brooding rims of the cloud of his shame had vanished from his heaven, and that a man may have sinned and yet be glad. He could give God thanks for the shame, whose oppression had led him to understand and hate the sin. For sin gives birth to shame, and in this child-bearing is cleansed. Verily there is One, I repeat, who bringeth light out of darkness, good out of evil. It comes not of the evil, but out of the evil, because He is stronger than the evil; and He, not evil, is at the heart of the universe. Often and often yet in the course of life, would Thomas have to be humbled and disappointed. But not the less true was the glow of strength that now pervaded his consciousness. It was that this strength, along with a thousand other virtues, might be perfected, that the farther trials were to come. It was true, so true that it was worth making fact.

But my young reader, who delights in the emotion rather than in the being of love, will grumble at these meditations, and say, "Why don't you go on? why don't you tell us something more of their meeting?" I answer,

"Because I don't choose to tell you more. There are many things, human things too, so sacred that they are better left alone. If you cannot imagine them, you don't deserve to have them described. We want a little more reticence as well as a great deal more openness in the world—the pulpit included. But against stupidity the gods themselves are powerless." Ah no! that is a heathen utterance. Let the stupid rage, and when they imagine, let it be vain things. The stupid, too, have a God that will slay their stupidity by the sword of his light. The time will come when even they will repent, not of their stupidity, for that they could not help, but of the arrogance of fancied knowledge that increased instead of diminishing it, and made them a thorn in the flesh of them that saw and would have opened their eyes. No doubt many of them that suppose they see, fancy it only in virtue of this same stupidity; but the end will show all. Meantime the tares and the wheat must grow together, and there are plenty of intellectual tares that spring from the root of the moral tares, and will be separated with them.

After awhile, when their feelings were a little composed, Thomas began to tell Lucy all his adventures. In the middle, however, Mrs. Boxall returned. She had most opportunely been calling on a neighbor, and if Thomas had not learned this from Mr. Kitely, he would have sent for Lucy instead of going in as he did. They heard her voice in the shop.

"Don't tell grannie anything about it yet," said Lucy. "She's much quieter in her mind now, and if we were to set her off again it would only do her harm. Any thing certain she has a right to know, but I don't think she has a right to know all that you are trying to do for her. That is your business. But you mustn't mind how she behaves to you, Tom dear. She thinks you and your father all one in the affair."

When the old lady entered she saw at a glance how things were going; but she merely gave a very marked sniff, and retreated to her chair by the window. She first seated herself, and then proceeded to take off her bonnet and shawl. But she could not keep silent long, and the beginning of speech as well as of strife is like the letting out of water.

"Thomas," she said—for people of her degree of education became more familiar in their address when they are angry—"is this room mine or yours?"

"Grannie," said Lucy, "Thomas has nothing to do with it. He was away from home, I assure you, when—when—things went wrong."

"Very convenient, no doubt, for both of you! It's nothing to you, so long as you marry him, of course. But you might have waited. The money would have been yours. But you'll have it all the sooner for marrying the man that turned your grandmother into the street. Well, well! Only I won't sit here and see that scoundrel in my room."

She rose as she spoke, though what she would or could have done she did not know herself. It was on Lucy's lips to say to her—"The room's mine, grannie, if you come to that, and I won't have my friend turned out of it." But she thought better of it, and taking Thomas's hand, led him into the shop. Thereupon grannie turned to Widdles for refuge, not from the pain of Thomas's presence, but from the shame of her own behavior, took him out of his cage, and handled him so roughly that one of the three wing feathers left on one side came off in her hand. The half of our ill-temper is often occasioned by annoyance at the other half.

Thomas and Lucy finished their talk in a low voice, hidden in the leafy forest of books. Thomas told her all about it now; how he wanted to find the man Jack Stevens, and how Robins and he had followed him to Lisbon, and found him there and brought him home; how he had had to part with her ring as well as his own watch for money to start them in their search, and how even then they had had to work their passage to Lisbon and back. But if the representation she and Mr. Fuller had given him of the state of the case was correct, he said, there could be no doubt but Jack's testimony would reverse the previous decision, and grannie would have her own.

"I can't help being rather sorry for it," concluded Tom; "for it'll come to you then, Lucy, I suppose, and you will hardly be able to believe that it was not for my own sake that I went after Jack Stevens. I've got him safe, and Robins too, at the Mermaid. But I can't be grand and give you up. If you were as rich as Miss Coutts, I couldn't give you up—though I should like to, almost, when I think of the money and my father."

"Don't give me up, Tom, or I'll give you up, and that would be a bad job for me."

Then they made it clear to each other that nothing was further from the intention of either of them.

"But what am I to do next, Lucy? You must tell me the lawyers that conducted your side of the case."

"I am afraid I can't ask *him* to do anything more."

"Who's *him*, Lucy?"

"Mr. Sargent."

"Sargent—Sargent—I think I have heard the name. He's a barrister. If you are not satisfied with him, the firm you employed will speak to another."

"He did everything, Thomas. But—"

Lucy hesitated. Thomas saw that she was blushing. Perhaps it was the consciousness of his own unworthiness that made him jealous.

"Oh, very well, Lucy! If you don't want to tell me, of course—"

"Thomas! Thomas! Can't you trust me yet? I have trusted you, Thomas."

He had the grace to feel ashamed of himself at once.

"Forgive me, Lucy," he said. "I was wrong. Only I love you so!"

"I will tell you all about it, Tom, dear."

"You shan't tell me a word about it. I can guess. But what are we to do?"

"I will go and consult Mr. Morgenstern."

"There is no time to lose."

"Come with me to his office, then, at once. It is not far to Old Broad Street."

They set out instantly, found Mr. Morgenstern, and put him in possession of the discovered evidence. He was delighted with the news.

"We must find Sargent at once," he said.

Lucy began to stammer out some objection.

"Oh! I know all about that, Lucy," said he. "But this is no time for nonsense. In fact you would be doing the honest fellow a great wrong if you deprived him of the pleasure of gaining his case after all. Indeed, he would feel that far more than your refusal of him. And quite right, too. Sargent will be delighted. It will go far to console him, poor fellow."

"But will it be right of me to consent to it?" asked Thomas, with hesitation.

"It is a mere act of justice to him," said Mr. Morgenstern; "and, excuse me, I don't see that you have any right to bring your feelings into the matter. Besides, it will give Mrs. Boxall the opportunity of making him what return she ought. It will be a great thing for him—give him quite a start in his profession, of which he is not a little in want. I will go to him at once," concluded Mr. Morgenstern, taking his hat.

CHAPTER LV
GUILD COURT AGAIN

I will not linger over the last of my story. Mr. Sargent was delighted at the turn affairs had taken—from a business point of view, I mean. The delight was greatly tempered by other considerations. Still he went into the matter mind and soul, if not heart and soul, and moved for a fresh trial on the ground of fresh evidence. Mr. Worboise tried the plan of throwing discredit on the witness; but the testimony of Robins and Thomas was sufficient to remove any influence that course might have had. The former judgment was rescinded, and the property was Mrs. Boxall's.

Mr. Worboise and Mr. Sargent met in the lobby. The latter, in very unlawyer-like fashion, could not help saying:

"You would have done better to listen to reason, Mr. Worboise."

"I've fought fair, and lost, Mr. Sargent: and there's an end of it."

The chief consolation Mr. Worboise now had was that his son had come out so much more of a man than he expected, having, indeed, foiled him at his own game, though not with his own weapons. To this was added the expectation of the property, after all, reverting to his son; while, to tell the truth, his mind was a little easier after he was rid of it, although he did not part with it one moment before he was compelled to do so. He made no advances however, toward a reconciliation with Thomas. Probably he thought that lay with Thomas, or at least would wait to give him an opportunity of taking the first step. My reader would doubtless have expected, as I should myself, that he would vow endless alienation from the son who had thus defeated his dearest plans, first in one direction, then in another; but somehow, as I have shown, his heart took a turn short of that North Pole of bitterness.

There is nothing to wonder at in the fact that Mrs. Boxall should know nothing yet of her happy reverse of fortune. They had, as I have said already, judged it better to keep the fresh attempt from her, so that if by any chance it should fail, she might not suffer by it, and, in any case, might be protected from the wearing of anxiety and suspense.

"Let's give grannie a surprise, Lucy," said Thomas, having hurried to her with the good news.

"How do you mean, Tom? We must be careful how we break it to her. Poor dear! she can't stand much now."

"Well, my plan will just do for that. Get Mrs. Whatshername, over the way—her old crony, you know—to ask her to tea this evening. While she's away, Kitely, Spelt, and I will get all the things back into the old place. There's nobody there, is there?"

"No, I believe not. I don't see why we shouldn't. I'll run across to the old lady, and tell her we want grannie out of the way for an hour or two."

She took care, however, not to mention the reason, or their surprise would have been a failure.

There were no carpets to fit, for the floor had been but partially covered, showing the dark boards in the newest fashion. Before Mrs. Boxall's visit was over, the whole of her household property had been replaced—each piece in the exact position it used to occupy when they had not yet dreamed of fortune or misfortune. Just as they were getting anxious lest she should come upon the last of it, Lucy, bethinking herself, said to the bookseller:

"Mr. Kitely, you must lend us Widdles. Grannie can't exist without Widdles."

"I wish you hadn't proposed it, miss; for I did mean to have all the credit of that one stroke myself. But Widdles is yours, or hers rather, for you won't care much about the old scaramouch."

"Not care about him! He's the noblest bird in creation—that I know, Mr. Kitely. He does not mind being bald, even, and that's the highest summit of disregard for appearances that I know of. I'm afraid I shouldn't take it so quietly."

"It don't much matter nowadays," said Mr. Kitely. "They make such wonderful wigs."

"But that's ten times worse," said Lucy.

"You don't mean to say you'd go with a bare poll, miss, so be that Providence was to serve you the same as Widdles?—which Heaven forbid!"

"I wouldn't bear a wig anyhow."

"What would you do, then, miss? Black and polish it?"

"What nonsense we are talking!" said Lucy, after a good laugh. "But I'm so happy I don't know what to do. Let's make a wig for Widdles, and grannie will think her bears' grease has made hair grow instead of feathers."

Whether this proposal was ever carried out, I do not know. But Widdles followed the furniture; and when grannie came home she found that all her things were gone. She stared. Nobody was to be seen. But all were watching from behind the defences of Mr. Kitely's book-shelves.

"Mr. Kitely," she called at last, in a voice that revealed consternation.

The bookseller obeyed the summons.

"I didn't expect it of you, Mr. Kitely," she said, and burst into tears.

This quite upset the conspirators. But Mr. Kitely kept them back as they were hurrying forward.

"We thought we could do a little better for you, you see, ma'am. It was a confined place this for the likes of you. So Miss Lucy and I made bold to move your things up to a place in the court where you'll have more room."

She said nothing but went up stairs. In both rooms she found utter emptiness. Mr. Kitely followed her.

"There's not a stick left, you see, ma'am. Come and I'll take you home."

"I didn't think you'd have turned me out in my old age, Mr. Kitely. But I suppose I must go."

It was with considerable exercise of self-denial that the bookseller refrained from telling her the truth, but he could not spoil the young people's sport. He led her up to the door of her own house.

"No, Mr. Kitely. I'll never set foot in that place again. I won't accept it from no one—not even rent-free."

"But it's your own," said Kitely, almost despairing of persuasion, and carried beyond his intent.

"That's just why I won't go in. It is mine, I know, but I won't have my own in charity."

"Thomas," whispered Lucy, for they were following behind, "*you* must tell her the good news. It will help her over her prejudice against you. Old people are hard to change, you know."

"Mrs. Boxall," said Thomas, going up to her, "this house is your own."

"Go away," returned Mrs. Boxall, energetically. "Isn't it enough that you have robbed me? Will you offer me my own in charity."

"Do listen to me, grannie," pleaded Thomas.

"I will not listen to you. Call a cab, Lucy. We'll drive to the nearest work-house."

Lucy saw it was time to interfere.

"What Thomas says is true, grannie, if you would only listen so him. Every thing's changed. Thomas has been over the seas to find a man who was in uncle's ship when it went down. He has given such evidence that the property is yours now."

"I don't care; it's all a trick. I don't believe he went over the seas. I won't take any thing from the villain's hand."

"Villains don't usually plot to give away what they've got," said Lucy.

"But it's Thomas Worboise you mean?"

"Yes; but he had nothing to do with it, as I've told you a hundred times, grannie. He's gone and slaved for you, and that's all the thanks you give him—to stand there on the stones, refusing to take what's your very own."

The light was slowly dawning on grannie's confused mind.

"Then you mean," she said, "that all my son Richard's money—"

"Is yours, grannie," said Lucy and Thomas in a breath.

"Only," added Lucy, "you've spoiled all our bit of fun by being so obstinate, grannie."

For sole answer the old woman gave a hand to each of them, and led them into the house, up the wide oak stair-case, and along the passage into the old room, where a fire was burning cheerfully just as in the old time, and every article of furniture, book-case, piano, settle, and all, stood each in its old place, as if it had never been moved.

Mrs. Boxall sat down in her own chair, "like one that hath been stunned," and for some moments gave no sign of being conscious of what was going on around her. At length a little noise at her ear attracted her attention. She looked around. On the edge of the little table which had always been beside her easy-chair, stood Widdles, the long feathers of whose wings looked like arms that he had tucked under his coat-tails, only there was no coat.

"Poor Widdles!" said the old woman, and burst into tears.

CHAPTER LVI
WOUND UP OR RUN DOWN

Thomas resumed his place in the office, occupying his old stool, and drawing his old salary, upon which he now supported himself in comfort and decency. He took a simple lodging in the neighborhood, and went twice a week in the evening to see his mother. In doing so, he did not run much risk of meeting his father, whom he neither sought nor avoided, for he was seldom home before midnight. His mother now lived on these visits and the expectation of them. And she began not only to love her son more and more for himself, but to respect him. Indeed, it was chiefly the respect that increased her love. If he was not converted, there must be something besides conversion that was yet good, if not so good. And she thought she might be excused if she found some pleasure even in that. It might be a weakness—it might be wrong, she thought, seeing that nothing short of absolute conversion was in the smallest degree pleasing in the sight of God; but as he was her own son, perhaps she would be excused, though certainly not justified. As Thomas's perception of truth grew, however, the conversations he had with her insensibly modified her judgment through her feelings, although she never yielded one point of her creed as far as words were concerned.

The chief aid which Thomas had in this spiritual growth, next to an honest endeavor to do the work of the day and hour, and his love to Lucy, was the instruction of Mr. Fuller. Never, when he could help it, did he fail to be present at daily prayers in St. Amos's Church. Nor did he draw upon his office hours for this purpose. The prayers fell in his dinner hour. Surely no one will judge that a quarter of an hour, though in the middle of the day, spent in seeking the presence of that Spirit whereby all actions are fitted to the just measure of their true end, was disproportioned by excess to the time spent in those outward actions of life, the whole true value of which depends upon the degree to which they are performed after the mind of that Spirit. What gave these prayers and exhortations a yet more complete fitness to his was their shortness. No mind could be wearied by them. I believe it very often happens that the length of the services, as they are called, is such that they actually disable the worshiper in no small degree from acting so after them as alone can make them of real worth to his being: they are a weakness and not a strength, exhausting the worshiper in saying "Lord, Lord," instead of sending him forth to do his will. The more he feels, the less fit is he, and the less fitting it is, to prolong the expression of his devotion. I believe this is greatly mistaken in all public services that I know anything about, which involve, in their length, an entire departure from good old custom, not good because old, but so good that it ought to have been older, and needs now to be raised from the dead that it may be custom once more. Thomas did not enjoy his dinner less, and did his work far more thoroughly and happily because of this daily worship and doctrine—a word which, I think, is never used by St. Paul except as meaning instruction in duty, in that which it is right to do and that which it is right not to do, including all mental action as well as all outward behavior.

It was impossible under the influence of such instruction that Tom should ever forget the friends who had upheld him in the time of his trouble. He often saw Captain Smith, and on one occasion, when he had a fortnight's holiday—the only one before his marriage—he went a voyage to Jersey in his brig, working his passage as before, but with a very different heart inside his blue jacket. The Pottses, too, he called on now and then; and even the unamiable Jim Salter came round to confess his respect for him, when he found that he never forgot his old mates.

As soon as Thomas resumed his stool in the counting-house Mr. Wither resigned his, and went abroad.

Mrs. Boxall of course recovered her cheerfulness, but her whole character was more subdued. A certain tenderness toward Lucy appeared, which, notwithstanding all her former kindness was entirely new. A great part of her time was spent in offices of good-will toward Widdles. She always kept her behavior to Mr. Stopper somewhat stately and distant. But he did his best for the business—for it was the best for himself.

My story leaves Mr. Spelt and Mr. Kitely each happy in a daughter, and Mattie and Poppie growing away at their own history.

One evening when Tom was seated with his mother, who had again recovered so far as to resume her place on the couch, his father came into the room. Tom rose. His father, without any greeting, said:

"Keep a lookout on that Stopper, Tom. Don't let him have too much of his own way."

"But I have no authority over him, father."

"Then the sooner you marry and take the business into your own hands the better."

"I'm going to be married next week."

"That's right. Make Stopper junior partner, and don't give him too large a share. Come to me to draw up the articles for you."

"Thank you, father. I will. I believe Mrs. Boxall does mean to make the business over to me."

"Of course. Good-night," returned Mr. Worboise, and left the room without speaking to his wife.

From this time Tom and his father met much as before their quarrel. Tom returned to the house for the week before his marriage, and his father made him a present of an outfit for the occasion.

"Oh, Tom! I can hardly believe it," said Lucy, when they came home from church.

"I don't deserve it," was all Tom's answer in words.

After their wedding-journey they went back to the old house in Guild Court, in which they had had one or two more rooms fitted up. Their grandmother, however, is now urging them to move to some suburb, saying she is quite willing to go with them. "And I don't believe you will have any objection either—will, you, old Widdles?" she generally adds.